D1572933

CER

ADDISON-WESLEY PUBLISHIN

AMICS

for the artist potter

by

F. H. NORTON

OMPANY, INC., CAMBRIDGE 42, MASS.

H738
N823c

Preface

The preparation of the manuscript for this book has extended over a number of years, with the help and encouragement of my friends and associates. Mentioned below are a few who have been particularly helpful; my thanks to others are no less sincere because they remain unnamed.

The sculptors George Demetrios and Walker Hancock have read part of the text and have loaned material for illustrations. Mr. Norman Arsenault of the Museum of Fine Arts in Boston has made many suggestions on the scope and plan of the book.

I am particularly indebted to Mr. and Mrs. Edwin Scheier, Miss Lydia Siedschlag, and Professor Charles M. Harder, who were kind enough to review the entire text and make many helpful comments.

I would also like to thank R. L. Stanton, who tried out the bodies and glazes, and Donald Fellows, who took many of the photographs.

The fine cooperation I received from the commercial suppliers of ceramic materials and equipment has been most gratifying.

F.H.N.

August, 1955

Contents

Part 1 How We Do It

Part 2 Why We Do It

How we do it

This section is especially written for those starting out in the field of pottery making, for here are illustrated the common methods used by the potter.

CHAPTER 1

Introduction

I. PURPOSE OF THIS BOOK

At the time of this writing, there are in this country literally thousands of enthusiastic beginners in the field of pottery, but comparatively few are fortunate enough to have the guidance of well-trained teachers. Of the others, some are guided by teachers with limited training, but many struggle along almost alone. During the past twenty-five years, the author has been tremendously impressed by the thirst for fundamental knowledge of the ceramic processes that is evident in the many potters who have visited him.

In Europe, the situation is somewhat different. There, the competent artist finds it fairly easy to make some sort of connection with a pottery. In many cases, the artist works out the designs for a skilled thrower to execute under his direction, or he may have a studio where he can produce his own pieces, with the invaluable technical aid of a professional potter. It is no wonder that in this atmosphere such fine ware is produced on the Continent, particularly in Sweden, Denmark, and Finland.

Dozens of books covering the field of art pottery are on the market. Some of these are excellent, but few of them, I fear, really answer many of the questions that plague the inexperienced potter. The books that cover the technical aspects of ceramics, on the other hand, are unsuited for the use of the average potter because they assume an extensive background of physics and chemistry. There seems to be a need for a book which explains the *why* as well as the *how* of doing things in terms simple enough for the beginner to understand, and yet complete enough to be of help to the teacher and the advanced potter. This is our aim in the present volume.

Because of the great number of inquiries from time to time, it is apparent that the beginner needs up-to-date information on where to buy materials and equipment, and how to build the things he cannot buy. This information is presented in a manner that should make it of real help to the potter.

There also seems to be a need for information on the make-up of bodies, glazes, and colors, so carefully and specifically given that they may be mixed by the amateur and used with a minimum of disappointment. The formulas in this book are accurate and complete, and have been carefully tested in the laboratory.

Finally, it is hoped that this book will point the way to suitable expressions of ideas in ceramics—that it will encourage good design and raise the standard of pottery produced in the studio.

In order to carry out the above purposes efficiently, this book is divided into two parts. The first is a series of well-illustrated chapters dealing with the various methods of pottery making, beginning with the simplest hand-molding, and ending with decoration of the pieces. These are the *how* chapters. The second part consists of chapters for those who wish to know more about the materials they are using, who want to explore the process of compounding their own bodies or glazes, or who wish to know more about design. These are the *why* chapters.

The book is concluded with a glossary. The reader should refer to it when he comes across an unfamiliar term either in this book or in the other literature on ceramics.

II. GENERAL REFERENCES

The following lists a few carefully selected books and periodicals dealing with the general field of pottery. More numerous and specific references are given at the end of each chapter.

Periodicals

Bulletin of the American Ceramic Society. Contains many articles on design and various phases of pottery making.

Ceramic Age. Although a trade journal for the industry, it contains numerous articles of interest to the artist potter.

Ceramic Monthly. A journal expressly for the artist potter. Contains authentic articles, but not too technical in nature.

Ceramic Industry. Another trade journal containing many articles on pottery making.

Ceramica (in Italian). A beautifully illustrated magazine that should be of great value to the ceramic artist.

Keramische Zeitschrift (in German). A pottery magazine containing authentic articles for the artist potter, well illustrated and well worth having, even for those with a limited knowledge of German.

Pottery Gazette. A trade publication for the English pottery industry, containing authentic articles on history and art.

Sprechsaal (in German). A technical trade paper, but containing some articles for the artist potter, and an excellent question and answer section.

Books

BINNS, C. F., *The Potter's Craft,* 3rd ed., D. Van Nostrand Company, Inc., New York, 1948. A very readable treatise on pottery making by one of our great potters.

BINNS, C. F., *The Manual of Practical Potting.* 5th ed., Scott, Greenwood and Son, London, 1922. A treasure house of formulas for all kinds of bodies, glazes, and colors.

BRONGNIART, A., *Porcelaine de Sèvres*, À Leleux, Paris, 1845. (In French.) A beautifully illustrated book, exhaustively covering Sèvres ware as made from 1770–1847.

COX, W. E., *Pottery and Porcelain,* Crown Publishers, Inc., New York, 1944. A complete history of pottery and porcelain. Profusely illustrated, but many cuts are so greatly reduced as to be nearly valueless. Lacks references, but readable.

DOAT, T., *Grande Feu Ceramics,* Keramic Studio Publishing Company, Syracuse, N. Y., 1905. (Translated into English.) A detailed and authentic description of all phases of making high-fired porcelain after the French school, which should be in the library of every serious potter.

FORSYTHE, G. M., *Art and Craft of the Potter,* Chapman & Hall, Ltd., London, 1934. A well-illustrated book on pottery making by one who had a great influence on art pottery in England.

GRANGER, A., *La Céramique Industrielle,* Gauthier-Villars & Cie, Paris, 1929. (In French.) An excellent book on European production methods.

HOME, R. M., *Ceramics for the Potter,* Chas. H. Bennett Company, Inc., Peoria, Ill., 1952. The reader will find a good discussion of artistic and technical developments in the potter's art.

KENNY, J. B., *Complete Book of Pottery Making,* Greenberg: Publisher, Inc., New York, 1949. One of the best books for a beginner in pottery making. The illustrations are excellent, showing each step in the processes discussed.

KENNY, J. B., *Ceramic Sculpture,* Greenberg: Publisher, Inc., New York, 1953. A well-illustrated book showing many simple processes for making sculpture in ceramics.

LEACH, B. H., *A Potter's Book,* Faber & Faber, Ltd., London, 1940. A study of the philosophy and practice underlying the production of fine pots, by a master craftsman.

McLaughlin, M. L., *China Painting,* Robert Clarke and Co., Cincinnati, 1877. A practical manual.

Optical Soc. of America, Committee on Colorimetry. *The Science of Color,* Thomas Y. Crowell Company, New York, 1953. A beautifully illustrated, clearly written treatise on color. Some parts require more scientific background than most artists have; nevertheless, it is a book even the nonscientist will find very helpful.

Piccolpasso, C. P., *The Three Books of the Potter's Art,* Victoria and Albert Museum, London, 1934. (English translation.) A detailed description of pottery-making in the Italy of the middle ages. Many of the methods and equipment may well be used today.

Rosenthal, E., *Pottery and Ceramics,* Penguin Books, Harmondsworth, 1949. An inexpensive little book, covering the whiteware field in a concise, authentic way, by one of the great ceramists of Europe.

Searl, A. B., *An Encyclopedia of the Ceramic Industries,* E. Benn, Ltd., London, 1930. A mine of information on bodies, glazes, potteries, and potters. A reference book of great value.

CHAPTER 2

Forming by Hand

I. INTRODUCTION

In this chapter, a few basic processes of forming by hand are described by the use of step-by-step photographs. The methods illustrated here have been found to give consistently good results, and are based on traditions of potting that reach back into the mists of prehistoric times.

Hand-forming methods are especially suited to the beginning potter because they require no investment in special equipment. All of the necessary items are common household articles. It is possible, too, for the amateur to make small pieces of reasonably good appearance right from the start. These simple methods are not very rapid, but through their use the beginning potter learns that only by exercising care and good workmanship in every step can a creditable piece be obtained.

The emphasis here is not on the final product, but on the method itself. The examples given are of simple, small objects, but these same methods may be applied to larger and more complicated pieces as the potter becomes more experienced.

II. CLAY

A complete description of clays and bodies is given in Chapters 15 and 17. However, at the start, all that is needed is a mixture with good working properties which will fire watertight at Cone 03. (The use of cones as temperature indicators will be described in Chapter 20.) This mixture can be obtained from a local clay deposit or from a pottery supply house.

Consistency of the clay. The consistency (wetness) of the clay is of prime importance. If the clay is of the proper firmness for the particular process at hand, it is easily worked, but if it is too wet or too dry, it can become completely intractable. Listed below are some properties of clay when it is in different stages of dryness:

(a) In a soft plastic condition, the clay may be readily formed, even in large masses, with relatively little pressure, but it is sticky and cannot support itself for any great height. The drying shrinkage is large.

(b) In a medium plastic condition, clay may be readily formed with reasonable pressure, will weld together, and will support itself for considerable heights. This consistency is most used for forming pots and sculpture.

(c) In a stiff plastic condition the clay is deformed only with considerable pressure and it is difficult to weld two pieces together. If the deformation is carried too far, cracking occurs. When clay is of this consistency, it may be carved or trimmed and small clay additions may be made. The drying shrinkage is much less than for the softer mixes.

(d) In the next stage of dryness, the clay becomes rigid and cannot be appreciably de-

Forming a pinch pot:

Fig. 2-7. The ball of clay.
Fig. 2-8. Pressing gently with the thumbs.
Fig. 2-9. Pressing the piece out to an even thickness.

Fig. 2-10. Scraping the bottom of the partially dried piece with a hacksaw blade.
Fig. 2-11. Finishing the partially dried piece by sponging.
Fig. 2-12. Easy-to-make pinch pots.

deforming. It can now be turned over and the bottom scraped flat, using an old hacksaw blade. The rest of the surface, inside and out, may be finished by smoothing lightly with a damp sponge.

Other shapes. Pinch pots need not be confined to circular forms. The so-called "free forms" are readily attained, provided the size is small. Several pieces of this kind are shown in Fig. 2–12, and many other designs may be worked out.

Larger pieces are made by first forming the base and then building up the wall by application of small pieces of clay, welded onto the previous piece by pinching. When the wall has been built to a height where it scarcely supports itself, it should be allowed to stand until it has stiffened somewhat, when the building may be continued. A pot as tall as a man has been built in this way, but a week or more was required to complete it. It is recommended, however, that pinch pots be confined to small pieces and that the coil method, described in the following section, be used for the larger ones.

IV. BUILDING A POT WITH COILS

This method is an ancient one, and is still used by primitive people such as the natives of South Africa and the Indians of New Mexico. It is interesting to note that pottery making by the coil method was the work of women in all primitive societies, but that when the potter's wheel was invented men took over this operation.

Because coiling permits the forming of excellent pieces with simple tools and without long training, this method has much to recommend it for the beginning potter. The process is relatively slow, however, and consequently the spontaneous shapes produced on the wheel are not possible. Coiling trains the eye and hands to achieve symmetry in working, and yet allows the originality of the hand-made piece to be retained. The sequence of operations in making a coil-built pot is illustrated in Figs. 2–13 through 2–25.

Clay for the coil method of forming. The clay for this process should have good plastic properties, and it should be well wedged to a uniform mass before the work is started.

Forming the bottom. Take a small plaster bat, place on its center a ball of clay about the size of a hen's egg, flatten it with the hand until it is about ½″ thick, and scrape flat. Next, cut a circle of cardboard of the diameter required for the outside of the base, lay it on the clay disk, and cut around it with a pointed tool held nearly vertical (an old dental tool is excellent for this purpose). A well-trimmed disk should result.

Making the coils. This is a simple process, but it is helpful to see it demonstrated by an instructor. Roll a piece of clay about the size of a large egg in the hands to form a rough cylinder about 1″ in diameter and 6″ long. Place the clay on a smooth table top (a linoleum surface is excellent), lay both hands on it lightly, and roll the cylinder back and forth. The pressure of the hands should be light and even, and the motion should be outward towards the ends of the cylinder. In a few rolls, the clay should be about ⅜″ to ½″ in diameter and roughly 30″ long. With practice, very even coils can be produced, although at first it may be difficult to maintain sufficiently uniform pressure to prevent thin spots. It is often advantageous to have the hands damp (not wet) to prevent too-rapid drying of the clay.

Coil-building a vase:

Fig. 2-13. The ball of clay for the bottom.
Fig. 2-14. Scraping the formed bottom flat.
Fig. 2-15. Cutting out the bottom around a
circular template.

Fig. 2-16. Rolling the coil from a rough clay
cylinder.
Fig. 2-17. The finished coil.
Fig. 2-18. Building the wall: the first coil.

Coil-building a vase (cont.):
Fig. 2-19. Welding the inner surface together with a plaster tool, while supporting the outside with the fingers.
Fig. 2-20. Welding the outer surface together, supporting the inside.
Fig. 2-21. Marking off the top of the roughly finished vase with dividers.

Some potters make all the necessary coils for a piece at one time and store them under a damp cloth until they are needed. Others prefer to make each coil as it is used.

Forming the wall. Pick up the first coil, being careful not to stretch it, and wind it around just inside the base disk, pressing it down lightly every ½″ or so. If the clay is of the correct consistency and the work proceeds at a normal pace, no water need be added at any time during the entire process.

When this first coil has been positioned all the way around the disk, it is continued for a second turn on top of the first one, pressing it lightly to weld it onto the first turn. Some potters prefer to cut the coil after one turn has been made, join the ends, and start a new turn for the second round. However, this takes longer and makes a weaker structure (because there are more joints), and therefore is not recommended. The little step in the coil as it passes over the starting point does no harm, and it serves to indicate the stopping place for the final coil. When the first coil has been wound around as far as it will go, the end is beveled and a new coil, also beveled, is joined to it. The process is continued until the wall is 2″ or 3″ high.

The potter should constantly bear in mind the shape of the piece that he hopes to make, and each coil should be so placed in relation to the one below as to give the proper final contour. Every effort should be made to maintain symmetry by turning the piece and looking at it from all sides as the work progresses. Some instructors recommend templates of cardboard or sheet metal to guide the beginner. However, the eye is more rapidly trained without them and, of course, the experienced worker does not need them.

Completing the wall. After the wall has reached the desired height, the coils should be welded into a homogeneous surface by sliding clay from one coil down over the next. This can be done with the tip of the finger or with a plaster tool, working first on the inside while supporting the wall with the other hand on the outside. Care must be taken to join the lower coil securely to the base. The process is repeated on the outside of the wall, taking care not to push it out of round.

Extension of the wall. If it is desired, the height of the wall may now be increased by adding more coils and welding them together in the same manner as described above. However, pieces of any great height will settle if the wall is built up too rapidly, and it is often necessary to allow the piece to dry out somewhat before continuing. Remember that the contour of the piece must be maintained as each coil is added.

Completing the top. When the desired height has been reached, the top is marked off to an even height with dividers and trimmed on the line with a thin knife. Now the piece may be allowed to dry until it is leather hard, but this must be a slow drying in a covered box or a damp chamber.

Finishing the piece. If the work has been well done up to this point, there will not be a great deal of finishing to do. The lip

Coil-building a vase (cont.):
Fig. 2-22. Trimming off the top.
Fig. 2-23. Finishing the leather-hard vase by scraping in different directions, like raking a flower bed.
Fig. 2-24. Recessing the bottom of the vase.
Fig. 2-25. Finishing with a damp sponge.

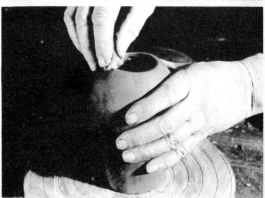

may be trimmed to give a rounded edge, and the sides may be scraped to give a more even surface. An old hacksaw blade is excellent for this purpose. The piece should then be turned over and the bottom scraped flat. If a more artistic foot is desired, a circle may be scribed on the bottom and the area inside the circle cut out to a depth of ⅛″ or ¼″ with a loop tool.

The final finishing of the surface is done in the leather-hard state. A damp sponge is used to soften the surface clay and to rub off the small lumps and fill in the small hollows, much as a gardener levels a seed bed with a rake. However, the sponging should no more be expected to correct large defects in the surface of pottery than sandpapering can be expected to conceal defective workmanship in a piece of wooden furniture.

V. COIL-BUILDING ON A WHEEL

This method, quite similar to that described in the previous section, has certain mechanical features that take it out of the freehand class, speed the process, and make it much easier to produce symmetrical pieces. The purist may scoff at using the wheel as described here, but the results are excellent. The steps in this process are shown in Figs. 2–26 through 2–33.

The wheel. The building is done on a light bench wheel used for banding plates (often called a "whirler"), which can be obtained from any pottery supply house.

Coil-building a bowl, turning the wheel by hand:
Fig. 2-26. Forming the base.
Fig. 2-27. Cutting the base.
Fig. 2-28. Truing up the base.
Fig. 2-29. Welding the coils together.

Forming the bottom. As before, the bottom is made from a ball of clay flattened into a disk. In this process, however, the disk is placed at the center of the wheel and is smoothed by shaving off the surface of the clay with a tool held steadily in one hand while the wheel is turned with the other. The edge of the disk is then trued up.

Building the wall. This is done in exactly the same way as described in the preceding section, except that the wheel is turned frequently to maintain symmetry. After the coils have been welded together, the inside and outside surfaces are scraped while the wheel is slowly turned. The upper rim is then trimmed and rounded off with a slender tool as the piece is rapidly turned.

Finishing. At this point, the piece is cut free from the wheel with a wire, and is allowed to dry until it is stiff. It can then be finished as described in the preceding section, but using the wheel for turning the bottom will accomplish the job much more quickly and precisely than hand carving. For this operation the piece is centered on the wheel head and held there by moistening or adding a few lumps of plastic clay. As the wheel is turned, the bottom is shaved off with a tool held steadily in one hand.

VI. DIFFICULTIES ENCOUNTERED IN COIL-BUILDING

One of the most common hazards in coil-building is the opening up of cracks in the

Coil-building a bowl (cont.):
Fig. 2-30. Trimming the top.
Fig. 2-31. Truing the top edge.
Fig. 2-32. Cutting the bowl free from the wheel with a wire.
Fig. 2-33. Recessing the bottom of the bowl.

drying and firing processes. When these appear between the coils they are usually caused by insecure welding of one coil with the next. Cracks may also appear where hollows have been filled in with a clay softer than the piece at the time of mending. This new clay shrinks more than the stiffer clay in the final drying, and so causes cracking.

Another common fault is lack of symmetry, caused by large hollows or humps, or by slumping of the piece. This is a fault that can be corrected only with experience. The potter must thoroughly know the characteristics of his clay—just how much it can be deformed without breaking, just how much weight it can stand without deforming.

VII. SLAB-FORMED PIECES—SOFT CLAY

By this method, a piece of plastic clay is cut into shapes which, when joined together, form the desired object. This also is a method that requires very little special equipment and no great amount of experience to turn out creditable pieces. It should be realized that this method of forming clay takes little account of its unique property of plasticity; slab-forming is usually more suited to wood or tin than to clay. However, we describe below the procedure for making a small covered box by slab-forming. The steps are shown in Figs. 2–34 through 2–46.

Rolling the clay sheet. The first step is to roll the clay into a sheet of uniform ¼" thickness, much as you would roll out a pie crust. A piece of damp cloth should be tightly stretched over the table to prevent clay from sticking to it, and the roller should be washed occasionally and wiped dry to avoid sticking to the clay. The rolling should be from the center of the clay to the outer edges. The finished sheet must be free from cracks or tears.

Cutting out the box. The next step is to make a pasteboard template for the combined bottom and sides of the box. Now place the template on the sheet of clay and use a slender knife or old dental tool to cut around the pattern. Remove the clay cutout (be careful not to stretch it!) and lay it on a plaster bat. Then cut a shallow groove around the bottom where the sides fold up, and, with a slender knife, bevel the edges to be joined.

Assembling the box. Now fold up the sides of the box and hold them in position with blocks of wood which are covered with damp cloth. Pinch the corners together to make a tight joint. It is a good idea to reinforce the corners on the inside with a thin roll of clay, worked into a smooth fillet.

Fig. 2-34. Rolling out a sheet of clay, using strips of wood to control the thickness.

Finishing. After the box has been standing for a few hours, it will be stiff enough to handle without deformation. The surface may then be scraped and sponged and the top edge squared off, with the wooden blocks acting as guides. The drying should be continued in a damp closet (with the wooden blocks still in place) to prevent the outside from drying too rapidly and causing the sides to bow in. This is a very common defect in slab-built ware.

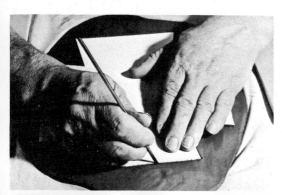

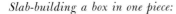

Slab-building a box in one piece:
Fig. 2-35. Cutting out the box, using a template.
Fig. 2-36. Scoring grooves around the base for folding.
Fig. 2-37. Beveling the corners.
Fig. 2-38. Joining the corners, with cloth-covered blocks supporting the sides.
Fig. 2-39. Reinforcing the corners.
Fig. 2-40. Supporting the sides for drying. The blocks make a convenient guide for trimming the top edge.

The cover. The cover for the box is cut out with the aid of a template, and is joined at the corners. A rim made from a narrow strip of clay is pressed onto the under side of the cover. The edges are trimmed after the cover has become leather hard. This should never be done freehand; the cover should be held on a square piece of masonite to guide the tool. If desired, a knob may be attached to the top. When partly dry, the cover is finished in the same way as the box.

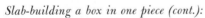

Slab-building a box in one piece (cont.):
Fig. 2-41. Cutting out the cover, using a template.
Fig. 2-42. Joining the corners of the cover.
Fig. 2-43. Adding a ridge to the underside of the cover.
Fig. 2-44. Trimming the edge of the cover, using a guide.
Fig. 2-45. Cover with knob attached.
Fig. 2-46. Finishing the box (note the well-designed knob).

VIII. SLAB-FORMED PIECES—LEATHER-HARD SLABS

In this process, the parts of the box are cut out of a rolled plastic clay sheet just as described in the preceding section, but instead of being joined immediately, they are allowed to dry slowly (in a damp box) to the rigid, leather-hard stage. They are then stuck together with clay slip, just as a wooden box is glued. The stages of this operation are shown in Figs. 2–47 through 2–53.

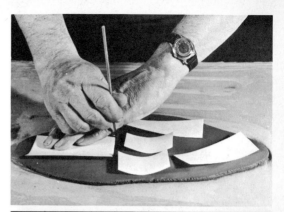

Cutting out the box. As an example, consider a simple open box. The base and sides are cut out of the flat clay sheet and are stored flat between damp plaster slabs, with cloth separators to prevent sticking. They are allowed to dry out very slowly for a few days. (During this time, the slip can be prepared by taking some of the clay used for the box itself, adding water gradually, and stirring until the mixture has the consistency of thick cream and is free of lumps.) When the clay slabs are stiff enough to be handled without deforming, the edges of the pieces are beveled by paring with a knife, so that all the parts fit together closely. It is helpful to use a wooden block, beveled on the side and end at 45°, to guide the knife. Accurate fitting is very important, for gaps cannot be filled with slip. The sections not being worked on should be kept covered so that they will not dry out too much.

Slab-building an open box:
Fig. 2-47. Cutting out the slabs, using templates.
Fig. 2-48. The slabs between damp plaster bats, with cloth separating the slabs to prevent sticking. They may be left in the damp box for a day.
Fig. 2-49. Beveling the edge of the slab to a 45° angle, using a guide block.
Fig. 2-50. Roughing the edge of the slab with a hacksaw blade, again using a guide block.

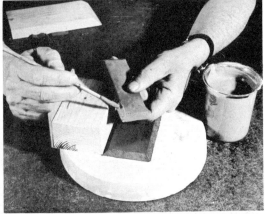

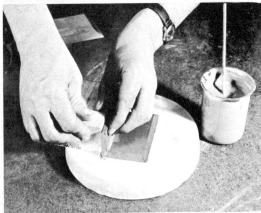

Slab-building an open box (cont.):
Fig. 2-51. Painting the edge with slip just before assembly.
Fig. 2-52. Joining one side and the bottom, using a block to keep the sides vertical.
Fig. 2-53. The box completely assembled, with the joints so closely fitted that no reinforcement is needed.

Assembling the box. The next step is to roughen all the edges to be joined by scratching with a toothed plaster tool, using the same guide board. This provides a better surface for the slip to adhere to. We are now ready for the actual assembly. Take the bottom and one side of the box, paint with slip the edges that are to be joined, press the two pieces together, and hold them in position for a few seconds until they are tightly joined, using a block to keep the side vertical. This must be done rapidly, so that the slip will not dry out before the pieces come together. The other sections are joined in the same manner. If the assembly is well done, no reinforcement is needed for the corners.

Finishing. The piece may now be finished in the same way as the covered box described in the preceding section.

IX. MOLDING OVER A FORM

With a little experience, excellent shallow pieces may be made by forming a sheet of clay on a simple mold. The beginner will find it helpful to try this method before becoming involved in the complexities of plaster work. The steps of this process are shown in Figs. 2–54 through 2–60.

Forming a free-form dish:
Fig. 2-54. The plasticine form.

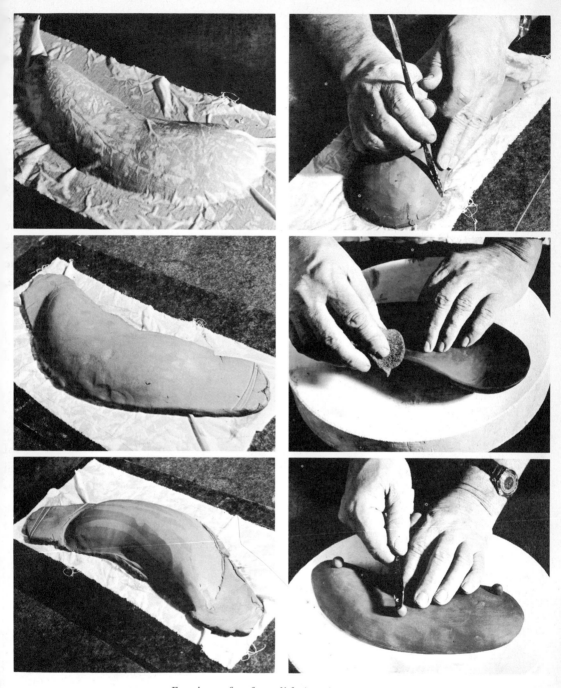

Forming a free-form dish (cont.):
Fig. 2-55. The form covered with a damp cloth.
Fig. 2-56. The sheet of clay laid over the form.
Fig. 2-57. The clay pressed down on the form.
Fig. 2-58. Trimming the edge.
Fig. 2-59. Finishing the dish with a sponge.
Fig. 2-60. Attaching feet to the finished dish.

The form. A sheet of masonite or any rigid material is used as a base, and on this a shape is molded to correspond to the reverse of the upper surface of the finished piece. The molding may be done in ordinary pottery clay or in plasticine. The form is then covered with a piece of damp cloth to prevent the clay from sticking to it.

Molding the clay. A sheet of clay is rolled out to a thickness of about ¼″, as previously described, and is lifted, inverted, and laid over the form. The clay is now gently rubbed down on the form, starting at the center and working toward the edge, to remove any air. Next, the edges are trimmed with a knife, and the piece is allowed to dry for a few hours.

Finishing. As soon as it is stiff enough to handle safely, the piece is lifted off the form and is finished with a scraper and sponge. If desired, small feet may be attached.

X. REFERENCES

1. BINNS, C. F., *The Potter's Craft*, 3rd Ed., D. Van Nostrand Company, Inc., New York, 1948 (Chapters II and III).

2. FORSYTH, G. M., *Art and Craft of the Potter*. Chapman and Hall, Ltd., London, 1934.

3. HYMAN, R., *Ceramics Handbook*. Fawcett Publications, Inc., Greenwich, Conn., 1953.

4. KENNY, J. B., *Complete Book of Pottery Making*. Greenberg: Publisher, Inc., New York, 1949 (Chapter 2).

5. LEACH, B. H., *A Potter's Book*. Faber and Faber, Ltd., London, 1940 (Chapter IV).

6. SANDERS, H. H., *Sunset Ceramics Book*. Lane Publishing Company, Calif., 1953.

7. DE VEGH, G., AND A. MANDI, *The Craft of Ceramics*. D. Van Nostrand Company, Inc., New York, 1949 (Chapters III, IV, and V).

CHAPTER 3

Forming on the Wheel

I. INTRODUCTION

The potter's wheel is probably the first machine that was developed by man. Just when and where it was conceived we do not know, but it certainly had a profound effect on the growth of civilization. The wheel is *the* tool of the potter, allowing him to use his skill to quickly produce beautifully shaped pieces, so that they have the freshness and vitality of quick sketches, rather than the labored effect obtained by coil-forming. Every serious potter must master the art of throwing on the wheel, or must have a good thrower working for him.

II. WHEELS

There are many kinds of wheels, and although some are easier to learn on than others, they all work on the same principle. The wheel consists of a vertical shaft on top of which is a wheel head, where the throwing is done. Wheels may be motor driven, or may be rotated by footpower.

The kick wheel. This wheel is driven by footpower, using either a revolving platform at the base of the shaft, or a treadle and crank. Many potters prefer the kick wheel because they feel that it provides better control than a motor-driven wheel. Obviously, however, the kick wheel is impractical for mass production.

The power wheel. Although the motor-driven wheel has not always found favor with the artist potter because it is more difficult to control the speed or because there is sometimes an appreciable vibration, a well-designed power wheel, such as that described in Chapter 30, is easier to learn on and, with experience, produces better work in less time than is possible with a foot-operated machine. The characteristics of a good power wheel are:

1. A smooth-running head about 12 inches in diameter.
2. A speed variation from 50 to 350 rpm.
3. Sufficient power to hold the set speed even on large pieces.
4. Good rests for both arms.
5. A bottom board that can be easily cleaned.

It is essential, too, to have a wedging table placed close to the wheel.

The head of the wheel. The head of the wheel should be of some rustproof material like brass, bronze, aluminum, or plastic. It is possible to use a head of hard wood that has been treated to resist moisture, and sometimes plaster is a satisfactory material. It is essential in every case that the head run true, and it is convenient to have concentric rings cut into it as an aid to centering.

It is desirable to form delicate pieces directly on a plaster bat which can be removed from the wheel head. These bats can be moistened and stuck to the wheel head with slip [Fig. 3–1(a)], but it is more convenient to have bats made to fit in a ring over the wheel head [Fig. 3–1(b)]. It is well worth while to make a plaster mold for casting these bats to an exact fit, to assure that they will not slip and are uniformly concentric.

If a piece has been thrown directly on the wheel head, it must be cut off by passing a wire under it and then taking it off with a pair of lifters, as shown for a pitcher later in this chapter. On the other hand, if the piece has been thrown on a plaster bat, there is no danger of distorting the most delicate piece. However, the bottom of the piece should be cut free with the wire, or it may crack on drying. Particles of plaster from the bat must never be allowed to get into the clay. These will expand on firing and may pop off a piece of the ware.

Mr. Norman Arsenault, of the Museum of Fine Arts in Boston, Massachusetts, has developed a simple method of removing pieces from the wheel head when bats are not used. Disks of fabricoid (such as used for automobile seats and tops) are cut to fit the head and are held in place by a small amount of plastic clay spread over the head. The disk is rubbed into place with a scraper and the throwing is then carried out in the usual manner. When the piece is finished, a fine wire is pulled between the disk and the wheel so that the disk and the piece, together, may be slid off onto a board. When the piece has partially dried, the disk is stripped off.

III. TOOLS

For efficient work, a few simple tools are required, as shown in Fig. 3–2.

Wire. A fine bronze wire (No. 28 gauge) with wooden handles on the ends is needed for cutting the piece loose from the wheel head.

Calipers and dividers. Large calipers and dividers are needed for precision throwing. These may be of metal or of wood.

Sponges. Sponges in a variety of sizes are needed for taking up excess water from the bottoms of pieces and for moistening the surface while throwing. A sponge tied to a stick is convenient for reaching into deep vessels.

Ribs. These tools are made of hard wood, preferably maple. They are fashioned in a number of different curves to enable shaping of the piece to the desired form.

Lifters. These tools are needed to lift a freshly thrown piece from the wheel head with a minimum of distortion. They should be available in several sizes. Tin, galvanized iron, and bronze are satisfactory materials.

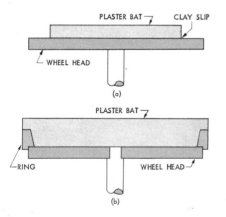

Fig. 3-1. (a) Plaster bat held on a wheel with slip. (b) Plaster bat held in a tapered ring resting on a wheel.

IV. CLAYS AND BODIES FOR THROWING

An experienced potter can throw small pieces from a great variety of clays and bodies. However, some materials are much easier to work

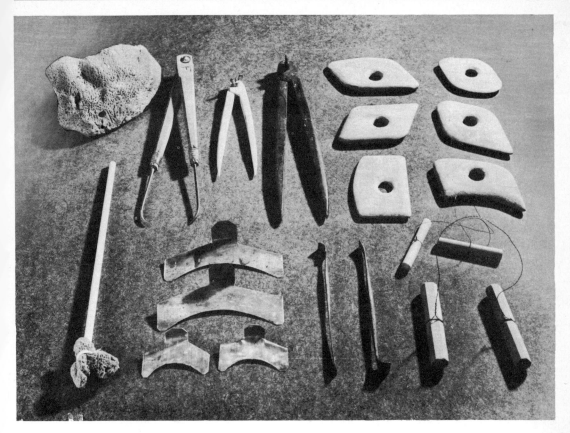

Fig. 3-2. Tools used in throwing: sponge, calipers, dividers, ribs, sponge on a stick, lifters, turning tools, and wires.

with than others, and the beginner should start with the more plastic bodies. A good throwing body should have a high degree of plasticity and the ability to absorb considerable water without slumping. Bodies of the stoneware type fall into this category; they are described in more detail in Chapter 17.

V. PREPARATION OF THE CLAY

It is assumed that a quantity of well-aged clay suitable for throwing is at hand. It cannot be emphasized too strongly that the clay must be thoroughly wedged shortly before it is to be used on the wheel. Methods of wedging are discussed in detail in Chapter 18, and need not be explained here. Much of the

trouble the beginner has in throwing is due to a lack of uniformity in the starting body. It is important to remember that discarded thrown pieces contain more water than the original body, and that therefore they must be very carefully worked into the clay batch.

An expert thrower can successfully work with clay of a variety of consistencies, but the beginner should strive for the particular value of water content that makes throwing easiest. Centering is more readily done when the clay is soft, but soft clay is unsatisfactory for thin walls because it will not stand up. Both ease of working and the nature of the piece must be taken into account in determining the consistency of the clay.

VI. THE THROWING OPERATION

Throwing is an art that is difficult to describe, for each potter develops his own individual way of working. For the beginner, there is no substitute for working with an experienced thrower. With good instruction, an apt pupil who conscientiously spends two hours a day on the wheel should be able to make creditable medium-sized pieces at the end of one month, and fairly large pieces at the end of three months. However, this can be accomplished only if a good throwing body is used on a well-designed wheel.

Few of our younger artist potters have any appreciation of the speed and precision of the old-time production throwers. Ed Donovan, the last of the old New England potters in the Paige Pottery in Danvers, Mass., was accustomed to throwing 10-inch flower pots for ten hours a day on a power wheel. Only thirty seconds were needed to form a pot so precise that it nested with the preceding ones. In another pottery, an Italian potter threw stoneware ginger jars at the rate of three a minute.

Throwing a vase. The various operations in throwing a vase are shown in Figs. 3–3 through 3–12. The steps are described in detail below.

Centering. The first operation in throwing is to center the lump of body on the revolving wheel head. Perfect centering must be attained before taking the next step, or a wobbly piece is bound to result. Because this is one of the hardest operations for the beginner, he is amazed to see an expert accomplish it in a few deft motions.

Perhaps the greatest aid to accurate centering is a good arm rest *for each arm,* which allows the clay to be rigidly guided, like a shaft in a bearing. It is true that many potters center without arm rests and may even do it with one hand, but arm rests make the operation quicker and surer, especially when a large quantity of stiff clay is being worked.

In all the throwing operations, and particularly in centering, good lubrication is needed, so that the clay flows through the hands easily. This lubrication is furnished by adding a coating of water to the clay on the wheel or, better, by using a slip of the same clay. The water or slip is splashed on or is applied with a sponge. How much to use is learned by experience—too little will not supply sufficient lubrication, too much will soften the clay.

The first step in centering is to form a ball of clay about the size of an orange, well-wedged and free from folds. This is thrown onto the center of the wheel, usually while the wheel is turning. The clay is then moistened and is caused to run true by containing it rigidly in the hands and, at the same time, letting the clay rise up in the center into a taller form. This form is repeatedly pushed down with the thumbs, and drawn up, in a wedging action, until all the clay has been worked into a symmetrical disk. Some potters do not run the clay up and down, but center at once and start the bottom.

Forming the bottom. The next operation is to form the bottom, and it is necessary to decide at this point what the bottom thickness is to be. It is almost impossible to change this dimension at a later stage. To form the bottom, the thumbs are pressed down through the center of the clay, with the fingers on the outside of the piece as guides. Only experience allows one to judge when the correct bottom thickness has been attained, because it cannot be seen. Plenty of lubrication is needed and, for large pieces, slip may be added more than once.

Throwing a vase on the wheel:

Fig. 3-3. A well-wedged ball of clay.

Fig. 3-4. The clay thrown on the wheel.

Fig. 3-5. Centering and drawing up the clay.

Fig. 3-6. Pushing the clay down, ready to start the vase.

Fig. 3-7. Forming the bottom.

Fig. 3-8. Opening up the clay.

Throwing a vase on the wheel (cont.):

Fig. 3-9. The first draft.   Fig. 3-11. Forming the vase.

Fig. 3-10. The second draft, forming a   Fig. 3-12. The final forming.

cylinder.

The next step is to open up the clay until the inner bottom diameter is correct, still using the fingers to guide the outside of the clay and the palm of the hand to guide the top edge. Throughout the entire throwing operation, one of the things to be kept in mind is that the clay must at all times be contained as fully as possible in the hands. If some slip remains inside after the bottom is formed, it should be removed with a sponge.

Making the draft. This operation consists of drawing the clay up into a cylinder of somewhat the height of the finished piece. Again lubrication must be applied to all surfaces of the clay. There are many ways to position the hands in making the draft, but the first step is usually carried out by using one or both hands, squeezing the lower wall between thumb and fingers and slowly pulling upward, at the same time guiding the upper edge.

The next draft may need further lubrication. The fingers of the left hand are placed inside the piece and a finger or knuckle of the right hand on the outside. Both hands are then raised together, with gentle pressure between them, to cause the wall to thin out and move upward. The upper edge should still be guided.

In making the last draft, many throwers use a rib on the outside to give a smoother surface. However, the use of a rib should not be overdone, or the piece will lose its handmade character.

Much practice is needed to get a thin, even wall. A beginning thrower should cut his pieces down with wire to see how even the walls really are. The expert produces thin walls at the bottom, always a sign of good workmanship.

Many years ago the author studied throwing with one of the old-time New England potters, 75 years old at the time, who was throwing pieces from local red-burning clay. It was remarkable to see him form these pieces as if by magic, so fast were his motions, and yet with such precision that each piece looked exactly like the next. When I had thrown what seemed to me to be a creditable piece, he would take hold of it with his powerful, sensitive hands, and draw it up to twice the height, cut it down with a wire, and show a thin, perfectly even wall.

The beginner should practice drawing up cylinders for a long time before going on to later operations. If a good cylinder is made, the final shaping is comparatively simple.

Shaping. This final operation is carried out by using the fingers inside and outside the cylinder, with both hands, or by using a rib.

Summary. The cross-sectional diagrams of Fig. 3–13 will help to clarify the verbal discussion above and the photographs showing the vase-throwing operations.

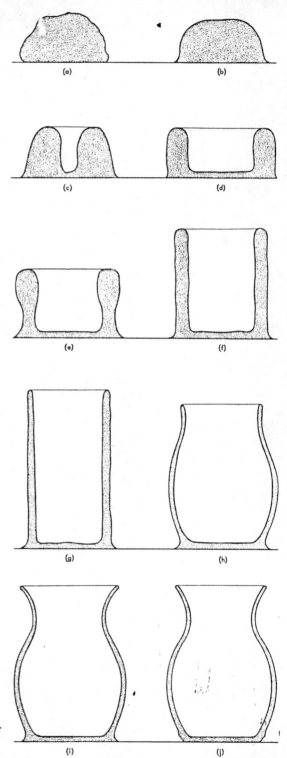

Fig. 3-13. Cross sections of the stages in the forming of a small vase.

Throwing a bowl. Figures 3–14 throug 3–16 show the forming of a bowl of simpl shape. Note that a rib is used on the outsid for finishing. Some skilled potters form bowl with one rib inside and one outside but this is not usual.

Necked pieces. Narrow-necked pieces must be closed in, as shown in Fig. 3–17. This is a final operation, as the hand, obviously, cannot be inserted in the piece after this is done.

Throwing duplicate pieces. Figure 3–18 shows the duplication of a vase by the use of guides, one for the maximum diameter and one for the upper lip. These guides are often used in production throwing.

Throwing a pitcher. Figure 3–19 shows a pitcher form, with a rib that is used for cleaning around the base. Figure 3–20 shows the operation of making the lip, which is not stretched right out, but is worked out by moving the finger, lubricated with slip, up and down. The handle is pulled out from the lump of clay as shown in Fig. 3–21, using slip for lubrication. The handle is attached as shown in Fig. 3–22, taking car not to distort the body of the pitcher. Figures 3–23 and 3–24 show the pitcher being cut off with a wire and removed with a pair of lifters.

VII. FINISHING

Some pieces require work to be done on them while in the plastic state, such as applying handles or forming lips, as described above for the pitcher, or adding beading or ridges with special tools. Finishing in the leather-hard condition is discussed in Chapter 5.

Throwing a bowl on the wheel:
Fig. 3-14. Starting from the first draft.
Fig. 3-15. Forming the bowl.
Fig. 3-16. Making the final form with a rib.

Fig. 3-17. Closing the neck of a vase.
Fig. 3-18. Throwing a piece to size, using guides.
Throwing a pitcher, starting with a vase shape:

Fig. 3-19. Cleaning around the base with a rib.
Fig. 3-20. Forming the lip.

Fig. 3-21. Pulling the handle from a lump of clay.
Fig. 3-22. Attaching the handle.

Throwing a pitcher (cont.):

Fig. 3-23. Cutting the piece free from the wheel head with a wire.

Fig. 3-24. Removing the piece, using a pair of lifters to avoid distortion.

VIII. JIGGERING

This operation is generally used in production work for making plates and other circular pieces. The artist potter may wish to use this process when making a number of identical pieces. The principle is much like that of throwing, except that one surface is formed against a plaster mold. This mold is set on the wheel head and must run true. A great deal of experience is needed to make good jiggered ware, especially in the larger sizes. It is not nearly as simple as it appears to be.

Making a saucer. The first step in making a saucer is to carefully draw a cross section, as shown in Fig. 3-25, allowing for the total shrinkage of the piece. A mold is then made in plaster to correspond to the inside surface, and a blade having the contour of the upper surface is formed. This blade is mounted on an arm (as described in Chapter 30), so that it may be pressed down over the mold while the mold is revolving.

Figures 3-26 through 3-34 show the necessary steps for making a saucer. First a disk of clay is made, a little thicker and a little greater in diameter than is desired for the finished saucer. This is done by placing a lump of clay of the correct size on a heavy, damp plaster block and striking it with a damp plaster tool to flatten it out. Much practice is required to get a bat of the correct thickness; a poor bat will not make a good saucer. Bats may also be made by rolling out the clay between strips, but this is a much slower process.

Next, the bat is carefully picked up and then slapped down on the mold, taking care to get it exactly centered. The bat is now wet with a sponge, the wheel is started, and the bat is pressed down with the fingers, working from the center toward the rim, to remove air. Next the blade is pulled slowly down

Fig. 3-25. Saucer to be made by jiggering.

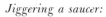

Jiggering a saucer:

Fig. 3-26. Ball of clay ready for batting out.

Fig. 3-27. Forming the bat with one blow of a cloth-covered plaster striker.

Fig. 3-28. Slapping the bat onto the plaster mold.

Fig. 3-29. The bat slapped down.

Fig. 3-30. Running the bat down to remove air.

Fig. 3-31. Finishing the saucer with the jigger tool. A sponge keeps the surface moist.

Fig. 3-32. Trimming the edge.

Jiggering a saucer (cont.):

Fig. 3-33. Removing the plaster mold and finished saucer, which will be free after a few hours of drying.

Fig. 3-34. Close-up of the saucer, showing the fine surface.

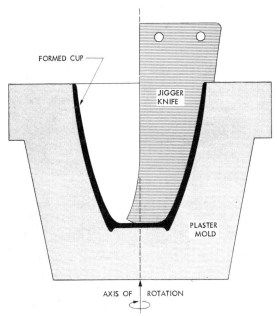

Fig. 3-35. Jiggering a cup.

to its correct position (against a stop). This operation forces the bat tightly against the mold and trims off any excess clay from the surface, leaving it smooth. The surface must be kept lubricated, just as in throwing. The next step is to trim off the excess clay from the edge of the saucer. The mold and saucer

are then removed from the wheel and allowed to dry, in the air, until the saucer is stiff enough to be removed from the mold. The mold is re-usable.

Making a cup. Cups may be jiggered by throwing a hollow blank of plastic body, placing it inside a revolving plaster mold, and using an inside blade for the working, as shown in Fig. 3–35.

Production work. Figure 3–36 shows a thrower forming uniform jars in large quantities. These will later be lathe-turned.

Figure 3–37 shows a team of production jiggermen at work. Today, automatic machines have largely taken their place.

IX. REFERENCES

1. ANON., Experiments in Jiggering, *Ceram. Ind.* April, 1951.

2. BINNS, C. F., *The Potter's Craft*, 3rd ed., D. Van Nostrand Company, Inc., New York, 1948 (Chapter III).

3. KENNY, J. B., *Complete Book of Pottery Making.* Greenberg: Publishers, Inc., New York, 1949.

Fig. 3-36. A skilled production thrower working in the Wedgwood Pottery at Stoke-on-Trent, England.

Fig. 3-37. A team of expert jiggermen in the Homer Laughlin Pottery at Newell, West Virginia.

CHAPTER 4

Forming
by Casting and Pressing

I. INTRODUCTION

The casting process. This process is used a great deal in making art pottery when shapes must be reproduced in large quantities. A clay slip is poured into a dry plaster mold and, after a short time, enough water has passed into the plaster to form a wall of solid clay against the mold. It is possible to form pieces with minute detail by this method, and it has the advantage of requiring little experience, providing the molds and the slips are right to start with. On the other hand, casting tends to be mechanical and the pieces therefore lack the individuality of thrown ware. There is also a tendency toward overelaboration, because details are so easily reproduced.

Casting has great versatility. The author has seen a tiny spray of vines and leaves, with stems no thicker than the lead of a pencil, cast in a mold at Copenhagen; and at Sèvres in Paris he has watched the casting of massive vases, eight feet in height.

The pressing process. This process consists of pressing plastic clay into a plaster mold to form a wall of relatively uniform thickness. Here again, fine detail may be reproduced, but it is a more time-consuming process than casting and requires more skill.

Large figures of terra cotta are made in this way, as well as such delicate sculpture as the bisque figures of Sèvres.

II. THE CASTING PROCESS

Ceramic casting may be divided into two classes: solid casting, where the mold is completely filled; and drain casting, where the mold is filled with slip which is poured out after a short interval, leaving a thin layer of clay against the mold.

The slip. The slip for casting is a thick suspension of clay in water, or a body mixture having the consistency of heavy cream. It is not feasible to make slip for this purpose by simply adding more water to the plastic clay, for other agents, called *deflocculants,* are needed to give good casting properties. Excellent casting slips may be purchased ready mixed, but for the potter who prefers to make his own, full directions are given in Chapter 18.

The mold. Casting is always carried out in plaster molds, so that the water from the slip is readily absorbed. For this reason, the plaster surface must have no treatment of any kind. Soap, shellac, or other similar coatings

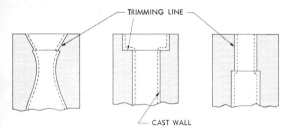

Fig. 4-1. Spares on the tops of casting molds.

will hinder the casting. The art of moldmaking will be taken up in Chapter 19.

The life of molds depends on the care with which they are used, the amount of detail, and the type of slip used. Finely detailed molds should give 20 casts, simple small molds 60 casts, and large molds 100 casts.

Spares. When casting, the level of the slip in the mold must be higher than the required height of the finished piece in order to allow for shrinkage of the slip during the casting process. This extra height is known as a *spare*. Figure 4–1 shows several kinds of spares on conventional molds. In every case the spare is planned to make it easy to trim the top of the piece in the mold.

Solid casting. Solid castings are made by pouring slip into the mold and leaving it there until it has cast solid. To make a good cast, extra slip must be available in the pouring cup to replace the shrinkage. Figure 4–2(a) shows a well-designed mold for solid casting. Figure 4–2(b) shows a poorly designed mold; because there is not an adequate supply of slip, a shrinkage cavity will form in the center. Solid casting methods are seldom used by the artist potter, and consequently they need no further discussion here.

Drain casting. In drain casting, the mold is completely filled with slip. A good mold,

with the correct amount of spare, is shown in Fig. 4–3. The casting action is chiefly due to water passing from the slip into the plaster mold and, in so doing, leaving a thin layer of firm body against the plaster surface. In other words, the plaster acts like a blotter, drawing the water from the slip through the layer of cast body. The longer the casting time in this process, the thicker the wall of the piece will be. The increase in thickness is not directly proportional to the length of time, however; the casting period must be increased about four times in order to double the thickness of the wall.

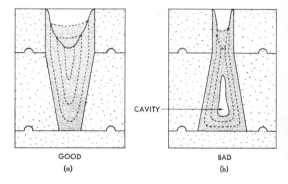

Fig. 4-2. Sections of solid-cast molds.

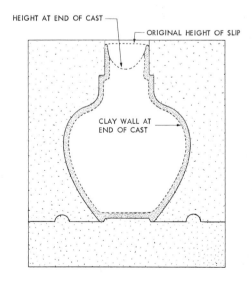

Fig. 4-3. Section of a drain-cast mold, showing the progress of the casting.

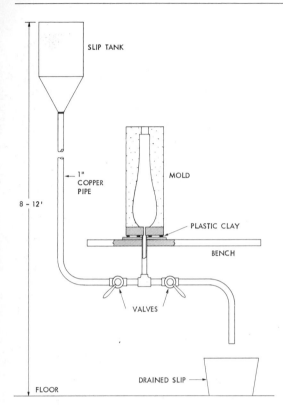

SLIP TANK

1"
COPPER
PIPE

MOLD

8 – 12'

PLASTIC CLAY

BENCH

VALVES

FLOOR

DRAINED SLIP

Fig. 4-4. Slip system for casting large vases by underpouring.

Underpour molds. When casting large pieces like garden vases or full-sized sculptured heads, it is desirable to introduce and to withdraw the slip from the bottom of the mold. This procedure makes it unnecessary to move the heavy mold, and there is no danger of the casting pulling away from the mold surface. A mold which has been set up to pour in this way is shown in Fig. 4–4. The small hole left in the bottom of the casting is plugged with a disk of the same body after the leather-hard stage is reached.

III. CASTING A VASE
The casting of a small vase is described in this section. The important steps are illustrated in Figs. 4–5 through 4–10.

Assembling the mold. The mold should first be thoroughly cleaned on the inside with a damp sponge, and when the parts are assembled they should be held firmly in place by clamps of some kind. This is an important precaution for there is nothing more discouraging than to have a mold leak during pouring. For light molds, a section from an old inner tube, used like an elastic, is quite satisfactory. A cord and wedge fastening is often used.

It should be remembered that a new mold may not work well the first two or three times it is used, until the surface has become conditioned. It is advisable to use old or lumpy slip to make the first several casts, and these can then be discarded.

Casting. The slip is readily poured into the mold from a pitcher. Care should be taken to pour the slip in a smooth, steady stream about the size of a lead pencil down the center of the neck, so that no slip strikes the walls. Spattered slip is apt to mar the finished vase. For small pieces, it is sometimes practicable to pour the slip down a rod.

Wreathing is a fault that is often found in castings when the slip is too thick or the pouring is too slow. In these cases, the level of the slip seems to rise in little jumps, and at each pause a faint line is left. Jarring or spinning the mold when pouring is a help, but the basic solution is to correct the slip.

The time required for the casting varies with the slip, the dryness of the mold, and the number of times the mold has been used. An average time is 15 minutes, but the inexperienced potter will use a trial-and-error method to find the exact time required for a given piece and adhere to it for each following cast.

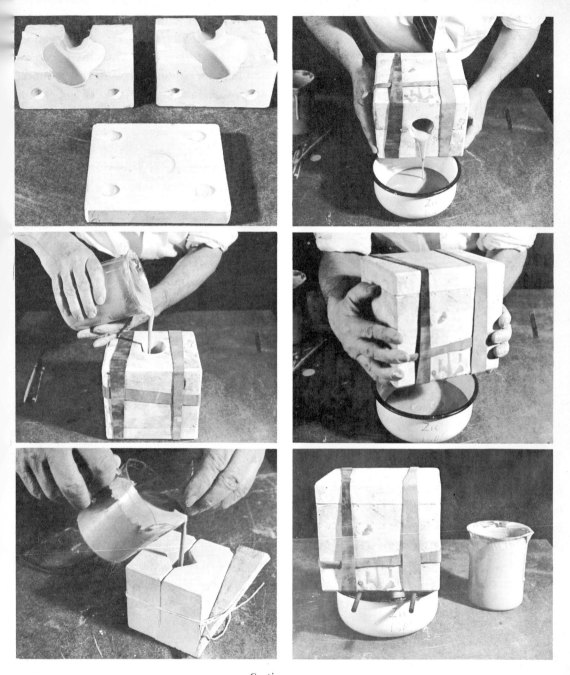

Casting a vase:

Fig. 4-5. A disassembled three-piece mold for a vase.

Fig. 4-6. Pouring the casting slip in an even stream into the assembled mold, held together with bands from an old inner tube.

Fig. 4-7. Pouring down a rod into a small mold.

Fig. 4-8. Draining the mold (after the slip has set for about 15 minutes).

Fig. 4-9. Shaking the mold upside down for even draining.

Fig. 4-10. Completing the draining by leaving the mold upside down on the pan for about 15 minutes.

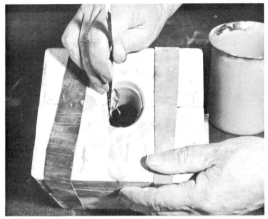

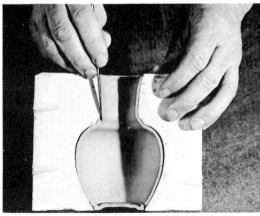

Casting a vase (cont.):
Fig. 4-11. Trimming the top of the vase by removing the spare.
Fig. 4-12. The opened mold, showing the cast vase.
Fig. 4-13. A cast vase that has been split in half by opening the mold too soon, to show the even wall thickness and trim line.

Draining. After the slip in the mold has built up to the correct wall thickness (estimated on the basis of time in the mold), the mold is inverted and the excess slip is poured out. A good slip will run out cleanly, but the mold should remain inverted for a few minutes to prevent any slip from running back into the mold and thickening the bottom. It often helps to gently shake the mold after draining to spread out any streamers.

When large pieces are drained, care should be taken to tip the mold gradually so that the slip will run out slowly as the air enters. Otherwise a vacuum which can suck in the whole side of a cast may be created. It is for this reason that bottom drainage for large pieces is desirable, as shown in Fig. 4-4.

Trimming. All cast pieces require some trimming, and it is good practice to always trim in the mold. In this way, little distortion occurs. Trimming may be done as shown in Fig. 4-11. A thin-bladed knife should be used, and care should be taken not to cut into the mold. This operation should be carried out at just the right time —if trimming is done too soon the piece will be distorted, and if it is done too late the piece will crack or tear.

Removing the piece from the mold. The vase is removed from the mold when it has become rigid and has shrunk away from the mold. If the clay sticks to the mold, the casting is not dry enough or the casting slip was not correctly deflocculated. When there are undercuts in a piece, it must be removed from the mold at exactly the right time; if the piece remains in the mold too long, it will shrink and crack.

Figure 4-12 shows the vase with the bottom and one side of the mold removed. The vase in Fig. 4–13 was cast in the same mold, but was opened before it was sufficiently dry. This was done deliberately here to show the even wall thickness and the trimming of the spare. Shrinkage has pulled the clay away from the mold in some places.

Handling drained slip and scrap. Slip drained from a mold is not the same as the original slip; it has lost water, and it is apt to be lumpy. Before using it again, it should be well blunged (mixed) and, if necessary, a little water added. It should then be put through a 100-mesh screen. The slip from molds should not, then, be drained back into the original slip supply, but into a separate container so that a large amount may be remixed and screened at one time.

Trimmings from the cast have lost even more water than excess slip has, and often, in addition, contain some plaster. It is best to keep all scraps together until a few pounds have accumulated and then blunge them with water, and screen. The action of calcium sulfate from the plaster may make it difficult to make a good slip from scraps, in which case the scraps should be thrown away.

IV. THE PRESSING PROCESS

The clay. Any plastic clay or body suitable for throwing may be used for pressing small pieces. For large pieces, however, a body containing grog is preferable because of its low shrinkage. The terra-cotta body described in Chapter 17 is quite suitable.

The mold. Molds used in the pressing process are very similar to those described for casting. However, a spare for the extra slip is not required. If a jointed mold is used, it is desirable to be able to reach inside to work on the joint.

Pressing with slabs. In this method, a sheet of clay is rolled out to the size of the mold, placed against the mold surface, and pressed firmly into place. This process produces a good surface, and is suitable for small- to medium-sized simple molds.

Pressing with small pieces. Here the clay is pressed against the mold surface in small pieces, each joined to the one before. This method is used for large or complicated pieces; it requires more skill than the slab method.

V. PRESSING A FIGURINE

The photographs of Figs. 4–14 through 4–20 show the steps for making a figurine by pressing in a mold.

Filling the mold. Sheets of clay are rolled to about ⅛″ thickness and are pressed into each half of the mold. The clay should be pressed down firmly everywhere, especially in the corners and hollows, but care should be taken not to let it become too thin over the projecting parts of the piece. More clay may be added locally if needed.

After the clay has stiffened somewhat, the edges are trimmed flush with the mold parting lines, care being taken not to trim below the plaster at any point. In fact, it is well to keep just above the line of the plaster, so that when the two halves of the mold are clamped together, the joint in the clay will be tight.

Assembling the mold. When the two halves of the mold are pressed together, they should be tied firmly, and a modeling tool should be used to work the inside of the joint together. In this figurine, it is impossible to reach the entire joint.

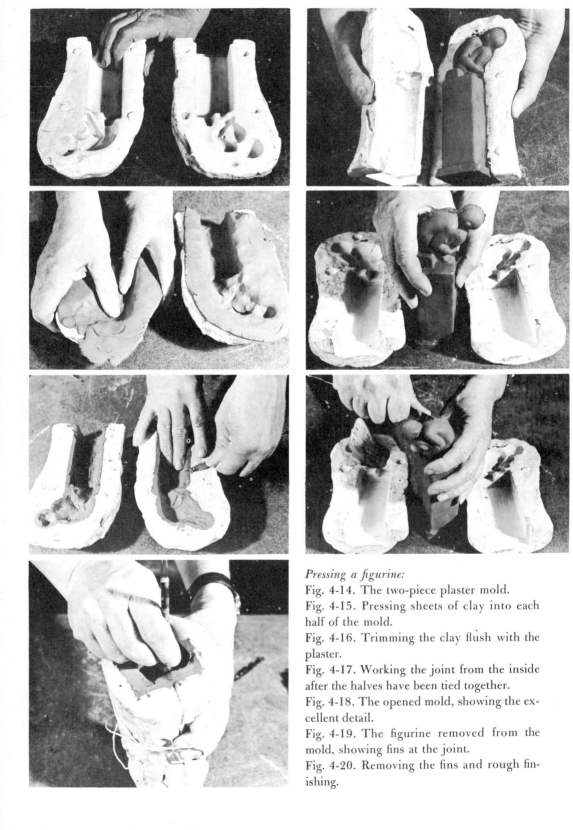

Pressing a figurine:

Fig. 4-14. The two-piece plaster mold.

Fig. 4-15. Pressing sheets of clay into each half of the mold.

Fig. 4-16. Trimming the clay flush with the plaster.

Fig. 4-17. Working the joint from the inside after the halves have been tied together.

Fig. 4-18. The opened mold, showing the excellent detail.

Fig. 4-19. The figurine removed from the mold, showing fins at the joint.

Fig. 4-20. Removing the fins and rough finishing.

Removing the figurine from the mold. The mold is easily pried apart along the joint, and this may be done very shortly after the initial pressing. When the mold is removed, the figurine should have an excellent surface.

Finishing. The last step is to work over the outside of the joint. Clay should be forced into any gaps in the joint and the joint should be scraped flush.

VI. PRESSING A TILE

In this section we shall describe the pressing of a simple tile, using the steps illustrated in Figs. 4–21 through 4–25.

Plastic clay or a terra-cotta mix is pressed into a mold in small pieces, each piece overlapping the preceding one. Considerable pressure is needed to force the clay well into the mold, to eliminate folds and air pockets. When the mold is filled, the cap is cut off

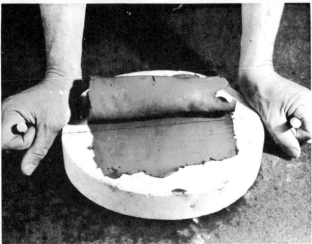

Pressing a tile:
Fig. 4-21. Starting to press clay into a plaster mold.
Fig. 4-22. Pressing the clay firmly into the filled mold.
Fig. 4-23. Cutting off the extra clay with a taut wire.

Pressing a tile (cont.):
Fig. 4-24. Scraping the surface smooth.
Fig. 4-25. The tile, removed from the mold and trimmed.

with a wire. The surface can then be scraped smooth with a hacksaw blade or other straight bar.

Removing the tile. To remove the tile, the mold is inverted on a frame consisting of a flat board with raised edges. After a few hours, the tile will shrink and fall on the board. If there are folds or air bubbles on the face of the tile, they may be easily filled with plastic clay. The fin on the back of the tile is then trimmed off, and the entire surface is sponged.

VII. PRESSING A MASK

This process is very similar to that for pressing a tile. The steps are shown in Figs. 4–26 through 4–29.

Filling the mold. The mold is lined with about ½ inch of clay, firmly pressed in (Fig. 4–26). Because it is difficult to gauge the thickness of the layer of clay, a tool like that shown in Fig. 4–27 is used to measure it. The partition across the piece is needed to

keep the sides from pulling in during drying and firing.

Removing the mask from the mold. After the clay has stiffened somewhat, the edges are trimmed off (Fig. 4–28). The mold is then inverted on a flat board like that described in the previous section. In about six to twelve hours the mask will drop out of the mold, and is ready to be finished (Fig. 4–29).

Finishing. The finishing process can be as elaborate as is desired. Figure 4–30 shows a mask with a black matte glaze.

VIII. REFERENCES

1. BRONGNIART, A., *Traité des Arts Ceramiques ou des Poteries.* Bechet, Paris, 1854.
2. GRANGER, A., *La Céramique Industrielle.* Gauther-Villars & Cie, Paris, 1929 (Chapter XIV).
3. KENNY, J. B., *Complete Book of Pottery Making.* Greenberg: Publishers, Inc., New York, 1949 (Chapter 6).

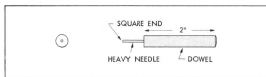

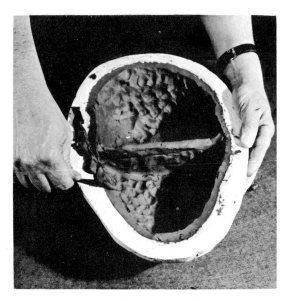

Pressing a mask:

Fig. 4-26. Covering the mold with clay and forming a partition.

Fig. 4-27. Front and side views of tool for gauging clay thickness. The needle is ½″ long for most work.

Fig. 4-28. Trimming the edges with a plaster tool. Note the wall thickness.

Fig. 4-29. Finishing the mask with a spatula.

Fig. 4-30. The finished mask, with a black semimatte glaze.

CHAPTER 5

Finishing

I. INTRODUCTION

Careful finishing is the sign of a good potter. On the other hand, no amount of finishing will make good ware from a poorly constructed piece, any more than a coat of paint will turn sloppy cabinet work into fine furniture.

II. TRIMMING

The first step in finishing is to trim the fins at the joints or edges, an operation often referred to as *fettling*. This operation must be performed at exactly the right stage—the "leather-hard" stage. At this point in the hardening process, the ware has not become too brittle, nor is it so soft that it will deform with handling.

The trimming is done with a thin-bladed knife or spatula, and no special instructions are needed, except that care must be taken to avoid splitting off large fragments, which might cause cracks in the piece. The trimming operation is illustrated in Figs. 4–20 and 5–1.

In some cases, trimming may be necessary over the entire surface of the piece, where it serves largely to remove lumps. This operation is shown in Fig. 2–23. Unglazed ware, such as parian porcelain or terra-cotta pieces, require this over-all finishing because worked-over areas present a different appearance than the cast or pressed surface.

III. TURNING

This operation is similar to that of trimming except that it is done on the wheel or lathe. The feet of thrown pieces are often finished in this way, but sometimes the whole piece is turned, inside and out, like Chinese eggshell porcelain.

Turning on the wheel. When a piece is to be finished on the wheel, it must be held firmly in place. A bowl, for example, may be held by wetting the metal wheel head (with a sponge) and pressing the piece down firmly. The suction of the water will hold the piece in place for several minutes. Properly centering the piece requires much practice, and it is almost miraculous to see how a skilled turner can center the piece on the wheel head with a few deft touches. The beginner must center the piece as best he can, using the concentric circles as guides. Then, as the piece revolves slowly, a pencil is used to mark the side farthest from the center. If the piece is not precisely centered, the wheel can be stopped to allow for adjustment. This process may need to be repeated.

If the piece is tall, it may be fastened by lumps of plastic clay, as shown in Fig. 5–2. If a number of pieces are to be turned, a cylinder can be thrown on the wheel, of the correct size to hold the piece. After the cylinder has become leather hard, any number of

Fig. 5-1. Fettling: trimming the fin off the edge of a saucer with a scraper.

Fig. 5-2. Turning the bottom of a vase on the wheel.

pieces can be turned with it, as shown in Fig. 5–3.

Turning on the lathe. For turning small pieces, a lathe will be found much more convenient than a wheel. Such a lathe (shown in Fig. 5–4) is easy to construct. A vacuum connection holds the pieces firmly against the face plate. In production work, wooden or plaster fixtures, called "chums," are used, as shown in Figs. 5–5 and 5–6.

Tools. Various tools are used for turning. The loop tool shown in Fig. 5–7, made by bending a piece of steel from a watch or clock mainspring into a circle and binding the ends with wire to a wooden handle, works well. The edges should be sharpened on a hand stone from time to time. Scrapers of various shapes, made from old files, hacksaw blades, or dental tools, give good results.

The turning operation. The turning operation itself requires experience and a gentle hand. It is very easy to accidentally catch the tool in the piece and pull it off the wheel.

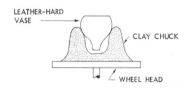

Fig. 5-3. Cross section of a vase held in a chuck so that its bottom can be turned. The chuck is made by throwing a form on the wheel and allowing it to become leather hard.

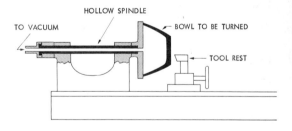

Fig. 5-4. A vacuum lathe for turning cups and bowls.

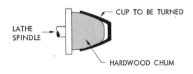

Fig. 5-5. Wooden chum for holding cups in the lathe.

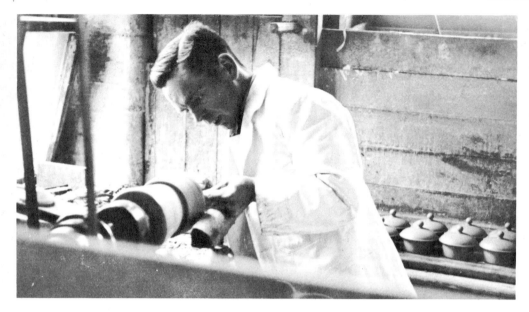

Fig. 5-6. Turning and burnishing teapot lids on the wheel. Note the wooden chum for holding the pieces.

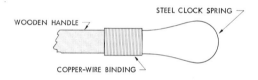

Fig. 5-7. Loop tool for turning.

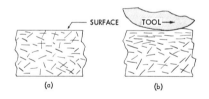

Fig. 5-8. Orientation of clay grains (a) before and (b) after burnishing.

The use of a guide stick pressed against the backboard will be very helpful (as described for plaster turning). With experience, a piece can be turned, inside and out, to produce a thin and even wall.

IV. BURNISHING

Burnishing is done on the piece when it is leather hard simply by rubbing the surface with a hard, smooth object such as a polished steel tool. This was the method used by primitive peoples to attain a polish on their ware. Our New Mexican Indians have produced some fine examples.

Although the theory of burnishing is not generally understood, it is really quite simple. The little plates of clay in the surface of a piece formed from a plastic body are arranged more or less helter-skelter, as shown in Fig. 5–8(a). The burnishing turns all these little plates so that they lie like shingles on a roof, as shown in Fig. 5–8(b). This rearrangement gives a polished surface which remains after drying, and even after firing at low temperatures. High temperatures largely destroy the polish, but even then a more than normal smoothness is apparent.

Burnishing may be carried out rapidly and evenly on the wheel or on the lathe, preferably directly after the piece has been turned. This is standard procedure in the production of some types of ware (such as cups).

V. WET FINISHING

This method of finishing is used for many types of ware, particularly for castings. A damp sponge wiped over the surface of the piece causes a thin layer of slip-like consistency to form on the surface and, as the sponge moves along, the high spots are dragged off and the low ones are filled, much as a road scraper levels a highway.

This kind of finishing is excellent if it is not carried too far. It is like using sandpaper on woodwork—too much rubbing takes off the corners and eliminates the detail. Figure 5–9 shows how the edge of a saucer is sponged to give a smooth rim; Fig. 5–10 shows the same operation in a large pottery. For small pieces, a soft wet brush is recommended for gentler action (Fig. 5–11).

Fig. 5-9.   Finishing plates in a large pottery.
Fig. 5-10. Finishing the edge of a saucer with a damp sponge.

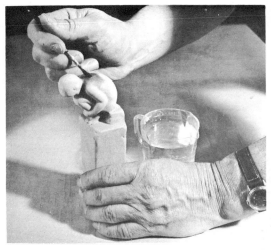

Fig. 5-11. Finishing a figurine with a wet brush.

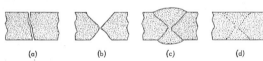

(a)   (b)   (c)   (d)

Fig. 5-12. Smoothing a dry surface with sand-paper.
Fig. 5-13. Truing up a dry slab box by rub-bing it on sandpaper.
Fig. 5-14. Repairing a crack, step by step.

VI. DRY FINISHING

When a piece is completely dry, finishing may be done with fine sandpaper (Fig. 5-12). This procedure takes off humps or ridges, but does not fill in the hollows. For flat surfaces, the sanding may be done by placing the sandpaper flat on a table and rubbing the piece over it, as shown in Fig. 5-13. After the sandpapering is completed, all dust should be removed from the piece, preferably by air-blasting.

The use of sandpaper should be confined to the finishing of rectangular pieces like boxes or flat bottoms. Extensive use of this method is associated with careless workmanship.

VII. REPAIRING A PIECE

Generally speaking, defective pieces should be discarded. However, occasionally so much work has gone into a piece that when a crack develops or a piece breaks off, repair may be justified. It should be clearly understood that pieces which are completely dry cannot be repaired unless they are first slowly moistened by sprinkling or sponging with water, and then are stored in a damp box until they attain the leather-hard state.

To successfully repair a broken section, both pieces must be brought to the same leather-hard state, with equal water content. The surfaces to be joined are then coated with slip (of the same composition as the body) and are quickly pressed together. The surface at the joint may then be smoothed out.

Cracks are best repaired by cutting a V from each side of the crack, painting the edges with slip, and then forcing in some body which is *as stiff as it can be worked.* If a soft plastic clay is used, it will, upon drying, shrink more than the body of the piece, and the crack will again open up. After the cracks are filled, the piece is allowed to set overnight in a damp box before the repair is scraped flush and sponged. The steps are shown in Fig. 5-14.

VIII. REFERENCES

1. BINNS, C. F., *The Potter's Craft*, 3rd ed. D. Van Nostrand Company, Inc., New York, 1948.

2. KENNY, J. B., *Complete Book of Pottery Making.* Greenberg: Publishers, Inc., New York, 1949 (Chapter 2).

CHAPTER 6

Drying

I. INTRODUCTION

Drying seems like a very simple process, but it often presents problems to the inexperienced potter because pieces that are dried too fast tend to crack, and pieces that have not been dried thoroughly enough explode in the kiln. In this chapter, some of the steps essential to good drying are discussed.

II. SHRINKAGE

Everyone knows that objects made from clay are smaller when dry than when they are first molded. This is due to the loss of the very thin films of water between the clay particles, which allows the whole mass to shrink (see Chapter 22). Some clays shrink a great deal, and some only moderately. For example, red stoneware body has an average lengthwise drying shrinkage of 5%; that is, a piece molded to 10 inches would shrink to 9½ inches. On the other hand, a terra-cotta body shrinks only 3% on drying. Shrinking occurs largely in the plastic range; once the leather-hard state is reached, little further shrinkage takes place.

III. WARPING IN DRYING

One of the most annoying problems encountered by the inexperienced potter is the warping of his pieces in drying. While this is discussed in detail in Chapter 22, it is well to give it some consideration here.

Cause of warping. In general, warping is caused by lack of uniformity in the body because of poor wedging, strains set up in molding, or nonuniform drying. It is comparatively easy to make the body uniform, but it is difficult to eliminate strains. For example, one face of a tile made in a plaster mold has had different treatment than the other face, and consequently the piece is likely to warp. In addition, when a piece is dried so that it loses water more rapidly from one side than from the other, warping is bound to occur.

Prevention of warping. If the piece has been uniformly made, warping is avoided by even drying; that is, every portion of the piece should be at the same stage of dryness at any given time. In the case of simple pieces with walls of even thickness, this is easy to accomplish, but when the piece has walls of varying thickness, uniform drying is more difficult. There are two ways of effecting evenness of drying: one consists of covering only the thin or exposed portions of the surface, to slow up their drying rate; the other retards the drying of the entire piece by means of a covering over the whole surface of the piece. The box shown in Fig. 2-40 would have warped badly if the drying of the outer surfaces had not been slowed by cloth-covered blocks.

49

IV. CRACKING IN DRYING

It is discouraging to find that a piece has cracked in drying. The causes are much the same as those for warping, but because of greater strains the piece cracks as well as warps. We describe below the causes of cracking, and precautions that should be taken.

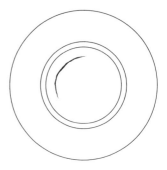

Fig. 6-2. Drying crack in the bottom of a jar.

Causes of cracking. Drying cracks are caused by differences in the shrinkage between various parts of a piece. For example, suppose that a bowl has been thrown on the wheel and dried rapidly in a warm place. After a few hours it would be apt to show a crack running down the rim, as shown in Fig. 6–1. This is because the rim has dried to the leather-hard stage before the thicker and better shielded base has dried hardly at all. A 5% shrinkage of the rim before the base has started to shrink at all sets up strains of such magnitude that cracks start at the rim and run down the sides.

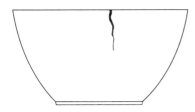

Fig. 6-1. Drying crack in the rim of a bowl.

Figure 6–2 shows a crack in the bottom of a piece. This has appeared because the outside of the bowl has dried and shrunk first, and has squeezed in the still soft bottom. When the bottom finally dries, the sides are rigid, and the inevitable result is a crack like that shown.

Prevention of cracking. To prevent drying cracks, precautions should be taken to assure that the molded piece is of the same consistency throughout. A vase with a moist bottom, a slab-built piece with one section drier than the others, or a joint in which soft clay has been squeezed between harder clay —all these conditions will lead to drying cracks. Slip should be used for joining leather-hard pieces only when the joint is so well fitted that the slip can be applied in a very thin layer.

When the piece is uniformly moist to start with, the drying must be carried out in such a way that the rate of drying is uniform throughout the piece. In general, the larger the piece, the more slowly it should be dried.

It will be found that some clays and bodies can safely be dried more rapidly than others. For example, bodies containing grog have less drying shrinkage than others, and therefore may be quite rapidly dried without danger of cracking.

V. DRYING METHODS

Drying large pieces. Successful drying by the studio potter is more often a problem of delaying the drying process than of accelerating it. The drying of a piece of any great size may be slowed by placing a cover over it, as shown in Fig. 6–3. This cover may be a tin can, or a box of thin, transparent plastic. The rate of drying is governed by the distance the cover is raised from the base.

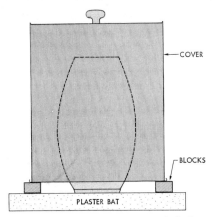

Fig. 6-3. Vase with a cover to retard drying.

For large bowls, the drying of the upper
edge may be delayed by covering with a
plastic sheet or aluminum foil, as shown in
Fig. 6–4. In fact, this method is recommended for slowing the drying of any thin
extensions on a piece, such as handles.

Drying small pieces. Small pieces may
be dried quite rapidly by exposure to the
air, provided the drying takes place uniformly. For example, the air cannot reach
the bottom of a piece if it is resting on a
board or bat. However, if it is raised as
shown in Figs. 6–5 and 6–6, the drying is
much more uniform and the time required
to dry the piece is lessened.

Fig. 6-4. Covering the edge of a large vase to retard drying.

Fig. 6-6. Placing a freshly molded tile on a screen
so that the sides will dry evenly.

Fig. 6-5. A vase raised on strips to allow the bottom to dry.

Fig. 6-7. Plaster setters used to keep bowls round while drying.

Drying setters. Bowls, or vases with wide mouths, should be dried on a plaster setter, as shown in Fig. 6–7, to keep them round.

VI. FINAL DRYING

At some time or other, I am sure that every potter, upon opening a kiln, has experienced the keen disappointment of finding a piece of ware exploded into fragments. I have been asked many times to explain the cause, for invariably the potter is sure that the piece has been around the pottery for several weeks before firing and consequently must have been thoroughly dry. The answer is that the piece has *not* completely dried by its exposure to the air. In humid weather, for instance, it is almost impossible for a piece to dry thoroughly. If the kiln is brought up to temperature very slowly, the final drying of small pieces can be accomplished in the kiln itself. For large pieces, however, the temperature rise must be considerably prolonged, because it takes longer for the water still in the clay to get through the pores, and the pressure of the steam which is generated is sufficient to explode even very strong pieces.

It is, perhaps, safer to accomplish the final drying of a piece by leaving it for several days in a warm place, such as over a radiator or stove, or the piece may be placed in an oven set at low heat overnight. If a number of pieces are to be dried, it might be worth while to build a simple dryer, as described in Chapter 30.

VII. REFERENCES

NORTON, F. H., *Elements of Ceramics.* Addison-Wesley Publishing Company, Inc., Cambridge, Mass., 1952 (Chapter 12).

CHAPTER 7

Biscuit Firing

I. INTRODUCTION

One of the most critical operations in the making of pottery is the firing. Here the potter is on trial, for any slipshod workmanship, no matter how well concealed, will be exposed. While many disappointments will be encountered in drawing the kiln, they are more than balanced by the satisfaction in taking out fine pieces.

As the kiln is the most costly item of the potter's equipment, particular care should be taken to select the model best suited to the work to be done. In this chapter we shall describe the firing process for biscuit ware and discuss the small kiln.

II. TYPES OF KILNS

There are many kinds and sizes of kilns on the market. On the other hand, it is quite simple for the potter to build his own. However, the quality of small commercial kilns has so greatly improved in recent years, and the prices are so reasonable, that it will scarcely pay for the potter to build his own unless he does it simply for the satisfaction of creating his own equipment, or because he needs a kiln with special characteristics.

Wire-wound electric kilns. This type of kiln is inexpensive to buy and operate, but it is limited to a maximum temperature of 1000°C (Cone 06) in most cases. (The use of cones as temperature indicators is described in Chapter 20.) It is possible to make a wire-wound kiln that will have a reasonable length of life at an operating temperature up to 1260°C (Cone 10) if heavy-duty windings like Kanthal are used, and if sufficient wire is installed to give a large radiating area. The most uniform temperatures are attained if the entire inner surface of the kiln chamber is covered with heating elements, but such a construction is more expensive than when only a portion (the four sides) of the kiln chamber is heated. However, when insulating refractories are used, the heat is quite uniform even when the heating units are localized.

Even in the best kilns, the heating units occasionally burn out, and one of the features to be looked for in a kiln is easy replacement of the winding. In the less expensive kilns the heater winding is laid in grooves cut in the insulating refractory, or it is molded into a light-weight refractory concrete, and replacement is easy. However, an edge of the groove can easily be broken off, and it is difficult to repair. The more expensive kilns and furnaces have removable heating elements which are easy to replace and which are very rugged.

Kilns are available with top openings, or with doors in the side. A kiln that opens at the top has the advantages that heating wire may be placed on all four sides and setting is made easier. However, there is much more danger of shaking dust onto the ware.

Figure 7–1 shows diagrammatically the common types of wire-wound kilns, and Fig. 7–2 shows the interior of a well-designed kiln for Cone 10 firing. It should be borne in mind that it may be more economical in the long run to use a well-insulated kiln at a higher initial cost than a thin-walled kiln whose operating costs are greater. For example, a well-insulated kiln will fire to Cone 4 on the same power as the thin-walled kiln will fire to Cone 06.

When selecting a kiln, the local electric company should be consulted, to make sure that the available wiring is adequate. The amount of power needed for wire-wound kilns can be figured, in kilovolt-amperes (kva), as follows. The kva is the current in amperes, times the voltage, divided by 1000.

Fig. 7-2. Interior of a wire-wound kiln for operation up to Cone 10.

For example, a small kiln using 15 amperes on a 110-volt line would be taking 1.65 kva. If the kiln needs more than this, special wiring will be required, much like that for an electric stove. Table 7–1 gives the power required for several sizes of kilns.

The smaller kilns are connected directly to a 110-volt line (regular house voltage), and are brought up to the required temperature over a period of several hours, and then are turned off. Care should be taken not to leave the heat on for too long a period, for this may cause the kiln to become overheated and the coils to burn out. The larger

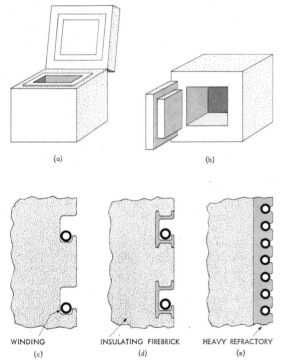

Fig. 7-1. Wire-wound kilns: (a) top-opening kiln, (b) side-opening kiln, (c) windings in grooves in insulating firebrick, (d) windings in reinforced grooves, and (e) removable heavy-duty element.

TABLE 7–1
POWER USED BY WIRE–WOUND KILNS

Kiln capacity in cubic feet	kva to reach Cone 06
0.5	1.1
1.0	2.2
2.0	4.5
4.0	9
8.0	18

kilns have two, three, or six different heats, controlled by means of switches, so that the heat may be brought up slowly and the required temperature can be maintained constant. For special firing, like that required for crystalline glaze work, a variable voltage transformer will give more perfect control.

If the potter is content with low- or medium-fired bodies and glazes, the wire-wound electric kiln is decidedly the first choice, for it has these advantages:

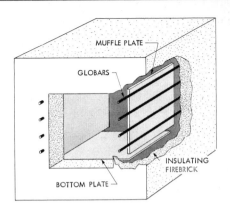

Fig. 7-3. Cutaway view of globar kiln (door removed).

Low first cost ($50 to $200 per cubic foot).
Simplicity of operation.
Safety (less danger from fire).
No need for flue connection.

Remember, though, that the greater cost of low-fired bodies may more than offset the initial saving in the cost of the kiln.

Globar electric kilns. These kilns have rods of silicon carbide (globars) as heating elements, instead of wire, which permits them to be fired to the higher temperatures required, for example, for work with porcelains. These kilns are ruggedly built and will give good service, but they are far more expensive than wire-wound kilns of similar capacity because of the more costly construction and also because a controlling transformer is absolutely necessary. Globar kilns, with the transformer, cost from $300 to $500 per cubic foot of working space.

Figure 7–3 is a sketch of the kind of globar kiln used for pottery, and Fig. 7–4 is a photograph of the same kiln.

Gas-fired kilns. Gas-fired kilns should be of the muffle type, so that combustion gases do not strike the ware. Figure 7–5 shows diagrammatically one type of muffle kiln. These kilns, when well designed, give uni-

Fig. 7-4. Globar kiln with door open, showing partly drawn ware.

form temperatures and may be used up to 1450°C (Cone 16). They are built both for side loading and for top loading. The latter (Fig. 7–6) permits the attainment of uniform temperature with greater ease.

The capacity of gas-fired kilns runs from 1 to 30 cubic feet. In the small sizes they are more costly than wire-wound kilns of the same capacity, but in the larger sizes the cost may be considerably less than for the corresponding electric kiln. The burners may be of the atmospheric type (like those used for a kitchen stove) or of the blower type,

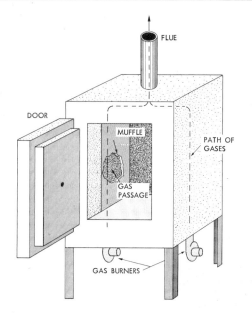

Fig. 7-5. Cutaway view of gas-fired muffle kiln.

Fig. 7-6. Gas-fired muffle kiln with pyrometer.

which are noisier but more suitable for larger kilns and higher temperatures. City gas, natural gas, or bottled gas may be used, but the burners must be adjusted for the particular kind of gas.

Most gas-fired kilns require a flue connection, or at least a ventilating hood to carry off the flue gases. These gases are somewhat hotter than those from a stove or a furnace, and the proposed installation should have the approval of the local building inspector and your fire insurance company.

To summarize: gas kilns can be used at high temperatures and are inexpensive to operate, but they require a flue connection, and because they generate considerable heat, they cause discomfort in hot weather, particularly in a small pottery.

Oil-fired kilns. These kilns are constructed like the gas-fired kilns, but they require more attention in firing and they are not as clean or as easy to control. Nevertheless, where gas is not available, oil-fired kilns are quite satis-

factory. They do require a flue connection and, in some cases, a chimney with a good draft.

Coal-fired kilns. Coal-fired kilns were once quite popular, but they are seldom used today because they are hard to control, dirty, and require an exceptionally efficient draft.

Wood-fired kilns. At one time wood-fired kilns were extensively used in rural areas where gas was not available and wood was plentiful. Excellent results can be obtained with a kiln that is well designed of insulating refractories. The highest temperature required for firing can be reached in such a kiln (for many years the porcelain of Copenhagen was wood-fired at 1500°C), and the firing of even a large kiln may be carried out in a single day. A wood-fired kiln does, however, require constant attention during firing. To obtain a uniform temperature throughout the kiln requires experience in firing and placing the saggers. An excellent kiln of this

Fig. 7-7. Wood-fired kiln made of insulating firebrick.

kind is shown on page 222 of *Elements of Ceramics,** and in the photograph of Fig. 7-7.

Continuous kilns. For the small pottery engaged in production, a continuous kiln may be found more efficient than the chamber kilns previously described. This type of kiln has a series of cars on which the ware is set, and the cars are moved in succession through a heated tunnel. The heat in the tunnel is low at the entrance, gradually increases to a maximum at the center of the tunnel, and then drops again so that the pieces slowly cool as they emerge.

A continuous kiln makes setting and drawing quite simple, since it is done in the open, and the fuel (or power) consumption is about half that for a chamber kiln of the same capacity. On the other hand, for maximum efficiency a continuous kiln must be kept running at full capacity night and day.

*F. H. Norton, *Elements of Ceramics.* Cambridge, Mass.: Addison-Wesley Publishing Company, Inc., 1952.

A continuous kiln of small capacity is shown in Fig. 7-8.

Summary. Although some years ago it would have been advisable for a potter to construct his own kiln because ready-made kilns were poorly constructed and expensive, the modern potter is well advised to purchase a kiln, unless he derives satisfaction from building his own equipment, or unless his kiln must have special features. Chapter 30 describes kilns that can be readily home-built.

Commercial kilns are of many sizes and the range of prices is great. Table 7-2 lists the types, sizes, prices, and operating characteristics of some of these.

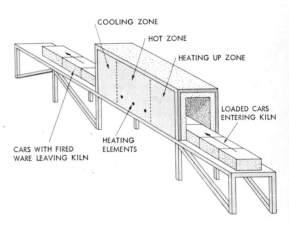

Fig. 7-8. Small continuous kiln.

TABLE 7-2
CHARACTERISTICS OF SMALL KILNS

Type	Size, cubic feet	Max. power required, kva	Max. safe temp.,°C	Cost in 1953, dollars	Cost of firing, dollars 1000°C	1150°C
Electric, wire wound	0.4	2	1000	40	0.25	
	0.8	4	1000	80	0.40	
	3.2	8	1100	240	1.00	
	2.5	8	1200	310	0.80	1.00
Electric, wire wound replaceable units	0.1	1	1200	50	0.08	0.11
	-0.9	4.5	1200	270	0.40	0.60
	1.9	7	1200	500	0.60	0.80
	3.3	8	1200	670	1.00	1.50
Electric, globar with transformer	0.1	2	1500	600	0.30	0.50
	6.2	20	1350	2500	5.00	8.00
	10.0	40	1300	5000	10.00	15.00
Gas-fired, muffle	3.3	------	1200	380	0.70	0.90
	30.0	------	1200	1250	6.00	8.00
	3.3	------	1300	730	0.80	1.10
	30.0	------	1300	1400	7.00	10.00
Oil-fired, muffle	3.3	------	1200	550	0.60	0.80
	30.0	------	1200	1570	5.00	7.00
	3.3	------	1300	740	0.70	0.90
	30.0	------	1300	2180	6.00	8.00

III. THE FIRING PROCESS

This process will be described in considerable detail in Chapter 22, but the beginner should know something of what happens in the kiln. When the clay or body is heated, the chemical water (the water in the crystal structure) is driven off at a red heat. Then, as the maturing temperature is approached, some of the body melts and forms glass, which pulls the particles of clay together and acts as a sort of glue to give the piece strength when it is cool.

Shrinkage in firing. Nearly all bodies and clays shrink during the firing process. Bodies fired to vitrification, like porcelain, may shrink as much as 11% in length (1% $= \frac{1}{100} = 0.01$), while bodies high in grog, like terra cotta, shrink only about 4%. For the finished size of a piece to be correct, shrinkage must be allowed for when the piece is first formed.

Warping in firing. Thin pieces are especially subject to warping in the firing process. The causes and prevention of warping are discussed in Chapter 22. Briefly, any unevenness or strain set up in molding, drying, or handling may cause warping. Tiles and slabs, particularly, must be handled with great care to maintain flatness.

Effect of firing on the absorption of the body. When the clay or body is fired, it gains strength and at the same time becomes less porous. Porosity is measured in terms of the weight of the water absorbed by a fired body compared with its dry weight. For example, if a tile weighs 100 gm when dry, and after soaking it weighs 110.6 gm, the gain in weight is $\frac{10.6}{100} \times 100 = 10.6\%$. This value is called the *absorption* of the body, and it runs from about 10% for earthenware bodies to 5% for stoneware bodies, and is zero for porcelain. If the absorption runs much over 10%, the body may well lack watertightness, a defect often found in studio ware. Even when unglazed, a piece should be able to hold water without seepage through the bottom. There is no excuse for making leaky ware or ware that must be temporarily sealed with wax or varnish; if the body does not make a watertight piece, either it should be fired to a higher temperature, or a body that matures at a lower temperature should be used.

Firing for translucency. At first, the beginner will not be working with porcelains, but when this type of body is used, translucency is important. Bodies develop translucency because of a large amount of flux or because of a high firing temperature. As mentioned above, a high firing temperature produces glass, which allows light to shine through the piece. It must be remembered that when a body is high in glass content, it tends to deform (sag) in the kiln, and therefore special supports (described in the next section) are needed.

IV. SETTINGS

The proper setting of ware in the biscuit kiln is important. While some very low-fired earthenware may be piled in the kiln helter-skelter, the setting of pieces in the kiln must usually be carefully planned to minimize warping and cracking.

The setting of earthenware. Figure 7–9 shows a typical setting for ordinary earthenware. The ware is set on refractory shelves which have been lightly coated with kiln wash to prevent sticking. A good kiln wash

Fig. 7-10. A partly loaded biscuit sagger (New Castle Refractories Co.).

Fig. 7-9. A kiln set with ware, showing the posts and shelves.

consists of 90% fine alumina and 10% Florida kaolin. The saggers shown in Fig. 7–10 are seldom used in a small kiln, but they are desirable in a wood-fired kiln.

Delicate pieces should be set on an unfired slab of the same composition as the piece, so that there will be no shrinkage strains. Thin-walled bowls are often set on bevel-edged disks to keep them round; sculptured pieces may need the temporary support of an un-fired body. To save space in the kiln, small pieces may be nested inside larger ones. Ware should never be placed less than one inch away from the heating elements, however, or it will warp toward the heat, as shown in Fig. 7–11.

The setting of stoneware. The procedure for setting stoneware is the same as that for earthenware, but more care must be taken to prevent sticking. If salt-glazing is used, each piece must have a little space around it, and one piece cannot be nested in another.

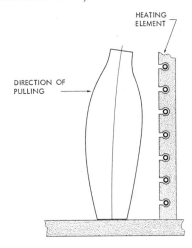

Fig. 7-11. A vase pulling toward the heating element during firing.

The setting of soft porcelain. These bodies tend to slump in the kiln as a considerable amount of glass is developed, and therefore must be well supported. Plates are usually set in a bed of flint or alumina which has been carefully formed to their shape. During the firing process, the piece sags to conform to this bed. Sometimes the plates are placed on fired setters coated with an alumina wash. Cups and bowls are usually inverted on an unfired disk, or are set with an unfired ring resting in the mouth. When they are well supported with drapery, figurines are set on an unfired disk, but if only the ankles support the figure, unfired supports are required.

The setting of hard porcelain. Because the firing temperature is so low, there is little shrinkage or distortion of hard porcelain biscuit, and therefore the setting presents no serious problem.

V. FIRING SCHEDULES

The value of preheating. In biscuit firing, it is always advisable to preheat the ware overnight at a temperature of 300°–500°C. This dissipates any remaining moisture in the ware and also warms the kiln, which facilitates the firing on the following day. As mentioned in Chapter 6, an imperfectly dried piece may explode in the kiln if the heating is too rapid. Even a completely dried piece may explode with too rapid heating because of the pressure of the steam that is built up by evaporation of the chemically combined water in the piece.

The rate of temperature rise. The rate of firing depends both on the size of the piece and the size of the kiln. In small kilns firing thin-walled pieces, the average schedule consists of setting in the afternoon, leaving on a low heat overnight, and then bringing the temperature to maximum firing heat in a period of from 4 to 8 hours the following day. Heavy pieces require longer firing times.

When the end of the firing period is approached, the rate of temperature rise should be decreased, so that the heat may soak evenly into the ware. It is advisable to hold the maximum temperature constant for about one hour. A pyrometer accurately determines the temperature of the kiln, but because many wire-wound kilns have no sensitive controls the firing must necessarily follow the kiln. However, this is usually no drawback, since the kiln rate naturally slows down towards the end of the firing period.

Cooling rates. If the ware is cooled with the kiln closed, no damage should result from the cooling, even when the kiln is small. Small kilns can be cooled overnight, while large kilns require at least 24 hours. A kiln should never be opened while the ware is still too hot to touch, otherwise there is danger of *dunting* (cracking). Even a natural cooling rate will cause dunting of large pieces when they are fired in light, wire-wound kilns, and in these instances the cooling must be artificially slowed.

Atmosphere control. Because biscuit firing is almost always a process of oxidation, no special atmospheric controls are required.

VI. REFERENCES

1. Granger, A., *La Céramique Industrielle.* Gauthier-Villars & Cie, Paris, 1929 (Chapter XIV).

2. Kenny, J. B., *Complete Book of Pottery Making.* Greenberg Publishers, Inc., New York, 1949 (Chapter 9).

3. Norton, F. H., *Elements of Ceramics.* Addison-Wesley Publishing Company, Inc., Cambridge, Mass., 1952 (Chapter 16).

4. de Vegh, G., and A. Mandi, *The Craft of Ceramics.* D. Van Nostrand Company, Inc., New York, 1949 (Chapter XI).

CHAPTER 8

Glazing

I. INTRODUCTION

The application of glazes is a simple process, but obtaining the correct thickness of the glaze is a matter of experience. We shall assume here that glaze slips are already on hand. (They may be purchased ready-made, or they may be made in the pottery, as explained in Chapter 24.)

II. METHOD OF APPLICATION

Brushing. The application of glaze by brushing has the advantage of requiring only a small amount of slip, but it is difficult to apply a really even layer by this method, especially when matte glazes, which do not flow easily in firing, are used.

The glaze is applied with a flat brush, just like a coat of paint, as shown in Fig. 8–1. Because the body absorbs moisture rapidly, the strokes must be quick and slightly overlapped; it is usually necessary to apply several coats to get the required thickness of glaze. Here the addition of gum to the glaze is invaluable, to prevent brushing off the first coat when applying the second; the second coat should be applied before the first one is quite dry.

Application of glaze by brushing is practical for trials and small pieces because it requires only a small amount of glaze slip, but this method is too slow for extensive use.

Dipping. This method is widely used for production work because it is possible to secure an even coating quickly. For the studio potter, however, its chief disadvantage is the large amount of slip required.

To apply glaze to a saucer by this method, the piece is immersed in a tub of glaze slip, as shown in Fig. 8–2, care being taken not to trap air bubbles on the surface. The saucer is removed from the slip as shown in Fig. 8–3, and is set on a screen to drain (Fig. 8–4). It is difficult to avoid dry spots on the edges where the piece has been held in the fingers, but these can be prevented by releasing the piece with a rotary movement of the fingers, allowing them to drag the glaze along the rim, or by spinning the piece as it is dropped onto the screen, thus spreading the glaze to the edge of the rim by centrifugal force. It is advisable for the beginner to improvise light tongs to hold the larger pieces as they are immersed, as shown in Fig. 8–5.

The consistency (specific gravity) of the glaze slip must be controlled to produce the correct thickness of glaze on the body. Dense bodies absorb little or no water and therefore require a thick slip, while porous pieces need a thin slip. If the piece is extremely porous, it may be necessary to soak the biscuit in water before dipping. In general, the specific gravity of the glaze slip should run

Glazing a vase and a saucer:

Fig. 8-1. Brushing glaze on a vase.

Fig. 8-2. Saucer immersed in glaze slip.

Fig. 8-3. Saucer removed from glaze slip; note the even coat.

Fig. 8-4. Wet saucer placed on a screen to drain and dry.

Fig. 8-5. Holding a plate with tongs for dipping.

from 1.3 for porous bodies to about 1.4 for dense bodies. (The measurement of specific gravity is described in Section VII of Chapter 18.)

Pouring the glaze slip. Less glaze is required for this method than for dipping, but the operation is slower. This is the only satisfactory method of glazing the inside of hollow ware, and external surfaces can sometimes be successfully glazed in this manner. The consistency of the glaze slip is the same as for dipping. The process of glazing the inside of a vase is shown in Figs. 8-6, 8-7, and 8-8. To glaze the outside of the piece, the vase was inverted over a dish, as shown in Fig. 8-9, and the glaze was poured over the surface.

Spraying the glaze. This method is by far the best for large pieces, as only enough glaze to actually cover the piece is required, and it is easy for the beginner to apply an even coat. A compressor, a paint sprayer, and a ventilated spray booth are required, and although this equipment is fairly expensive, any serious pottery project should be so equipped. The spray attachment of a vacuum cleaner is often satisfactory.

By this process, the glaze slip is atomized by air pressure into a fine mist of globules which are projected at high velocity onto the surface of the biscuit, as shown in Fig. 8-10. These particles form a smooth film of uniform thickness when the spraying is correctly done. However, if the spray gun is held too far from the piece, the globules will partially dry before they hit, and a loose, fluffy layer which will not fire down to a good glaze will result. On the other hand, if the gun is held too close to the piece, or is held too long in one place, the layer of

Glazing the inside of a vase:
Fig. 8-6. Pouring the glaze slip in.
Fig. 8-7. Turning the vase to distribute the glaze slip evenly.
Fig. 8-8. Pouring the excess glaze slip out.

GLAZE SLIP

Glazing the outside of a vase:
Fig. 8-9. By pouring.
Fig. 8-10. By spraying. Note the well-lit spray booth.
Fig. 8-11. By dipping.

glaze becomes very wet and is apt to slough off. It takes experience to do a good job of applying glaze by spraying. Most commercial pottery is glazed in automatic spraying machines.

A satisfactory setup for spraying is illustrated in Chapter 30. Note that the piece to be sprayed should be set on a revolving table or whirler, and that the spraying should be done in a well-ventilated enclosure, to prevent inhalation of the glaze.

Other glazing techniques. When a piece is to be glazed with one color on the inside and another color on the outer surface, the simplest method is to pour the glaze for the inside into the piece, making certain that all of the surface is covered, and then to pour it out. The mouth of the piece is then sponged clean on the outer edge, and the piece is carefully immersed in the second glaze up to the rim, as shown in Fig. 8-11. This process is used for commercial work, and is carried out quickly and neatly with a little practice. A more even dividing line can be obtained by making two glost fires (see Chapter 10). After the inside glaze is applied, the outside glaze can be sprayed on, if desired (a stopper is first placed in the mouth, to prevent the spray from spattering onto the inside glaze).

Mottled glazes such as the Rockingham type are obtained by glazing in the usual way with a uniform light color and then spattering on a darker color by flipping dark glaze from a stiff brush.

Scroddled glazes are made by flowing a series of overlapping colored glazes onto a flat disk of plastic clay, which is then jolted to cause any desired degree of intermingling while the colors are still wet. Streaks of colored, fluid glazes are sometimes combed across the clay body with a quill to obtain interesting effects. After the glaze has become firm, the disk is molded over a plaster form to make a platter or a plate.

Flow glazes of various colors used on vertical surfaces are applied thickly in splashes with a brush. When the piece is fired, the glazes flow down and the colors intermingle to give a variegated effect.

Other glazing methods are described and illustrated in Chapter 24.

Glazing one-fired ware. For some types of ware, it is possible to fire the glaze and biscuit at the same time. By this method, the body is glazed while it is green, usually by spraying. No special precautions are necessary.

III. THE THICKNESS OF THE GLAZE LAYER
Judging glaze thickness by volume. After some experience, it is possible to judge the thickness of the glaze quite closely, but the beginner usually gets it too thin. A good rule of thumb is to allow a specified volume of glaze slip for each unit area of biscuit. The values in Table 8–1 are reasonably correct; however, some of the stoneware and porcelain glazes may be much thicker.

Judging glaze thickness by translucency. Another method of judging the thickness of the glaze is by the appearance of the underglaze decoration as the glaze is applied. When the wet glaze layer is of the correct thickness, the decoration should be just

Fig. 8-12. Sponging the foot of a glazed vase.

faintly visible. If there is no underglaze pattern, pencil marks made on the biscuit will serve (these will disappear on firing).

IV. PRODUCING AREAS BARE OF GLAZE
It is often desirable to leave certain areas of a piece free of glaze. This is particularly true of the foot of a piece, which is apt to stick in the glost firing. The glaze is removed by scraping after it is dry, and the last traces are removed by sponging, as shown in Fig. 8–12. A piece of carpet stretched on a board is useful for rubbing the area clean.

Another method of leaving certain areas free of glaze is to paint those portions with hot paraffin before glazing. The glaze will not adhere to the paraffin, and after firing these areas are quite bare.

V. APPLICATION OF VAPOR GLAZES
This method of applying glaze is excellent for delicately sculptured pieces, because it leaves only a very thin film of glaze on the surface. The inside of a sagger is coated

TABLE 8–1

GLAZE THICKNESS

Type of glaze	Vol. of glaze slip, in cc per sq cm of surface	Thickness of dried glaze, in mm	Thickness of fired glaze, in mm
Clear glazes	0.1	0.6	0.3
Opaque glazes	0.2	1.2	0.6
Matte glazes	0.2	1.2	0.6
Crystalline glazes	0.3	2.0	1.0
Flow glazes	0.3	2.0	1.0

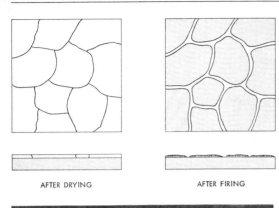

AFTER DRYING   AFTER FIRING

Fig. 8-13. Crawling, a glaze defect.
Fig. 8-14. An extreme case of crawling, which might, though generally considered a defect, give an interesting effect if properly controlled.

with glaze and the biscuit piece is placed inside it. On firing, the vapors from the glaze deposit a very thin coat onto the piece. Conversely, if a glazed piece of ware is placed in a new sagger, it will lose some of its glaze to the sagger wall and will appear "dry." For this reason, new glost saggers are often glazed on the inside before being used.

Vapor glazing requires the use of highly volatile constituents, like borax and common salt, in the glaze composition.

Salt glazing. This method of glazing was used on much of the fine English tableware produced about the middle of the 18th century. It gives a delicate orange-peel surface of great distinction. It was also used in Colonial days for stoneware, often with cobalt blue decorations. The glaze is applied by bringing the piece up to about Cone 7 (1200° C) and then adding to the fire common salt, which at once volatilizes and combines with the clay surface. Low-firing bodies cannot be glazed by this method; it is reserved for stoneware. Salt glazing requires a special kiln that must be used only for this kind of firing.

VI. GLAZE DEFECTS AND THEIR ELIMINATION

Crawling. The inexperienced glazer has his greatest trouble with the defect known as crawling, and an understanding of the cause will suggest remedies. In firing, this imperfection is evidenced by a crawling up of the glaze into separated areas of the piece, with exposed portions of the body in between, as shown in Fig. 8–13; in extreme cases (Fig. 8–14) the glaze forms in little beads. Actually, the trouble has not started with the firing, but can be traced back to the drying of the glaze, where shrinkage caused a network of cracks, often so fine that they are invisible except upon close scrutiny. When the piece is fired, surface tension causes the separated areas to draw together into beads, just as water forms in droplets on an oily surface.

The remedy is either to reduce the drying shrinkage, or to toughen the glaze film so that it will not crack. Drying shrinkage can be lessened by reducing the amount of raw clay in the glaze to not over 5% or by lessening the amount of grinding in the preparation of the glaze. The glaze can be toughened by adding gum to the glaze slip.

Crawling is sometimes caused by dust or grease on the biscuit, which prevents the glaze from adhering to the surface. Care must be taken to be sure that the biscuit is really clean. In handling, the fingertips will sometimes deposit enough grease to cause trouble.

Pinholes. Pinholes are usually due to air that has been trapped in the body slip as bubbles, which are forced into the glaze in the glost firing. Pinholes are sometimes caused by too rapid firing, which does not allow sufficient time for the glaze to completely mature.

Dust and dirt. Specks that appear on the upper surfaces of glazed pieces are usually grit from the kiln or particles of dust from the air. Glazed pieces should be carefully protected from dust until they are set, and it is good practice to blow out the kiln with compressed air before it is used.

Colored spots. These are caused by impurities in the glaze. A copper screen may cause green spots, and an iron utensil is apt to cause brown spots.

Uneven surfaces. Wavy or pebbly surfaces are caused by uneven application of the glaze slip or by glost-firing at too low a temperature.

Crazing. This common defect is a network of fine cracks which develops in the glaze immediately after cooling, or sometimes after a long period of time. This difficulty can be avoided by purchasing well-tried glazes; if the potter makes his own glazes, the question of fitting must be explored, as discussed in Chapter 25.

VII. PRECAUTIONS

It is essential to remember that some of the materials used in glazing are poisonous, particularly the lead compounds, and care must be taken to keep them away from the mouth and to breathe as little of their vapors as possible. The use of lead-containing frits instead of lead oxides greatly reduces this hazard, and actually there is no cause for undue alarm, since many white paints in common use contain greater amounts of lead than do glazes.

VIII. REFERENCES

1. DANIELSON, R. R., The Crawling of Glazes, *Bull. Am. Cer. Soc.* **73**, 1954.

2. DOAT, T., *Grande Feu Céramics*, Keramic Studio Publishing Company, Syracuse, N. Y., 1905 (Chapter IV).

3. SELLERS, T., Glazing Techniques, *Ceramic Monthly* **1**, No. 9, 24 (1953); **1**, No. 12, 25 (1953).

4. DE VEGH, G., AND A. MANDI, *The Craft of Ceramics*, D. Van Nostrand Company, Inc., New York, 1949 (Chapter X).

CHAPTER 9

Underglaze Decoration

I. INTRODUCTION

Underglaze decorations have been used for as long as the process of glazing has been known, for it was a quite natural step to adopt the colored-slip technique from the pre-glaze era. At the outset natural colored clays were used; later, slips colored with earth colors came into use.

Underglaze decorations have a high degree of durability, since they are protected from the wear and tear of handling by the layer of glaze. The overlay of glaze also gives the colors a depth that is never attained with overglaze methods. However, the range of colors is somewhat limited, because it is not possible to use the less stable colors in a glost fire. The palette of colors becomes smaller and smaller as the glost temperature is raised.

II. COMPOSITION OF UNDERGLAZE COLORS

Stains. Stains will be fully discussed in Chapter 28. For underglaze use they must be stable under the particular glaze used, because any dissolution will not only alter the color, but may also allow it to diffuse in the glaze and prevent sharp delineation of the color pattern.

Diluents. A strong stain may be mixed with a white compound to form pale colors, or a colorless mix may be colored with only a small amount of stain to achieve the same result. Adding white to a strong stain is the more flexible method, for a whole series of shades can be produced from one batch; however, very fine grinding and intimate mixing are essential. Ground whiteware body, kaolin (raw or calcined), alumina, feldspar, and flint are common diluents.

Fluxes. Because the underglaze color must have such specific properties as the ability to adhere to the body after firing, a porosity very close to that of the body so that the glaze will be evenly absorbed, and about the same wetting properties for the glaze as the body itself, it is usually necessary to add a small amount of flux and a suspending agent. Additions of 5% glaze and 5% clay are typical; for low temperatures, a more active flux may be needed.

III. COMMERCIAL UNDERGLAZE COLORS

Commercial underglaze colors cover a wide range of hues and are thoroughly reliable. The novice studio potter is urged to buy his colors rather than attempt to mix them. Here again it is true that as the firing temperature increases, the range of usable colors decreases.

Underglaze colors are much the same as the glaze stains listed in Tables 28–8 and 28–9. It must be remembered that zinc in the glaze is detrimental to chrome-tin pinks, and that chrome greens cannot be used with glazes containing tin. On the other hand, copper turquoise stains can be successfully used under glazes containing zinc.

IV. APPLICATION OF UNDERGLAZE COLORS

Media. Because underglaze material is almost devoid of plasticity, it must be supported in a suitable medium to permit easy application. It is usual to blend the color into a so-called fat oil or essential oil mixture by working them together on a glass plate, using a spatula, as shown in Fig. 9–1. The color is sometimes mixed with gum arabic and water to give a good brushing consistency, or glycerin solutions may be used as vehicles.

Brushing on the color. The studio potter generally uses a brush to apply the underglaze colors, and suitable brushes are obtainable from any ceramic supply house. Even an expert cannot do good work with a poor brush, and it is therefore good economy to buy the best brushes and to take good care of them. They must be thoroughly washed with alcohol or turpentine each time they are used.

It is difficult to verbally explain the art of applying underglaze with a brush; the beginner is well advised to work with an experienced person until his technique is developed. If simple designs are chosen at first, creditable work can be turned out after some practice.

One helpful piece of equipment for this work is an armrest to steady the hand. A low rest is used for painting on large pieces, such as the tile shown in Fig. 9–2. A higher rest, such as the one shown in Fig. 9–3, is useful for such work as banding a plate on a whirler.

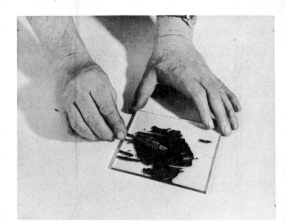
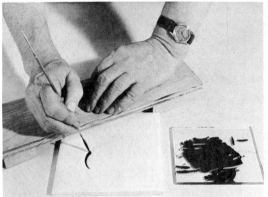

Fig. 9-1. Mixing an underglaze color and a medium with a spatula on a glass plate.
Fig. 9-2. Decorating a tile with a brush, using a handrest.
Fig. 9-3. Painting a band on a plate, using a wheel and an armrest.

Spraying on the color. When underglaze color is applied with an airbrush, a fairly dilute suspension must be used. With a little practice, uniform areas can be covered, or the color can be shaded. Figurines are often decorated in this way. Underglaze may be locally removed, to form white areas, by erasing when dry.

More intricate designs can be made by applying a thin paper stencil (frisket) to the biscuit surface with a gum solution and then spraying the entire surface of the piece, as shown in Fig. 9–4. When the color is partially dry, the frisket is carefully peeled off, leaving a clean design (Fig. 9–5). A similar effect can be achieved by painting a design with a liquid-rubber resist; the resist is peeled off after the color has partially dried.

Printing a design. Decalcomania transfers are used to a considerable extent in decorating commercial ware, because they permit the use of a number of colors simultaneously. However, because of the cost of making the transfers, this method is not feasible for the studio potter unless he wants to purchase commercial designs. Copper plates are uneconomical for the same reason; they are practical only for production runs.

Silk-screen printing, however, is a practical method of application for the studio potter because he can easily make his own stencils. Only one color can be applied at a time, but by careful registering, a second color can be used after the first one has dried. This process is described in detail in Chapter 29.

Fig. 9-4. Spraying underglaze color on a plate with an airbrush. A paper frisket has been stuck to the center of the plate.

Fig. 9-5. Peeling off the frisket, showing the cleancut pattern.

Fig. 9-6. Tile decorated with underglaze crayons (by Louise Shattuck).

Underglaze crayons. Biscuits may be decorated with crayons, formed by mixing underglaze colors with wax. Skill is quickly acquired, and this method is therefore especially recommended to the beginner. The method is illustrated by the tile shown in Fig. 9–6, made by Louise Shattuck, a noted Boston potter.

V. BURNING OFF

It is the usual practice to fire underglaze colors to red heat in order to decompose the oils or gums and burn off the carbon before glazing. This is done to prevent glaze blistering, caused by gases forming in the glost fire. When the glost fire is very slow or when the vehicle is low in organic matter, burning off is not required.

VI. REFERENCES

1. KENNY, J. B., *Ceramic Sculpture.* Greenberg: Publishers, Inc., New York, 1953 (Chapter 8).

2. MARTZ, K., Decorating with Engobes, *Ceramics Monthly* 1, No. 2, 21 (1953).

3. NORTON, F. H., *Elements of Ceramics.* Addison-Wesley Publishing Company, Inc., Cambridge, Mass., 1952 (Chapter 23).

CHAPTER 10

Glost Firing

I. INTRODUCTION

Glost firing is often the last operation in forming the finished piece, and since a great deal of time has now been spent on the piece, every effort must be made to have no defect show up in this final stage. Every potter, no matter how experienced, feels a thrill of anticipation as he draws the kiln; will he find a masterpiece, just passable ware, or a complete failure?

II. MATURING THE GLAZE

As we have explained, the unfired glaze layer is a series of fine particles loosely held together. These particles melt upon heating, and interact to form glass, which acts as a bond. If the glaze is not brought to a high enough temperature, the surface is apt to be pebbly or wavy; on the other hand, if the glaze is fired at too high a temperature, it will flow down vertical surfaces. Each kind of glaze has a recommended maturing temperature, and this should be closely followed.

III. FIRING SCHEDULES

In general, any glaze may be brought to maximum temperature quite rapidly. The limiting factors are the rate of heating of the kiln itself and the ability of the body to stand a quick rise of temperature. Small tiles can be glost-fired in an hour, but most pieces require a much longer time.

Standard glazes. It will be found convenient to set the kiln for glost firing late in the afternoon and to maintain a low heat during the night, so that the kiln will have reached red heat by morning; the kiln is then brought up to the maximum maturing temperature during the day (just as for firing biscuit). In this way, low-firing glazes can be fired in the morning, and those (such as porcelain) requiring very high temperatures can be left in the kiln all day.

Most of the glazes used by the studio potter are fired in an oxidizing atmosphere (a kiln free from smoke), but hard porcelains are finished off in a reducing (smoky) atmosphere, to give greater whiteness to the finished piece. The beginner should confine himself to an oxidizing fire, because the kiln is then easier to control, and because some colors are spoiled by reduction.

Special glazes. Crystalline glazes must be fired according to a special schedule, tabulated in Section III of Chapter 26. Because pyrometric cones do not provide sufficient control, a pyrometer is essential for these glazes.

Copper red glazes must be fired with alternate oxidation and reduction, as explained in Section III of Chapter 26. In gas- or oil-fired kilns, it is possible to control the atmosphere by varying the secondary air supply by

Fig. 10-2. Stilts, pins, and spurs.

means of dampers, but other methods are required for electric kilns. One way is to introduce a small amount of gas into the bottom of the kiln; another is to drop carbonaceous solids such as coke or naphthalene (mothballs) into the kiln.

IV. SETTING METHODS

The proper setting of ware in the glost fire is an important step, because a piece that tips over is not only itself spoiled, but is apt to spoil several others. Special settings must be used in glost firing hard porcelain because the required temperature is so high that warping readily occurs.

Setting flat ware. One of the simplest ways to set a piece of flat ware, such as a plate, is on a stilt, as shown in Fig. 10–1(a). These stilts are obtainable from any ceramic supply house, and they come in many sizes. The three marks left on the bottom of the plate when the stilt is knocked off after firing the piece may be ground out if desired.

Spurs like those shown in Fig. 10–1(b) may also be used. These stilts and spurs are very inexpensive, and are used only once. Other commonly used setters are shown in Fig. 10–2.

When it is not necessary to glaze the foot of a piece, the glaze can be sponged off this part and the setting can be done directly on a refractory shelf. The shelf should be first coated with a wash of powdered alumina or flint with about 10% kaolin added, to prevent sticking if the glaze should accidentally run. A layer of coarse flint (bitstone) is sometimes quite satisfactory.

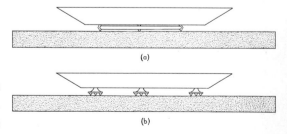

(a)

(b)

Fig. 10-1. Setting of glost ware on (a) stilts and (b) spurs.

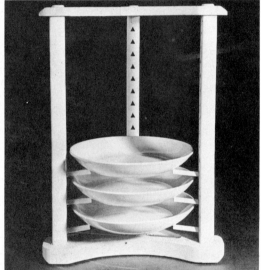

There are a number of different ways of setting when many plates are to be fired at one time. The glost sagger shown in Fig. 10–3 supports each piece on three triangular pins set in sockets in the sagger wall. In setting, the lower group of pins is placed first and a plate is set on them, and subsequent groups of pins are similarly filled. The marks left by the pins can be polished off if desired.

The open setting shown in Fig. 10–4 is quite satisfactory for muffle or electric kilns and has the advantage of being lighter and smaller than the sagger. The thimble setting shown in Fig. 10–5 gives the advantage of flexibility; the height can be varied to suit the purpose.

Setting hollow ware. Cups, bowls, and vases are usually set on stilts, as shown in Fig. 10–6(a). However, the stilts must be large enough to comfortably accommodate the pieces; that shown in part (b) of Fig. 10–6 is too small for safety. If the glaze is removed from the foot of a piece, it can be set on an alumina-washed plate.

Great care must be taken in the setting of pieces with flow or crystalline glazes, as the glaze tends to gather thickly at the bottom of the piece, and may even drip off. A stilt set on a disk of insulating firebrick may be used in these cases; the disk will absorb considerable glaze and yet may be broken away after firing.

Setting tiles. When only a few tiles are to be fired at one time, they may be set on a kiln

Fig. 10-3. A 24-plate glost sagger with three plates set (New Castle Refractories Co.).
Fig. 10-4. Setting rack for plates (Louthan Manufacturing Co.).
Fig. 10-5. Thimble setters for holding glost plates (Louthan Manufacturing Co.).

plate if care is taken to remove all the glaze from the back of the tile. If a number of tiles are to be fired at once, the setter shown in Fig. 10–7, which holds 24 tiles, is practical.

A very flexible tile setter can be made from two strong insulating firebricks (B&W, K-28), as shown in Fig. 10–8. These bricks are handy for making kiln furniture on the spur of the moment, because they are easily cut with a saw (Fig. 10–9). It is desirable to paint the setter with a wash of 20% kaolin and 80% alumina to prevent dusting. The top tile should be set first; working downward will prevent dust from getting into the glaze.

Fig. 10-6. Stoneware bowl set on stilts (a) properly and (b) improperly. The bowl in (b) is likely to tip over in the kiln because the stilts are too small.

Fig. 10-7. Twenty-four-tile refractory setter.
Fig. 10-8. Tile setter made from insulating firebrick.
Fig. 10-9. Cutting insulating firebrick with an old hacksaw blade.

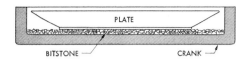

Fig. 10-10. High-fired porcelain plate set in a crank for the glost fire.

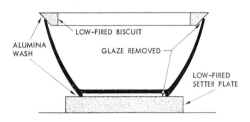

Fig. 10-12. High-fired porcelain bowl with setter to hold rim circular.

Fig. 10-11. Setters for vitrified ware. The glost pieces rest on a dry foot (Louthan Manufacturing Co.).

Setting sculpture. The glost setting of sculpture presents no serious problems. In this section we shall consider only glost firing of ware that has been previously biscuited at somewhat higher temperatures.

Sculptured heads, or any of the more compact pieces, may be set on washed kiln plates after the glaze has been sponged from the base of the piece. Relief plaques may be set on plates if the back is free of glaze, or should be set on stilts if it is not.

Setting hard porcelain pieces. Hard porcelain pieces must be carefully supported to avoid distortion due to the high temperatures required for firing, which cause considerable shrinkage. In general, the supports should be similar to those used for biscuit firing of vitreous ware, but here we have the added complication of a glazed surface.

Porcelain flatware can be set on an alumina-washed plate or on coarse silica grain (bitstone), after the foot has been cleared of glaze. There will be some sagging or lifting of the rim, but this has been allowed for in the original design, if the piece was correctly formed. Each plate is held in its own sagger

or crank, as shown in Fig. 10–10. Modern potters often use special setters, like those shown in Fig. 10–11.

Porcelain hollow ware is often set on an unfired disk (the foot must be free of glaze). For high-grade ware, when the rim must be kept perfectly round, a setter is placed on the rim as well, as in Fig. 10–12. Here again, the glaze must be carefully removed from the rim before the setter is applied.

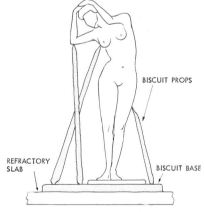

Fig. 10-13. Porcelain figurine with supports for the glost fire.

After firing, the unglazed rim may be polished, or the piece may be refired without the setter. There will be no additional shrinkage and little if any warping in this second firing.

The extended parts of sculptured pieces of porcelain must be carefully supported with props of biscuit-fired body, as shown in Fig. 10–13. These props are pointed at the upper end, so as to make only small contact with the glazed surface, and are painted with alumina to prevent sticking. The small marks made by the props can be polished off after firing.

V. REFERENCES

1. ANON., Glost Firing of Ware, *Ceram. Ind.* **44**, 132 (1945).

2. ANON., Placing of Ware for Glost Firing, *Ceram. Ind.* **44**, 82, 84 (1945).

3. DOAT, T., *Grande Feu Céramics,* Keramic Studio Publishing Company, Syracuse, N. Y., 1905 (Chapters VI and VII).

CHAPTER 11

Overglaze Decoration

I. INTRODUCTION

European decorators. Soon after white glazed earthenware and porcelain were introduced in Europe, European craftsmen seized upon the idea of using it as a background for painting in vitrifiable colors. Although some of the designs were very simple, extremely elaborate work was produced at the potteries of Spode, Meissen, and Sèvres, noted for their complicated floral designs. While we admire the amazing skill of the better flower painters, we cannot always be enthusiastic over the design as a whole. Some of the finest pottery has no decoration at all; shape, color, and texture serve to attract the eye.

China painting in the United States. At about the beginning of the 19th century china painting was extremely popular in this country. Many schools were established, and some of the excellent work done compared favorably with European ware. For the most part, the pottery itself was imported from abroad, and only the painting was done here. For this reason there was, more often than not, a lack of unity between the basic form of the piece and its decoration. Popular enthusiasm for china painting had almost died out by 1910.

Today there is much fine work being done by contemporary artists, but the trend is toward simpler patterns closely tied in with the basic design of the piece, and the artist usually both makes the piece and decorates it. This is certainly as it should be, if the result is to be an artistic piece that is pleasing to the eye. The great quantities of gaudy ware made for the gift trade, of course, are another matter, and certainly leave much to be desired in the way of design and technique.

II. COMPOSITION OF OVERGLAZE COLORS

These colors are generally made up of stains (described in Chapter 28), a flux (soft glass) to make the color vitrify and adhere to the glaze, an opacifying agent, and a vehicle to give good brushing consistency.

III. COMMERCIAL OVERGLAZE COLORS

Here again, the colors available from commercial suppliers are thoroughly reliable, and they may be purchased in almost any hue. They come as dry powders, to be mixed with the vehicle supplied by the colormaker. The vehicle is usually a fat oil, thinned with spirits of turpentine, although soluble gums are used by some decorators.

It is well to obtain all of the colors to be used on a single piece from the same supplier, so that the colors will be certain to blend well and mature at the same temperature.

IV. APPLICATION OF OVERGLAZE COLORS

Brushing on the color. Again we must stress the ultimate economy of purchasing the best brushes and taking good care of them, and we must emphasize that there is no substitute for a good teacher.

Remember, too, that the beginner should try simple patterns first. There is much more satisfaction in doing a simple design well than in doing a poor job on a complicated pattern. Figure 11–1 shows a simple but effective overglaze decoration, applied with a brush on a crackle glaze.

Other methods of application. In production work overglazes are applied by silk-screen printing, decalcomanias, and with a spray. These and other methods are described in Chapter 29, along with the overglaze processes of gilding and lustering.

Thickness of application. To give best results, overglaze colors must be of the correct thickness; the more translucent the color, the thicker the application must be. Experience is the best guide in this respect.

V. FIRING OVERGLAZE COLORS

These colors were often referred to as "muffle" colors, for they should not be subjected to the flames in a kiln. A modern electric kiln, of course, needs no muffle.

The colors are fired at about Cone 016 (735°C), which is just above red heat. As we

Fig. 11-1. Simple overglaze design painted on a crackle glaze (Dedham Pottery).

have mentioned previously, some colors will not blend with each other, and it may therefore be necessary to fire some of the colors, add others, and fire again. Some of the porcelain plaques made at Sèvres are fired as many as fifteen times to handle the great number of colors used.

The overglaze colors must fuse into the glaze somewhat, and for this reason it is usual to fire ware with high-fire glazes at somewhat greater temperatures than are used for soft glazes. The following data will serve as a guide: hard and electrical type porcelains with glazes maturing at Cones 12 to 16 (1310° to 1450°C) should have the overglaze fired at Cone 013 (825°C); bone china, frit porcelain, and white earthenware, with glazes maturing at Cones 4 to 6 (1165° to 1190°C), should be fired at Cone 016 (735°C); low-fired art ware with glazes maturing at Cone 06 to 03 (1005° to 1080°C) should be fired at Cone 019 (630°C).

In all cases, overglaze colors are fired in an oxidizing atmosphere, since any trace of reduction (smoky fire) will spoil some of the colors.

During the firing process many colors change—some become more intense, some fade, and some change in hue. An experienced artist makes allowances for these changes, and he also knows which colors will blend with others, and which will react and spoil the effect.

VI. SPECIAL OVERGLAZE EFFECTS
Special effects that can be obtained in overglazing are described in Chapter 29. These include lusters, gilding, ground laying, encrustations, and many others. The discussion is delayed until a later chapter because most of these methods of decoration are beyond the capabilities of a beginner.

VII. REFERENCES
1. Holst, Z. S., Overglaze Decoration, *Ceramic Monthly* 2, No. 4, 25 (1954).

2. Mann, K., *China Decoration,* Pitman Publishing Corporation, New York, 1953.

PART 2

Why we do it

This section is, first, for those who wish to know something of the reasons behind the various processes used in making pottery; second, for those who plan to advance beyond the routine making of pots; and lastly, for those who want to break away from the beaten path and find new trails to follow.

CHAPTER 12

Historical Development of Pottery Making

I. INTRODUCTION

Of the many excellent reference books dealing with the development of pottery making in all parts of the world, a few are listed at the end of this chapter. Many more will be found in the libraries. Because of this wealth of reference data, no attempt will be made to go into historical detail here, but the more significant developments, both aesthetic and technical, are briefly discussed to give a background against which to judge contemporary work.

II. HANDMADE EARTHENWARE

Prehistoric pottery. Pottery making extends so far back in time that it is useless to attempt to place its beginnings in any one region. One of the remarkable things about primitive pottery making is its almost universal association with early man over the whole surface of the earth, and because communication was practically nonexistent, we are led to the conclusion that it evolved independently in many regions. It was quite natural that pottery making should follow closely on the heels of the discovery of fire, for the hardening effect of fire on natural clay is easily observable.

Prehistoric pottery was made of impure clay that could be fired at low temperatures in an open fire, much as is done today by the Indians of New Mexico, although sometimes temporary walls were placed around the fire to form a kind of kiln. The first pieces were probably utilitarian, and were followed by ceremonial objects. These, of course, were all formed by hand, probably over a rounded stone or in a basket at first, and later built freehand, as is done today by primitive peoples.

Figure 12–1 shows a piece of early pottery from northern Chile which is a good example of primitive work.

Pottery in the Mediterranean area. With the growth of culture in the areas around the Mediterranean Sea, pottery began to rise from its crude state. In Asia Minor, glazed ware was made as early as 5000 B.C., and the art soon spread to Egypt, Cyprus, and Crete. Although the body was soft and low-fired, glazes and decorations of incising and slip painting were developed along many lines. The art progressed from the making of simple pots and bowls to the making of figurines, usually for religious purposes, but occasionally as toys. Tiles and decorative bricks were produced for buildings, especially in Asia Minor.

Pottery in the Far East. In the Far East pottery was first entirely handmade from local clays, and was confined in its early stages to

Fig. 12-1. Chilean bowl showing simple, effective decoration. (Courtesy
of the American Museum of Natural History, New York.)

the making of architectural and votive pieces. Some glazing was used, but most of the decoration was by surface modeling.

Pottery in the New World. The American Indian is believed to have originally come to the New World from northern Asia over the Bering Straits in Neolithic times, but undoubtedly the cultures of Central and South America were augmented by the influx of knowledge from the Orient. In any event, handmade ware of low-fired local clay was produced, exclusively by women, in many places on these two continents. Although glazing was rarely, if ever, used, excellent sculpture and pots, both slip-decorated and polished, were common. The Indians of New Mexico still make excellent pottery of this type. A thorough description of the method is given by Guthe (39),* and a 16th century bowl from Peru is shown in Fig. 12-2.

_____

*Numbers in parentheses are those of the references at the end of this chapter.

III. WHEEL-THROWN EARTHENWARE

The potter's wheel probably originated in the Near East about the year 3000 B.C., but it took over a thousand years for its use to spread to Egypt, China, and adjacent areas. This invention not only caused a revolution in pottery making, but changed a whole way of life. Here was man's first machine, which was to develop in future centuries into the complex forms that make modern life possible.

While handmade pottery was always the work of women, the men took over the potter's wheel, and only in recent times have women ventured to use it.

Fig. 12-2. Sixteenth-century Peruvian polished black bowl. (Courtesy of the American Museum of Natural History, New York.)

Pottery making in Greece. The potter's wheel permitted the formation of clay ware with much more rapidity and freedom than was possible before its invention. In ancient Greece the wheel was used to form many utilitarian vessels, which were later put on the wheel a second time and shaved to very precise dimensions. Our museums are filled with examples of this ware, often superbly painted with red or black figures in a sort of thin glaze. Many of the shapes, however, were derived from metal forms, and do not have the feeling of the plastic clay.

Pottery making in China. Here the wheel was used at a very early date, probably about 2000 B.C. The first known earthenware of China was confined to rather heavy pieces, sometimes with sculptured decorations.

Pottery making in Egypt. In this area, the potter's wheel was used as early as 1500 B.C. to form soft earthenware.

Pottery making in Europe. The potter's wheel was introduced to Europe by the Ro-

mans. Until the 18th century, most of the pottery produced there was made of a red or buff earthenware body of local clay. When occasionally glaze was used, it was of a crude lead type.

Pottery making in the United States. It is believed that the first ware made in this country (other than by Indians) was fired at Jamestown about 1610. Soon after, many small redware potteries sprang up all over the East. In New England, it was an exceptional town that did not have a small pottery whose wares were peddled from house to house by wagon. During the war of 1812, when imports from Great Britain were cut off, the industry flourished. For example, the town of Peabody, Massachusetts, had more than 60 potteries operating at one time. The ware was very similar to that made in England one hundred years earlier, but our pottery had distinctive shapes and some interesting raw lead glazes. This ware is probably our only folk pottery. It is well described by Watkins (21), and a typical piece is shown in Fig. 12–3.

Fig. 12-3. Fine piece of New England redware with an orange and green glaze.

Fig. 12-4. Chinese stoneware bowl of the Sung dynasty. (Courtesy of The Metropolitan Museum of Art, New York.)

IV. STONEWARE

The weakness and porosity of earthenware must have been long recognized by early potters, but the low-firing temperatures of crude kilns prohibited the production of harder pieces. When a totally enclosed kiln finally became a reality, the superior strength of hard-fired pieces was evident.

Stoneware in China. At about the start of the Christian era, a true stoneware was made in China from clays containing feldspar, or to which feldspar was added. Glazes of the lime-feldspathic type were used, and for the first time we find pottery that is watertight and strong, with the rugged charm that is evident in the piece shown in Fig. 12–4. This ware gradually evolved into porcelain, as will be discussed later.

Stoneware in Japan and Korea. The art of making stoneware spread from Korea to Japan, where it developed an individual character, as clearly described by Bowes (52) in his excellent book.

Stoneware in Germany and the Low Countries. From the 15th century on, natural clays were used in Northern Europe for making stoneware. Utilitarian articles like jugs and steins were the chief products, and at about this time the newly discovered salt glaze replaced the slip-type glaze previously used. In general, this stoneware was well made of a strong, dense body, as described by Blacker (22).

Stoneware in England. The ware produced in England between 1720 and 1780 was a distinctive, white, salt-glazed stoneware, more delicately shaped than that previously produced, and often decorated with enamel colors. However, this was soon displaced in popularity by smoother-glazed earthenware. A fine piece of salt-glazed earthenware is shown in Fig. 12–5.

Stoneware in the United States. In this country, much utilitarian salt-glazed stoneware was produced by the Dutch as early as 1735, in the New York area. The art spread

Fig. 12-5. Salt-glazed white stoneware teapot, made in England about 1740. (Courtesy of The Metropolitan Museum of Art, New York.)

until many potteries were in operation in the East, nearly all of them using clay from New Jersey. One pottery in Nashua, New Hampshire, for example, imported its clay by way of the Middlesex Canal and the Merrimac River. This ware, mostly jugs and crocks, was often decorated by stamping or by cobalt slip, and the better examples are much in demand by collectors. A fine jar is shown in Fig. 12–6.

Modern stoneware. Many modern potters have turned to stoneware as the medium best suited to express their ideas. Good stone-

ware has a down-to-earth feeling that the more sophisticated porcelain lacks. In this country, some fine examples are the pieces made by Binns at Alfred, New York (Fig. 12–7), by Russel Crook at Boston, and more recently by the Scheiers in New Hampshire. Recently the Scandinavians have turned to this medium to produce some of the very finest modern ceramics, as shown in Figs. 12–8 and 12–9.

V. PORCELAIN
This white, translucent ware gradually evolved in China in the first few centuries

Fig. 12-6. Stoneware jar made in Charlestown, Massachusetts, about 1840.
Fig. 12-7. Stoneware vase made by C. F. Binns at Alfred, N. Y., about 1915.
Fig. 12-8. Fine stoneware vase made by Stid Lindberg at Gustavsberg, now
owned by the King of Sweden.

Fig. 12-9. Modern bowl designed by A. C. Percy and made by the Gävle Porcelain Manufactory in Sweden. (Courtesy of The Metropolitan Museum of Art, New York.)

A.D. (61). When specimens appeared in Europe, they were the envy of every potter, and many tried unsuccessfully to duplicate this ware. From these attempts, however, evolved translucent bodies with glass as a flux which were a considerable refinement over the ware previously produced, although they did not compare with the Chinese porcelain. Not until 1709 did the German chemist Böttger make a real porcelain from kaolin, quartz, and feldspar. Although he hoped to keep the formula secret, the knowledge soon spread over all of Europe.

Chinese porcelain. This ware was first made during the Tang Dynasty (618–906) and reached its greatest perfection during the Ming Dynasty (1368–1644). The ceramic art had never before, and has seldom since, reached such heights. To understand this achievement, it is necessary to know something of the environment that made it possible. Because the potters were subsidized by the Emperor, they were able to try innumerable experiments with body, glazes, and decorations. Pure materials were available, high-temperature kilns had been developed, and there was no pressure for mass output. It was a leisurely art.

A former student of the author, from Ching-tê Chên, had at his home a pair of vases with dragons crawling up their sides— dragons finished in such detail that every scale was in place. The eyeballs were tiny spheres, black on one side and white on the other, and they were loose in their sockets, so that when the vases were moved the eyes would twinkle and the dragons seemed to come to life. My student thought it not at all odd that the potter had taken half a lifetime to produce this exquisite pair of vases.

There is not space here to even begin to enumerate the magnificent glazes that came out of this golden era. Even now, many of them are reproduced only with the greatest difficulty. These fine examples of the ceramic art are worthy of the closest study, and every potter should visit our museums for just this purpose. A vase from the Kang Hsi period is shown in Fig. 12–10.

Modern hard porcelains. The porcelain bodies developed in Europe and elsewhere after the 17th century were composed of the three main ingredients kaolin, quartz, and feldspar, but the raw materials and the proportions varied from factory to factory. Table 12–1 lists the compositions of a number of porcelains.

One of the finest and highest-fired modern porcelains is that made at Copenhagen (47). The porcelains developed scientifically at Sèvres are excellent, especially that used for their bisque figures. Parian porcelain has been used in England for excellent small sculptured pieces.

Few modern artist potters have turned to porcelain as a medium, largely because they have no means for the necessary high firing. A notable exception is Adelaide Robineau,

who worked in this country at the beginning of the 20th century. One of her vases is shown in Fig. 12–11.

Soft porcelains. The attempts to duplicate Chinese porcelain in Europe resulted in the development of a low-fired translucent body using glass as a flux. These bodies were not very strong or resistant to temperature shock, but from them developed such excellent bodies as that made by Belleek in Ireland and Lenox in this country.

About 1748, a soft porcelain called bone china was developed in England, probably at Bow (36). The name is derived from the major ingredient—calcined bones. While this ware is hard to make because of its low plasticity and low unfired strength, it is highly translucent and very strong when fired. Because it is not a good body for throwing on the wheel, it has not been used much by studio potters. A representative bone china piece is shown in Fig. 12–12.

More recently, soft porcelain bodies using nepheline-syenite as a flux have been used in this country. They are useful to the artist potter because they may be fired in low-temperature kilns, but they cannot compare with high-fired porcelains in the range of glazes that can be used with them. The compositions of some typical porcelains are shown in Table 12–1.

TABLE 12–1

COMPOSITION OF PORCELAIN BODIES

Type of body	Materials						
	Clay mins.	Feldspar	Flint	Bone ash	Frit	Talc	Whiting
Hard porc., Limoges	42.1	36.8	19.5	-----	-----	----	1.6
Hard porc., Sevres	66.4	15.1	12.1	-----	-----	----	6.4
Hard porc., Limoges	47.4	26.0	26.6				
Hard porc., Japan	32.3	26.8	40.9				
Hard porc., Carlsbad	51.8	17.3	29.6	-----	-----	----	1.3
Hard porc., Berlin (1877)	54.9	21.6	23.5				
Hard porc., Chinese	47.0	25.0	27.0	-----	-----	----	1.0
Parian bisc. (Copenhagen)	52.0	45.0	2.0	-----	-----	----	1.0
Bone china	12.0	16.0	33.0	39.0			
Belleek	48.0	-----	22.0		30.0		
Talc porcelain	30.0	35.0	28.0	-----	-----	7.0	

Fig. 12-10. Porcelain vase made in China during the Kang Hsi period
(1662–1722). (Courtesy of The Metropolitan Museum of Art, New York.)

Fig. 12-11. Tall porcelain vase made by Adelaide Alsop Robineau, about 1910. (Courtesy of The Metropolitan Museum of Art, New York.)

Fig. 12-12. Bone-china cup probably made in Liverpool, England, about 1780.

VI. WHITE EARTHENWARE

A compounded white earthenware body was not regularly produced until the middle of the 18th century. This ware, first made in England, had many advantages in ease of manufacture and sales appeal, and consequently it rapidly displaced much of the older type of ware. It was known as Queen's ware, and much of it was imported to this country in the 19th century (23).

Potters in this country at first used the English method of producing white earthenware, using English materials. A denser body later became more or less standard in the greatly expanding industry in the East, while West Coast manufacturers, because they have excellent talc available, produce lower-fired bodies both for production and for art work.

VII. CONCLUSIONS

The artist potter should take every opportunity to study the work of ceramic craftsmen of earlier times, just as a musician practices the works of the great composers, or a painter studies the products of the old masters. Many well-illustrated books in this field are to be found in our public libraries, and our museums abound with excellent specimens for study. Such study should not be undertaken with the thought that the potter will attempt to imitate these pieces, but rather so that he may acquire a feeling of what is suitable for the medium of clay.

Table 12-2 summarizes our knowledge of the development of pottery throughout the world. There are, of course, many gaps yet to be filled.

VIII. REFERENCES

The list of references given below is only a small part of the available literature on the subject of ceramics, but these will serve as a starting point. Public and school libraries contain many books on this subject, and the reader may extend his knowledge as far as he desires.

Periodicals

1. *American Journal of Archeology,* Concord 1885 +. Occasionally articles may be found here dealing with the early pottery of North and South America.

2. *Antiques,* New York, 1922 +. Many articles may be found here dealing with ceramics of the early United States and Europe.

3. *Connoisseur,* London, 1901 +. Occasional well-illustrated articles dealing with ceramics may be found here.

4. *Illustrated London News,* London, 1842+. This periodical is useful in keeping informed on excavations of early pottery.

5. *Keramische Zeitschrift* (in German), Lübeck, 1948 +. Some well-illustrated articles in this journal deal with European ceramics.

6. *Transactions of the English Ceramic Circle,* London, 1833 +. This publication is wholly comprised of scholarly articles dealing with early English ceramics.

TABLE 12-2 (a)

WORLD HISTORY OF POTTERY

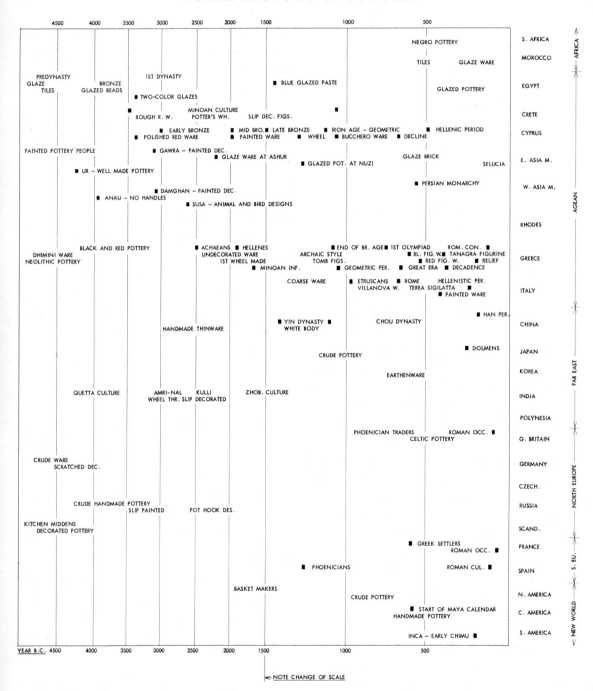

TABLE 12-2 (b)

WORLD HISTORY OF POTTERY

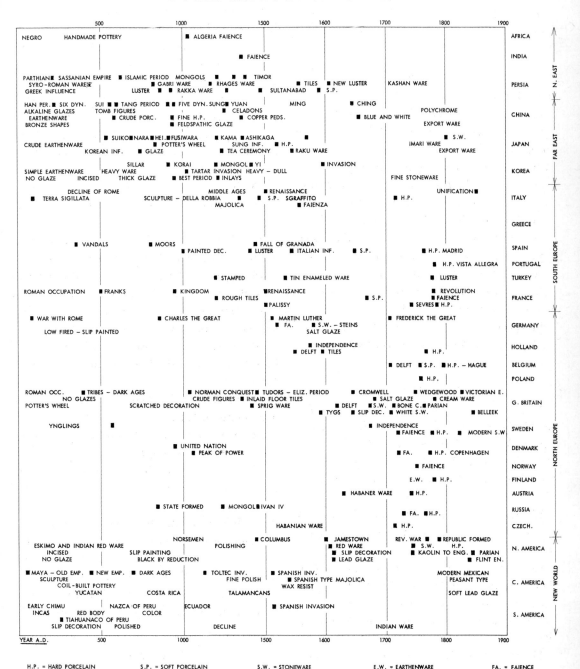

H.P. = HARD PORCELAIN   S.P. = SOFT PORCELAIN   S.W. = STONEWARE   E.W. = EARTHENWARE   FA. = FAIENCE

7. *Transactions of the Oriental Ceramic Circle* (in English), London, 1921 +. This contains articles written by experts in the field of ancient Chinese and Japanese pottery and porcelain.

General

8. BURTON, W., *A General History of Porcelain*, Cassell & Co., Ltd., London, 1922.

9. CHAFFERS, W., *Marks and Monograms on European and Oriental Pottery and Porcelain*, 14th ed, Borden, Los Angeles, 1946.

10. COX, W. E., *Pottery and Porcelain*, 2 vols., Crown Publishers, Inc., New York, 1944.

11. HOBSON, R. L., *Potteries and Porcelains*, Encyclopedia Britannica, 14th ed., 1929, p. 338.

12. HONEY, W. B., *European Ceramic Art*, Faber & Faber, Ltd., London, 1950.

13. PICKMAN, D. L., *The Golden Age of European Porcelain*, Boston, 1936.

14. PRIME, W. C., *Pottery and Porcelain*, Harper & Brothers, New York, 1878, 1929.

United States

15. ANON., *Pottery and Porcelain of New Jersey, 1688–1900. An exhibition held April 8, 1947*, Newark Museum, Newark, N. J., 1947.

16. BARBER, E. A., *Pottery and Porcelain of the United States*, G. P. Putnam's Sons, New York, 1893.

17. HOUGH, W., *An Early West Virginia Pottery*, Government Printing Office, Washington, D.C., 1901.

18. RAMSEY, J., *American Potters and Pottery*, Hale, Cushman and Flint, Boston, 1939.

19. SPARGO, J., *Early American Pottery and China*, Appleton-Century-Crofts, Inc., New York, 1926.

20. SPARGO, J., *Potters and Potteries of Bennington*, Houghton Mifflin Company, Boston, 1926.

21. WATKINS, LURA, *Early New England Potters and Their Wares*, Harvard University Press, Cambridge, Mass., 1950.

England

22. BLACKER, J. F., *The A.B.C. of English Saltglaze Stone-ware*. Stanley Paul and Company, London, 1922.

23. BURTON, W., *A History and Description of English Earthenware and Stoneware*, Cassell & Co., Ltd., London, 1904.

24. BURTON, W., *Josiah Wedgwood and His Pottery*, Cassell & Co., Ltd., London, 1923.

25. CHURCH, A. H., *English Porcelain Made During the 18th Century*, Wyman and Sons, Ltd., London, 1904.

26. EARLE, C., *Earle Collection of Early Staffordshire Pottery*, A. Brown and Sons, Hull, Mass., 1915.

27. GARNER, F. H., *English Delftware*, D. Van Nostrand Company, Inc., New York, 1948.

28. GRANT, M. H., *The Makers of Black Basalts*, Blackwood and Sons, London, 1910.

29. HASLEM, JOHN, *The Old Derby China Factory*, George Bell and Sons, London, 1876.

30. HAYDEN, A., *Spode and His Successors*, Cassell & Co., Ltd., London and New York, 1925.

31. HURLBUTT, F., *Bristol Porcelain*, Medici Soc., London, 1928.

32. KING, WILLIAM, *Chelsea Porcelain*, Benn Brothers, Ltd., London, 1922.

33. LANCASTER, H. B., Liverpool Pottery for the American Market, *Connoisseur* **107**, 208 (1941).

34. RACKHAM, B., *Medieval English Pottery*, Pitman Publishing Corporation, New York, 1948.

35. READ, H., *Staffordshire Pottery Figures*, Gerald Duckworth & Co., Ltd., London, 1929.

36. SOLON, L. M., *The Art of the Old English Potter*, John Francis Company, New York, 1906.

Classic Period

37. LANE, A., *Greek Pottery*, D. Van Nostrand Company, Inc., New York, 1949.

38. WALTERS, H. B., *History of Ancient Pottery —Greek, Etruscan, and Roman*, John Murray, London, 1905.

Primitive

39. GUTHE, C. E., *Pueblo Pottery Making,* Yale University Press, New Haven, Conn., 1925.

40. HOLMES, W. H., *Aboriginal Pottery of the Eastern United States,* Government Printing Office, Washington, D.C., 1903.

41. LAVACHERY, H. A., *Les Arts Anciens D'Amerique,* Anvers Editions "De Sikkel," 1929.

42. MARTIN-VEGUF, G. B., Nazca Pottery at Florida State University, *Am. J. of Arch.* **53,** 345 (1949).

43. MERA, H. P., *Style Trends of Pueblo Pottery,* Waverly Press, Baltimore, 1939.

44. WASSERMAN, B. J., (Ed.) *Ceramicas del Antiguo Peru,* Priviti Pub., San Blas, Peru, 1938.

Continental Europe

45. BALLOT, M. J., *French Pottery, Palissy, and the XVIth Century Factories,* Morancé, Paris, 1924.

46. FROTHINGHAM, A. W., *Lustreware of Spain,* Hispanic Society of America, New York, 1951.

47. HAYDEN, ARTHUR, *Royal Copenhagen Porcelain,* T. Fisher Unwin, London, 1911.

48. HONEY, W. B., *Dresden China,* A. & C. Black, Ltd., London, 1934.

49. NEURDENBERG, E., *Old Dutch Pottery and Tiles,* translated by B. Rackham, Ernest Benn, Ltd., London, 1923.

50. RACKHAM, B., *Early Netherlands Maiolica,* Geoffrey Bles, Ltd., London, 1926.

51. SOLON, L. M., *The Old French Faience,* Cassell & Co., Ltd., London and New York, 1903.

Far East

52. BOWES, J. L., *Japanese Pottery,* Edward Howell, Liverpool, 1890.

53. COLLIE, J. N., Notes on Some Chinese Glazes on Pottery and Porcelain, *Trans. Eng. Ceram. Soc.* **15,** 160 (1915-16).

54. FUNK, W., Technical Production of Chinese Porcelain, II. Colored Decoration, *Ber. Deut. Keram. Ges.* **23,** 197, 326 (1942).

55. HETHERINGTON, A. L., *The Early Ceramic Wares of China,* Charles Scribner's Sons, New York, 1922.

56. HETHERINGTON, A. L., Catalogue of the Exhibition of Celadon Wares, *Trans. Oriental Ceram. Soc.* **21,** 31 (1947–48).

57. HOBSON, R. L., *The Wares of the Ming Dynasty,* Charles Scribner's Sons, New York, 1923.

58. HOBSON, R. L., *The Later Ceramic Wares of China,* Charles Scribner's Sons, New York, 1925.

59. HOBSON, R. L., *Eumorfopoulos Collection,* 6 vols. Ernest Benn, Ltd., London, 1925.

60. HUGHAN, R. R., Early Chinese Ceramic Glazes, *Ceramic Age* **56,** No. 2, 40 (1950).

61. LAUFER, B., *The Beginnings of Porcelain in China,* Field Museum of Natural History, Anthropological Series **5,** No. 2 (1917).

Near East

62. KELEKIAN, D. K., *Potteries of Persia,* Catalogue of the Kelekian Collection, Herbert Clarke, Paris, 1909.

63. POPE, A. U., *An Introduction to Persian Art Since the Seventh Century,* Charles Scribner's Sons, New York, 1931.

64. REITLINGER, G., Sultanabad Classification and Chronology (Persia) *Trans. Oriental Ceram. Soc.* **20,** 25 (1944–45).

65. STARR, R. F. S., *Indus Valley Painted Pottery,* Princeton University Press, Princeton, N. J., 1941.

CHAPTER 13

Principles of Design

I. INTRODUCTION

To design is to plan an object to best suit its purpose, to seem most pleasing to the senses of those who come in contact with it, and to be most harmonious with its surroundings. It means the conscious assembly and purposeful arrangement of various elements into a satisfactory whole. Design underlies the successful production of a painting, a piece of sculpture, a pot, a bridge, or an airplane.

A good design may evolve slowly over many years by the gradual improvement of an object without any conscious knowledge of correct design principles. This is true of the folk pottery developed prior to the machine age. However, a knowledge of the principles of design enables the artist to arrive more quickly at a satisfactory arrangement of the various elements, gives the work a greater perfection, and, most important, allows for greater individuality.

The master plan. To those who have studied design, there seems to be a universal master plan, and while we catch glimpses of it from time to time, it eludes us in its entirety. It is possible, however, to take certain definite steps in its direction.

Approaches to the understanding of design. During certain periods in the development of our civilization, artists, architects, and designers seemed to have a firmer grasp on the principles of good design than at other times; the 5th century B.C. in Greece, the Tang and Sung Dynasties in China, and the Gothic period in Europe are examples. Careful study and analysis of the works of these periods will yield much insight into the bases of good design.

Good books and bad have been written on the principles of design; the references at the end of this chapter have been selected because they present stimulating ideas. By studying the approach of these authors to the problem, it is possible to learn certain universally accepted principles on which new ideas may be founded.

It should be emphasized that no two designers approach a problem in the same way, and there are many avenues along which one may travel and reach a pleasing result. It is this great variety, this endless possibility of combinations, that makes design so baffling and yet so fascinating and rewarding. (Take a look around your own backyard; the myriad of forms found there will serve as an inexhaustible pool of ideas.)

In this chapter an attempt is made to outline a rational approach to design which can serve as a starting point, but only by diligent practice and under the guidance of a stimulating teacher may one become a competent designer.

II. BASIC ATTRIBUTES OF DESIGN STRUCTURE

While writers on the technique of design use varied terminology and have diverse views on details, there is general unanimity on three basic attributes of good design. Indeed, these are universally accepted in literature and music, as well as in ceramics. Although these three attributes may be expressed in different terms, as shown in Table 13–1, they have substantially the same meaning.

Unity. *Unity* requires that all elements of a design must be directed to one end; there must be nothing superfluous, and no diversion of interest. A design that lacks unity creates a feeling of frustration in the observer when his eye travels about trying to find the underlying theme. Let us consider a few examples of unity of design.

The design of an airplane has unity. A streamlined fuselage has wings flowing out to the sides, repeating in their cross sections the larger form, and the tail section repeats the design of the wings on a smaller scale. The observer at once feels that the whole is tied together for a single purpose—to navigate the air.

A great painting gives a feeling of complete unity, whether it be a group by Cézanne, where all details contribute to the central motif, or a portrait by Vermeer, where all of the accessories serve to strengthen the expression of the face.

Good sculpture is unified in its presentation. For example, the frieze in the Parthenon shows a procession that, with less skilled treatment, might easily have been only a succession of separate elements, but here each figure is so cleverly related to the next by means of parallel lines, attitudes of the horsemen, and other transitions that a definite feeling of unity is the result.

Unity is no less important in the art of pottery making; here, too, all of the separate elements should reinforce the main theme. For example, the vase in Fig. 13–1 gives the feeling that the handles are growing out from the body, not just tacked on. The pitcher in Fig. 13–2, on the other hand, lacks unity, because interest is divided between the main shape and the unrelated dog on the handle.

We reiterate that, above all, a good design must have *unity;* there must be no diversion of interest among extraneous elements. Every good designer is in agreement on this point.

Order. In its broadest sense, *order* in design means that there must be a readily discernible relationship among the various elements. This relationship may be a balance between the several parts, symmetry about a line or a point, simple proportions between the elements, or harmony of color.

The classic Greeks believed the measure of beauty to be the amount of order in relation to the total number of elements discernible in a design. More recently, Birkhoff has

TABLE 13-1

SHOWING THE UNIFORMITY OF DESIGN PRINCIPLES IN ALL THE ARTS

Types of Art		Basic Attributes		
		Oneness	Orderliness	Diversification
Sculpture Graphic arts Architecture	(Design in space)	Unity	Order	Variety
Literature Poetry	(Design in time)	Unity	Coherence	Emphasis
Music	(Design in time)	Unity	Form	Variety
Drama Ballet	(Design in time and space)	Unity	Coherence	Richness

attempted to measure beauty by establishing a mathematical relationship between complexity and order in a design, and while his results are not completely satisfying, they at least show a trend that is inescapable. In conformity with Birkhoff's concepts, the series of polygons in Fig. 13–3 shows increasing order from left to right. This element of order, so much appreciated by the classic school of thought, is less appreciated by the contemporary designer.

Variety. The attribute of *variety* gives richness to the design. It leads the eye about as it

Fig. 13-2. Bennington (Vermont) hound-handled pitcher, showing lack of unity.

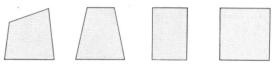

Fig. 13-3. Polygons showing increasing order from left to right.

continually reveals new relations, new associations, and new interests. An observer is as repelled by monotonous repetition of elements in a design as he is by a monotonous diet!

Variety is achieved by changing forms, lines, spacing, and background areas. This variety, however, should have a basic plan —a central motif that gives unity, with paths to lead the eye to the main theme. The design of Fig. 13–4 has such a central point of interest, with lines leading the eye toward it from all sides. A design without such a plan leaves the observer with a sense of frustration.

III. TOOLS FOR ACHIEVING THE THREE BASIC ATTRIBUTES

In this section we shall discuss the most important of the many properties of design that are essential in attaining the three basic at-

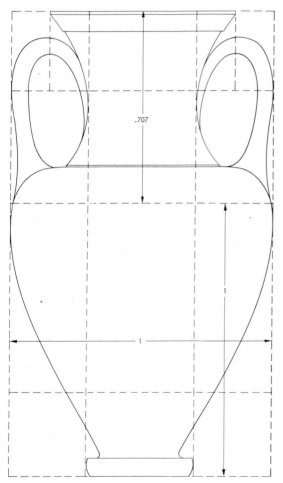

Fig. 13-1. Greek amphora, showing harmonious proportions and unity.

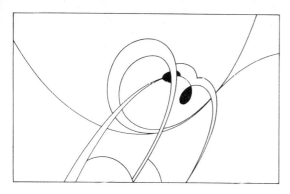

Fig. 13-4. Abstract design, showing a center of interest and lines leading the eye to it.

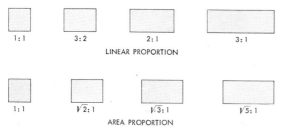

Fig. 13-5. The two types of proportion.

The method of area proportion was evidently used in the classic period of Greece, as shown by Hambidge (5) and others. There is no space here to expound the theory of dynamic symmetry as propounded by Hambidge, but his book is an excellent reference for those who are interested. Modern designers, for the most part, are not enthusiastic about this theory.

Balance. *Balance* is an important element of order, and it is essential to good design. Balance means an equality of interest about an axis, and is often associated with the equalization of gravitational forces. For example, the old-fashioned well sweep is in perfect balance, for the short and heavy weighted end precisely equals the long, slender end holding the bucket, as shown in Fig. 13–6(a). In a similar way, the abstraction in Fig. 13–6(b) shows perfect balance. All great paintings have a sense of balance.

tributes described above. These properties are just as much tools of the designer as are the modeling tool, brush, or pen. Like a good carpenter or machinist, the artist must learn to use all of his tools properly if he is to produce good work.

Proportion. *Proportion* is a very powerful tool for gaining unity and order. There are two general methods of obtaining correct proportions: (1) the linear method, that is, in proportions of 1:1, 3:2, 2:1, 3:1, etc., and (2) the method of proportioning by area, that is, in ratios of 1:1, $\sqrt{2}$:1, $\sqrt{3}$:1, $\sqrt{5}$:1, etc. Both of these methods are illustrated in Fig. 13–5. Whichever method is used, the results must be *visually satisfying;* we should be able to see clearly the proportions of the complete design. We must not, however, allow a rigid adherence to proportion to dull spontaneous and stimulating ideas.

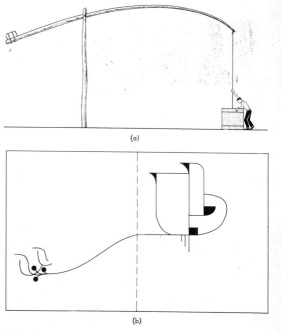

Fig. 13-6. Unsymmetrical (occult) balance (a) in a well sweep and (b) in an abstract design.

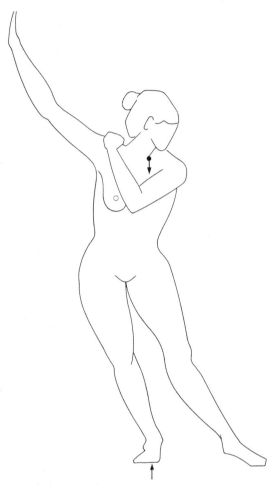

Fig. 13-7. Balance in a sculptured figure.

In pottery making, complete balance is usually achieved by symmetry, but even free-form pieces, no matter what the shape, must have this attribute. And every piece of sculpture, no matter how complex, must show the good balance illustrated in Fig. 13-7.

There are two kinds of balance: symmetrical and unsymmetrical (or occult). The first consists of two equal elements or groups of elements equally distant from a center point [as the two children of equal weight on the see-saw shown in Fig. 13-8(a)], while the second consists of unequal elements at different distances from the center [the fat boy,

Fig. 13-8(b), who must sit nearer the center than his partner, to achieve balance].

Symmetrical balance is most often found in pottery, where each half is the mirror image of the other, resulting from the fact that the piece is a surface of revolution. However, balance may also be attained in surface designs in which two-, three-, four-, five-, or sixfold symmetry is found.

Rhythm. *Rhythm,* or repetition of elements, is another factor associated with order. The hand is a thing of beauty because the fingers are a repeating theme. However, unlike the keys on a piano, for instance, they are not all exactly the same—instead, they have a graded variety. Hair is also a study in pleasing repetitive design, for although similar locks follow one after another, they are never exactly alike. Another example is the frond of a fern, where the pinnules repeat, but vary slightly. Figure 13-9 shows an abstract design in which similar forms are repeated.

It is not strange that we should look for rhythm in design, when this property is so evident in our daily lives. The rhythm of music, the rotation of the earth, the change of seasons, the movement of the tides and of waves, the sequence of hunger and of satisfaction of it are all examples of common rhythmic experiences.

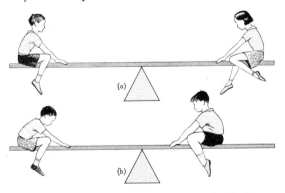

Fig. 13-8. Symmetrical and unsymmetrical balance.

In pottery making, repetition occurs most frequently in surface decorations, where the consecutive elements suggest the shape as a whole, as in the vase of Fig. 13–10.

Harmony. The property of *harmony* is important to an orderly design. In this sense, harmony means compatibility between the various elements of the design. Compatability may be achieved in many ways; for example, by the use of related sizes, related shapes, and harmonious color combinations.

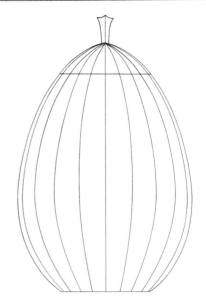

Fig. 13-10. Fluted jar, showing repetition of elements in harmony with the over-all shape.

Alignment of elements. One of the more important of the remaining relations contributing to unity and order is *alignment* of the elements, to give strength to the final composition. The life drawing of Fig. 13–11 clearly shows this attribute in the alignment of the head, arm, and leg, which gives both unity and order. The pieces illustrated in Fig. 13–12 show a form of alignment that helps the eye to follow the salient points of symmetry.

Clarity of design. There can be no evidence of fumbling in a good design; the idea expressed must be clearly apparent. For example, the rectangle of Fig. 13–13(a) is clearly just that, and the trapezoid of Fig. 13–13(b) is definitely a trapezoid, but the shape in Fig. 13–13(c) is slightly tapered, so that one is not quite sure whether a trapezoid is intended or whether the design is an unworkmanlike rectangle. Sizes of adjacent elements should be exactly the same or distinctly different; there should be no ambigu-

Fig. 13-9. Above, frond of a Christmas fern, showing gradative repetition of the pinnules; below, abstraction based on the same principle.

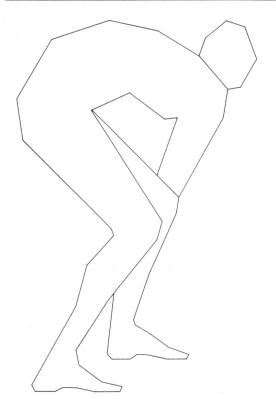

Fig. 13-11. Alignment of leg, arm, and head, giving unity and order.

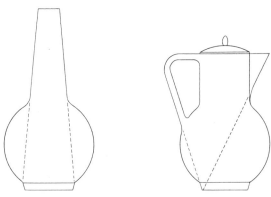

Fig. 13-12. Vase and chocolate pot, showing how alignment of elements gives unity and order.

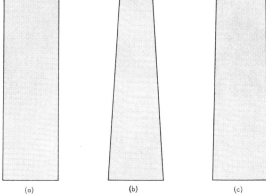

(a)   (b)   (c)

Fig. 13-13. (a) and (b) are definite forms, but (c) leaves some doubt as to whether the taper was intentional.

ity. Similarly, values and colors that differ should have sufficient contrast so that the observer is sure that separate hues are intended.

Accenting the design. *Accent* is a device to draw the eye to the single most important feature of the design, and serves also to relieve monotony. One form of accent is the use of a change of color, form, or texture; movement also tends to accent the central theme by leading the eye about the design. To express motion, something that is ordinarily associated with movement must be portrayed; for instance, an arrow, a wave, or a runner (see Fig. 13–14). Figure 13–15 is an abstract design with a sense of motion upward and to the right, for this is the direction of greatest interest.

IV. THE ELEMENTS OF GOOD DESIGN

The elements that are assembled to produce a good design may be lines or areas in a surface, or lines, planes, and solids in space.

The line. The *line* is the most fundamental of all the elements. It forms the boundaries of areas on a surface, it may be the outline of a solid when viewed in silhouette, or it may enclose and define forms. Lines can be straight, curved, or a combination of the two.

Let us first consider straight lines. It will be readily seen that the direction of a line can be used to express an idea. For example, a horizontal line suggests tranquillity or

Fig. 13-14. Means of expressing motion.

Fig. 13-15. Abstract design, showing movement upward and toward the right.

Fig. 13-16. Value produced by parallel straight lines. By varying line widths and spacing, values ranging from white to black can be produced.

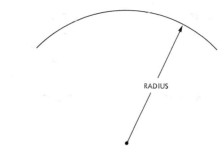

RADIUS

Fig. 13-17. Arc of a circle.

Fig. 13-18. Curve with regularly changing curvature.

Fig. 13-19. Reverse curve, sometimes called the "Hogarth line."

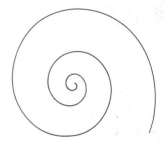

Fig. 13-20. Logarithmic spiral.

repose, because we associate it with a reclining person or a surface of tranquil water. On the other hand, a vertical line suggests a living, vital thing, such as a standing person or a growing tree. A slanted line suggests motion, like that of a falling stick, or of a person starting to walk. Closely spaced parallel lines, however, are used to indicate value over an area, as in Fig. 13–16.

Curved lines form a part of nearly every design. The simplest is that of constant curvature, like that of an arc (Fig. 13–17), but this suffers from lack of variety. The curve with regularly changing curvature, like the parabola of Fig. 13–18, is used a great deal. This curve combines strength and beauty, and it is found in such streamlined forms as the airplane, the human body, fish, and pottery. It is derivable from mathematical forms, as described in the next chapter. The reverse curve, shown in Fig. 13–19, is sometimes called the "Hogarth line" or "line of beauty." It is found in the female figure and is used in many vase forms. However, this curve lacks the strength that is evident in one with regularly changing curvature.

Fig. 13-21. Spiral border from a Greek vase.

The logarithmic spiral shown in Fig. 13–20, which Thompson (12) calls the "curve of life," is found in many living things. Seashells are a common example. The spiral was used for decoration on much of the early pottery, and it lends itself to a variety of patterns, as shown in Fig. 13–21.

The solid. A *solid* may be a simple shape like a cube, or a more complicated form, such as a wheel-thrown vase, a free-form piece, or a sculptured figure. A simple form can be diagramed on paper as an outline or a silhouette; a more complicated solid can be approximately delineated by several views, or cross-sections.

The pattern. A pattern is a design in which the motif is repeated at regular intervals. These are of three kinds: border patterns, a central motif, and all-over patterns. Although the artist seems to shy away from anything mathematical, it will be helpful to consider patterns by the logical step-by-step approach used by the crystallographer.

A single symbol (Fig. 13–22) may be taken as a starting point, and various operations can be performed upon it to give a basic pattern (the sample symbol was selected solely for demonstration purposes, and there has been no attempt to form particular patterns).

The simplest operation is a translation, or step-by-step movement, in a straight line (Fig. 13–23), especially suitable for a border.

Fig. 13-22. In Figs. 13-23 through 13-31, this single symbol is used in various ways.

Fig. 13-23. Translation in steps.

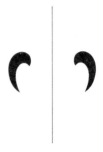

Fig. 13-24. Reflection about a line (like a mirror image).

Fig. 13-25. Rotation about a point.

Figure 13–24 shows reflection about a line, where one symbol is the mirror image of the other.

Rotation about a point is an interesting operation that can be carried out in a number of ways. Figure 13–25 shows a symbol that is rotated by one-half a revolution, or 180°, in each step. Three-, four-, five-, and sixfold rotations are shown in Fig. 13–26.

It is also possible to combine several of the above operations, as reflection and rotation are combined in Fig. 13–27, reflection and translation in Fig. 13–28, rotation and translation in Fig. 13–29, reflection and alternate translation in Fig. 13–30, and rotation, reflection, and translation in Fig. 13–31.

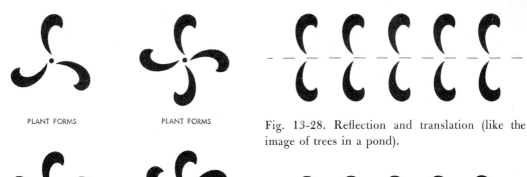

PLANT FORMS

PLANT FORMS

Fig. 13-28. Reflection and translation (like the image of trees in a pond).

STARFISH

SNOWFLAKE

Fig. 13-26. Three-, four-, five-, and sixfold rotations.

Fig. 13-29. Rotation and translation.

Fig. 13-27. Reflection and rotation.

Fig. 13-30. Reflection and alternate translation.

Fig. 13-31. Reflection, rotation, and translation.

A little study will reveal many interesting patterns that can be developed by the simple operations listed above. However, they are more easily visualized by comparison with examples from nature:

Reflection is demonstrated in all of the higher animals, including man; it is this bilateral symmetry, among other things, that differentiates them from the lower orders. Designs based on the property that the right side is a mirror of the left are especially pleasing; see, for example, the maple leaf of Fig. 13–32.

Examples of *translation* are common in nature; see the leaf edge of Fig. 13–33. But nature is never monotonous, and the translation is not uniform for any great distance.

Most plant forms show *rotation* in one form or another, as in Fig. 13–34, and they are models for some of our most pleasing designs. Snowflakes are another example.

Allover patterns must be based on interlocking triangles, squares, or hexagons (Fig. 13–35), because these are the only regular polygons that will completely fill a flat space. It should be observed that a hexagonal (honeycomb) pattern differs from the square or triangular pattern in that it has no continuous lines extending through it. A design may be developed inside each polygon, and this is often done in such a way as to relate each polygon to its neighbors. The polygons themselves are not evident in the final design; they simply form a skeleton on which to build. An example of a good allover design is shown in Fig. 13–36. White spaces, of course, form a pattern, as well as black ones, and they must be given equal consideration. The painters of classic Greek vases were especially skilled in the use of white space, and their work is well worth studying. Figure 13–37 indicates how easily the emphasis can be changed from a black to a white pattern.

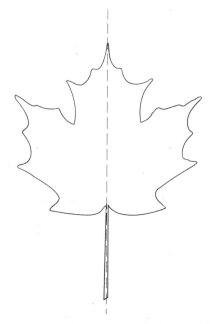

Fig. 13-32. Leaf of a sugar maple, showing bilateral symmetry.

Fig. 13-33. Edge of a leaf.

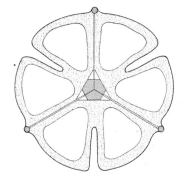

Fig. 13-34. Section of a seed pod from a wood lily, showing threefold rotation.

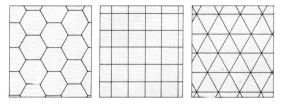

Fig. 13-35. The three regular polygons, each covering an area, form the basis for an over-all pattern.

Fig. 13-36. Allover pattern using a spiral motif based on whirligig beetles on a pond surface.

Fig. 13-37. A pattern of black on white (at the top) changing to white on black (at the bottom), showing the importance of the "background."

Values. *Value,* which is the degree of lightness or darkness of the surface, is extremely important in good design and, of course, the full range from black to white is available to the artist. Gradations of value may be obtained by crosshatching, stippling, or by even application of the medium. A sculptor often obtains different values by orienting the surfaces of a piece to cast shadows. Gradations of value give unity, variety, and accent.

The use of color. The use of color is such a broad topic in itself that only a few aspects of it can be touched on here. Colors are selected and combined for the sole purpose of achieving a pleasing result, and such combinations are those that are found in nature. I well remember walking along a woodland path on an autumn morning and enjoying the carpet of leaves, with its happy combinations of browns, golds, and crimsons. Suddenly I became aware of a discordant note, and discovered that a gaudy cerise ribbon had found its way among the leaves. Nature could never have made such a mistake!

The soft earth colors are always suitable for pottery, and they can be combined in many simple ways to give pleasing effects. This is not to say that brilliant colors should never be used, for striking effects are obtained if color is used with skill. However, one tends to tire of garishly decorated pottery, while the quieter colors continue to please the eye.

The use of texture. The surface texture of a piece is an integral part of the design, for it may be varied over wide limits to give many interesting effects. Ceramics is particularly suited to gradations of texture, from highly polished glaze to rough, pebbly effects. Pueblo pottery, with contrasting areas of polished and matte surfaces, is a good example.

V. DESIGN BASED ON FUNCTION

L. H. Sullivan, noted architect, has said, "Function determines form, and form determines function." This is one way of saying that the interaction of every object with its environment either brings form and function into harmony, or the object cannot long exist. Teague (11), one of the most stimulating of the modern designers, strongly believes that function is a very important attribute of design.

All living organisms are closely associated with their environments, so much so that their very existence depends on the stability of their surroundings. For example, trout need cool water to exist, and if the mean temperature of a lake where they abound should permanently be raised even a few degrees, the trout will die and such fish as bass and pickerel, more at home in warmer waters, will take their place. Plants and animals also adapt themselves to their environment: the bat has developed powers of flight quite different from that of birds, and his radar-type equipment enables him to pursue and capture flying insects in complete darkness. The woodpecker has a strong bill and a long tongue that is especially adapted to catching insects under the bark of trees. The bee has developed a complicated social life, to enable it to store honey and so live through the long winter. These are not isolated examples; *every* creature in our world is adapted to a particular niche, and it is interesting to note that competition is so keen that only those best adapted can long exist.

Of all living things, man alone is capable of controlling his environment, and then only to a limited extent. Our progress from barbarism to civilization, however, is measured largely by the extent of this control.

Because everything in nature is exactly, and often ingeniously, fitted to its surroundings, it is logical that we should consider pleasing, man-made objects that are well fitted for their function, made from suitable materials and by suitable methods.

Designing for purposeful use. Many feel that beauty is greatest when an object best serves its purpose. The modern airplane, for example, is a thing of beauty because each part is fashioned to do a particular job in relation to the whole; nothing is superfluous, nothing is sham. Note also that the form of an airplane is largely determined by the properties of the air through which it must move.

A great bridge, with its towers and arches, is beautiful because every member is designed to take just the stress imposed, and the entire structure is prescribed by the conditions of use—the span, the load, the wind forces, etc.

The teapot in Fig. 13–38 is beautiful because it serves its purpose so well. The spherical body holds the heat of the tea, for its surface area is a minimum in relation to its volume. The spout pours cleanly, and the handle fits the hand to give good balance in pouring. There are no superfluous features.

Fig. 13-39. Flower holder.

The flower holder of Fig. 13–39 is designed to facilitate the arrangement of flowers; its appearance without flowers is of no importance.

Automobiles built strictly for sport or for racing, with their smooth, streamlined bodies, are things of beauty, but the cars sold to the motoring public, which have evolved from the carriage, are seldom completely satisfying as to design. The gaudy and useless chrome trimmings, the meaningless excrescences, the unnecessary body length, all mar its beauty and tend to bring the automobile down to the level of that most horrible example of modern design, the juke box!

Using suitable materials. For the most part, the old crafts evolved slowly, because the materials used were dependent upon availability and cost, as well as suitability. For example, early furniture was made exclusively of wood, which was the only suitable material that could be worked with hand tools.

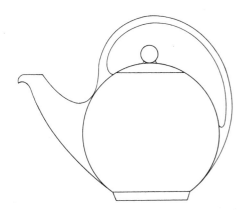

Fig. 13-38. Functional teapot.

Soft wood such as white pine was used for low-stressed parts like chair seats and table tops, while maple, birch, and hickory, which are much stronger, were used for chair backs and legs. Metal was scarce and glue was unreliable, and it was therefore a difficult problem to obtain strong joints. Pinned tennons and dovetailing were commonly used. The development of strong waterproof glues and metal fittings has made it possible to use wood far more efficiently, as evidenced by some of the modern Scandinavian furniture.

The art of pottery making displayed a similar evolution. At first only low firing temperatures were possible, and it was necessary to use soft, weak bodies in thick sections. As higher temperatures became attainable, strong vitreous bodies could be used, and thin, delicate designs became possible.

In planning on the material to be used, the designer of pottery must consider the function of the proposed piece. It is just as inappropriate to make a heavy-walled piece of porcelain as it is to make a delicate piece of soft earthenware.

One of the cardinal virtues of good design is honesty—one kind of material should never masquerade as another. We are all familiar with metal furniture that has been grained to look like wood, and with wooden furniture that is painted to look like metal; we have all seen roll siding for houses that has been embossed to imitate brick or stone, and we are familiar with birch and maple (themselves beautiful!), stained to look like mahogany. Nearly every material, if properly used, has a beauty of its own, and should not be hidden under a cloak of pretense.

Suitable manufacturing methods. Methods of manufacture have evolved as a result of the properties of available material. For example, the plastic nature of clay made forming on the potter's wheel possible, and the various methods for producing wrought-iron work, basketry, and wood carvings are similar examples.

When new materials become available, fabrication is usually first attempted by the current methods. Plastics were first handled like sheets of wood, for example, but new methods of forming in dies now permit tremendous production rates. And modern welding techniques permit production of iron objects far more economically and efficiently than was possible by the blacksmith.

Pottery making is no exception: tiles pressed in steel molds can be made of material so low in plasticity that they could not possibly have been formed by hand.

VI. LESS TANGIBLE ASPECTS OF DESIGN

A design may meet all the requirements of a perfect structure, based on the rules given above, and still not be quite satisfactory. On the other hand, a design that seems to definitely violate one or more of the basic attributes sometimes has great appeal. It is hard to say why this is so; there is an intangible something about a successful piece that is impossible to analyze, and that is lacking in the piece that does not quite make the grade.

One of the nebulous aspects of design is good taste. Some designers instinctively know what is in good taste and what is not, and others must acquire this judgment by careful study.

VII. SUMMARY

A good design is the purposeful assembly of various elements into a whole that delights the eye of an observer either because it evokes pleasant memories, is simply pleasing to look at, or because it is particularly well suited to its purpose. To reach the heights of excellence, a design:

1. Must have the three basic attributes of good structure—unity, order, and variety.

2. Must be suited to the purpose of the piece, suited to the material used, and be manufactured by an appropriate method.

3. Must have interest, association, and good taste.

Good design can be achieved only by long and arduous practice and a study of the good designs of others. Working with a good teacher is of inestimable value in reaching the goal.

VIII. REFERENCES

1. BIRKHOFF, G. D., *Aesthetic Measure*, Harvard University Press, Cambridge, Mass., 1933.

2. BROD, FRITZI, *Two Hundred Motifs and Designs*, Stephen Daye Press, New York, 1945.

3. DEWEY, JOHN, *Art as Experience*, Minton, Balch & Co., New York, 1934.

4. GRAVES, M., *The Art of Color and Design*, McGraw-Hill Book Company, Inc., New York, 1941.

5. HAMBIDGE, J., *Dynamic Symmetry, The Greek Vase*, Yale University Press, New Haven and New York, 1920.

6. KLEINSCHMIDT, O., Das Einformverfahren für drehende Gefässe, *Keram. Zeit.* **5**, 229 (1954).

7. NEWTON, N. T., *An Approach to Design*, Addison-Wesley Publishing Company, Inc., Cambridge, Mass., 1951.

8. OSBORNE, H., *Theory of Beauty*, Philosophical Library, Inc., New York, 1953.

9. RUSKIN, J., *The Seven Lamps of Architecture*, E. P. Dutton and Company, New York, 1932.

10. SANTAYANA, G., *The Sense of Beauty*, Charles Scribner's Sons, New York, 1896.

11. TEAGUE, W. D., *Design This Day*, Harcourt, Brace and Company, New York, 1940.

12. THOMPSON, SIR D. W., *On Growth and Form*, University Press, Cambridge, England, 1948.

CHAPTER 14

Application of Design Theory to Pottery

I. INTRODUCTION

It is difficult to state in words exactly how the principles of good design can be successfully applied to the actual manufacture of ceramic pieces. We shall, however, attempt to outline some of the steps in this chapter.

The successful application of design theory requires much thought and many trials, and some failures will inevitably ensue. The beginner should remember that his first concern must be to develop his own sense of good design and good taste; the production of a masterpiece comes later! Again we stress the value of studying the work of others and of working with a good teacher whenever possible.

Mass production vs. studio production. The mass producer of consumer goods, whether radio cabinets, automobiles, suits, or tableware, must attune his design very closely to the public taste, or he will soon find himself out of business. Unfortunately, it has been found that any sudden, radical change, even when based on better design, is nothing less than suicide. Only by gradual education and good example can the good taste of the average buying public be raised.

Fortunately, the artist potter usually sells his ware to a flexible and discriminating clientele, and consequently has more leeway to express his own concepts. In this field there is much opportunity for good design, and there is less condemnation of the new and unusual.

Traditional vs. modern design. As in all forms of art, we have proponents of the traditional forms of pottery and proponents of modern design. Traditional forms have evolved over a long period of time, and have survived because they suit a particular purpose. Therefore these forms have an easily recognized soundness, although they are sometimes a little dull, too! It should be borne in mind, however, that originality in itself is not enough for good design, and although many fine modern pieces are being produced, the basic principles of good design are inherent in these pieces as well.

II. CLASSIFICATION OF POTTERY AS TO USE

There are many approaches to functionality in the design of pottery. A few of the more obvious are discussed here; many others will occur to the designer. Nearly all pottery can be classified into a few simple groups, based on function.

Bottles (for storing liquids). These containers are characterized by a small mouth that can be tightly stopped with a cork or cap. Earthenware and stoneware bottles have been used since time immemorial to hold wine, olive oil, water, and other liquids. Since the beginning of the 20th century these have been largely replaced by glass bottles, although stoneware bottles are still used for purely decorative purposes and for flower holders.

Jars and crocks (for storing granular solids or solids in a liquid). These containers have wide mouths, and sometimes covers. They have long been used for storing grain, olives, pickles, salted meat, and other items that require complete protection. Stoneware crocks are still used to a considerable extent.

Pitchers, teapots, and ewers (for dispensing liquids). These vessels are still commonly used in our homes. They have small lips or spouts, but usually cannot be tightly sealed. They appear in many forms, but all have the characteristic of being able to pour small amounts of liquid in a smooth stream.

Cups and bowls (for dispensing solids and liquids). Bowls are used as serving dishes in the larger sizes, and for individual service in the smaller sizes. Cups are used to drink liquids from directly. Both have large, open mouths and are seldom covered.

Plates (for dispensing solids). These pieces are quite flat and are not covered. They are made in a great variety of shapes, and may be purely decorative, as well as utilitarian.

Other forms. Flower holders may be specifically designed for the purpose, or may be adapted from bottles or jars. Candlesticks are usually specially designed for this purpose,

and are seldom made of pottery. Lamp bases are today quite often made from bottles and jars, but they are also especially designed in ceramic ware. Ash trays are a kind of small plate, specifically designed for the purpose. Ornamental pieces for the interiors or exteriors of buildings may well be in the form of traditional bottles, jars, or bowls, but they often consist of sculptured pieces, as well. Tiles are used for walls and floors, around fireplaces, and sometimes for table tops.

Figure 14–1, which shows typical examples of the above categories, will point up the differences and similarities.

III. DESIGN BASED ON FITNESS FOR USE

Proper operation. A well-designed piece is built to carry out its proper function: a pitcher must pour cleanly, a flower holder should hold flowers in the desired positions, and a teapot cover should stay in place when tea is being poured. The designer must proportion the several parts so that the intended function is easily carried out. This is one of the most important aspects of design for all but strictly ornamental pieces.

Stability. A stable form stands firmly on its base, even when subject to considerable disturbance. The pieces in Fig. 14–2 show increasing stability from left to right. A strictly ornamental piece may require little stability, but tableware needs it to a high degree.

Ruggedness. A piece of pottery must not only *be* strong enough to stand up under use; it must also *look* strong enough. Cox points out that even a delicate piece should never look as though it could be easily mutilated by the chipping off of extended parts. Like the one-horse shay, it should remain intact or break completely.

Fig. 14-1. Classification of pottery according to use.

Fig. 14-2. Increasing stability from left to right.

Washability. An often-neglected feature of pottery is ease of washing. A pebbly glaze, a porous body, delicate ornamentation, or undercut areas all make washing difficult. The decline of salt-glazed tableware in the 18th century was largely due to the difficulty of keeping it clean.

Compatibility with surroundings. A designer does not always know where a piece is going to be used, but he should design his pieces with particular kinds of locations in mind. For example, ware to be used on an outdoor terrace can be heavy in section and gay in color, while ware for a formal setting should be more delicate and sophisticated, with sufficiently subdued coloring to allow blending with colors of other objects on the table.

Originality. This feature will greatly enhance sales if the changes from conventional style are really sound.

IV. DESIGN WITH RESPECT TO MATERIAL

The potter must always keep in mind the old precept, "Work with the material, not against it." For example, if plastic material is being used, it should be formed into shapes that it naturally takes, rather than into shapes more suited to cast bronze or stamped steel.

Advantages of plastic materials. The potter has much greater freedom in creating forms than workers with more intractable materials. Just as a life drawing made rapidly with a few sure strokes is often far more effective than a tight, detailed drawing that takes considerable time, so a piece thrown freely on the wheel may be more pleasing than one copied from a design laid out on the drawing board. Many of our great ceramic artists, however, do not themselves form pieces on the wheel, but rather have a skilled artisan work under their immediate supervision.

Thickness of sections. It is well to repeat here the admonition that the wall thickness or weight of a piece must be appropriate to the material: it must feel right when it is lifted; it must give the impression that it is strong enough for its purpose and yet not be too heavy or clumsy. This is why it seems right for porcelain to be thin and light, and for earthenware to be thicker and heavier.

Edges and corners. Shapes that are quite appropriate for metal are often not at all suitable for pottery. For example, sharp edges and corners on pottery not only chip easily, but are hard to cover evenly with glazes. Strong vitreous bodies may suitably have more delicate edges than softer bodies and, in the same way, purely decorative ware may be lighter than ware planned for hard usage. One of the chief criticisms of Greek vases is that the sharp edges readily chip.

V. DESIGN WITH RESPECT TO METHOD OF MANUFACTURE

In general, an article does, and should, give evidence of its method of manufacture. A finished pewter bowl still shows hammer marks, a piece of fine furniture obviously has dovetailed joints, and a piece of wheel-thrown pottery shows the concentric marks of throwing.

Hand-molding. Hand-molded pieces, whether coil-built or modeled, have a primitive quality, but they offer the utmost freedom to achieve any desired form, unhampered by restrictions of symmetry. To scrape and sponge a handmade piece to give it the perfect form of a wheel-thrown piece may be clever, but it certainly defeats the purpose of using hand-forming in the first place.

Wheel-throwing. By this method, the skilled potter can form almost any shape that is a solid of revolution. If proper guides are used, piece after piece can be rapidly thrown in an almost identical pattern. In this country, very little of this kind of ware is made in production, and in many of our larger potteries, not a man can be found who has a knowledge of wheel-throwing.

Jiggering. In this process one surface is formed by a plaster mold and the other by a template, and so no variation from the original design is possible. Jiggering processes put some restrictions on designing which are learned only by long experience.

Casting. This reproductive process is suited to a great variety of shapes. Drain castings give walls of uniform thickness, and consequently there is no independent control of both surfaces. For example, if the outer surface has a raised design, the inner surface will have the negative of it, minus most of the fine details.

Solid casting, on the other hand, allows control of both surfaces, but is difficult to use for pieces having thin walls. One of the useful characteristics of the casting process is that it makes possible the reproduction of fine surface details.

Pressing. Pieces that are pressed in molds have advantages similar to those of cast pieces, and are subject to much the same restrictions.

VI. DESIGN WITH RESPECT TO SHAPE

The purpose of a piece imposes certain restrictions on its shape, but even within these restrictions hundreds of shapes may be used. It is the purpose of this section to show how various pleasing shapes are derived by following the basic principles outlined in the previous chapter.

Correct proportion is one of the most obvious attributes of a good design, especially the over-all proportion, which is based on the proportions of such component parts as the foot, the neck, and the handles of a piece. Generally speaking, the more consistently a system of proportions is followed throughout the whole of a design, the more pleasing the result.

Linear proportion. In Chapter 13 we discussed the simple 1:1, 2:3, etc., ratios of linear proportion, and to illustrate these a single vase form that has been given several different linear ratios of height to width is shown in Fig. 14–3. Which of these is best depends on the purpose for which the vase is intended.

4:1   3:1   5:2   2:1   3:2   1:1   2:3   1:2   2:5   1:3   1:4

Fig. 14-3. A single vase form drawn with various linear proportions.

In Chapter 13 we also mentioned that the aesthetic value of a piece was increased when a great many of the elements showed a discernible interrelationship. For example, if the diameter of the lip of the T'zu vase of the Sung Dynasty shown in Fig. 14–4 were taken as one unit, other dimensions could be expressed as simple multiples of it:

Diameter of foot	2 units
Maximum diameter	4 units
Height to shoulder	8 units
Height to maximum diameter	6 units
Height of neck	1 unit

These relations, which give a feeling of order to the whole piece, are recognized by the eye almost unconsciously. Actually, the relationships need not be as exact as in this example, for the eye would not quickly recognize small departures.

The stoneware "Ko Yao" Sung bowl shown in Fig. 14–5 is another example of correct proportioning; the diameter of the foot is equal to the height, while the diameter of the mouth is three times that of the base.

Figure 14–6 shows a piece of recent Scandinavian stoneware whose dimensions are simply related.

Area proportion. Because they could be simply laid out with the aid of a knotted cord, area proportions were carefully followed by the early Egyptians and Greeks. The usual ratios are $1:\sqrt{2}$, $1:\sqrt{3}$, $1:\sqrt{5}$, and 1:1.618 (the whirling square). The significance of these area ratios is illustrated by the "root-two" rectangle of Fig. 14–7, on two sides of which are applied squares, one of which has an area twice that of the other. These proportions may be readily laid out by starting with a square and rotating the diagonal down to the base, as shown in Fig. 14–8. The only tool required is a piece of string.

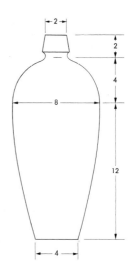

Fig. 14-4. T'zu vase of the Sung dynasty, showing simple linear proportions.

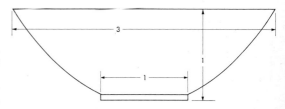

Fig. 14-5. Ko Yao bowl, showing linear proportions.

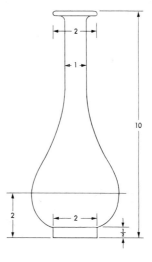

Fig. 14-6. Modern Scandinavian vase, showing linear proportions.

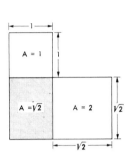

Fig. 14-7. Derivation of the root-two rectangle.

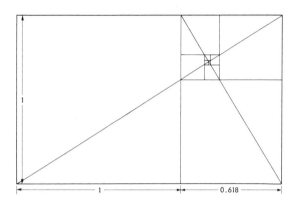

Fig. 14-9. The whirling square.

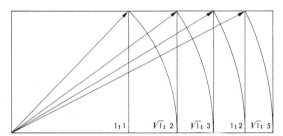

Fig. 14-8. Derivation of other area ratios.

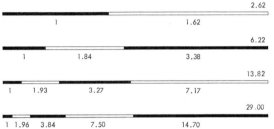

Fig. 14-10. The harmonious division of a line into two, three, four, and five parts.

The whirling square is particularly interesting because it is closely associated with growing things. The 1:1.618 ratio of length to width occurs in the Fibonacci series of numbers 0, 1, 1, 2, 3, 5, 8, 13, 21, 34, 55, 89, 144, 233, ... Each number is the sum of the two preceding ones, and any number divided by its predecessor gives approximately 1.618. This proportion is found in leaves and seeds (a sunflower head is a good example). Figure 14–9 shows a whirling-square rectangle with the resulting spiral plan of ever-decreasing sizes.

If a line is to be divided into two parts, so that the ratio of the smaller is to the larger as the larger is to the whole, then we find the same ratio of 1:1.618, called by the Greeks the "golden mean." This division was used not only by the Greeks, but by painters of the Renaissance era as well, sometimes in-

advertently because it is a *pleasing* ratio, and sometimes by intent. Modern artists also use it a great deal.

A line may be harmoniously divided into 3, 4, 5, or more parts, as shown in Fig. 14–10. The greater the number of divisions, the more closely the ratio approaches 1:2. Figure 14–11 shows patterns where the areas have been harmoniously divided into five parts.

Figure 14–12 shows a vase form with varying area proportions, all of them admittedly pleasing. Many paintings have a height-to-width ratio of $1:\sqrt{2}$. Hambidge has analyzed the structure of many Greek vases. A typical example is the kylix shown in Fig. 14–13, where the unit of design is the root-two rectangle. In spite of the fact that contemporary designers pay little attention to the Hambidge theory, the student should find it helpful to orderly thinking.

Shapes based on the straight line. The straight line may be used to create forms of great simplicity and strength. Do not be afraid to use it. One of the simplest ceramic forms is the cylinder, which has.only one possible variable, the ratio of height to diameter, although a foot and neck are often added. A few arrangements of this form are shown in Fig. 14–14. Conical shapes are also simple and pleasing. It is possible to vary the angle of the cone and the amount of truncation, and to combine cones, as shown in the examples of Fig. 14–15. The straight line is also used for creating asymmetrical (free) forms.

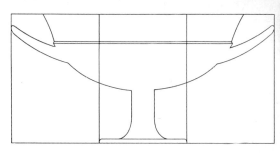

Fig. 14-13. A kylix, shown enclosed in three root-two rectangles. (Hambidge, *Dynamic Symmetry*, p. 53.)

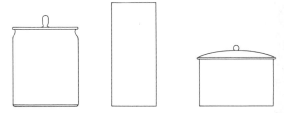

Fig. 14-14. Vase forms based on the cylinder.

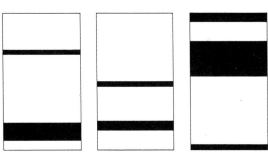

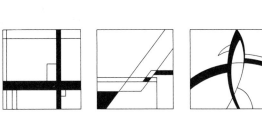

Fig. 14-11. Above, spaces divided vertically into five harmonious parts; below, abstractions based on the same harmonious divisions.

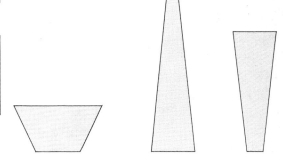

Fig. 14-15. Vase forms based on the cone.

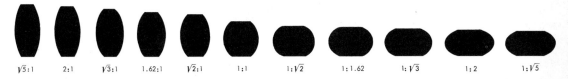

| $\sqrt{5}:1$ | 2:1 | $\sqrt{3}:1$ | 1.62:1 | $\sqrt{2}:1$ | 1:1 | $1:\sqrt{2}$ | 1:1.62 | $1:\sqrt{3}$ | 1:2 | $1:\sqrt{5}$ |

Fig. 14-12. A single vase form drawn with various area proportions.

Shapes based on the circular arc. Most ceramic shapes are based on curves, since the plasticity of the material used favors such forms. Curved forms have a most satisfying quality—perhaps because the human body is made up of curves. The potter need not be a mathematician to use curves properly, but he should know how typical curves are formed by simple, graphical methods. Because the circle has uniform curvature, it is not as interesting as other curves, but it may be used to produce spherical shapes such as those shown in Fig. 14–16.

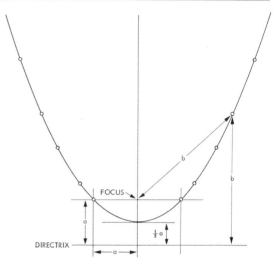

Fig. 14-17. Parabola.

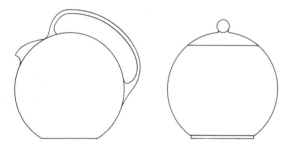

Fig. 14-16. Forms based on the sphere.

Shapes based on the parabola. Several curves with uniformly changing curvature are most useful of all for forming ceramic shapes, for they have both strength and grace. The basic curve of the parabola is shown in Fig. 14–17. It will be recognized as the form used for the reflector of an automobile headlight, a familiar object. This curve can be readily formed by using a compass to locate a set of points equidistant from the focus and directrix, as shown in the figure. Figure 14–18 shows how well this curve lends itself to pleasing pottery designs.

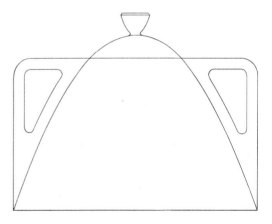

Fig. 14-18. Shape based on the parabola.

Shapes based on the catenary. This is the curve formed by a hanging chain, as shown in Fig. 14–19. It is much like the parabola, and its shape may be easily determined by hanging a light chain from two

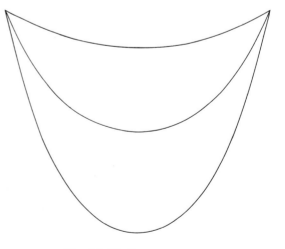

Fig. 14-19. Catenary curves.

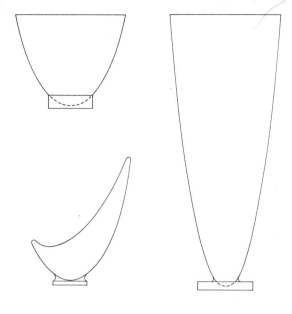

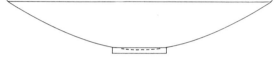

Fig. 14-20. Shapes based on the catenary.

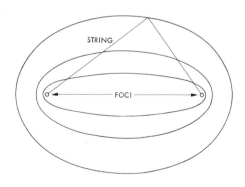

STRING

FOCI

Fig. 14-21. Ellipse.

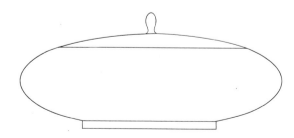

Fig. 14-22. Form based on the ellipse.

points on a vertical wall and tracing the resultant curve. By altering the lengh of the chain, a whole series of curves can be produced. Figure 14–20 shows examples of its use in the design of pottery.

Shapes based on the ellipse. This curve is readily formed by tying a thread between two pins placed as shown in Fig. 14–21, and then drawing a pencil around the inside of the thread. A whole series of ellipses can be produced by altering the length of the thread, and the shape can also be distorted by enlarging one end to give an "egg shape." An example of the use of ellipses is given in Fig. 14–22.

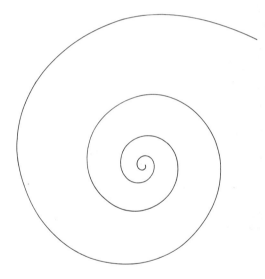

Fig. 14-23. Logarithmic spiral.

Shapes based on the logarithmic spiral. This very important curve is often found in nature (Fig. 14–23). Shells are a good example. Sir D'Arcy Wentworth Thompson calls it the "curve of life," and, indeed, it has many interesting properties. Figure 14–24 shows an adaptation of this curve to a pottery shape.

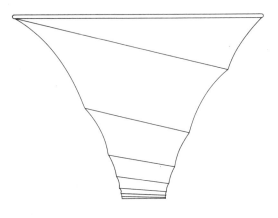

Fig. 14-24. Shape based on the logarithmic spiral.

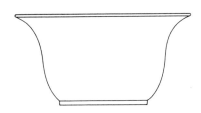

Fig. 14-25. Vase form using an S-curve.

Shapes based on the S-curve. This curve, shown in Fig. 13–19, is often referred to by artists as the "line of beauty" or the "Hogarth line." Because it is found in the female figure, it is associated with grace, but it lacks the strength of other curves. Although the S-curve is often used in shaping pottery, it is not as satisfying as curves with regularly changing curvature. An example is shown in Fig. 14–25.

VII. ORNAMENTATION

How much ornament should a piece have? Of what should the ornamentation consist? These are questions that a designer must face, and the answer depends a great deal on the proposed use and the prospective buyer. When a vase is perfectly proportioned, it needs no surface decoration to enhance its beauty—shape, color, and texture are all that are needed. Is the beauty of the human figure enhanced by covering its surface with tattooing?

There is not sufficient space here to cover the specific uses of surface ornamentation. Remember, however, that it is always better to use too little than too much, and where ornamentation is used, it should first of all be subordinated to the main shape, and secondly, be in harmony with it.

VIII. CONCLUSION

There can be no hard and fast rules for applying the principles of design to ceramic pieces, for even though all the rules are closely followed, the finished piece may lack the intangible something that gives it appeal. Perhaps it is the personality of the potter that makes the difference. However, until he has established his own style and is successful with it, it is certainly necessary for the beginner to follow these principles closely and to study the work of the great potters.

We cannot do better than to quote from an article in *Arts and Crafts* by Edwin and Mary Scheier:

"There is no material more satisfactory than clay; and no material can be more dangerous.

"A facile medium, immediately responsive, it allows more than most for trite and immediately pleasing effects. Mistakes can be hidden—too easily—under unrelated decoration. In other arts subject matter may give strength and interest, at least for a time; in a basically abstract art like pottery, it cannot. Clay is no medium for the craftsman unsure of himself."

IX. REFERENCES

1. ALBERT, J., Design—The Role of the Small Pottery, *Bull. Am. Ceram. Soc.* **29**, 419 (1950).

2. ANON., Masterpieces in Pottery, *Studio.* London and New York, **136**, 186 (1948).

3. BARRINGER, L. E., Ceramic Art and Education, *Bull. Am. Ceram. Soc.* **15**, 1 (1936).

4. HARDER, C. M., Functional Design, *Bull. Am. Ceram. Soc.* **21**, 174 (1942).

5. HOME, R. M., *Ceramics for the Potter,* Chas. A. Bennett Company, Inc., Peoria, Ill., 1952.

6. LEACH, B., *The Potter's Book,* Faber & Faber, Ltd., London, 1940.

7. LESTER, K. M., *Creative Ceramics,* Chas. A. Bennett Company, Inc. (formerly The Manual Arts Press), Peoria, Ill., 1948.

8. MEYER, F. S., *Handbook of Ornament,* Wilcox & Follett Co., Chicago, 1945.

9. PERKINS, D. W., Notes on Foot Design for Ceramic Ware, *Ceramic Age* **52**, No. 6, 342 (1948).

10. RUSSELL, G. What We Mean by Good Design, *Bull. Am. Ceram. Soc.* **28**, 292 (1949).

11. SHEPARD, A. O., Symmetry of Abstract Design with Special Reference to Ceramic Decoration, *Carn. Inst. Wash. Pub. No. 574,* 209 (1948).

12. WINGFIELD DIGBY, G. F., *The Work of the Modern Potter in England,* John Murray, London, 1952.

CHAPTER 15

Clays

I. INTRODUCTION

Clay is the backbone of the ceramic arts. This remarkable mineral has the property of excellent workability when it is mixed with water, and the resultant mass seems to be just asking to be formed into an interesting shape. When the clay is dried, it is strong enough to be handled, and firing fixes the plastic form into an enduring shape.

Although clays are found nearly everywhere on the earth's habitable surface, they vary widely in their properties. Some are well suited to pottery making just as they are, while others must be purified or mixed with suitable ingredients to make them workable.

The potter needs a general knowledge of the kinds of clay that are suited to the ceramic arts, so that he may select and blend them intelligently to form the mixtures that are best for his purpose. In this chapter, we shall attempt to give a thorough, but readable discussion of this fascinating subject.

II. WHAT IS CLAY?

Clay is made up of tiny crystals, many of them so small that they cannot be seen under the highest power of an ordinary microscope. These crystals are composed mainly of a mineral called *kaolinite* ($Al_2O_3 \cdot 2SiO_2 \cdot 2H_2O$), whose composition approximates

> 47% silica (SiO_2)
> 39% alumina (Al_2O_3)
> 14% water (H_2O)

The average size of these crystals is so small that no ordinary scale will measure them. If they were laid end to end it would take about 50,000 of them to make an inch, and their thickness is about $\frac{1}{10}$ of their length. In shape they are like tiny plates, more or less hexagonal in outline and with flat faces.

The newly developed electron microscope makes it possible for us to actually see and study these fine clay particles. Figure 15–1 shows some typical specimens. It is the plate-like nature of clay that gives it its plastic properties when mixed with water; the plates glide over one another, with the water acting as a lubricant.

Other clay minerals. Besides the kaolinite mentioned above, there are a number of other clay minerals that are quite similar in their properties, but because they are only minor constituents of ceramic clays, we need not consider them in any detail. The only ones that are of interest to us are *montmorillonite* and *halloysite,* which are even finer than kaolinite and are sometimes used in small quantities to enhance the working properties of other ceramic materials.

Other minerals in clays. Even the purest of natural clays contains free particles of materials that may be thought of as sand or grit. The most common is quartz (SiO_2), found in a great variety of particle sizes. Feldspars ($K,NaO \cdot Al_2O_3 \cdot 6SiO_2$) act as grit in the plas-

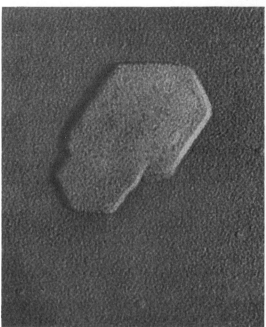

Fig. 15-1. Platelike particles of kaolin magnified 50,000
times. Note the smaller crystals on the face.

tic clay, but become fluxes during firing. Tiny flakes of mica are frequently found in small quantities, and the iron-containing minerals that are often present may cause discoloration of the fired clay.

Organic matter in clays. Some clays, especially ball clays, contain organic matter in the form of lignite (a type of coal) and waxes. These generally burn out on firing, but they influence the plasticity and dry strength of the clay.

III. THE ORIGIN OF CLAY

Clay is a secondary product in the earth's crust; that is, it results from decomposition by weathering of the older rocks of the feldspar type. Some clays, like English china clays, are found where they were formed, while others, such as ball clays, are found in deposits far removed from the parent rock.

These latter have been washed out of the partially decomposed parent rock and laid down in swamps and ponds, and for this reason consist mainly of relatively fine particles.

IV. KINDS OF CLAY

Many kinds of clay are available to the ceramist, and it seems fitting to spend a little time in describing them briefly.

Kaolins. These are the whitest of all the clays, because of their low iron content, and therefore they are the principal ingredient of white earthenware and porcelain bodies. Because kaolins are not very plastic, have a low dry strength, and are extremely refractory, they are not suitable for pottery making except when mixed with other ingredients. Ball clay is added for plasticity, and fluxes are added to make them less refractory.

Residual kaolins, such as those found in North Carolina and in Cornwall (England), must be treated to remove undecomposed rock fragments, and after this is done the clay is extraordinarily pure and white. The so-called sedimentary kaolins have already been washed by nature to give a reasonably pure clay, but for best results they are washed again. The immense deposits found in Georgia are typical of sedimentary kaolins.

An unusually fine-grained kaolin with more plasticity and greater dry strength than those discussed above is found in some of the lakes of northern Florida. After treatment, this clay is of high purity and can be fired to an excellent degree of whiteness. It is often used in mixtures for whiteware bodies.

Ball clays. These important ceramic clays, so named because in the early days they were sold in the form of balls, are found only in rather small areas of Kentucky, Tennessee, and southern England. They are fine-grained and therefore highly plastic, and they have a high dry strength. Both drying and firing shrinkage are unusually great for this kind of clay, and for this reason it cannot be used alone. Also, the fired color is not as white as that of the kaolins. Ball clays are nearly always added to American whiteware bodies to give improved working properties, but because they impair translucency, they are seldom used in European hard porcelain bodies.

Ball clays are not water washed, as are the kaolins, but grit and organic matter can be screened out of the slip when it is made up for the body.

Stoneware clays. There are many kinds of stoneware clays that contain sufficient feldspar, combined with a plastic clay, to give both good working properties and a dense body when fired. These clays are widely used by the artist potter because they can be readily thrown on the wheel or pressed into molds. They are an important ingredient in many bodies, as well as being satisfactory for use alone.

Red brick clays. These are the clays that are used for building bricks, and they are found nearly everywhere in the eastern United States. In Colonial times redware pottery was made from this kind of clay, but it is difficult to make a watertight body when it is used alone. On the whole, red brick clays impart good working properties when they are used as an addition to low-firing bodies, and they give a warm red or orange color to the fired piece (depending on the amount).

Other clays. Of the many types of clay found in nature, those mentioned in the preceding paragraphs are the ones of chief interest to the potter. Very fine-grained bentonites might be mentioned also; these are sometimes used in small amounts to enhance the plasticity of a body.

V. TREATMENT OF CLAYS

Nearly all clays contain too much grit in their natural state, and they must therefore be washed before being used. The process is quite simple. The clay is blunged (mixed) with water to form a thin suspension, and is then passed through a fine screen to remove the coarse grit. The suspension is allowed to stand until the fine grit settles out, and the suspended clay is then filtered or dried to remove the water.

Kaolins usually come already washed, but ball clays, brick clays, and some stoneware clays must be treated by the potter. Because a composition containing quartz and feldspar filters much more readily than the clay alone, the body is usually made up before the washing is done. Washing methods are discussed more fully in Chapter 18.

Ball clays and kaolins that have been "air-floated" are available from suppliers. This means that the clays have been ground and the coarser particles removed by an airstream. Clays treated in this way can be used in dry-pressed bodies, but lump clay should be used for plastic bodies and casting slips.

VI. CHEMICAL COMPOSITION OF CLAYS

This section may appear too technical for the tastes of some readers, and it can be omitted without loss of continuity in the general discussion of clays. However, if one is to embark seriously into the field of ceramics, it is necessary to have some knowledge of methods of calculation for making up bodies and glazes. This section is intended as an introduction to the more extended use of formulas later in this book. It should be emphasized here that a chemical background is not required for carrying out ceramic calculations; only the most elementary arithmetic is needed.

Chemical analysis of a clay tells us something about what we may expect when it is used in a body, particularly how it will be-have on firing. For example, highly pure kaolins are very refractory and cannot be fired to a dense structure in the pottery kiln; on the other hand, stoneware clays, which contain potash and lime, will fire quite readily. Analysis of the amount of iron oxide present in the clay tells us what the fired color will be. While each clay is not always specifically analysed, it is well to have a general knowledge of the composition of typical clays.

Composition of typical clays. Table 15–1 gives the chemical analyses of some of the typical clays used for pottery.

Chemical elements. A chemist reports the chemical composition of a clay as though the elements were combined with oxygen in their normal oxide. For example, silicon (Si) is reported as SiO_2, aluminum (Al) as Al_2O_3, and iron (Fe) as Fe_2O_3 or FeO. The chemist uses a kind of shorthand to indicate the elements by symbols, and the reader should become familiar with the symbols for the common elements. The amount of each oxide is expressed as a percent of the whole, and the total of all the elements should be 100%, or close to it.

Table 15–2 shows the sums of the basic oxides (FeO, MgO, CaO, Na_2O, K_2O), the neutral oxides (Al_2O_3), and the acid oxides (SiO_2, TiO_2). This classification is useful in

TABLE 15–1

CHEMICAL ANALYSIS OF TYPICAL CLAYS, IN PERCENT

Constituent	English china clay[1]	N.C. kaolin[1]	Florida plastic kaolin[1]	Ky. ball clay	Tenn. ball clay	N.J. stoneware clay	Red brick clay
Silica (SiO_2)	48	46	47	53	61	68	57
Alumina (Al_2O_3)	38	36	37	29	25	22	19
Iron oxide (Fe_2O_3)	0.5	0.6	0.8	2	1	1.6	7
Magnesia (MgO)	–	0.4	0.2	0.3	0.1	0.2	3
Lime (CaO)	–	0.4	0.2	0.4	0.1	0.3	4
Titania (TiO_2)	–	0.4	0.2	0.8	1.3	–	1
Alkalies (K,NaO)	2	0.7	0.3	2	2	2.5	5
Combined water	12	13	15	12[2]	10[2]	6	4
Basic oxides	2.5	2.1	1.5	4.7	3.2	4.6	19
Neutral oxides	38	36.4	37.2	29	25.0	22.0	19
Acid oxides	48	46	47.0	53.8	62.3	68.0	58

[1] Washed. [2] Includes some organic matter.

evaluating a clay, because the higher the percentage of basic oxides, the lower the maturing temperature required for firing.

Atoms. All matter is composed of "building blocks" known as *atoms*. Atoms are not all exactly alike; in fact, there are at least one hundred different kinds found in nature. Of these, less than half are common enough to interest us here. It is necessary to know some-

TABLE 15-2
ATOMIC WEIGHTS OF COMMON ELEMENTS

Element	Symbol	Atomic weight	Element	Symbol	Atomic weight
Aluminum	Al	26.97	Magnesium	Mg	24.32
Antimony	Sb	121.76	Manganese	Mn	54.93
Arsenic	As	79.91	Molybdenum	Mo	95.95
Barium	Ba	137.36	Nickel	Ni	58.69
Beryllium	Be	9.02	Nitrogen	N	14.01
Bismuth	Bi	209.00	Oxygen	O	16.00
Boron	B	10.82	Phosphorus	P	30.98
Cadmium	Cd	112.41	Platinum	Pt	195.23
Calcium	Ca	40.08	Potassium	K	39.10
Carbon	C	12.01	Silicon	Si	28.06
Chlorine	Cl	35.46	Silver	Ag	107.88
Chromium	Cr	52.01	Sodium	Na	23.00
Cobalt	Co	58.94	Strontium	Sr	87.63
Copper	Cu	63.57	Sulfur	S	32.06
Fluorine	F	19.00	Tin	Sn	118.70
Gold	Au	197.20	Titanium	Ti	47.90
Hydrogen	H	1.00	Tungsten	W	183.92
Iron	Fe	55.84	Uranium	U	238.07
Lead	Pb	207.21	Zinc	Zn	65.38
Lithium	Li	6.49	Zirconium	Zr	91.22

thing about these atoms if we are to understand how they combine to form the substances used in ceramics.

The sizes of atoms do not vary greatly, but their weights vary considerably. It is impossible to "weigh" an atom by ordinary means, but it is quite simple to determine the *relative* weights of different atoms if we use the lightest one, hydrogen, as unity (one). This results in a series of values from 1 through 92 or more, called *atomic weights* (see Table 15-2). The simplicity of this method of measurement is apparent when we note that any one of these values, expressed in grams, contains exactly the same number of atoms—six, with twenty-three zeros after it! This figure is so enormous that it cannot be visualized, but that does not matter. What *is* important is to

know, for example, that 16 grams of oxygen contain the same number of atoms as 56 grams of iron.

Atoms have another important property. Each atom can carry one or more units of electricity, called a *charge*. Some atoms (the metals, like aluminum, silicon, iron, etc.) can carry positive charges, and some (the nonmetals, like oxygen, chlorine, etc.) can carry negative charges. These charges are always whole numbers. Some atoms can carry only one particular charge, while others may carry different numbers of charges, depending on the environment. The number of charges is indicated by plus (positive) or minus (negative) signs to the right and slightly above the symbol for the element: $O^{(--)}$, $Fe^{(++)}$, $Si^{(++++)}$, $Al^{(+++)}$, etc.

Molecules. *Molecules* are formed by a combination of atoms. Such combinations are never haphazard, but follow exact rules. Positively charged atoms must combine with negatively charged atoms in such a way that the positive charges are just balanced by the negative charges. A few examples will make this clear.

Lime (calcium oxide) is formed by the combination of calcium atoms with an equal number of oxygen atoms:

$$Ca^{(++)} + O^{(++)} \rightarrow CaO.$$

The combining weights would then be one atomic weight of calcium and one atomic weight of oxygen, as shown in the following equation:

$$40 \text{ grams } Ca^{(++)} + 16 \text{ grams } O^{(--)}$$
$$\rightarrow 56 \text{ grams CaO.}$$

Remember that there are the same number of atoms in 40 grams of calcium as in 16 grams of oxygen.

Take another example. Silica is formed by the combination of silicon and oxygen as follows:

$$Si^{(++++)} + 2\,O^{(--)} \rightarrow SiO_2.$$

Since the silicon has four positive charges, two doubly charged oxygen atoms must be combined with it. The combining equation is:

$$28 \text{ grams } Si^{(++++)} + 2(16) \text{ grams } O^{(--)}$$
$$\rightarrow 60 \text{ grams } SiO_2.$$

Another example is alumina, Al_2O_3:

$$2\,Al^{(+++)} + 3\,O^{(--)} \rightarrow Al_2O_3,$$

or

$$2(27) \text{ grams } Al^{(+++)} + 3(16) \text{ grams } O^{(--)}$$
$$\rightarrow 102 \text{ grams } Al_2O_3.$$

As previously mentioned, some atoms can hold a variable number of charges. One of these is iron. For example:

$$Fe^{(++)} + O^{(--)} \rightarrow FeO \text{ (ferrous oxide)},$$

or

$$2\,Fe^{(+++)} + 3\,O^{(--)} \rightarrow Fe_2O_3 \text{ (ferric oxide)}.$$

One may well ask, "How do we know how many charges an atom will have under a particular set of conditions?" There is no simple answer, but the compounds used in ceramics are so few and so uncomplicated that we can soon learn the specific combinations.

Complex molecules are formed by combining the simple ones. For example, lead disilicate is formed as follows:

$$PbO + 2\,SiO_2 \rightarrow PbO \cdot 2\,SiO_2,$$

and potash feldspar is formed by

$$K_2O + Al_2O_3 + 6\,SiO_2$$
$$\rightarrow K_2O \cdot Al_2O_3 \cdot 6\,SiO_2.$$

The combining weights are simple additions, as before:

$$94.3 \text{ grams } K_2O + 101.9 \text{ grams } Al_2O_3$$
$$+ 6(60.1) \text{ grams } SiO_2$$
$$\rightarrow 556.8 \text{ grams } K_2O \cdot Al_2O_3 \cdot 6\,SiO_2.$$

556.8 grams is the *formula weight* of potash feldspar. This is a useful term in ceramic calculations and is simply the sum of all the atomic weights in the formula. The most frequently used formula weights are given in Table 15–3.

Equivalent weight. The term *equivalent weight* sometimes causes confusion, but it is simple to understand if it is viewed logically. The equivalent weight of a substance is that weight which will yield a formula weight of any portion of the substance in which we are interested. There is therefore no one equivalent weight for a single compound. A few examples will help to make this clear.

Potash feldspar $(K_2O \cdot Al_2O_3 \cdot 6\,SiO_2)$ has a formula weight of 556.8 grams; therefore this weight of feldspar will produce one formula weight of potassium oxide, one of alumina, and six of silica. If we need to supply one formula weight of potassium oxide or alumina, then it follows that 556.8 grams of feldspar, its equivalent weight, must be used; if we wish to supply one formula weight of silica, then we must use 556.8/6 or 92.9 grams of feldspar, which is its equivalent weight in terms of silica.

Suppose that one formula weight of boric oxide (B_2O_3) is required, and the raw material is borax $(Na_2B_4O_7 \cdot 10H_2O)$. This may be rewritten as $Na_2O \cdot 2\,B_2O_3 \cdot 10H_2O$, with a formula weight of 381.4 grams. To supply one formula weight of B_2O_3 would then require 381.4/2 or 190.7 grams of borax. Therefore the equivalent weight of borax is 190.7 if we are interested in B_2O_3, but it is 381.4 if we are using it to supply soda.

On the other hand, a simple oxide such as quartz (SiO_2) would have an equivalent weight of 60.1, the same as its formula weight.

Equivalent weights are listed in Table 15-3.

Calculation of the mineral content of clays.

To obtain real insight into the value of a clay for a particular purpose, we need to know exactly what minerals are present and in what proportions. These may be roughly divided into the clay minerals that give plas-

tic properties, the quartz that gives lowered shrinkage, and the feldspar that serves as a flux to bind the mass together on firing. It is possible to precisely determine the amounts of these minerals by x-ray and microscopic techniques, of course, but these are too specialized to discuss here. However, for our purposes, it is sufficient to approximately determine the amounts by calculations from the chemical analysis.

As an example, let us analyze New Jersey stoneware clay. First, we convert the percent weights listed in Table 15-1 for this clay to equivalent weights of the oxides, and then recombine these to determine the amount of clay and other minerals. It must be recalled that soda and potash are to be found in the feldspar (potash may also be present in the mica, but we shall neglect this) and that feldspar also contains some of the alumina. The remainder of the alumina combines with silica to form the clay minerals, and any residue of silica is left as quartz. Iron oxide is assumed to be present as such, and the amounts of lime and magnesia are so small that we can neglect them in our calculations. The method of calculation is shown in Table 15-4.

TABLE 15-3

FORMULA AND EQUIVALENT WEIGHTS OF CERAMIC MATERIALS

Material	Formula	Formula weight	Equivalent Weight		
			Basic oxides	Neutral oxides	Acic oxides
Alumina	Al_2O_3	101.9		101.9	
Aluminum hydrate	$Al_2O_3 \cdot 3H_2O$	155.9		155.9	
Ammonium carbonate	$(NH_4)_2CO_3 \cdot H_2O$	114.1	114.1		
Arsenious oxide	As_2O_3	197.8		197.8	
Barium carbonate	$BaCO_3$	197.4	197.4		
Boracic acid	$B_2O_3 \cdot 3H_2O$	123.7		123.7	
Boric oxide	B_2O_3	69.6		69.6	
Borax	$Na_2B_4O_7$	381.4	381.4		190.7
Calcium carbonate[1]	$CaCO_3$	100.0	100.1		
Calcium oxide (lime)	CaO	56.1	56.1		
Calcium fluoride	CaF_2	78.1	78.1		
Chromic oxide	Cr_2O_3	152.0	76.0	152.0	
Clay (kaolinite)	$Al_2O_3 \cdot 2SiO_2 \cdot 2H_2O$	258.2		258.2	129.1
Clay (calcined)	$Al_2O_3 \cdot 2SiO_2$	222.2		222.2	111.1
Cobaltic oxide	Co_2O_3	165.9	83.0	165.9	
Cryolite	Na_3AlF_2	210.0	140.0	420.0	
Cupric oxide	CuO	79.6	79.6		
Feldspar (potash)	$K_2O \cdot Al_2O_3 \cdot 6SiO_2$	556.8	556.8	556.8	92.9
Feldspar (soda)	$Na_2O \cdot Al_2O_3 \cdot 6SiO_2$	524.5	524.5	524.5	87.6
Flint (quartz)	SiO_2	60.1			60.1
Ferrous oxide	FeO	71.8	71.8		
Ferric oxide	Fe_2O_3	159.7	79.8	159.7	
Lead carbonate[2]	$2PbCO_3 \cdot Pb(OH)_2$	775.6	258.5		
Lead oxide[3]	Pb_3O_4	685.6	228.5		
Lithium carbonate	Li_2CO_3	73.9	73.9		
Magnesium carbonate	$MgCO_3$	84.3	84.3		
Magnesium oxide	MgO	40.3	40.3		
Manganese dioxide	MnO_2	86.9	86.9		86.9
Nickel oxide	NiO	74.7	74.7		
Potassium carbonate	K_2CO_3	138.0	138.0		
Sodium carbonate	Na_2CO_3	106.0	106.0		
Sodium nitrate[4]	$NaNO_3$	85.0	170.0		
Strontium carbonate	$SrCO_3$	147.6	147.6		
Tin oxide	SnO	150.7			150.7
Titanium dioxide	TiO_2	80.1			80.1
Zinc carbonate	$ZnCO_2$	125.4	125.4		
Zinc oxide	ZnO	81.4	81.4		
Zirconium oxide	ZrO_2	123.0	123.0		

[1] Whiting   [2] White lead   [3] Red lead   [4] Niter

TABLE 15-4

CALCULATION OF MINERALS IN STONEWARE CLAY

Oxide	Weight percent of oxide in clay	Relative number of equivalent weights of oxide in clay [1]
Silica (SiO_2)	68.0	1.13
Alumina (Al_2O_3)	22.0	0.217
Ferric oxide (Fe_2O_3)	1.6	0.010
Alkalies (K, NaO)	2.5	0.032

[1] Obtained by dividing weight percent by formula weight (Table 15-3).

Equivalents of oxides in clay	1.130 SiO_2	0.217 Al_2O_3	0.010 Fe_2O_3	0.032 Alkalies
0.032 Equiv. feldspar	0.192	0.032	———	0.032
Difference	0.938	0.185	0.010	0
0.185 Equiv. clay mineral	0.370	0.185		
Difference	0.568	0	0.010	
0.568 Equiv. quartz	0.568			
Difference	0	———	0.010	
0.010 Equiv. ferric oxide	———		0.010	
Difference	———		0	

First, the weight percents of the oxides are converted to the correct number of equivalents (the assumption is made that one half of the alkali is soda and the other half is potash). These figures are set up at the head of a table, and 0.032 equivalent of feldspar is subtracted to eliminate the alkalies. This procedure reduces the alumina and the silica at the same time. Next, 0.185 equivalent of clay mineral is subtracted, which eliminates the alumina and leaves 0.568 equivalent of silica, which is taken out with 0.568 equivalent of quartz. Finally, 0.010 equivalent of iron oxide is subtracted to account for all of the minerals. The water is automatically accounted for in this method of calculation, and need not be given special consideration.

We have now determined the relative number of equivalents of the various minerals of which this clay is composed, and these are now converted to weight percent, as shown in Table 15–5.

TABLE 15–5

CALCULATION OF WEIGHT PERCENT OF MINERALS

Mineral	Rel. No. of equiv.	Relative weight[1]	Weight percent
Clay mineral	0.185	47.8	47.4
Feldspar	0.032	17.3	17.2
Quartz	0.568	34.1	33.8
Hematite	0.010	1.6	1.6
Total		100.8	100.0

[1]Obtained by multiplying figures in the preceding column by each formula weight.

An analysis such as that shown in Table 15–5 tells us a great deal about the ceramic properties of a particular clay. For example, the clay mineral gives good workability and dried strength; the feldspar and iron oxide form glass on burning, to give fired strength; and the quartz acts as a skeleton to reduce both drying and firing shrinkage.

Another useful way of expressing the composition of a clay is by the Seger or equivalent formula, where the relative numbers of equivalents of the component oxides are arranged in three columns: (1) the basic oxides, (2) the neutral oxides, and (3) the acid oxides. For stoneware clay, the formula would be

$$\begin{matrix} 0.032 \text{ Na,KO} \\ 0.010 \text{ Fe}_2\text{O}_3 \end{matrix} \quad 0.22 \text{ Al}_2\text{O}_3 \quad 1.13 \text{ SiO}_2.$$

It is usual to make the sum of the neutral oxides equal to unity and to express the other quantities relative to this. Again for stoneware clay, the formula would then read

$$\begin{matrix} 0.145 \text{ Na,KO} \\ 0.045 \text{ Fe}_2\text{O}_3 \end{matrix} \quad 1.00 \text{ Al}_2\text{O}_3 \quad 5.15 \text{ SiO}_2.$$

When the proportion of basic oxides in a clay or body is high, the maturing temperature in the kiln must be low, and therefore this information permits at least an estimate of what firing temperature to use.

It will be found instructive to work out the equivalent formulas for the other clays listed in Table 15–1.

Figure 15–2 shows graphically the mineral content of a few typical clays, together

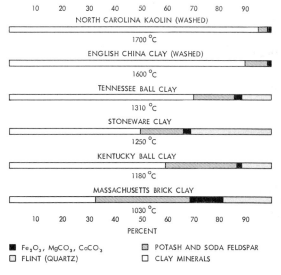

Fig. 15-2. Mineral composition of some typical clays, and their firing temperatures.

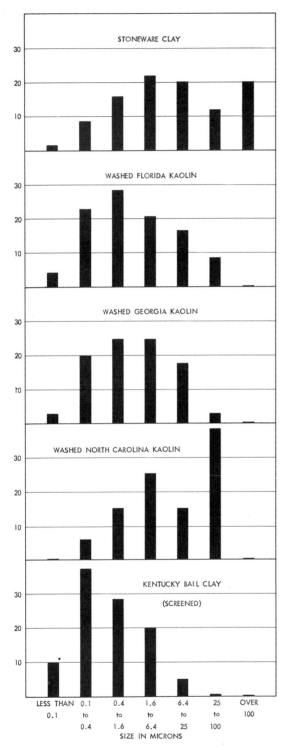

Fig. 15-3. Particle size of various clays.

with the temperatures at which they reach zero porosity. It will be seen that as the amounts of feldspar and other basic minerals ($MgCO_3$, $CaCO_3$, and Fe_2O_3) increase, the maturing temperature steadily decreases. It must be remembered that because some elements are much more powerful than others, the total amount of fluxing minerals does not give us the whole story. However, this information does give us a reasonably good picture.

VII. PHYSICAL PROPERTIES OF CLAYS

Particle size. Some of the properties of clays are greatly influenced by the sizes of the particles of which the clay is composed, and their distribution. The graphs of Fig. 15–3 show the sizes of particles found in four typical clays, expressed in microns. The micron is an extremely small unit; there are approximately 25,000 microns in one inch.

Ball clay which has been passed through a fine screen to remove the lignite (organic matter) and coarse grit, but which has not been water washed, is the finest of the clays. Ten percent of the particles in this clay are less than 0.1 micron in size, and these extremely small particles contribute to high drying shrinkage and great strength. The effectiveness of these particles in this respect is largely due to their combined surface area, which increases in direct proportion to the smallness of the particles. In this case, the total surface area of the finest 10% of the particles is approximately equal to the total surface area presented by the remaining 90%.

Stoneware clay is not so fine as ball clay; about 20% of it is made up of such coarse material as the grit of quartz, feldspar, and mica. Washing would remove these coarse particles. This clay is quite workable, and does not shrink excessively.

Florida kaolin is a water-washed clay and therefore has no coarse particles. It has fewer very fine particles than the ball clay, however, and is usually made up of particles of medium size. Florida kaolin is not so strong as ball clay, but its strength and its working properties are good.

North Carolina kaolin has practically no extremely fine particles, but about 40% of its particles are in the 25–100 micron range. The coarsest particles are washed out. This clay is not sufficiently workable to be used alone.

The sizes of the particles of washed Georgia kaolin fall somewhere between those of the Florida and North Carolina kaolin.

Plastic properties. The plastic properties of a clay play a very important part in the successful application of the forming process, such as throwing on the wheel. There is no sure way of measuring plasticity quantitatively, but an experienced potter is able to judge it fairly accurately by feeling the plastic mass or by actually throwing it on the wheel.

Of the natural clays, stoneware is the most workable, although some of the red-burning brick clays are almost as good. The kaolins are too "short" (i.e., crumbly) for good working, and the ball clays are usually too sticky, and although some of them can be thrown on the wheel quite readily, they cannot be dried and fired without warping and cracking. However, suitable combinations of kaolin, ball clay, and nonplastic materials have excellent workability (see Chapter 22).

Drying properties. When formed by ordinary methods, all clays and bodies shrink in drying, because of the removal of the thin films of water from between the particles.

The finer the particles, the more films of water, and the greater the shrinkage. Consequently, fine ball clays shrink a great deal, while the coarse kaolins shrink very little. As we shall explain in Chapter 22, the addition of nonplastic grog (fireclay particles) or feldspar decreases the shrinkage of a clay.

Table 15–6 lists the shrinkages of various clays from the plastic to the fully dry condition. The percent shrinkage as listed is based on the plastic length; for example, a clay molded into a tile 10 inches long will be, let us say, 9.5 inches in length when dried. The percent shrinkage is then

$$\frac{10 - 9.5}{10} \times 100 = 5\%.$$

TABLE 15–6
DRYING SHRINKAGE AND DRY STRENGTH OF TYPICAL CLAYS

Type of clay	Linear shrinkage, in percent of plastic length	Dry strength (modulus of rupture, lb per sq in.)
N.C. kaolin, washed	4.5	200
Florida kaolin, washed	6.0	300
Georgia kaolin, washed	3.0	65
Ky. ball clay	11.0	700
N.J. stoneware clay	7.5	450
Glacial brick clay	5.0	400

Table 15–6 also lists the dry strengths of the various clays. Note that the fine-grained ball clays are very strong, while the kaolins are less so. Since few of these clays are used alone, the individual properties are important only as a guide to the proper combination of clays for a body with suitable characteristics.

Firing properties. The firing properties of greatest interest are the color, the shrinkage, and the porosity.

The fired color depends to a large extent on the amount of iron minerals present. The washed residual kaolins, with 0.5% iron oxide, are very white; the sedimentary kaolins, with 0.7% iron oxide, show a faint cream color; the ball clays, with 1% iron oxide, fire a definite cream color; and stoneware clay, with 2.5% iron oxide, fires gray or buff. The brick clays, which contain about 7% iron oxide, fire red.

Although the amount of iron in a clay has the greatest influence on the fired color, other factors also affect the color. For example, lime acts as a bleach for the iron reds.

Firing shrinkage, as explained above, is closely allied with the size of the particles in a particular clay.

The porosity of a clay is determined by measuring the amount of water that has been absorbed by the fired clay after it has been boiled for one hour and has remained immersed for 24 hours. For example, if an unglazed plate weighs 196 grams when dry and 220 grams after the above water treatment, its absorption is

$$\frac{220 - 196}{196} \times 100 = \frac{24}{196} \times 100 = 12.8\%.$$

The absorption value is important for judging the suitability of a clay for a particular purpose. Tight-burning clays help to reduce the firing temperature required; open-burning clays tend to increase the absorption of the body in which they are used.

VIII. CLAY DEPOSITS

Local clays hold an appeal for the artist potter for several reasons: (1) they are readily available, usually at low cost; (2) there is a feeling of satisfaction in carrying through the process of pottery making from start to finish, even to the point of obtaining the raw materials; (3) there is a special charm and sentiment to ware that is made of local clays.

The map of Fig. 15–4 shows the regions where pottery clays are to be found. This map is by no means complete, because new deposits are continually being developed.

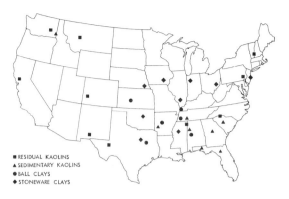

Fig. 15-4. Pottery clays of the U. S.

When raw materials are not available locally or when the local clay is not suitable, clay may be purchased, either in the correct proportions for direct use, or separately for combination by the potter himself.

IX. SELECTION OF SUITABLE CLAYS

The properties of various ball and stoneware clays are listed in some detail in this section, to assist the potter in making a proper selection for his purpose. Included is a list of sources of supply. Although some producers of clay are very cooperative in furnishing specific data on the properties of their products, it would be helpful if more complete information were available on all commercial clays.

Ball clays. Table 15–7 lists the properties of American ball clays. It will be noted that these properties vary considerably. For example, the dry modulus of rupture runs from 150 lb/in^2 to more than 1000 lb/in^2. The fineness of the clay, on which the plastic properties largely depend, causes considerable variation in drying shrinkage. The firing shrinkage for these clays is high in every case (from 6 to 13%), which is an indication that they cannot be successfully used unless mixed with other kinds of clay.

The clays listed vary considerably in porosity when fired. Some are tight-firing (i.e., they reach zero absorption at Cone 9 or less), while others are quite open-firing. The fired color also varies, and this is an important consideration in the selection of a clay for a particular purpose.

Table 15–8 lists properties of a few of the many English ball clays. In general, the dry strength of these clays is somewhat higher than for American clays, and they are tighter-firing; most of them are fairly well vitrified at Cone 9.

Summary. It may be said that:

(1) Dorset ball clays (English) have the highest drying shrinkage.

(2) English ball clays, in general, have higher dry strengths than American clays.

(3) Kentucky ball clays are lowest in carbonaceous matter.

(4) Dorset ball clays are high in carbonaceous matter and difficult to oxidize in firing.

(5) English ball clays vitrify at lower temperatures than American clays.

(6) Tennessee ball clays, in general, are the whitest in color when fired.

TABLE 15-7

PROPERTIES OF AMERICAN BALL CLAYS

Producer	Brand	Particle size[1]	Dry strength[2]	Drying shrinkage[3]	Firing shrinkage Cone 9[4]	Absorption at Cone 9	Fired color	SiO$_2$	Al$_2$O$_3$	Fe$_2$O$_3$	TiO$_2$	CaO	MgO	K$_2$O	Na$_2$O	H$_2$O
Bell Clay Co.	Dark ball	77.0	770	8.3	9.3	4.6	White	53.03	30.38	0.91	1.40	0.35	0.36	1.01		12.63
"	Dresden	78.5	930	9.3	9.6	0	Ivory	54.04	30.65	1.62	1.07	0.44	0.51	0.31		11.46
"	Gray ball	56.0	440	8.1	9.9	7.0	Cream	56.22	29.97	1.05	1.81	0.26	0.24	0.79		9.90
"	Special	66.5	610	8.2	9.6	5.8	Cream	54.62	30.17	0.98	1.60	0.30	0.30	0.90		11.27
"	Universal	77.6	840	8.7	9.4	2.7	Cream	53.43	30.49	1.19	1.27	0.39	0.42	0.73		12.16
"	Superior	77.6	810	8.5	9.5	3.4	Cream	53.28	30.44	1.08	1.32	0.37	0.40	0.84		12.33
Cooley Clay Co.	Thomas	-	380	7.0	10.9	3.5	White	50.8	29.0	1.1	1.6	0.3	0.8	0.6	0.7	15.3
"	Cooley No. 2	-	150	6.0	9.8	5.5	Ivory	53.3	31.5	1.6	1.6	0.3	0.4	1.14		10.7
Ky. Clay Min. Co.	No. 1 ball	-	430	11.2	13.6	4.2	Gray	53.4	28.6	2.2	0.8	0.4	0.3	1.78		13.54
"	No. 5 ball	-	390	9.9	10.6	6.2	Gray	59.5	23.3	2.3	2.3	0.8	0.3	1.78		11.63
"	K. C. M. ball	-	360	9.5	10.2	6.2	Gray	58.8	22.2	2.5	0.8	0.2	0.2	1.83		11.13
"	No. 600	-	390	10.2	11.5	5.5	Gray	58.1	24.7	2.3	0.8	0.3	0.3	1.85		12.10
Old Hickory Clay Co.	No. 2 ball	43.0	380	7.6	6.0	7.8	White	51.6	33.7	0.8	1.3	0.1	0.2	0.2	0.1	11.9
"	No. 3 ball	-	600	8.0	10.0	0	Gray	54.2	29.9	1.7	1.6	0.5	0.8	0.3	0.6	16.7
"	No. 6 ball	43.0	500	8.0	8.0	0	Gray	50.1	33.0	0.9	1.3	1.4	0.3	0.4	0.7	12.0
Ky.-Tenn. Clay Co.	Old mine #4	35.0	460	6.6	9.5	4.0	Cream	51.7	31.2	1.2	1.7	0.2	0.5	0.4	0.6	12.1
"	Special	34.0	680	7.8	9.0	7.5	Cream	48.3	29.6	1.0	2.3	0.3	0.6	0.5	0.3	17.3
"	No. 12 black	29.0	530	7.8	9.2	10.5	Cream	47.6	31.0	1.1	1.7	0.2	0.6	0.1	0.4	17.4
"	K-T ivory	29.0	320	5.5	6.5	12.0	Ivory	57.9	26.4	0.7	2.4	0.2	0.4	0.1	0.4	11.5
"	No. 5 ball	10.0	330	4.5	10.5	0.5	Gray	51.8	31.3	1.0	1.4	0.3	0.2	1.4	0.9	11.7
"	Wade No. 5	36.0	480	5.8	12.5	0.2	Gray	43.8	35.9	1.0	0.7	0.1	Tr.	2.0	0.4	16.0
"	Martin No. 5	8.0	280	6.0	7.5	6.0	Cream	60.7	25.5	0.7	1.4	0.1	Tr.	1.7	0.4	9.4
"	Ball No. 9	-	305	4.0	9.5	6.0	Cream	51.6	29.4	1.0	1.8	0.7	0.8	1.3	0.4	13.4
"	Ball No. 10	-	210	3.4	10.2	5.6	White	49.7	33.2	1.0	1.8	0.1	0.2	0.7	0.4	12.9
"	No. 7 ball	-	210	4.5	9.5	4.7	White	47.8	36.3	0.7	1.2	Tr.	0	0.9	0.6	12.6
"	S. G. R. No. 1	-	220	4.1	11.2	7.0	Cream	47.3	34.9	0.6	2.8	Tr.	0	1.0	0	13.1
"	Miss. H. + P.	-	1000+	5.6	9.5	0	Ivory	57.0	27.9	2.2	1.3	0.5	0.3	0.5	0.4	9.8
H. C. Spinks Clay Co.	Challenger	46.0	360	8.3	9.5	9.0	Ivory	54.1	28.9	1.1	1.7	0.2	0.2	0.3	0.2	13.3
"	Black Charm	16.0	250	6.3	6.5	9.5	Ivory	62.9	22.6	1.6	0.2	0.3	0.3	1.2	0.3	10.6
"	Bandy black	8.0	220	5.4	8.5	3.0	Ivory	59.2	25.1	1.0	1.3	0.1	-	1.9	0.4	10.9
"	Bandy tan	14.0	-	4.8	8.0	3.3	Ivory	61.1	24.6	1.2	1.3	0.3	0.6	1.8	0.4	8.7
"	Gizmo	20.0	170	6.4	4.0	8.0	Ivory	66.5	22.7	1.5	-	0.4	0.5	1.3		8.2
United Clay Mines	Imperial	67.8	750	-	-	5.6	Ivory	52.9	27.1	1.0	1.9	0.1	0.2	0.4	0.2	16.4
"	Rex	23.0	240	-	8.4	0	Ivory	56.2	28.5	1.1	1.7	0.1	0.7	1.9	0.4	9.3
"	Royal	36.1	510	-	9.5	0	Ivory	52.8	28.9	0.9	1.7	0.2	0.3	1.7	0.3	13.2
"	Victoria	56.3	580	-	-	4.1	Ivory	56.9	27.9	0.9	1.8	0.1	0.1	1.9	0.4	9.8
"	Yankee	60.5	700	6.8	8.5	0	Ivory	57.3	24.5	1.8	1.0	0.1	0.8	2.8	0.3	11.4

[1]Weight percent of clay below 0.5 micron.   [2]Modulus of rupture, lb per sq in. (plus 50% flint).   [3]Linear shrinkage based on plastic size.   [4]Linear shrinkage based on dry size.

TABLE 15-8

PROPERTIES OF ENGLISH BALL CLAYS

Producer	Brand	Particle size[1]	Dry strength[2]	Drying shrinkage[3]	Firing shrinkage Cone 9[4]	Absorption at Cone 9	Fired color	SiO$_2$	Al$_2$O$_3$	Fe$_2$O$_3$	TiO$_2$	CaO	MgO	K$_2$O	Na$_2$O	H$_2$O
Moore + Munger	M and M	-	510	5.0	13	0	Cream	47.88	31.72	1.03	1.01	0.20	0.52	0.52	2.36	14.62
"	Ivory fat	-	330	4.5	10	0	Ivory	54.89	30.90	0.95	1.40	0.39	0.41	0.16	2.50	8.94
"	Great beam	-	480	5.6	15	0	-	47.51	34.14	1.00	1.30	1.18	0.41	1.64		12.75
"	No. 11	-	430	6.4	13	0	-	50.00	33.35	1.00	0.90	0.56	0.41	0.87	3.61	9.50
United Clay Mines	Bedminster	66	-	5.0	10	0	-	52.10	32.47	1.47	1.31	0.24	0.55	0.48	2.20	9.13

[1]Weight percent of clay below 0.5 micron.   [2]Modulus of rupture, lb per sq in. (plus 50% flint).   [3]Linear shrinkage based on plastic size.   [4]Linear shrinkage based on dry size.

TABLE 15-9

PROPERTIES OF AMERICAN KAOLINS

Producer	Brand	Particle size[1]	Dry strength[2]	Drying shrinkage[3]	Firing shrinkage Cone 9[4]	Absorption at Cone 9	Fired color	Chemical analysis								
								SiO_2	Al_2O_3	Fe_2O_3	TiO_2	CaO	MgO	K_2O	Na_2O	H_2O
Southern Clay Inc.	No. 27	–	25	4.00	8.0	16	White	–	–	–	–	–	–	–	–	–
"	No. 600	–	651	7.80	10.0	24	White	–	–	–	–	–	–	–	–	–
United Clay Mines	Kingsley	17	74	–	10	17	White	46.09	37.89	0.53	1.09	0.10	0.16	0.15	0.46	13.66
"	Monarch	18	24	–	9	14	White	46.26	38.18	0.31	1.17	0.09	0.14	0.17	0.37	13.58
"	Layton	26	948	–	17	7	White	47.96	36.62	0.33	1.23	0.22	0.74	Tr.	0.31	12.84
"	Putnam	38	–	–	18	10	White	46.90	37.56	0.82	0.18	0.05	0.36	0.09	0.43	13.72
Whittaker C. + D.	609[5]	–	–	–	–	–	White	46.95	36.75	0.80	0.18	0.15	0.20	0.10	0.14	14.95
"	1431[6]	–	–	–	–	–	Ivory	44.0	40.0	0.5	1.0	0.5	–	–	–	13.25
"	1433[6]	–	–	–	–	–	Ivory	44.0	39.0	1.0	1.0	0.5	–	–	–	13.25
"	1434[6]	–	–	–	–	–	Ivory	44.0	40.0	0.5	1.0	0.5	–	–	–	13.25
"	1479[6]	–	–	–	–	–	White	44.5	39.5	0.75	0.5	0.25	–	–	–	14.25
"	38[6]	–	–	–	–	–	Ivory	44.99	39.95	0.34	0.73	Tr.	Tr.	0.10	0.12	13.82
Kaolin, Inc.	Kamec[7]	27	275	4.5	8.2	19	V. White	46.18	38.38	0.57	0.04	0.37	0.42	0.10	0.58	13.28
Edgar Pl. Kaolin Co.	Florida[5]	33	400	6	–	–	White	46.95	36.75	0.80	0.18	0.15	0.20	←0.24→		14.95
Edgar Bros Co.	No carb.[6]	5	21	2	–	25	White	44.95	38.67	0.40	1.35	0.03	0.02	0.05	0.48	13.84
"	Klondike[6]	17	65	3	–	–	White	42.01	41.48	0.30	0.72	0.60	0.47	←0.47→		13.65
Georgia Kaolin	Pioneer[6]	22	327	5.7	9	8.8	White	45.34	37.29	0.61	1.54	0.25	0.22	0.10	0.35	13.38
"	Velvacast[6]	7	56	5.1	17.5	8.0	White	45.12	38.12	0.63	1.35	0.03	0.22	0.3	0.31	13.75

[1] Weight percent of clay below 0.5 micron.   [2] Modulus of rupture, lb per sq in. (plus 50% flint).   [3] Linear shrinkage based on plastic size.   [4] Linear shrinkage based on dry size.
[5] Florida   [6] Georgia   [7] South Carolina

TABLE 15-10

PROPERTIES OF ENGLISH CHINA CLAYS

Producer	Brand	Particle size[1]	Dry strength[2]	Drying shrinkage[3]	Firing shrinkage Cone 9[4]	Absorption at Cone 9	Fired color	Chemical analysis								
								SiO_2	Al_2O_3	Fe_2O_3	TiO_2	CaO	MgO	K_2O	Na_2O	H_2O
Paper Makers I. Co.	V C-1	12	100	7.5	–	37	White	–	–	–	–	–	–	–	–	–
"	A-1	–	120	8.5	–	35	White	–	–	–	–	–	–	–	–	–
"	M + M China	7	150	9.0	–	31	White	–	–	–	–	–	–	–	–	–
"	Richardsons	–	120	9.0	–	34	White	–	–	–	–	–	–	–	–	–
"	M + M Import	–	160	9.2	–	30	White	–	–	–	–	–	–	–	–	–
Moore + Munger	M. G. R.	–	42	4.0	6.8	16.8	White	45.17	40.86	Tr.	None	0.39	0.31	←0.72→		12.53
"	M. W. M.	–	54	4.5	5.8	16.0	White	46.40	38.12	0.68	None	0.25	Tr.	1.18	0.40	12.32
"	No. 44	–	41	4.2	8.8	16.7	White	46.81	37.71	1.21	0.13	0.50	0.25	1.62	None	12.23
"	No. 17	–	70	5.0	10.0	12.0	White	47.00	38.24	0.87	0.24	0.16	0.03	0.78	0.44	12.68
Whittaker C. + D.	372	–	–	–	–	–	White	47.40	38.01	0.59	–	Tr.	0.41	1.26	0.29	11.69

[1] Weight percent of clay below 0.5 micron.   [2] Modulus of rupture, lb per sq in. (plus 50% flint).   [3] Linear shrinkage based on plastic size.   [4] Linear shrinkage based on dry size.

TABLE 15-11

PROPERTIES OF AMERICAN STONEWARE CLAYS

Producer	Brand	Particle size[1]	Dry strength[2]	Drying shrinkage[3]	Firing shrinkage Cone 9[4]	Absorption at Cone 9	Fired color	Chemical analysis								
								SiO_2	Al_2O_3	Fe_2O_3	TiO_2	CaO	MgO	K_2O	Na_2O	H_2O
United Clay Mines	Preston	32	560	4.9	11	.2	–	73.52	16.05	1.16	1.05	0.16	0.26	1.87	0.60	5.40
"	Principio	52	820	–	19	0	–	59.40	25.04	2.80	0.91	0.25	0.15	2.14	0.67	8.58
"	Yankee ball	52	830	–	19	0	–	57.66	26.60	2.22	1.02	0.23	0.35	2.21	0.66	9.11
"	Benton	54	290	–	18	0	–	57.72	23.64	6.01	1.09	0.23	0.54	1.97	0.65	8.31
"	Enfield	65	1100	6.5	10	0	–	51.28	33.63	1.13	1.00	0.52	0.59	2.60	0.26	9.19
Western Stoneware Co.	Monmouth	–	–	–	–	0	Buff	56.80	28.56	–	–	0.30	0.33	0.30	1.34	12.20
United Clay Mines	Hanover	52	817	←19→		0	–	59.40	25.04	2.80	0.91	0.25	0.15	0.67	2.14	8.58

[1] Weight percent of clay below 0.5 micron.   [2] Modulus of rupture, lb per sq in. (plus 50% flint).   [3] Linear shrinkage based on plastic size.   [4] Linear shrinkage based on dry size.

Kaolins. Table 15–9 lists the properties of some of the kaolins produced in this country. In comparison with ball clays, they are coarser and whiter firing, and they require much higher temperatures for vitrification. The Florida kaolins are finer than the others, and are closer in properties to the coarser of the ball clays. The residual kaolins, in general, are whiter when fired (they contain less titanium dioxide, TiO_2).

Table 15–10 lists the properties of some English kaolins (called china clays). In gen-eral, they are whiter firing than American sedimentary kaolins and are comparable to our residual clays. English kaolins contain somewhat more feldspar than American kaolins, and they consequently fire a little tighter.

Some kaolins are now produced with con-trolled particle sizes.

Stoneware clays. Table 15–11 lists the properties of some of the American stone-ware clays.

Suppliers. The following producers of clays are listed in the *Ceramics Data Book;* they are reliable sources. The per-pound price of clay is less for large lots than for small; 100-lb bags are economical units for the small potter. It is necessary to specify whether lump or pulverized clay is desired; usually either kind is available.

Kaolins and china clays:

Edgar Plastic Kaolin Company
Metuchen, N. J.

Georgia Kaolin Company
Elizabeth, N. J.

Moore & Munger
33 Rector Street
New York 6, N. Y.

United Clay Mines, Inc.
101 Oakland Street
Trenton 6, N. J.

Whittaker, Clark & Daniels, Inc.
260 W. Broadway
New York 13, N. Y.

Huber Corporation
101 Park Avenue
New York 17, N. Y.

English China Clays Sales Corporation
551 Fifth Avenue
New York 17, N. Y.

Ball clays:

Bell Clay Company
Gleason, Tenn.

United Clay Mines, Inc.
101 Oakland Street
Trenton 6, N. J.

Spinks Clay Company
First National Bank Building
Cincinnati 2, Ohio

Moore & Munger
33 Rector Street
New York 6, N. Y.

Kentucky Clay Mining Company
Mayfield, Ky.

Old Hickory Clay Company
Paducah, Ky.

Kentucky-Tennessee Clay Co.
Mayfield, Ky.

Stoneware clays:

United Clay Mines, Inc.
101 Oakland Street
Trenton 6, N. J.

Potters Supply Co.
East Liverpool, Ohio

American Art Clay Company
Indianapolis, Ind.

Western Stoneware Company
Monmouth, Ill.

X. REFERENCES

1. BLEININGER, A. V., Properties of American Bond Clays and Their Use in Graphite Crucibles and Glass Pots, *Nat. Bur. of Standards Tech. Paper No.* 144, 1920.

2. KLINEFELTER, T. A., AND W. W. MEYER, Properties of Some American Kaolins and a Comparison with English China Clays, *J. Am. Ceram. Soc.* **18**, 163 (1935).

3. KLINEFELTER, T. A., *et al.*, Some Properties of English China Clays, *J. Am. Ceram. Soc.* **16**, 269 (1933).

4. MEYER, W. W., AND T. A. KLINEFELTER, Substitution of Domestic for Imported Clays in Whiteware Bodies, *J. of Res. Nat. Bur. of Standards* **65**, 1937 (RP 1011).

5. NORTON, F. H., *Elements of Ceramics.* Addison-Wesley Publishing Company, Inc., Cambridge, Mass., 1952 (Chaps. 2 and 3).

6. REIS, H., *Clays, Their Occurrence, Properties and Uses,* 3rd ed., John Wiley & Sons, Inc., New York, 1927.

7. SORTWELL, H. H., American and English Ball Clays, *Nat. Bur. of Standards Tech. Paper No.* 227, 1923.

CHAPTER 16

Nonplastic Ceramic Materials

I. INTRODUCTION

In this chapter we shall discuss the properties of materials other than clays which are necessary to the successful production of pottery.

II. SILICA

Purpose. Silica, in the form of quartz, is used in nearly all ceramic bodies for three reasons: (1) to reduce the drying shrinkage and thus help prevent cracking of the piece, (2) to give better firing qualities by reduction of the firing shrinkage, and (3) to act as a sort of skeleton to hold the shape of the piece in the kiln.

Deposits. Silica in the natural state is usually in the form of quartz. We are all familiar with the quartz crystals found in rocks and in sand. However, only a few deposits supply quartz that is sufficiently pure to be useful in ceramics. The map of Fig. 16–1 shows the locations of sources for the comparatively pure silica necessary for this purpose.

Preparation. Quartz may be found in massive crystals or in the form of a friable sandstone. The latter is more useful because it is easily crushed and ground. The great bulk of this sandstone is used in the glass industry, but some of it is fine-ground for use in whiteware bodies and glazes.

The sandstone is ground in a silica-lined ball mill with silica pebbles, to give a pure, extremely fine quartz powder, often called "potter's flint," although it is not true flint. This powder is so fine that all but a very small portion of it will pass through a 325-mesh screen. The iron oxide content is held below 0.02%, and because the silica content makes up the balance (over 99%), this commercial product may be considered 100% silica (SiO_2) for purposes of calculation.

Flint. Flint, which is a form of silica, is widely used in Europe for ceramic ware. Flint is obtained from the flint pebbles frequently found in the chalk beds on both sides of the English Channel. Like quartz, flint is silicon dioxide (SiO_2) of high purity, and the fineness of its crystals makes it highly suitable for use in ceramics. This product is the true "potter's flint."

III. FELDSPAR

Purpose. Feldspars are used as a flux in ceramic bodies. When the body is fired, the feldspar melts and forms molten glass which causes the particles of clay to cling together; when this glass solidifies it gives strength and hardness to the body. The translucency of

- GLASS SAND
- FELDSPAR
- TALC

Fig. 16-1. Silica, feldspar, and talc deposits of the U. S.

porcelain bodies is attributable to this glass, as discussed elsewhere. Feldspars are useful also because they are a good source of soda and potash; they are one of the very few water-insoluble compounds of these two materials.

Deposits. Feldspar is a common constituent of many rocks. Granite, for example, contains about 60% feldspar. Feldspar is mined in massive form; many of the deposits are high in purity. The map of Fig. 16–1 shows the location of some of the more important deposits.

Composition and preparation. Feldspars vary widely in composition, and it is a credit to the millers that the commercial product is so uniform in its properties. Ceramic feldspars are composed of the following minerals:

Albite	$Na_2O \cdot Al_2O_3 \cdot 6SiO_2$
Microcline } Orthoclase	$K_2O \cdot Al_2O_3 \cdot 6SiO_2$
Anorthite	$CaO \cdot Al_2O_3 \cdot 2SiO_2$
Quartz	SiO_2
Kaolinite	$Al_2O_3 \cdot 2SiO_2 \cdot 2H_2O$

Compositions which are high in potash (K_2O) are used in clay bodies, while those with a high soda (Na_2O) content are used in glazes. Some typical feldspar compositions are given in Table 16–1.

For exact calculations in bodies and glazes, the analysis of a particular feldspar can be obtained from the supplier.

The lump feldspar is ground in ball mills, and to obtain uniform composition the various grades are carefully blended. Powerful magnets are used to remove iron particles, to avoid discoloration of the fired body. The resulting powdered feldspar is so fine that more than 95% of it will pass through a 325-mesh screen.

TABLE 16-1

COMPOSITION OF FELDSPARS

Constituent	A	B	C	D	E	F	G
Silica (SiO$_2$)	73.4	69.8	71.5	66.1	66.0	70.0	60.2
Alumina (Al$_2$O$_3$)	15.0	17.1	16.6	18.7	18.7	18.1	23.7
Ferric oxide (Fe$_2$O$_3$)	0.1	0.1	0.1	0.1	0.1	0.1	0.1
Lime (CaO)	0.2	Tr.	0.3	0.2	0.2	1.5	0.4
Magnesia (MgO)	Tr.	None	Tr.	Tr.	Tr.	Tr.	0.1
Soda (Na$_2$O)	3.1	3.5	3.7	3.0	2.8	6.5	10.1
Potash (K$_2$O)	8.0	9.4	7.5	11.8	12.0	3.5	5.0
Loss on ign.	0.2	0.2	0.3	0.3	0.2	0.3	0.5
Microcline	48	56	45	69	70	21	20
Albite	26	30	32	25	23	55	54
Anorthite	1	None	2	1	1	8	None
Quartz	22	12	18	3	4	13	None
Nepheline	–	–	–	–	–	–	22
Other mins.	3	2	3	2	2	3	4

A Topsham, Me. (Consolidated Feldspar Co.)
B Portland, Conn. (Eureka Flint and Spar Co.)
C Kona, N. C. (Consolidated Feldspar Co.)
D Rochester, N. Y. (Derry Feldspar)
E Kingman, Arizona (Mojave Feldspar)
F North Carolina (Glaze Spar)
G Nepheline–Syenite (Am. Nepheline Corp.)

Sources. Feldspar is obtainable at most pottery supply houses, or from the following firms:

International Minerals & Chemical Corp.
Trenton Trust Building
Trenton 8, N. J.

Eureka Flint and Spar Co.
Trenton 8, N. J.

United Feldspar and Minerals Corporation
10 E. 40th Street
New York 16, N. Y.

Bell Clay Company
Gleason, Tenn.

IV. OTHER FLUXES

Nepheline-syenite. This mineral is much like feldspar, but it is a more powerful flux and is commonly used in low-temperature, vitreous bodies. The raw material comes from Canada, and is milled in this country. An analysis of this mineral is given in Table 16–1.

Limestone and magnesite. These minerals are the carbonates of calcium ($CaCO_3$) and magnesium ($MgCO_3$). They are used in small amounts as a flux in some vitreous bodies, and as an ingredient in many glazes. They are obtainable in pure, finely powdered form from chemical manufacturers.

V. TALC

Purpose. Talcs are used for fillers and coatings in many industries, but about one-fourth of the entire output is used in ceramic whiteware bodies. Because bodies made from talc are highly resistant to heat shock, talc is used for making electrical units, in low-fired artware bodies, and for making ovenware and kiln furniture.

While small amounts of talc have been used in vitreous bodies for many years, only comparatively recently have large quantities been used in low-fired earthenware bodies. California potters have been the leaders in this development, perhaps because pure talcs are plentiful in that region.

Talc bodies are desirable because they may be fired as low as Cone 06 and still give considerable strength. Glazes fit these bodies with no delayed crazing, and the ware is quite resistant to sudden heating and cooling. Good casting slips can be made with high-talc bodies, but plastic bodies that are high in talc are not quite as workable as the normal whitewares.

Composition. Theoretically, the formula for talc is $3MgO \cdot 4SiO_2 \cdot H_2O$, but its purity seldom approaches this level in fact. The following minerals (known as "talc minerals") are often associated with pure talc:

Tremolite $\quad$ $2CaO \cdot 5MgO \cdot 8SiO_2 \cdot H_2O$
Anthophyllite $\quad$ $Mg,CaO \cdot SiO_2$
Diopside $\quad$ $Mg,CaO \cdot 2SiO_2$
Serpentine minerals

In addition, there may also be small amounts of quartz (SiO_2), calcite ($CaCO_3$), magnesite ($MgCO_3$), or dolomite ($Ca,Mg \cdot CO_3$).

The talcs also differ physically among themselves. Some, such as soapstone, are massive, and when ground give rounded particles that are soft and translucent. Others are fibrous and platy, and are used to a considerable extent in the paint industry. A third type contains a great deal of comparatively hard tremolite, which is an advantage when talc is used for ceramic bodies.

The talcs used for ceramics may be roughly classified as the high-lime type used for artware bodies and the low-lime type used for electrical porcelains. Analyses of a few talcs are given in Table 16–2, locations of some of the important deposits are indicated on the map of Fig. 16–1, and particle sizes are given in Fig. 16–2.

TABLE 16–2
COMPOSITION OF CERAMIC TALCS

Constituent	A	B	C	D	E	F	G
Silica (SiO_2)	53.1	58.3	56.7	51.8	58.3	57.9	57.0
Alumina (Al_2O_3)	2.7	1.6	2.1	2.0	0.9	1.7	1.9
Ferric oxide (Fe_2O_3)	0.3	0.9	0.4	0.4	0.3	0.4	0.3
Lime (CaO)	6.0	0.5	6.1	6.5	5.9	9.1	8.6
Magnesia (MgO)	30.3	32.6	26.6	29.5	28.8	27.9	27.0
Soda (Na_2O)	0.2	–	–	–	–	–	–
Potash (K_2O)	0.7	–	–	–	–	0.4	0.3
Loss on ign.	7.1	5.8	8.3	9.6	5.8	2.4	4.4
Size[1]	89	96	87	76	–	95	96

A Ceramic Talc (Southern California Minerals Co.)
B No. 486 Talc (Southern California Minerals Co.)
C W. S. Ceramic Talc (Kennedy Minerals Co.)
D D. V. Ceramic Talc (Kennedy Minerals Co.)
E Ceramitalc (International Talc Co., Inc.)
F C. B. Ceramic Talc (Sierra Talc Co.)
G L. S. Silver Talc (Sierra Talc Co.)

[1]Percent which passes through a 325–mesh screen.

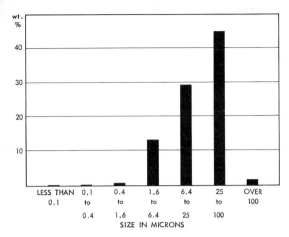

Fig. 16-2. Particle size of talc.

VI. GLAZE MATERIALS

Glaze materials are usually pure chemical compounds, and they will be considered in Chapters 23 and 24.

VII. REFERENCES

1. KNIGHT, F. P., JR., Commercial Feldspars Produced in the United States, *J. Am. Ceram. Soc.* **13**, 532 (1930).

2. *Industrial Minerals and Rocks,* 2nd ed., American Institute of Mining and Metallurgical Engineers, New York, 1949.

3. Ladoo, R. B., *Non-Metallic Minerals,* Mc-Graw-Hill Book Company, Inc., New York, 1925.

CHAPTER 17

Ceramic Bodies

I. INTRODUCTION

A ceramic body must have some rather unique properties to make it useful: it must have good working properties in the plastic state, so that it may be modeled, thrown on the wheel, or cast; it must dry reasonably fast without cracking; it must fire to a strong, dense structure without undue shrinkage; and the finished product must have the desired color and translucency.

Improvement of any one of these properties may mean sacrificing something of the others. As with almost everything in life, we must compromise to obtain the best over-all results. For example, if the firing temperature must be low because of the limitations of kiln equipment, then whiteness of color and translucency are impaired, and low shrinkage can be achieved only by some sacrifice of workability. These are the reasons for such a great variety of body compositions, and the serious potter must understand them if he is to be in a position to select those which are best suited to his purpose.

Quite naturally, the novice asks, "Why do we use several clays in combination with nonplastics to make up a body, rather than a single well-selected clay?" In the first place, not many natural clays have both good working and good firing properties, and almost none combine these two properties with a good white color. A combination of several clays, with each one contributing to some specific desirable property, and with the ad-dition of flint to reduce shrinkage and of feldspar to act as a flux, gives a happy compromise. And if one of the ingredients should deviate slightly from what is anticipated, the total effect on the body will be small.

II. NATURAL CERAMIC BODIES

Although natural clays with sufficient quartz and feldspar to fire into a good body are not uncommon, they are not ordinarily used, chiefly because correct combinations of ingredients can almost always result in a better product.

Natural bodies used by the ancient Chinese. The ceramic industry in ancient China was largely based on the use of natural clay —a partially decomposed pegmatite. This clay was ground, screened, and aged to produce the very fine ware that was typical of that era. However, many historians believe that uncontrollable variations in the supply of this natural clay contributed heavily to the deterioration of the industry.

Single clays as bodies. Many of the stoneware clays found in this country could be used just as they come from the ground, but although they have excellent workability and fair firing properties, they are invariably improved by addition of other minerals. Red-burning glacial clays, whose firing range is often narrow are also improved by the addition of other materials.

Partially decomposed rock. In this country there are a few deposits of partially decomposed rock which are very similar to the natural clay used by the ancient Chinese. The sandy kaolin found in Bennington, Vermont, is an example. When finely ground, this kaolin has a fair degree of plasticity and produces a porcelain-type body on firing. An analysis is given in Table 17–1. The rock known as Plastic Vitrox, mined in California, is of a similar nature, but it sometimes contains too much iron to give a good white body, and this is true of other similar deposits. Table 17–1 gives an analysis of stoneware clay for comparison with these other minerals.

TABLE 17–3

CALCULATION OF MINERALS IN WHITEWARE BODY

Oxide	Relative weight[1]	Relative No. of equivalents[2]
Silica (SiO$_2$)	69.6	1.153
Alumina (Al$_2$O$_3$)	19.9	0.197
Ferric oxide (Fe$_2$O$_3$)	0.8	0.0050
Magnesia (MgO)	0.1	0.0025
Lime (CaO)	0.3	0.0054
Potash (K$_2$O)	2.1	0.0223

[1] From Table 17–2. [2] 1st column divided by equiv. wts., Table 15–3.

Pure materials added, in equiv.	Relative equivalents of oxides (last column above)					
	1.153 SiO$_2$	0.1970 Al$_2$O$_3$	0.0050 Fe$_2$O$_3$	0.0025 MgO	0.0054 CaO	0.0223 K$_2$O
0.0223 Feldspar						0.0223
Difference	1.019	0.1747	0.0050	0.0025	0.0054	0
0.175 Clay min.	0.350	0.1747				
Difference	0.669	0	0.0050	0.0025	0.0054	0
0.0025 MgCO$_3$				0.0025		
Difference	0.669	0	0.0050	0	0.0054	0
0.0045 CaCO$_3$					0.0054	
Difference	0.669	0	0.0050	0	0	0
0.0050 Fe$_2$O$_3$			0.0050			
Difference	0.669	0	0	0	0	0
0.669 Quartz	0.669					
Difference	0	0	0	0	0	0

TABLE 17–1

NATURAL BODIES

Constituent	Plastic vitrox[2]	Sandy kaolin[3]	Stoneware clay[4]
Silica (SiO$_2$)	75.56	65.34	73.52
Alumina (Al$_2$O$_3$)	14.87	24.59	16.05
Ferric oxide (Fe$_2$O$_3$)	0.09	0.78	1.16
Lime (CaO)	0.22	–	0.16
Magnesia (MgO)	0.20	–	0.26
Soda (Na$_2$O)	0.29	–	0.60
Potash (K$_2$O)	6.81	2.31	1.87
Loss on ign.	2.04	6.98	5.40
Dry strength	140 lb per sq in.	100 lb per sq in.	560 lb per sq in.
Drying shrinkage	4.5%	3.2%	4.9%
Firing shrinkage[1]	15.4%	10.0%	12.0%
Fired color	White	Cream	Buff

[1] Fired at Cone 10.
[2] From Cal. — milled so 80% passed 325–mesh screen.
[3] From Bennington, Vt. Milled 10 hr.
[4] Preston brand (United Clay Mines).

III. CALCULATION OF THE MINERAL CONTENTS OF BODIES

Analysis of an unfired body. The proportionate amounts of minerals in a body made up of several ingredients can be determined by the same method used for computing the make-up of a single clay (Chapter 15).

As an example, let us examine an ordinary whiteware body composed of.

Kentucky ball clay	28%
Georgia kaolin	24%
Potter's flint	34%
Potash feldspar	14%

The chemical analyses of the above ingredients are given in Table 17–2. The first figures in each column represent the weight percent, and the second group of figures represents the relative amount of the material added to the body.

The relative weights of the amounts of oxides as given in the last column of Table 17–2 may now be used to calculate the actual amounts of minerals added, as shown in Tables 17–3 and 17–4.

TABLE 17–2

COMPOSITION OF BODY INGREDIENTS

Constituent	Ky. ball clay		Georgia kaolin		Potter's flint		Potash feldspar		Total
	%	% x .28	%	% x .24	%	% x .34	%	% x .14	
Silica (SiO$_2$)	53.0	14.8	45.8	11.0	99.8	34.0	69.5	9.5	69.6
Alumina (Al$_2$O$_3$)	29.0	8.1	38.5	9.3	0.2	0	17.5	2.5	19.9
Ferric oxide (Fe$_2$O$_3$)	2.0	0.5	0.7	0.2	–	–	0.1	0	0.8
Lime (CaO)	0.4	0.1	–	–	–	–	0.8	0.2	0.3
Magnesia (MgO)	0.3	0.1	–	–	–	–	–	–	0.1
Potash (K$_2$O)	2.0	0.5	–	–	–	–	11.7	1.6	2.1

TABLE 17-4

CALCULATION OF MINERALS IN WHITEWARE BODY

Mineral [3]	Rel. No. of equiv.	Relative weight [1]	Weight percent [2]
Clay mineral	0.175	45.2	45.6
Feldspar	0.022	12.2	12.5
Hematite	0.0050	0.9	0.9
Lime	0.0054	0.3	0.3
Magnesia	0.0025	0.1	0.1
Quartz	0.669	40.2	40.6
Total	–	98.9	100.0

[1] Obtained by multiplying first column by equiv. weights, Table 15-3.
[2] The second column divided by 98.3.
[3] These are theoretically pure – not those in Table 17-5.

The equivalent formula for this whiteware body is

$$0.0223 \; Na,KO$$
$$0.0054 \; CaO$$
$$0.0025 \; MgO \qquad 0.197 \; Al_2O_3 \qquad 1.153 \; SiO_2$$
$$0.0050 \; Fe_2O_3$$

Converting to unit Al_2O_3, we get:

$$0.119 \; Na,KO$$
$$0.022 \; CaO$$
$$0.013 \; MgO \qquad 1.0 \; Al_2O_3 \qquad 5.86 \; SiO_2$$
$$0.025 \; Fe_2O_3$$

It is interesting to compare these results with the analysis of stoneware clay, which fires at about the same temperature. They are surprisingly alike, although in the whiteware body the content of feldspar and iron oxide is somewhat less, and that of lime and magnesia (neglected in the calculations for the stoneware clay, for simplicity) is somewhat higher.

Calculation by analysis of the fired body.

The composition of the original batch of clay can be determined by analyzing the resultant fired body. Analysis by Meyer and Klinefelter of an electrical porcelain produced the following information:

Basic oxides	5.30%
Neutral oxides	24.00%
Acid oxides	70.70%

In this procedure, certain assumptions must be made. For good working properties, it is assumed that 25% of the batch must have been ball clay, and we know that best results are obtained when two ball clays are used, rather than one; therefore we can start with the premise that two ball clays, totaling 25% of the clay body, are present.

Let us choose the raw materials shown in Table 17–5, and set up Table 17–6 much as we did before, with the percentages of basic, neutral, and acid oxides of the fired body at the top. Now we subtract each raw material until nothing remains. Unlike our previous examples, this calculation is based on percentage weights rather than equivalents.

TABLE 17-5

CHEMICAL ANALYSIS OF RAW MATERIALS

Constituent	Kentucky ball clay	Tennessee ball clay	Maine feldspar	Georgia kaolin	Potter's flint
Silica (SiO_2)	49.9%	50.3%	72.7%	45.7%	100.0%
Alumina (Al_2O_3)	31.4	31.5	15.1	38.7	–
Ferric oxide (Fe_2O_3)	0.6	0.6	0.1	0.3	–
Titania (TiO_2)	1.5	1.3	0.1	1.4	–
Lime (CaO)	0.2	0.2	0.3	0.2	–
Magnesia (MgO)	0.3	0.3	–	–	–
Potash (K_2O)	1.2	2.0	8.3	–	–
Soda (Na_2O)	0.2	0.3	3.1	–	–
Loss on ign.	14.7	13.6	0.3	13.7	–
Basic oxides	1.9	2.8	11.7	0.2	–
Neutral oxides [1]	32.0	32.1	15.2	39.0	–
Acid oxides	51.4	51.6	72.8	47.0	100.0

[1] The Fe_2O_3 is included in the neutral oxides.

TABLE 17-6

CALCULATION OF ELECTRICAL PORCELAIN BODY

Raw Materials	Fired Body		
Parts	Basic oxides	Acid oxides	Neutral oxides
	5.30%	70.70%	24.00%
0.125 Ky. ball clay [1]	0.24	6.43	4.00
Difference	5.06	64.27	20.00
0.125 Tenn. ball clay	0.35	6.45	4.01
Difference	4.71	57.82	15.99
0.398 Me. feldspar [2]	4.66	28.97	6.05
Difference	0.05	28.85	9.94
0.255 Ga. kaolin	0.05	16.84	9.94
Difference	0	16.84	0
0.1684 flint		16.84	
Difference	-------	0	-------

[1] This is one-half of the 25% ball clay allowed for.
[2] An amount of feldspar and kaolin must be selected to give (together) the correct value of basic and neutral oxides still unaccounted for. These figures are readily obtained by algebra, but a trial-and-error method may be used.

	Material	Parts	Percent [1]	
	Ky. ball clay	0.125	11.67	
	Tenn. ball clay	0.125	11.67	
	Me. feldspar	0.398	37.16	
	Ga. kaolin	0.255	23.81	
	Flint	0.168	15.69	
	Total	1.071 [2]	100.00	

[1] Number of parts divided by 1.071 and multiplied by 100 gives percent.
[2] This total exceeds 1.000, for the clay loses water in firing.

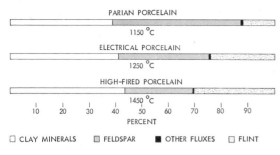

Fig. 17-1. Mineral content of typical porcelain bodies.

Application of calculations. Let us again emphasize the advantages of being able to analyze ceramic bodies before they are used. When we know within reasonable limits the workability of a body, the maturing temperature it requires, and what the properties of the fired body will be, costly trial-and-error experiments are avoided.

We know that 40% clay mineral content gives a reasonable amount of plasticity, for example, and that 50% gives excellent workability. Good parian bodies may run as high as 50% in feldspar content, while high-fired porcelains need as little as 20%. Flint may run as low as 10% in the parians and up to 30% in hard porcelains. (These percentages, of course, refer to actual mineral content, not to the amounts of the material added to the batch.)

Figure 17–1 shows graphically the mineral composition of three typical porcelain bodies, and indicates how a change in composition influences the maturing temperature.

IV. CLASSIFICATION OF CERAMIC BODIES

The potter will find it useful to have a good general knowledge of the various types of ceramic bodies. These can be classified in many ways; only the most important classifications are given here.

Classification according to structure. Pottery bodies are often classified according to structure as follows:

    Earthenware (over 3% absorption)
        red-firing
        red grog bodies (terra cotta)
        white-firing
            feldspathic
            talc
    Stoneware (1–5% absorption)
        red-firing
        gray-firing
        black-firing (basalt)
        colored (Jasper ware of Wedgwood)
        grog bodies (terra cotta)
    Porcelain (0–2% absorption)
        feldspar
            nepheline-syenite, low-fired
            parian
            normal
            high-fired
        bone china (English)
        frit porcelain (Lenox, Belleek)

Classification according to firing temperature:

    Low-fired (1010°C, Cone 06)
        red earthenware
        talc body
    Medium-fired (1150°C, Cone 4)
        red stoneware
        parian porcelain
        nepheline-syenite porcelain
        red terra cotta
    High-fired (1230°C, Cone 8)
        gray stoneware
        white earthenware
        porcelain
    Very high-fired (1450°C, Cone 16)
        high-fired porcelain
        refractories

TABLE 17-7
EARTHENWARE BODIES

Raw materials	Red earthenware (1)	Terra cotta (2)	White earthenware (3)	Talc body (4)	Sculpture body (5)
Potter's flint	90	-----	340	-----	250
Me. feldspar	-----	-----	140	-----	320
Nepheline–syenite					40
Glacial brick clay	800	100	100		
Plastic vitrox				163	
Edgar (N.C.) plastic kaolin	-----		120		
Edgar (N.C.) kaolin	-----	80	120	-----	210
Lundy (N.C.) kaolin					
Ky. special ball clay	-----	-----		24	
Bell's dark ball clay	-----	-----	100		
Ky. Old Mine #4 ball clay	100	110	180	163	
Tenn. #1 ball clay	-----	-----		163	180
Bentonite	-----	60			
Talc (Warm Springs)	-----			487	
Grog 14–35M	-----	320			
Grog 35–100M	-----	120			
Grog –100M	-----	170			
Barium carbonate	10	40			
Water	1500	150	1200	1200	800
Mixing	Mill 15 hr	Soak + wdg.	Blunge	Blunge	Mill 1-1/2 hr
Screening	100 M	None	100 M	100 M	100 M
Filter	✓		✓	✓	✓
Drying shrinkage	6%	2%	5%	-	1.5%
Firing temp.,°C	1000-1020	1145-1165	1225-1250	1000-1050	1015
Firing, Cone	06-05	3-4	8-9	06-05	06
Firing shrinkage	4%	4%	9%	-	1.5%
Absorption	9%	11%	4%	-	20%

Summary. Both the structure and the firing temperature are important considerations when the body for a particular piece is selected. At first the beginning potter should use commercial bodies, or should stick to formulas that are known to be suited both to his purpose and to his kiln equipment. Experience will allow modification of standard formulas for a particular result, and then the following general points should be kept in mind.

Keep in mind the limitations of your kiln equipment; these determine the limits of the firing temperature. Remember that you must decide beforehand whether your piece requires minimum shrinkage, whether you want maximum or only fair translucency, and what the final color is to be. All these items have an important bearing on the body to be used.

V. EARTHENWARE

Because earthenware bodies are easy to handle and do not require high firing, these are most commonly used by the beginner. However, even with these bodies, there is no excuse for making such a highly porous piece that it will not hold water. The compositions of some of these bodies are given in Table 17–7, and some of the properties are discussed below. It is suggested that the novice at first use the formulas given in the table, and after he has gained experience small systematic changes can be made in an attempt to develop a body that is exactly what he requires.

Red earthenware. A good red-colored earthenware can be made from a glacial brick clay with a little flint and ball clay added. Grinding in a ball mill gives better working properties and a tighter body when fired. Although this body can be thrown on the wheel, it is not as suited to this method as higher-temperature bodies. Its chief advantage is that it can be fired to a watertight condition in a wire-wound kiln.

Low-firing talc bodies. These are particularly popular on the West Coast. This kind of body is reasonably plastic and gives an excellent white color.

Red terra cotta. This body contains a large proportion of grog (fragments of fired clay). It is not suitable for wheel throwing, but is excellent for pressing or direct modeling of large pieces, because of its good workability. The grog content of this body reduces the drying and firing shrinkage to a considerable extent, so that there is little danger that even large pieces will crack on firing.

White earthenware. A strong, white, earthenware body may be used for high-temperature firing. This body is quite plastic and may be readily thrown and jiggered, or it can be used in the form of a slip for casting. Many of our large potteries produce an excellent commercial body of this type.

VI. STONEWARE

Stoneware bodies are denser and stronger than earthenware bodies, and the higher "ring" they give when struck indicates higher vitrification. Because of the higher firing temperatures, a wider range of glazes can be used than for earthenware. Stoneware, however, fires watertight without a glaze. Compositions of some of the stonewares are given in Table 17-8.

TABLE 17-8
STONEWARE BODIES

Raw materials	Red stoneware (6)	Gray stoneware (7)	Basalt (8)	Jasper (9)	Grog stoneware (10)
Me. feldspar	– – – –	– – – –	20	– – – –	– – – –
Potter's flint	290	225	10	70	100
Hanover clay	600	475	440	– – – –	375
Glacial brick clay	100				
Bell's dark brick clay		300	– – – –	300	225
Ochre	– – – –		440		
Manganese dioxide	– – – –		90		
Barium carbonate	10	– – – –		630	
Grog 14–35 M					300
Water	1200	1200	1100	1000	150
Mixing	Blunge	Blunge	Mill 12 hr	Mill 12 hr	Wedge
Screen	100 M	100 M	100 M	100 M	
Filter	√	√	√	√	–
Drying shrinkage	5%	5%			
Firing temp., °C	1145–1165	1225–1250	1100	1260	1225–1250
Firing, Cone	3–4	8–9	2	10	8–9
Firing shrinkage	9%	8%	8%	8%	5%
Absorption	6%	5%	2%	2%	7%

Red stoneware. The fired color of this stoneware is buff or light red, depending on the brick clay used. Its plasticity compares favorably with that of the best modeling clay, and it can be thrown on the wheel or successfully used for small sculptured pieces. This body can be fired at Cones 3–4.

Gray stoneware. The working properties of this body are the same as those of red stoneware, but it fires at Cones 8–9, and the fired color is gray. A wide variety of raw glazes can be used at these firing temperatures. Gray stoneware can also be salt-glazed.

Basalt ware. Basalt ware is actually black stoneware, made from a body high in iron oxide and fired in a reducing atmosphere. This body is not recommended for use by beginners.

Jasper ware. This stoneware body was developed by Wedgwood in its colored form (it may also be white). It contains a large amount of barium carbonate or sulfate. This body, also, is not recommended for beginners.

VII. PORCELAIN

Few ceramic artists in this country work with porcelain, largely because equipment for firing at the necessary high temperatures is not readily available. Porcelain bodies are hard and strong, and have hard porcelain glazes. The greatest charm of porcelain is its translucency, especially in thin sections, which gives life and depth not found in other bodies. Compositions of some porcelain bodies are given in Table 17-9.

Parian ware. Parian bodies are simple in composition. They are high in feldspar content and are self-glazing. The name stems from the marble found on the Greek island of

TABLE 17-9
PORCELAIN BODIES

Raw materials	Parian porcelain (11)	Syenite porcelain (12)	Electrical porcelain (13)	High-fired porcelain (14)	Frit porcelain (15)
Potter's flint	– – – –	60	190	220	190
Me. feldspar	600	– – – –	370	300	270
Nepheline–syenite		540			
Edgar (N.C.) plastic kaolin	150	80	70	80	70
Edgar (N.C.) kaolin	– – – –	80	220	280	220
Lundy (N.C.) kaolin	150	80			
Bell's dark ball clay	– – – –	80			
Ky. Old Mine #4 ball clay	100	80	150	120	150
Frit	– – – –	– – – –	– – – –	– – – –	100
Water	1500	1500	1500	1500	1500
Mixing	Mill 15 hr	Mill 15 hr	Mill 15 hr	Mill 15 hr	Mill 5 hr
Screen	100 M	100 M	100 M	100 M	100 M
Filter	√	√	√	√	√
Drying shrinkage	5%	4%	4%	4%	4%
Firing temp., °C	1145–1165	1145–1165	1225–1250	1450	1150
Firing, Cone	3–4	3–4	8–9	16	3–4
Firing shrinkage	10	9	11	11	10
Absorption	0	2	0	0	1

Paros. Parian bodies fired at Cones 3–4 give a good white surface with a slight sheen and excellent translucency, but because plasticity is low, pieces are generally cast.

Low-fired porcelains. When nepheline-syenite is used as a flux, it is possible to obtain a vitreous, translucent body which can be fired at Cone 4. Because of the low clay content, the workability is not especially good, and the chief advantage of this body is that it matures at such a low temperature.

Medium-fired porcelains. These bodies are much like the electrical porcelains used in industry, and they are excellent as a starting point for the artist interested in vitreous bodies. They are white and translucent when fired, and the working properties, though not quite comparable to those of stoneware bodies, are good.

High-fired porcelains. These bodies are strong, white, and translucent, but the high firing temperature required (Cone 16) necessitates special kiln equipment. European high-fired porcelains seldom contain ball clays; sufficient plasticity for working is attained by fine grinding and aging, because ball clays do reduce translucency and often impair the color.

Bone china. Bone china, which is composed largely of calcined bones (calcium phosphate), is extensively used to produce a fine translucent body. England is especially noted for its fine bone china ware. Because of its low plasticity and low dry strength, great skill is required in handling the body. Bone china also tends to deform in firing. This body is not recommended for a beginner.

Frit porcelain. Highly translucent pieces are produced from frit porcelain bodies; Lenox and Belleek ware are good examples. This porcelain body is also not recommended for use by beginners.

VIII. REFRACTORY BODIES

Refractory bodies are useful for making kilns and kiln furniture, but they require higher firing temperatures than are ordinarily available.

Fire-clay bodies. These are a mixture of plastic fire clay and grog. They are low in shrinkage and may be used successfully for large pieces.

Alumina bodies. For refractory uses that require extremely high temperatures, a mixture of fused alumina grog and a plastic fire clay gives good results, but this body is more expensive than that described above.

Silicon carbide bodies. These bodies are excellent for muffles and setting plates, because of their high thermal conductivity and great resistance to cracking. However, it is more economical to purchase commercial muffles and setting plates than to form them in the studio.

Insulating bodies. These bodies, as the name implies, are used for insulating kilns, among other things. However, here again, the potter is advised to purchase insulating firebricks rather than to attempt to fashion his own insulation.

IX. COMMERCIAL BODIES

Many excellent bodies can be purchased already prepared, and although the total cost may be a few cents a pound more than the combined cost of the necessary ingredients, the savings in equipment and in time more than compensates. We list below some of the fine commercial bodies that are available in this country.

1. Cone 010 bodies containing frit, with rather low plasticity.

2. White-firing talc bodies, which mature at Cones 06–03 and are much in demand in California for artware. They cast well and may also be modeled, but they lack the workability of good stoneware bodies.

3. White-firing nontalc bodies. These bodies usually contain nepheline-syenite, and they fire at about Cone 06. They may be vitrified at higher temperatures than this, but low firing results in a whiter finished product.

4. Buff-burning bodies which have fair to good plasticity, and fire at Cones 06–2.

5. Red-burning bodies which fire at Cone 02.

6. White-burning bodies of standard white earthenware composition which fire at Cone 4.

7. Terra-cotta bodies with grog, which fire at Cones 02–4.

Few high-fired bodies are available commercially in this country, although the supply houses of Europe carry a great variety of whiteware bodies for the high-temperature range. Below are listed some of the manufacturers who supply commercially prepared bodies.

United Clay Mines, Inc.
Trenton, N. J.

American Art Clay Co.
Indianapolis 24, Ind.

Ferro Corp.
Ceramic Arts Supplies Division
214 Northfield Road
Bedford, Ohio

B. F. Drakenfeld & Co., Inc.
45 Park Place
New York 7, N. Y.

The O. Hommel Company
Pittsburgh 30, Pa.

Pemco Corp.
Pottery Arts Supply Division
5601 Eastern Avenue
Baltimore 24, Md.

X. REFERENCES

1. ANON., Laboratory Course in Pottery, 2. How to Make a Body. *Ceram. Ind.* **50**, No. 3, 118 (1948).

2. ANON., What is a Good Low-Cone Body? *Ceram. Ind.* **42**, No. 6, 68 (1944).

3. BINNS, C. F., *Manual of Practical Potting*, 5th ed., Scott, Greenwood & Sons, London, 1922.

4. COLLINS, P. F., Auxiliary Fluxes in Ceramic Bodies, *J. Am. Ceram. Soc.* **15**, 17 (1932).

5. COX, P. E., Why Use More Than One Clay in a Body Mixture, *Ceram. Age* **52**, No. 4, 202 (1948).

6. FUNK, I. W., Technical Production of Chinese Porcelains, *Ber. Deut. Keram. Ges.* **22**, 163 (1941).

7. KOENIG, C. J., Nepheline Syenite in Low Temperature Vitreous Wares, *Bull. No.* 112, Ohio State University Experimental Station, July, 1942.

8. LOOMIS, G. A., AND A. R. BLACKBURN, Use of Soda Feldspar in Whiteware Bodies, *J. Am. Ceram. Soc.* **29**, 48 (1946).

9. MEYER, W. W., AND T. A. KLINEFELTER, Substitution of Domestic for Imported Clays in Whiteware Bodies, *J. of Res. Nat. Bur. of Standards* **65** (1937), (RP 1011).

10. NEWCOMB, REXFORD, JR., *Ceramic White-wares*, Pitman Publishing Corporation, New York, 1947.

11. ROSENTHAL, ERNEST, *Pottery and Ceramics*, Harmondsworth, Middlesex, 1949.

12. SEARLE, A. B., *An Encyclopedia of the Ceramic Industries*, Ernest Benn, Ltd., London, 1929.

13. WATTS, A. S., Some Whiteware Bodies Developed at the Ohio State University, *J. Am. Ceram. Soc.* **10**, 148 (1927).

14. WOLF, J., Keramische Massen, dargestellt nach ihren mineralischen Zusammensetzungen und als Silikate, *Sprechsaal* **60**, No. 43, 785 (1927); **60**, No. 44, 807 (1927); **60**, No. 45, 827 (1927).

CHAPTER 18

Preparation of Bodies

I. INTRODUCTION

Preparation of the ceramic body is the first important step in the fabrication of a fine piece of ware. Negligence in carrying out this operation will surely cause trouble in later stages. In this chapter, preparation of the body is described in considerable detail, and it is strongly recommended that the potter study these steps carefully.

II. MEASURING THE INGREDIENTS

Reasonably accurate measurement of the ingredients is essential if the body is to have the required properties, but it is a waste of time to measure more precisely than is necessary.

Scales. Of the many kinds of scales available, some are simple and inexpensive while others are more precise but costly. The artist potter needs reasonably accurate scales, but not precision instruments.

For small batches of clay, a double- or triple-beam balance is convenient. Balances with a total capacity of 600 grams, which are sensitive to within 0.1 gram and which have no loose weights to be misplaced, are commercially available. These balances are easily and quickly read, and it is simple to weigh small quantities of ingredients to be added together for a large batch of clay. This balance will therefore conveniently handle batches with a total dry weight of one or two

kilograms and yet is sensitive enough for making up small batches of glaze.

For larger weighings, a small platform balance with a capacity of 35 kilograms (75 lb) and a sensitivity of 30 grams (1 oz) is satisfactory.

The metric system. You will note that we speak of "grams" and "kilograms" in describing the balances above. This is the metric system of measurement, and it is recommended that all measurements be made in these units. Most batch formulas are expressed in terms of grams and multiples of a gram, but a table of conversion factors is given below, for those cases when the units are given in pounds and ounces:

1 kilogram	= 2.205 pounds
1 kilogram	= 35.34 ounces
1 pound	= 0.454 kilogram
1 pound	= 454 grams
1 ounce	= 28.35 grams

It is apparent that there are 1000 grams in 1 kilogram and, if necessary, the gram may be easily divided into further units of 10. For example, a batch of clay that weighs 1.073 kilograms is said to weigh 1073 grams, which is the same thing. Manipulation of quantities is simpler in the metric system than in the English system.

Weighing the dry ingredients. Precise weighing of the dry ingredients is extremely

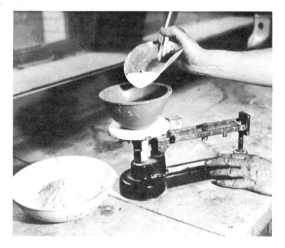

Fig. 18-1. Weighing a small batch of clay.

Fig. 18-2. Weighing a large batch of clay.

important if the batch of clay is to have the anticipated properties. A pan or a similar container must be placed on the scales to hold the ingredient to be weighed, and the first step is to determine the weight of the pan and to record it so that it may be referred to again and again (it is convenient to mark it directly on the pan).

Let us assume that the pan weighs 68 grams, and that we need 226 grams of clay for the batch we are preparing. The scale weights are set to 68 + 226 = 294 grams, and clay is added to the pan on the other side of the balance until the scale beam floats at its mid-point of swing, as shown in Fig. 18–1. The clay is then dumped into the blunger and a second ingredient is weighed out in the same manner. Always read the balance weights before weighing and *check them after weighing*. It is impossible, of course, to correct mistakes after the batch has been made up. Figure 18–2 shows how to weigh the ingredients for a large batch of clay.

Measuring the water. Water for the body can be measured either by volume or by weight, that is, either in a graduated flask or

on a balance. In the metric system, a unit *weight* of water (1 gram) is conveniently equivalent to a unit *volume* of water (1 cubic centimeter). Graduated flasks or pitchers can be obtained from any chemical or photographic supply house.

Precision of measurements. To weigh ingredients more precisely than is necessary is a waste of time, but our measurements must be reasonably accurate. The following "rule of thumb" is helpful:

When required quantity is	Weigh to nearest
1 to 100 grams	¹⁄₁₀ gram
100 to 1000 grams	1 gram
Over 1000 grams	10 grams

Allowance for moisture. Some ceramic materials, like feldspar and quartz, have negligible amounts of moisture, while lump ball clay may contain as much as 15% of free moisture (based on dry weight). When a formula calls for 1000 grams of ball clay, it means *dry* clay, and therefore some correction must be made for the moisture content.

One thousand grams of an ordinary moisture-containing clay would yield only 870 grams of dry clay, an amount much too small to give proper results.

It is necessary to determine the moisture content of each batch of clay, and then to keep it constant by storage in a tight container. Moisture content is determined as follows.

A 100-gram sample of the clay is placed in an open dish and is dried in a 110°C oven until it reaches a constant weight. This may take as long as 24 hours. The dry sample is then weighed again and the amount of remaining moisture is calculated as below:

Weight of dish	210 grams
Weight of dish and wet clay	308 grams
Weight of wet clay	98 grams
Weight of dish and dry clay	298 grams
Weight of dry clay	88 grams
Weight of water in clay	10 grams

The percentage of water in the clay, based on the dry weight, is then expressed as follows:

$$\frac{\text{Weight of wet clay} - \text{weight of dry clay}}{\text{Weight of dry clay}}$$
$$\times 100 = \frac{98 - 88}{88} \times 100 = 11.4\%.$$

In other words, if 1000 grams of this dry clay were needed for a batch, 1114 grams of the wet clay would be weighed out, for 114 grams would be water.

Now let us see how a complete batch formula would be worked out. Suppose that we use the example in the first column of Table 18-1. No correction is needed for the flint and the feldspar, because they contain no moisture. The weights of the clays are determined as follows:

Weight of clay + weight of water
$$= \text{weight of wet clay.}$$

Florida kaolin:
$$120 + 120 \times 5/100 = 126 \text{ grams,}$$
or, more simply,
$$120 \times 1.05 = 126 \text{ grams.}$$

North Carolina kaolin:
$$120 \times 1.02 = 122 \text{ grams.}$$

Kentucky ball clay:
$$180 \times 1.15 = 207 \text{ grams.}$$

Bell's ball clay:
$$100 \times 1.12 = 112 \text{ grams.}$$

The last column of Table 18-1 summarizes the calculations for this batch.

It should be kept in mind that clay stored in warm places, even though covered, continues to dry slowly. Consequently, new checks of the water content must be made from time to time. It is desirable to retain some moisture in clays (especially the ball clays), because completely dry materials are difficult to combine into a plastic mass.

III. PLASTIC MIXING OF THE BODY

When water is added to the dry ingredients and the mass is kneaded at the same time, care must be taken to add the water slowly enough so that the mixture does not become too sticky. Very careful mixing is required to work out all of the lumps in this process. It will be found easier, if time permits, to first mix the dry ingredients thoroughly, add the correct amount of water, and allow the batch

TABLE 18-1
CORRECTION FOR MOISTURE IN RAW MATERIALS

Raw materials	Batch formula	% Moisture	Corrected batch
Potter's flint	340	0	340
Me. feldspar	140	0	140
Fla. plastic kaolin	120	5	126
N.C. kaolin	120	2	122
Ky. Old Mine #4 ball clay	180	15	207
Bell's dark ball clay	100	12	112

Fig. 18-3. Blunging a small batch of slip.   Fig. 18-4. Blunging a large batch of slip.

to soak for 24 hours. The mass can then be readily mixed by hand kneading. The raw materials must be thoroughly washed or air-floated before mixing if a smooth working body is to result, because there is no way of screening out grit or other impurities in this process of mixing.

After the first mixing, the body should be thoroughly wedged by the method described in the next section.

IV. BLUNGING INTO SLIP

The best way to make up a body is to add enough water to the dry ingredients to form a mixture of the consistency of thin cream (slip), pass this mixture through a screen to remove the grit, and then extract enough of the water to bring the mass into a plastic state. This method has the following advantages: (1) the ingredients are more thoroughly mixed than by other methods, (2) the grit, lignite, and other coarse matter are removed,

(3) many of the soluble salts (that may later cause scum) are removed with the water.

For small batches, the mixing of the dry ingredients with the water can be accomplished with an eggbeater or a household electric mixer, as shown in Fig. 18-3. A smooth mixture is more easily obtained if the dry ingredients are slowly added to the water, rather than the reverse. The mass must be stirred until all of the lumps are removed, and this may take several hours.

Commercial blungers that will handle 10 gallons of slip at one time are available for mixing large batches (Fig. 18-4).

The amount of water necessary to attain the proper consistency varies with the kinds of clay used but, in general, 1200 to 1500 cc of water are required for each 1000 grams of dry body.

To avoid discoloration, the use of iron utensils must be avoided in making up the slip. Vessels should be of heavily tinned steel, wood, or stoneware.

Screening the slip. After blunging, the slip should be passed through a screen to remove coarse particles and lumps. The usual mesh sizes are 80, 100, and 120 per inch. If the batch is very lumpy or contains a great deal of coarse material, it should be passed through a 35-mesh screen first, to avoid clogging the fine screen.

There are many kinds of screen commercially available, but for small-scale work in the pottery, the wooden riddle with bronze wire is most satisfactory. The screen may be shaken by hand when small batches of slip are to be screened (Fig. 18–5), but a mechanical vibrator facilitates the screening of large batches. *Clean* your screen immediately after it has been used. A gentle stream of water from a tap or hose will usually do it easily and quickly. A soft brush may be used; a coarse brush or too vigorous scrubbing will spoil a fine screen.

Fig. 18-6. The author pouring slip through a magnetic separator.

Magnetic separators. Figure 18–6 shows slip being poured between magnets to remove iron specks. This is particularly important for porcelain bodies.

Removing the water. Although water can be removed from slip by simply drying in an open pan, this method fails to remove the soluble salts, and dirt is apt to fall into the mixture. A slightly better method is to suspend the slip in a cloth bag until most of the water has dripped out (like making jelly!), and then to spread the slip in an open pan for completion of the drying. A third method, for small quantities of slip, is to pour the mixture into a heavy plaster dish and allow the plaster to draw out the moisture. This has the disadvantages that plaster may get into the slip, and that the absorption of lime by the slip contaminates it.

Fig. 18-5. Screening a small batch of slip.

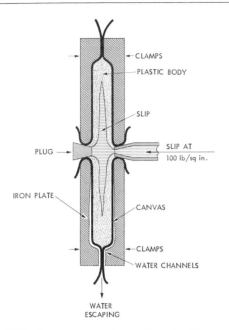

Fig. 18-7. Cross section of one plate of a filter press, showing its operation.

Fig. 18-8. Small laboratory filter press, holding 30 pounds of body.

Commercially, water is removed from slip by pumping it into a canvas filter pocket, as shown in Fig. 18–7, and then applying pressures of 80 to 120 lb/in². This process is fairly rapid. Small presses for use in the studio are available (Fig. 18–8), but they must be carefully adjusted for good results.

It has been the author's experience that the use of vacuum filters is by far the most satisfactory method of removing water from small batches of slip. Figure 18–9 shows a standard filter capable of handling several hundred grams of slip at one time. The filtering is done on filter paper supported on a porcelain plate, so that there can be no contamination of the slip. The vacuum is supplied by an ordinary sink pump. The operation is shown in Fig. 18–10.

Large batches of slip are filtered in a similar manner, with cloth supported by heavy screens replacing the filter paper. These filters are easy to construct, easy to use, and

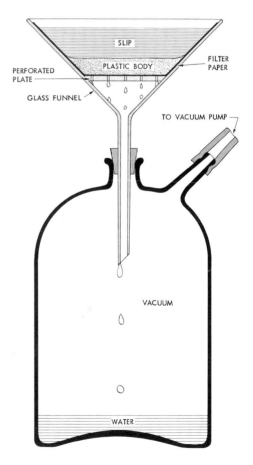

Fig. 18-9. Cross section of filter for handling small batches of slip.

Fig. 18-10. The author filtering a small batch of slip.

With practice, this becomes a rhythmic process that goes quickly and easily.

An examination of the cut surface will indicate when the wedging is complete; there should be no sign of lumps or blobs of air. It is instructive for a beginner to wedge two lumps of body, one black (stained with 2% lamp black) and one white, until the mass is a uniform gray; the length of time required is apt to be surprising. The steps in this process are shown in Figs. 18–13 through 18–17.

easy to clean. They greatly simplify the preparation of the body. This operation is explained in detail in Chapter 30.

Wedging. After the water has been removed, the clay must be thoroughly worked (wedged) for two reasons: (1) to distribute the remaining moisture evenly throughout the mass, and (2) to remove all the air from the body.

For small batches, hand wedging is quite satisfactory. The procedure is as follows:

(1) Take a ball of the plastic clay about the size of a cantaloupe and pass it over a stretched wire to bisect it (Fig. 18–11).

(2) Place one half of the ball, cut side up, on a damp, firmly supported plaster bat.

(3) Throw the second half, also cut side up, down onto the first (Fig. 18–12).

(4) Now, bisect the new lump at right angles to the first cut and repeat the process twenty to thirty times.

Wedging clay:
Fig. 18-11. Cutting the lump of clay in half.
Fig. 18-12. Slapping the two halves together, ready to repeat the operation.

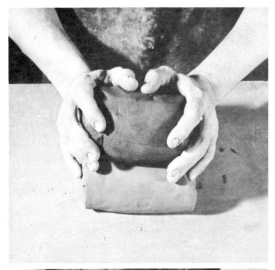

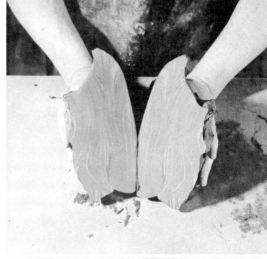

A wedging demonstration:

Fig. 18-13. A lump of darkened clay and a lump of light clay ready to be wedged together.

Fig. 18-14. The cut surface of the clay after three cycles of wedging.

Fig. 18-15. The cut surface after six cycles.

Fig. 18-16. The cut surface after twelve cycles.

Fig. 18-17. The cut surface after thirty cycles, showing perfect uniformity.

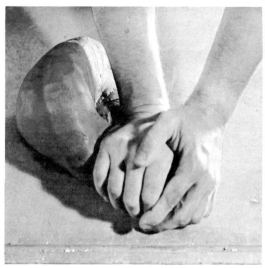

Fig. 18-18. "Jelly-roll" wedging: the roll is deformed by the pressure of both hands, turned 90°, and pressed again.

Fig. 18-19. Oriental wedging: the rhythmic pressure from the right hand makes the clay flow around.

There are other methods of wedging. The "jelly roll," shown in Fig. 18–18, consists of pressing the clay down with both hands, turning it, and pressing again. The Oriental method shown in Fig. 18–19 becomes very efficient when the correct rhythmic motion is learned so that the clay flows around smoothly.

For large batches, hand wedging is time-consuming, and machines are commercially available for the wedging operation. The small pug mill and auger with a vacuum attachment shown in Fig. 18–20 is convenient, but somewhat costly. When the body is passed through this apparatus several times the air is completely removed and excellent uniformity is attained.

V. BALL MILLING

In this method of mixing, the dry materials and water are placed in a ball mill, and the mill is run for several hours. This process is particularly good for vitreous bodies, because the grinding action reduces the aver-

age particle size, as well as thoroughly mixing the ingredients. After the milling, the slip is screened and the water is removed by the methods described in the previous section. Porcelain slips should also be run through the magnetic separator to remove iron specks.

Fig. 18-20. A small vacuum auger for preparing a plastic body.

The mill. A ball mill is invaluable to the potter, because it may be used not only for preparation of the body, as described above, but for the blending of glazes and for any general grinding operation. The mill consists of a cylindrical container, usually of porcelain, that rotates slowly about its axis. The container is about half filled with flint pebbles or porcelain balls, and the charge to be ground fills the voids between the pebbles. The rotary motion, illustrated in Fig. 18–21, grinds the charge by impact and by rubbing it between the pebbles. Mills come in various sizes. For mixing bodies, a capacity of 50 lb of charge is convenient (Fig. 18–22). The grinding rate is directly linked with the speed of rotation, and the manufacturer's recommendations should be closely followed. Table 24–2 lists the characteristics of a number of ball mills.

Fig. 18-22. A ball mill for grinding bodies. Note the drain pan underneath.

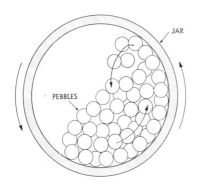

Fig. 18-21. Cross section of a ball mill in operation.

Ball-mill drives. There are many ways of driving a ball mill. The larger sizes, because they are heavy to handle, are mounted on permanent bearings. Sizes up to 2 gallons may be placed on rollers, as shown in Chapter 30.

The procedure. The pebbles to be used in a ball mill should be 1″ to 1½″ in diameter, and should occupy roughly one-half the volume of the cylinder. They must be thoroughly clean, of course. The dry charge is placed in the mill, with sufficient water (about 1500 cc for each 1000 grams of dry charge) to make a creamy slip (Fig. 18–23). If too little water is used, the body will stick to the balls and the grinding process will be inefficient. The total volume of the balls, the body, and the water should be about one-half that of the container. The mill must be tightly sealed with a cover clamped over a rubber gasket (Fig. 18–24). After the mill has been running for a short time, it should be opened, to make sure that the clay has not become so gummy that it is sticking to the balls.

Cleaning the mill. Removing the slip from the mill can be a very messy job unless it is properly done. Large mills have

Fig. 18-23. Filling the ball mill.

Fig. 18-24. Clamping the cover on the ball mill. Note the rubber gasket for tight sealing.

doors in the sides. When the grinding is completed, the door can be replaced by a screen that will hold back the pebbles and allow the slip to pass through as the mill is rotated (Fig. 18–25). To cleanse the mill thoroughly after the slip has been removed, a small amount of water is put into the container, the mill is again rotated with the door in place, and then the remaining diluted slip is run out through the screened door, as before.

If the next batch of clay to be ground in the mill is the same as the first batch, the procedure above is sufficient, but if a different body is to be ground, the cleaning proc-

Fig. 18-25. Ball mill with draining plate in place.

ess must be repeated until the balls are thoroughly clean. If a colored body has been ground in the mill, it is advisable to mill a charge of white sand and water overnight and then flush the mill thoroughly. This method leaves the mill absolutely clean.

VI. MIXING BODIES CONTAINING GROG

Bodies which contain grog, such as those for terra-cotta pieces or refractories, must be made up in the plastic state. For small lots, mixing and wedging can be done by hand, but this laborious procedure for large lots can be avoided by using a machine. The best kind of machine is the so-called "wet pan" shown in Fig. 18–26, which is obtainable in small sizes; they are fairly expensive.

Grog bodies benefit by aging, and they should be made up ahead of time and stored until they are to be used.

VII. CASTING SLIPS

Casting slips are of the same, or similar, composition as the equivalent plastic bodies. The water content is the same as that for the plastic body, but the slip is made more fluid by the addition of a chemical agent called a deflocculant.

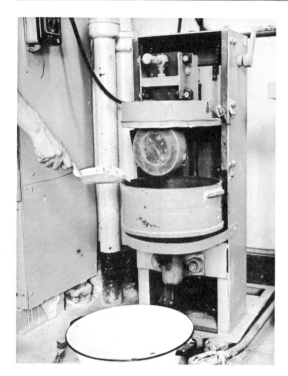

Fig. 18-26. Filling a small wet pan (with the muller raised) for a terra-cotta mix.

Deflocculants. There are many kinds of deflocculating agents, one of which is made by adding 8 grams of sodium carbonate (anhydrous) to 50 cc of hot water, stirring until the crystals are dissolved, and then adding 25 cc of "N" brand silicate of soda, stirring again, and adding sufficient hot water to bring the total volume to 100 cc. The solution should be cooled and then stored in a tightly stoppered bottle. Only high-grade, carefully stored chemicals should be used, and the solution should not be used when it is more than one month old.

The action of a deflocculant is not completely understood, but it undoubtedly affects the forces between the clay particles and increases the fluidity of the water film. One may well ask, "Why use a deflocculant rather than increase the water in the plastic mass?" The use of a deflocculant has two advantages: (1) A deflocculated slip has little tendency to settle, and therefore the bottom of a cast piece is no thicker than the top; (2) a deflocculated slip with a low water content casts a firm wall and the slip drains out cleanly.

Measurement of water content. The amount of water present in a slip is directly related to the specific gravity of the slip as a whole (see Chapter 24 for calculation of specific gravity). Table 18–2 shows this relationship, and Table 18–3 tells us how the water content of a slip should be varied to increase or decrease the specific gravity. (The values apply to lead-glaze slips only approximately, because of the high density of the lead compounds.) Water used in making slip must be soft or distilled water.

Amount of deflocculant to be added. Without specialized laboratory equipment it is difficult to determine the exact amount of deflocculant required for a given slip, and yet we must avoid adding either too little or too much. Too little deflocculant results in a thick, gummy slip that will not pour; too much will cause the cast to stick tightly to the mold surface and may well "burn" the mold so that it cannot be used again. The following procedure is recommended.

TABLE 18–2

SPECIFIC GRAVITY AND WATER CONTENT OF SLIPS

Specific gravity	Percent water (wet wt)
1.40	48.0
1.45	45.5
1.50	43.0
1.55	40.5
1.60	38.0
1.65	35.2
1.70	33.0
1.75	30.5
1.80	28.0
1.85	25.5
1.90	23.0
1.95	20.5
2.00	18.0
2.05	15.5
2.10	13.0

Fill the mixer or blunger about half full of water, and calculate the amount of dry body needed to give a specific gravity of 1.75 (Table 18–2). Then add to the water 1 cc of the deflocculating solution for every 125 grams of dry body. Now add the dry body slowly to the fluid in the blunger, and mix for one-half hour. If the slip is too sticky after this length of time, add just a few drops of deflocculating solution and mix again. If the slip is still not sufficiently thinned, keep adding very small quantities of deflocculant until the slip is thin enough to pour. It is important to know just how much deflocculant is added altogether—no more than 1.7 cc for each 125 grams of dry body should ever be used.

Conversely, if the slip is too thin after the first half hour of mixing, dry body should be added in very small quantities until the specific gravity is raised to its proper level. Normally, the specific gravity should be between 1.70 and 1.80 for best results. The following numerical calculation will illustrate the above procedure.

Start with 1000 cc of water in the blunger. Table 18–2 tells us that a specific gravity of 1.75 corresponds to 30.5% of water based on the slip weight.

Then, in our example, 1000 cc of water is 30.5% of the total weight (1 cc of water weighs 1 gram) and therefore the total weight of the slip is to be

$$\frac{1000 \times 100}{30.5} = 3280 \text{ grams.}$$

Consequently, the weight of the dry body to be added is

$$3280 \text{ grams} - 1000 \text{ grams} = 2280 \text{ grams,}$$

and the amount of deflocculating solution required is

$$\frac{2280}{125} = 18 \text{ cc.}$$

Thickness of the slip. There are instruments capable of measuring the viscosity (thickness) of casting slips, but the artist potter usually must rely on other means of measurement. With a little experience, the consistency can be readily judged by dipping a spoonful of slip from the well-mixed batch and allowing it to pour from the edge of the spoon. When the slip pours in a smooth,

TABLE 18–3

CORRECTION OF SLIP SPECIFIC GRAVITY

Desired specific gravity of slip (rows) vs. Original specific gravity of slip (columns). Right-side values = cc water to be added to 100 cc original slip; lower-left values = grams of solid to be added to 100 cc of original slip.

Desired \ Original	1.20	1.25	1.30	1.35	1.40	1.45	1.50	1.55	1.60	1.65	1.70	1.75	1.80	1.85	1.90	1.95	2.00	2.05	2.10	2.15	2.20
1.20		19	50	80	100																
1.25	8		18	43	60	85	95														
1.30	21	9		17	35	51	66	82	100												
1.35	35	22	10		15	30	43	58	70	88											
1.40	48	36	24	11		13	25	37	50	63	77	87									
1.45	60	49	37	26	12		12	22	32	45	57	66	78	90	100						
1.50	75	62	50	39	27	13		11	18	30	41	50	61	70	80	93					
1.55	95	78	65	52	40	28	14		10	17	27	36	46	55	66	73	85				
1.60		97	83	68	54	42	30	15		9	16	25	33	43	52	61	66	76	85		
1.65			100	88	72	59	45	31	16		8	15	23	31	40	48	54	62	70	77	85
1.70					94	76	63	47	32	17		7	14	21	29	36	43	50	57	65	70
1.75						100	80	66	50	34	18		7	14	20	27	33	40	48	54	60
1.80							108	86	71	54	37	20		6	13	18	25	31	38	45	50
1.85									95	76	58	40	22		6	11	17	23	29	36	42
1.90										104	83	63	43	24		5	11	17	22	28	34
1.95												91	68	47	26		5	11	16	21	26
2.00													100	74	50	30		5	11	16	
2.05														113	60	56	33		5	10	15
2.10															125	88	63	37		5	10
2.15																150	78	69	40		5
2.20																	166	111	75	43	

NOTE: This Table is computed for an average specific gravity of the solids of 2.5.

thick stream, it is of the correct viscosity. Generally speaking, slips for solid castings can be more viscous than those for drain castings.

Clays for casting slips. The properties of a casting slip are directly allied with the kinds of clay used. For example, coarse-grained kaolins make a fast-casting body, while ball clays slow the casting but give a tougher layer. The kinds of clays must be used in the proper proportions to give the required results, and it is best for the beginner to use well-tested formulas.

Commercial casting slips. Many ready-mixed varieties of casting slips are available commercially, most of them for use in low-fired kilns. Some sources of supply are listed in Chapter 17.

Slip formulas. Table 18–4 lists the formulas for and the properties of some of the casting slips that have proved satisfactory.

VIII. STORING AND AGING OF CERAMIC BODIES

Storing. In the small pottery it is most convenient to store plastic bodies in 6- or 8-gallon stoneware crocks which can be tightly covered. The body should be wedged in balls or cylinders of convenient size before being stored, to facilitate removal from the crocks. Each type of body should have its own crock, carefully marked. If the crocks are made completely airtight by sealing the cover with a rubber gasket, the body will probably keep indefinitely without attention. However, it is sometimes necessary to add a little water when body is stored over a long period of time. Thin plastic bags are often used for storing small batches of clay.

TABLE 18-4
CASTING SLIPS

Body	No. of cc of deflocculating sol. for 1000 grams dry body [1]	Specific gravity	Linear drying shrinkage from mold size, %
White earthenware Table 17–7 No. 3	8.5	1.78	4
Talc body Table 17–7 No. 4	7.0	1.70	4
Parian body Table 17–9 No. 11	8.5	1.75	5
Syenite body Table 17–9 No. 12	8.5	1.72	4
Electrical porcelain body Table 17–9 No. 13	11.0	1.80	4
High-fired porcelain Table 17–9 No. 14	8.0	1.72	4

[1] This solution consists of 100 cc water, 8 grams of sodium carbonate, and 25 cc of "N" brand sodium silicate.

Aging. All bodies become more workable after aging, for it takes time for the water to penetrate all the interstices of the clay and to build up stable films. It is believed that bacterial action also helps to develop the plasticity of stored clay.

Our American potteries seldom take the necessary time for aging their ordinary clays, but bone china and hard porcelain bodies are almost always aged before they are used. Early Chinese potters, on the other hand, considered aging so important that it is said that they made enough body for their own and their sons' lifetimes.

When maximum workability is desired, it is helpful to rewedge the body from time to time during the aging process.

IX. REFERENCES

1. Granger, A., *La Céramique Industrielle*, Gauthier-Villars et Cie, Paris, 1929 (Chap. V).

2. Hall, F. P., The Casting of Clayware—A Résumé, *J. Am. Ceram. Soc.* **13**, 751 (1930).

3. Hyman, R., *Ceramics Handbook*, Fawcett Publications, Inc., New York, 1953.

4. Newcomb, R., Jr., *Ceramic Whitewares*, Pitman Publishing Corporation, New York, 1947 (Chap. IV).

5. Norton, F. H., *Elements of Ceramics*, Addison-Wesley Publishing Company, Inc., Cambridge, Mass., 1952 (Chap. 11).

CHAPTER 19

Mold Making

I. INTRODUCTION

In the pottery industry, molds are universally made from gypsum plaster, for this material takes an accurate impression, is reasonably hard and strong when set, and, most important, is porous enough to readily absorb water.

Molds are used for forming plates by jiggering, for casting pieces of any shape, and for making pressed pieces. Although molds are primarily used for quantity reproduction of pieces, it is often necessary to make a mold for a single piece.

It is difficult to describe mold making, and here again the beginner is urged to work with an expert maker of molds, in order to learn the tricks of the trade. We shall attempt to give only an outline of the processes used, and the reasons for their use.

II. PLASTER FOR THE MOLD

Composition. Plaster is made from gypsum rock, which is composed of $CaSO_4 \cdot 2H_2O$. The rock is heated in huge kettles until part of the water is driven off, leaving the finished plaster, $CaSO_4 \cdot \frac{1}{2}H_2O$.

There are many grades of plaster, which vary in the time of set, the hardness, and the amount of expansion on setting. For ceramic molds, "pottery plaster" is commonly used; the kind known as "molding plaster" is similar and is more readily available. Hard-surfaced plasters containing soluble materials cannot be used for models or molds. How-

ever, a hard plaster like "hydrocal" may be used for models not requiring high absorption. High-expansion plasters are sometimes used to compensate for later shrinkage.

Time for setting. As is commonly known, when plaster is added to water, part of it dissolves, but soon the entire mass crystallizes in intermeshing needles until a solid body results (considerable heat is given off in this process). Pottery plaster sets in about 20 minutes after it is mixed, and although this time may be decreased by very thorough mixing, or increased by little or no mixing, it is important to bear in mind that there is a limit to the time available for forming the desired mold. The plaster can be formed with a spatula as it becomes increasingly stiff.

Mixing the plaster. Small batches of plaster may be mixed in bowls by hand, as shown in Figs. 19–1 through 19–5. The dry plaster is sifted through the fingers into the water in the bowl until all of the free water is taken up. The plaster must never be dumped into the water if lumping is to be avoided. The mix should be allowed to set for about 2 minutes, and then should be mixed for roughly 3 minutes with the hands, a spoon, an eggbeater, or an electric mixer. (A mixer that can be contrived from an electric drill is described in Chapter 30.) After a thorough mixing, the bowl should be firmly

Mixing plaster:

Fig. 19-1. Sifting dry plaster into water in the mixing bowl.

Fig. 19-2. Stirring the plaster mix after it has soaked for a few minutes.

Fig. 19-3. Using an electric mixer for a smooth mix.

Fig. 19-4. Jarring the bowl to make bubbles rise.

Fig. 19-5. Skimming the bubbles off the surface. The plaster is now ready to use.

Fig. 19-6. Preparing to mix a large batch of plaster. The plaster and water have been weighed out.

jarred to bring air bubbles to the surface, where they can be skimmed off. Although the plaster is already beginning to stiffen, it can be used for about 10 or 15 minutes before it becomes too stiff to handle.

Bowls made of rubber (one half of a rubber ball makes a good bowl), of plastic, or of thin brass are excellent, because they can easily be cleared of set plaster by squeezing.

Large batches of plaster must be weighed for mixing, to assure proper consistency. One hundred pounds of plaster requires about 60 to 75 pounds of water. The mixture should soak for 2 minutes before mixing, and then should be mixed for 3½ minutes with a motor-driven mixer like that shown in Fig. 19–3 or the larger mixer shown in Fig. 19–6. The plaster is ready to use when the air bubbles have been removed.

Remember that plaster expands approximately 0.02 inch in every 10 inches, and therefore it must *never* be cast *inside* a solid mold. Learn to be neat in using plaster; it is a messy substance to clean up. It is simple to cover the working surface with several layers of newspapers to catch the waste. Plaster must never be allowed to drip down the drain of a sink, of course; sooner or later the drain will clog.

Separators. Unless the hardened plaster surface is treated in some way, it is impossible to apply a second layer of plaster without having it stick. Many kinds of separators can be used, but for ceramics nothing is better than a solution of English Crown Soft Soap, which is composed of 500 grams of soap added to 1000 cc of boiling water. This solution can be made in reasonable quantities and stored for future use.

The solution is applied to the dampened plaster surface with a brush or a sponge until a good lather is worked up, and then it is washed off; the process should be repeated a second and third time, and every trace of soap removed. If soap gets into the liquid plaster being applied, it will prevent setting. If the soaping has been well done, the plaster surface will have a polish like that of ivory, for the soap forms an insoluble calcium oleate with the plaster surface. Because the soap causes a chemical reaction, it must never be used on the surface of a mold that is to come in contact with the clay body.

Tools for plaster work. A few of the tools needed for working plaster into molds are shown in Fig. 19–7.

III. FORMING THE MODEL FOR THE MOLD

Calculation of mold size. We know that all clays and bodies shrink to some extent when dried and fired, and it is therefore necessary to make the mold somewhat larger than the required size for the finished piece. Potters who do not know how to calculate shrinkage values use time-consuming cut-and-try methods to determine the correct size for the mold, but it is not difficult to learn to make the necessary calculations.

We have already discussed drying and firing shrinkages of various clays in Chapters 15 and 17. The shrinkage values given there are expressed as percentages of the length of the original body. Drying shrinkage is based on the plastic or mold size, while firing shrinkage is based on the green (dried) size. A clay with 5% drying shrinkage, for example, would have a green length corresponding to the mold size less 5% (5/100). In calculating the mold size, we must determine the shrinkage, which is based on a size that we have not yet measured. If we know algebra, this calculation is simple, but even without this tool, the calculation is not too difficult.

Let us take an example. A tile is to be made exactly 10 inches long when fired from a body with 3.6% drying shrinkage and 11.3% firing shrinkage. We must work backwards in two steps: from the fired size to the green size, and then to the mold size.

Green size:

Green size − firing shrinkage = fired size

or

Green size − 11.3/100 × green size = 10

or

1 − (11.3/100) × green size = 10

or

0.887 × green size = 10;

therefore

Green size = 10/0.887 or 11.3 inches.

Mold size:

$$\text{Mold size} = \frac{11.3}{1 - (3.6/100)}$$

$$= \frac{11.3}{0.964} = 11.7 \text{ inches.}$$

Calculation check:

Mold size × 3.6/100 = drying shrinkage

or

11.7 × 3.6/100 = 0.4.

Green size = mold size − drying shrinkage

or

11.7 − 0.4 = 11.3.

Green size × 11.3/100 = firing shrinkage

or

11.3 × (11.3/100) = 1.3.

Fired size = green size − firing shrinkage

or

11.3 − 1.3 = 10,

which checks.

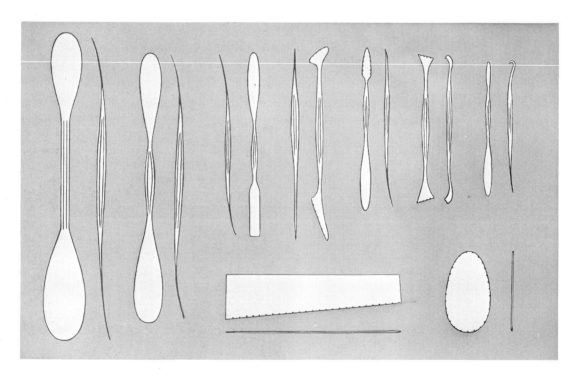

Fig. 19-7. Tools for working plaster (U.S. Gypsum Co.).

Summary. The following rules summarize the above procedure.

(1) Divide the fired size by 1 minus 1/100 of the percent firing shrinkage, which gives the green size.

(2) Divide this figure by 1 minus 1/100 of the percent drying shrinkage, which gives the mold size.

Wheel-turned model. This is the simplest method of making models which are circular in shape.

A plaster chuck, with its surface well soaped, is set up on the wheel head. The lower flange of the chuck should extend about one inch beyond the maximum diameter of the model, and the boss of the chuck should be smaller than the base diameter of the piece. A cottle (sheet of linoleum) is wrapped around the flange of the chuck and tied with heavy twine. The height of the cottle should be a few inches more than the required height of the model.

The plaster is poured into the cottle, nearly to the top (Fig. 19–8). Remember that it is better to have a little more plaster than you feel will be needed, since too little plaster will spoil the cast. Excess plaster can be poured into bat molds if these are kept handy.

As soon as the plaster in the cottle becomes just firm enough to stand by itself, the cottle is removed and the plaster is roughed down to nearly the final size as quickly as possible (Fig. 19–9). At the start, the turning can be done with a hand tool, but as the

Forming a plaster model for a bowl:
Fig. 19-8. Pouring plaster into a cottle tied on the wheel head.
Fig. 19-9. Rough-turning the shape as soon as the cottle has been removed, before the plaster is fully set.
Fig. 19-10. Finish-turning the shape.

plaster becomes harder a scraper steadied against a pointed stick resting against a backboard is used. The final turning to the desired shape (Fig. 19–10) is done very carefully, perhaps using a template as a guide. Care must be taken not to apply so much pressure to the model that it falls off the chuck.

The turned model, which is now reasonably hard, is tapped loose and lifted from the chuck. After it has thoroughly dried it may be returned to the wheel for finishing with fine sandpaper.

Lathe-turned model. Wheel turning is not suitable for fashioning models with bases of small diameter. For these, the following procedure should be followed.

A cylinder of plaster is cast around a steel rod, with one end of the rod projecting about one inch outside the plaster, and the other end just flush with the plaster. The model

can then be mounted in a lathe and readily turned to size. A light, inexpensive lathe is quite satisfactory for this purpose.

Template forming. In this method the model is built up around a rotating shaft, and is formed by a sheet-metal template that has been cut from 20-gauge galvanized iron and filed to exact size. The first coat of plaster applied to the shaft should be rather stiff, and then thinner coats are added until the proper size has been reached. If this process is correctly carried out, the model will be mirror smooth. The method requires practice, but it has proved to be the most satisfactory way of making models. The photographs of Figs. 19–11 through 19–15 make the steps of this process clear.

This method is not confined to circular pieces; rectangular, hexagonal, and many other shapes can be produced by moving a template over a bed of soft plaster. A simple

Forming a plaster model for a vase (Hedrick-Blessing Studio): Figs. 19-11 through 19-15
Fig. 19-11. The armature and template in position.

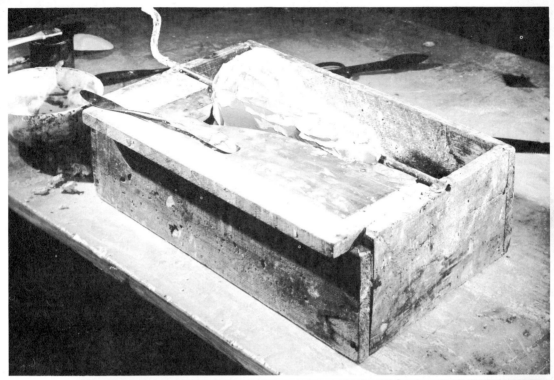

Fig. 19-12. The first coat of plaster.
Fig. 19-13. Applying the second coat.

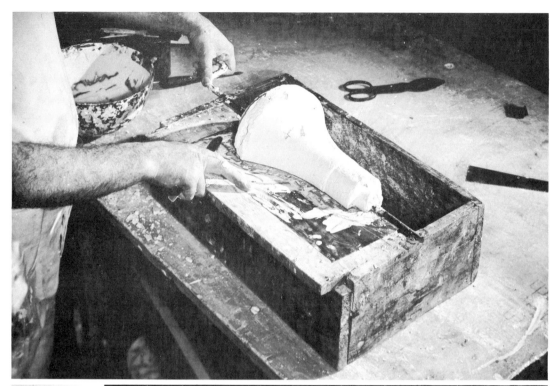

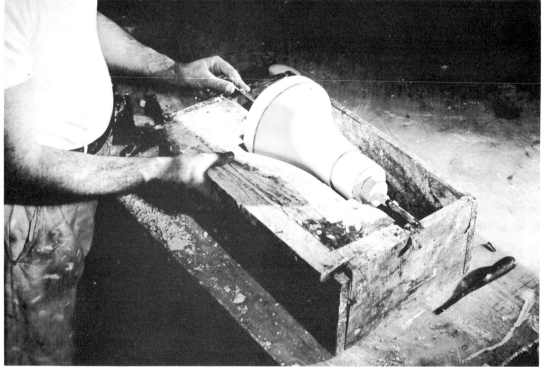

Fig. 19-14. Finishing the form.
Fig. 19-15. Removing the finished model.

machine for this purpose is commercially available, but the studio potter can rig up a slide board that will serve equally well.

IV. MAKING THE MOLD

After the model is made, the mold must be cast around it. The mold may be cast in one piece for a simple article like a bowl, but usually several pieces must be cast.

Three-piece mold. As an example, let us consider the model of a simple vase. We shall make a mold consisting of two sides and a bottom, as shown in Figs. 19–16 through 19–27.

The first step is to locate lines to divide the mold exactly through the axis, for if one half of the mold is even slightly larger than the other, it cannot be removed from the model without chipping. The best method is to use compasses to find the center at each end of the model, as a guide for the lines.

The model is now mounted horizontally on a marble slab or a piece of plate glass, using plasticine or damp clay as an adhesive. The compasses should again be used to level the vase so that the center points marked on the ends are exactly the same height, and a line is scribed on each side of the model by drawing the compass along.

After the dividing lines have been established, division walls must be erected. The simplest method is to cast a sheet of plaster about ¼ inch thick on plate glass. This is cut into templates which roughly fit the model. Any small openings can be filled with plasticine, using the dividing line as a guide. Irregularities in the form of hollows are not important, because if plaster enters them they can be scraped smooth; however, it is impossible to correct humps in the plasticine.

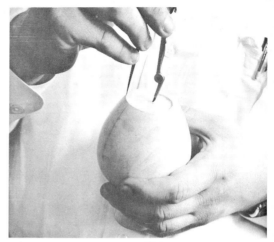

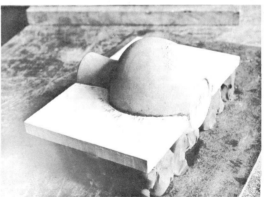

Pouring a mold:

Fig. 19-16. Putting center marks on the end of the model.

Fig. 19-17. Putting on the centerline with compasses.

Fig. 19-18. Plaster templates placed to divide the vase into halves. The space between the templates and the model is filled with plasticine.

Pouring a mold (cont.):

Fig. 19-19. The model boxed in with marble blocks. Both model and templates have been soaped and are ready for pouring.

Fig. 19-20. Pouring the plaster to form the first half of the mold.

Fig. 19-21. The marble slabs removed, showing the half mold.

Fig. 19-22. Scraping the outside of the mold smooth.

Fig. 19-23. Cutting keys (natches) in the first half of the mold.

Fig. 19-24. Beveling the corners to prevent later chipping.

The next step is to place a frame around the entire assembly. Strips of soapstone or marble are useful for this purpose, but blocks of soaped plaster or waterproof ply-wood are satisfactory. Any remaining cracks should be filled, and clay should be run up the outsides of the joints to make them smooth. The entire model, including the dividing walls, should now be well soaped and the excess wiped off.

Plaster should now be carefully poured into this box; splashing should be avoided because of the danger of trapping air and causing bubbles. After the plaster has set, the dividing slabs are removed and the half-mold is pulled from the model and scraped smooth on the outside. Using a spoon or a spatula, notches are cut into the edges that are to be joined with the second half of the mold. The outside corners of the mold are then beveled to a depth of about ⅛ inch with a scraper and file, to prevent chipping.

The model is now replaced in the half-mold in its original position, the frame is re-placed, and the edges of the first half are soaped. The second half of the mold is now poured, removed, and cleaned, and the en-tire mold is reassembled on the model pre-paratory to pouring the bottom. When the bottom has been cast and cleaned, the com-plete mold is assembled. It is necessary to tie the three parts of the mold together until they are completely dry, and grooves are cut to hold the cord for this purpose.

Pouring a mold (cont.):
Fig. 19-25. The model back in the mold, with the mold soaped and the marble slabs replaced, ready for pouring the second half of the mold.
Fig. 19-26. The two halves of the mold assembled with the model and the marble slabs, ready for pour-ing the bottom. Note the keys (natches).
Fig. 19-27. The finished mold assembled. Note the grooves for the tying cords.

Simple relief mold. A relief mold for a tile with a modeled surface is modeled in plasticine or clay. The model is placed on a plate glass or marble slab, a fence is built around it, and a negative is poured in plaster. This negative can be used directly for pressing plastic clay, but it is difficult to clean the plasticine out of the mold completely and it is more convenient to work on the negative plaster cast to smooth out details.

A positive is now made from this negative after soaping. Note that the edges of the tile must be beveled so that it can easily be released from the model, or expansion of the plaster will lock it in tightly. Scrapers can be used on this positive to smooth out the details; it is soaped, and the finished negative mold is made. Professional sculptors often make as many as a dozen positive and negative casts, in order to greatly refine the details.

V. WASTE MOLDS

When it is desired to make a plaster model of a complicated clay or plasticine original piece, a "waste" mold is used (i.e., a mold that is chipped away from the finished cast in small pieces, and so is wasted). As an example of a waste mold, let us consider the figurine in Fig. 19–28.

Making a waste mold. *Dividing the mold.* The first step is to divide the piece into a sufficient number of sections so that the plasticine or clay can be easily cleaned out. In this instance an area in the back was separated, as well as areas along each arm (like trapdoors), as shown in Figs. 19–29 and 19–30. These divisions are made with pieces of copper about 1″ × ½″ × 0.005″, cut from a copper strip with shears. (The copper should be wiped with an oily cloth, so that it will not

Fig. 19-28. A plasticine figure.

stick to the plaster.) The copper pieces are pushed into the plasticine to about half the depth of the copper, to form a fence. It is not necessary to make this "fence" straight; in fact, a degree of waviness is desirable, to give keying action later. The copper strips should be nearly at right angles to the model surface. After the strips are all in place, place balls of plasticine about the size of peas over the joints between the strips. These not only hold the copper pieces together, but are an aid later in trimming the plaster.

Adding the blue coat. In order to distinguish between mold and model at a later stage, the latter is colored with a few drops of bluing. This plaster is applied evenly to the surface of the piece, including the fence, with a soft brush. At first, much of the plaster will run off the vertical surfaces, but as it begins to set it can be built up to about 1/16 inch in thickness. The coat should be kept as even in depth as possible; too thin a coat may peel off with the plasticine, and the blue color will be lost in these spots. Figure 19–31 shows this stage of the process completed.

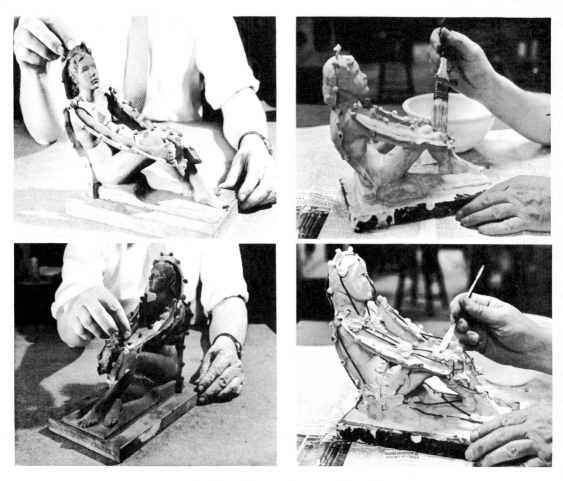

Casting a figure, using a waste mold:

Fig. 19-29. Dividing the figure with copper strips.
Fig. 19-30. Another view of the divided figure. Note the balls of plasticine on the joins of the copper pieces.

Fig. 19-31. Brushing a thin blue coat on the figure.
Fig. 19-32. Adding reinforcing wires to the surface of the blue coat and securing them with plaster.

Wiring the piece. Pieces of soft galvanized wire, about 1/16 inch in diameter, are now bent to fit closely over the coat of blue plaster. A small mix of very thick plaster (white) is applied with a spatula to fix these wires in place, as shown in Fig. 19–32. This small mold on which we are working needs very few wires; a large mold needs to be carefully reinforced in all directions, especially along the division lines. Very large molds need heavy wire, and a life-sized figure requires ½-inch pipe.

Adding the white coat. A small batch of white plaster is now mixed for application to the blued surface. Many mold makers prefer to wash the blue surface with a very thin clay slip to give a parting line between the layers. Professional casters flip the plaster onto the surface with their fingers, but this takes considerable skill. For small pieces, this coat may be applied with a spatula. At first the plaster will run down the sides, but it will hold in place as it starts to stiffen. Here again, even thickness should be main-

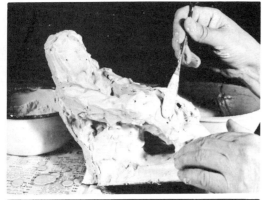

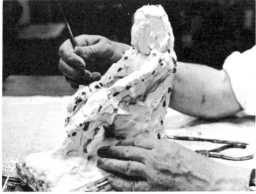

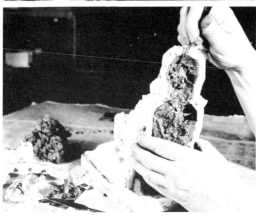

Using a waste mold (cont.):
Fig. 19-33. Adding the white coat over the reinforcing wires.
Fig. 19-34. Trimming the plaster along the coppers as soon as the plaster has started to set. Note the plasticine balls half cut through and the edges of the coppers showing between them.
Fig. 19-35. Opening the mold to remove the plasticine.

tained; about ⅛ to ¼ inch will suffice for small pieces—that is, just enough to completely cover the wires. Molds that are too thick are undesirable, for reasons that we shall discuss later.

Be sure that the plaster is even with the coppers, to give a strong parting edge, as shown in Fig. 19-33. As soon as possible, trim the plaster from the coppers, cutting halfway through the small plasticine balls. The mold is now complete, as shown in Fig. 19-34.

As soon as this white coat is set (this may be determined by its temperature, for it heats up appreciably during the setting period) the coppers are pulled out one by one with pliers. The spaces left by the plasticine balls facilitate this operation. Now the sections of the mold can be separated fairly easily by applying a little force.

Removing the plasticine. After the above operations, it will usually be found that the original model has been torn or distorted, and probably cannot be used again. Now the plasticine must be removed from the mold itself with a modeling tool, as shown in Fig. 19-35. This must be done very carefully, so as not to mar the mold surface. The last bits of plasticine can be sucked out of the crevices by pressing a lump of the same material firmly against the plaster surface and then withdrawing it. Now the inside of the mold must be thoroughly soaped with a brush or a sponge; be sure to cover every bit of the surface thoroughly. As before, the suds are then carefully removed. This operation is shown in Fig. 19-36.

The armature. Unless it is very squat and compact, a figurine needs a wire armature much in the shape of a skeleton; that is, with wire running up the back from the base of the spine into the head, and with wires run-

ning down the arms and legs. These wires
are of galvanized iron about 1/16 inch in diameter, and are held in place with dabs of
stiff plaster, as shown in Fig. 19–37. Care
must be taken to keep the wires from touching the mold surface; otherwise they will
show in the finished piece. Some casters dip
the armature in plaster before inserting it
into the mold.

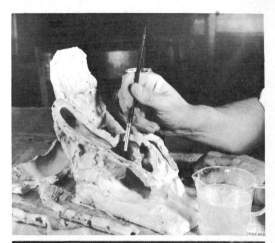

Assembly. Simple molds, like those for
heads, can be held together with a layer of
stiff plaster along the seams and then are tied.
Strips of burlap are cemented along the joints
of large molds, to withstand the pressure of
the liquid plaster when the mold is used.
The author recalls the case of two students
who tried to make a cast of a life-sized figure
with insufficient tying of the mold. After several hundred pounds of plaster had been
poured into the mold, the joints opened up,
and the plaster ran out on the floor, under
the door, down a flight of stairs, and into a
lawyer's office below. Two days of hard work
were required to clean up the mess! A large
figure, of course, should never be cast solid.

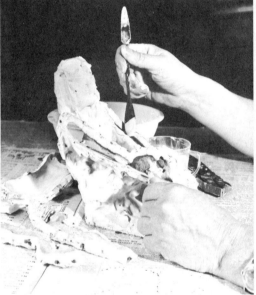

Filling the mold. Because the arms of the
figurine we are making are rather slender,
there is a possibility that the plaster will not
completely fill them when it is poured from
below. It is wise to fill the arms first, squeeze
the trapdoors into place, and then fasten
them, as shown in Fig. 19–38.

Now the mold is inverted and filled with
plaster of normal consistency, as shown in
Fig. 19–39, and is then shaken, rocked, and
bumped to release any trapped air. After a

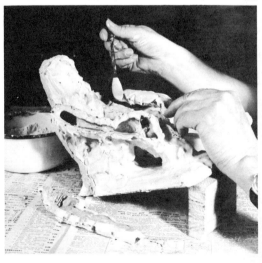

Using a waste mold (cont.):
Fig. 19-36. Soaping the inside of the mold.
Fig. 19-37. Fastening a wire armature in the
arms and legs with dabs of plaster.
Fig. 19-38. Filling the arms with plaster (the
back of the mold has been fastened in place).

 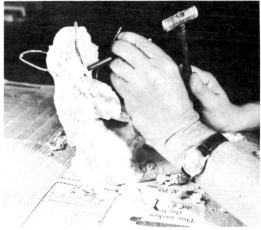

Casting a figure, using a waste mold (cont.):

Fig. 19-39. Pouring plaster into the bottom of the mold (the parting lines have been sealed over with plaster).

Fig. 19-40. Chipping off the mold. The head is shown exposed.

short time the plaster is poured out of the mold, and then returned to it, with more vigorous shaking. This process may be repeated a second time, and this time the plaster should be flush with the base of the mold. After the plaster has started to set, the bottom can be scraped flat.

The removal of air from the mold, as described in the preceding paragraph, is extremely important. Many a student has been dismayed to find that he has cast a head without a chin, or a figure without elbows!

Removing the mold. After the plaster has set, the mold is removed by uncovering the ends of the wire by careful chiseling and then pulling the wires out with pliers. Usually most of the mold will come off with the wires, leaving only the blue coat, and any remaining portions are removed by careful chipping with a dull chisel and a light hammer, as shown in Fig. 19–40. Care must be taken not to chip the piece itself, and special care must be taken in removing the mold around slender parts like the ears, fingers, and nose.

If the piece is inadvertently chipped, it should be patched at once with "killed" plaster, which is made by adding plaster to water without stirring. Killed plaster is very slow in setting and will not become too hard when used in patches, as normal plaster does.

Summary. Although the process of waste molding may seem long and laborious, it can be carried through quite rapidly when experience has been gained. The beginner, as always, should start with simple pieces and progress to the more complicated ones. It is unfortunate that the number of professional mold makers is rapidly dwindling in this country, chiefly because this craft does not appeal to the young people.

VI. PIECE MOLDS

The plaster model made by the waste-mold process can now be used to form a piece mold in which a ceramic form may be cast or pressed. The advantage of a piece mold is that each piece may be drawn away from the model without sticking.

Fig. 19-41. A figurine modeled in plaster by Walker Hancock. Its shellac coating must be removed before it can be used as a model for a mold.

Making the divisions. As a simple example, let us examine the small figurine of the hitchhiker recently modeled by Walker Hancock, and shown in Fig. 19–41. The back is one piece, and forms the master section. The beginner may have difficulty in finding a dividing line, but the simple setup in Fig. 19–42 works very well. The piece is set on a flat surface with a lump of plasticine to hold it in place, and a vertical rod set in a block is moved around it, as shown. Pencil carbon paper clearly marks the equator.

The first piece. After soaping, set the figure face down in plasticine, carefully modeling up to the dividing line. Be sure that the surface nowhere extends below the line, or the mold will catch. So far as possible, the surface of the plasticine should be kept at right angles to that of the figure. When the plasticine has been carefully worked all around the figure, set up a wall about ½ inch high around the outside, as shown in Fig. 19–43.

Now plaster is brushed on all of the exposed parts of the figure (Fig. 19–44), the plaster mold is filled to a thickness of about ½ inch (Fig. 19–45), and the surface is smoothed (Fig. 19–46). After the plaster has

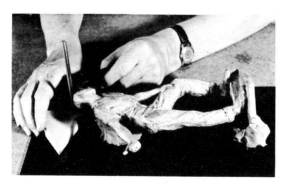

Making a piece mold:

Fig. 19-42. The figurine mounted on its back with plasticine. The centerline is drawn by pressing a vertical rod against a piece of carbon paper.

Fig. 19-43. Plasticine modeled up to the centerline. Note the wall to contain the mold.

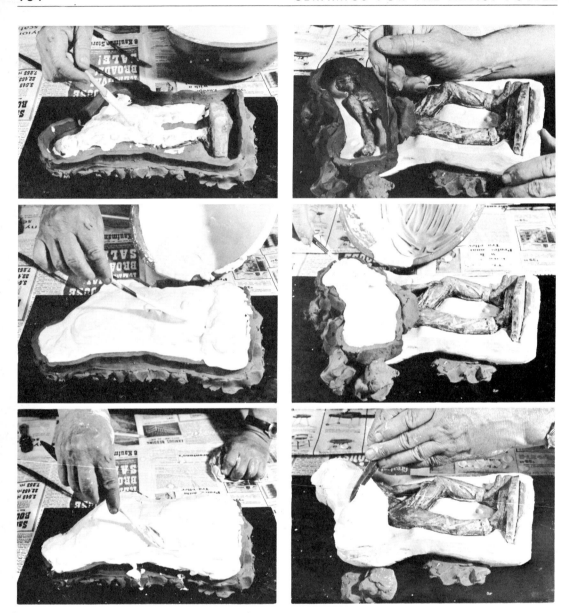

Making a piece mold (cont.):

Fig. 19-44. Brushing plaster onto the model.

Fig. 19-45. Pouring on more plaster to form the first piece of the mold.

Fig. 19-46. Smoothing the mold before it has set.

Fig. 19-47. After the figure has been removed from the first piece of the mold and the edges of the mold have been trimmed and soaped, the mold and figure are reassembled as shown and the wall for the second piece of the mold is put in place.

Fig. 19-48. Pouring the second piece of the mold.

Fig. 19-49. Scraping it smooth.

 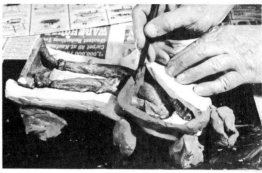

Making a piece mold (cont.):

Fig. 19-50. Putting the trimmed, soaped piece back in place.

Fig. 19-51. Setting up the wall for the third piece of the mold.

set, the figure is turned over, the plasticine is removed, and the first mold piece is taken off. If the soaping has been properly done and the division correctly made, it should be easily removed. The edges of the piece are now scraped smooth, leaving a sharp corner in contact with the figure. Keys are notched in the edges.

The second piece. The first mold piece is replaced on the figure (be sure there are no chips of plaster under it), and the assembly is placed on the table figure side up. The edges of the figure and of the mold are now soaped. A clay wall is fashioned as shown in Fig. 19-47, to outline the second piece. This piece should be as large as it is possible to make it and still have it easily released. Efficient dividing techniques are developed with experience; it does no harm to have more divisions than will later be found necessary.

This second mold piece is now filled with plaster, as shown in Figs. 19-48 and 19-49. After it has set, it is removed (Fig. 19-50) and the edges against the clay wall are scraped smooth. Be careful not to touch the sides that join the first piece.

Additional pieces. The second mold piece is now replaced on the figure, and the clay wall for the third piece is set up as shown in Fig. 19-51. This process is repeated until the figure is completely enclosed. When this has been done, all of the pieces are removed, assembled without the model, and tied together ready for use.

Simplified piece mold. Figure 19-52 shows a four-piece mold for casting the porcelain peacocks of Fig. 19-53.

Piece mold for a head. The simple piece mold shown in Fig. 19-54 was used for the head of Fig. 21-20. The disassembled pieces in Fig. 19-55 show the divisions.

Complicated piece molds. Figure 19-56 shows a mold with some 25 pieces (a portion of the case has been removed for purposes of illustration), and Fig. 19-57 is the same mold with some of the pieces removed. It was necessary to form a case outside the small pieces to hold them in place. This kind of mold is far beyond the capacities of a beginner.

Many sculptured pieces are so complicated that it is impractical to make a piece mold from them in their entirety. The figure modeled by George Demetrius and shown

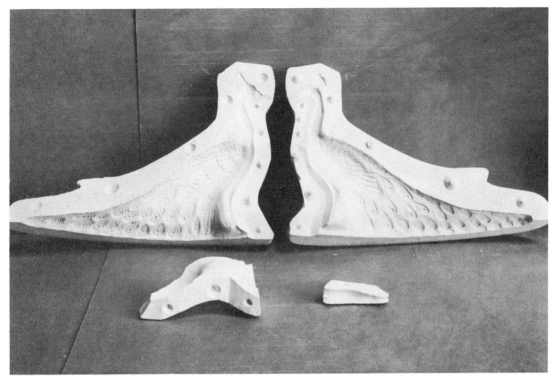

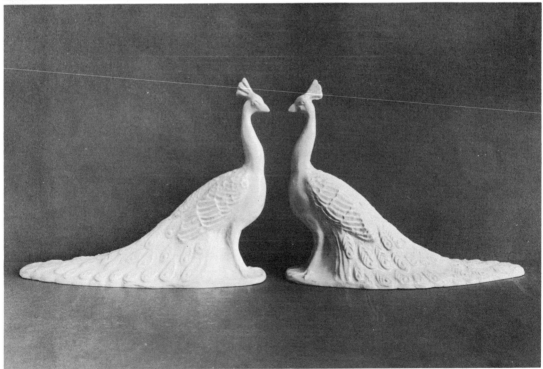

Fig. 19-52. A simple four-piece mold.
Fig. 19-53. A pair of porcelain peacocks made from the mold in Fig. 19-52.

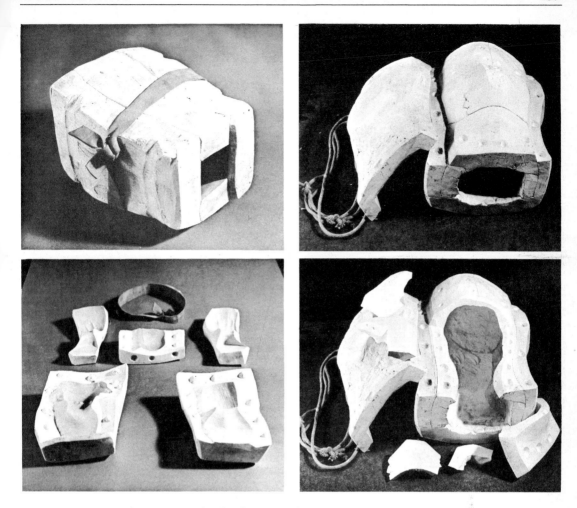

Fig. 19-54. A simple piece mold for a small head.
Fig. 19-55. The mold of Fig. 19-54 disassembled.
Fig. 19-56. A complicated piece mold for a full-size head, with the top of the case removed.
Fig. 19-57. The mold of Fig. 19-56, with several pieces removed.

in Fig. 21–22 is a case in point. In this case, the head, arms, and legs were cut from the plaster model with a fine saw, and separate piece molds were made for each. Some of the Sèvres biscuit groups are cut into 20 or 30 parts, each with its own piece mold.

Precautions. When making piece molds for casting ceramics, care must be taken to remove the top pieces first. It is easy to see that if the bottom pieces are removed first, the weight from above may cause the cast to collapse.

Shellac should never be used on the original plaster model, because this necessitates parting with mutton tallow, which later prevents water entering the mold surface when it is used for ceramic purposes.

VII. REPLACING A MOLD

Plaster molds are good for reproduction of roughly 50 to 100 pieces before a new mold is needed. It takes a long time to make a new mold from the model, but it is comparatively easy to make a mold from each piece of the original mold, from which as many new molds may be made as desired. This process is not described here because the studio potter seldom has use for it.

VIII. REFERENCES

1. BINNS, C. F., *The Potter's Craft*, 3rd ed., D. Van Nostrand Company, Inc., New York, 1948 (Chaps. VI and VII).

2. KENNY, J. B., *Complete Book of Pottery Making*. Greenberg: Publisher, Inc., New York, 1949 (Chaps. 4, 5, and 7).

3. PERKINS, D. W., Turning a Plaster Model, *Ceram. Age* **52**, No. 37, 149 (1948).

4. OFFUTT, J. S. AND C. M. LAMBE, Plasters and Gypsum Cements for the Ceramic Industry, *Bull. Am. Ceram. Soc.* **26**, 29 (1947).

5. YOUNG, M. K., Recent Developments in Plaster Mold Making, *Bull. Am. Ceram. Soc.* **33**, 83 (1954).

CHAPTER 20

Temperature Measurement

I. INTRODUCTION

In any baking process, it is necessary to know the temperature of the oven, and to remove the baked goods at just the right time. The correct degree of heat in the oven is even more important to the ceramist than to the baker, and because it is not always feasible to open the kiln to check on the progress of the firing, some sort of temperature indicator is necessary.

There are three methods of checking the temperature in the kiln: (1) by means of a thermometer, called a pyrometer, which gives a direct reading of the temperature; (2) by use of a fusible mixture, called a pyrometric cone, which softens when a certain degree of heat is attained; and (3) by means of draw trials, which are small samples pulled from the kiln from time to time during the firing.

II. IMPORTANCE OF TEMPERATURE MEASUREMENTS

Bodies. As a ceramic body is fired to higher and higher temperatures, more and more glass is formed, the piece continues to shrink and becomes more dense, and eventually the piece will soften and deform. The range of temperatures between the point where a body is sufficiently hard and the point where it begins to soften and deform is rather extensive for many bodies. On the other hand, bodies that are high in lime, for example, pass quickly from the point of reasonable strength to the melting point. Obviously, this kind of body requires accurate temperature control.

Both the degree of temperature and the length of time a body is fired at a particular temperature are important. The length of time varies inversely with the temperature; that is, the longer the time of firing, the lower the temperature, and conversely. Table 20–1 gives data on a porcelain body fired to the same degree of maturity at different temperature levels.

Glazes. Like bodies, glazes have the best properties when they have been fired just to a particular point. If underfired, they lack gloss and evenness of surface, while overfiring will cause the glaze to flow off the piece.

Here again, the firing ranges vary considerably with the kind of glaze. Fritted glazes, for example, have a wide temperature range, while close temperature control is necessary for many other types.

Because glazes require a certain interval of time at maximum temperature to free themselves of bubbles, time becomes a very important factor in the firing of glazes.

III. TEMPERATURE SCALES

The centigrade scale. Throughout this book, temperatures are given in degrees centigrade, where $0°$ is the melting point of ice and $100°$ is the boiling point of water (see Fig. 20–1).

TABLE 20-1

INFLUENCE OF TIME ON MATURING PORCELAIN

Time at maximum temperature	Maximum temperature to just reach zero porosity
10 minutes	1225°C
100 minutes (1.7 hr)	1200°C
1000 minutes (17 hr)	1175°C
10,000 minutes (167 hr)	1150°C

TABLE 20-2

MELTING POINTS

Substance	Melting point, °C
Ice	0
Tin	232
Aluminum	660
Copper	1083
Nickel	1455
Platinum	1774

Determination of the temperature scale.
Temperature scales are determined by fundamental laws of physics, and are based on certain fixed points. Some of these are listed in Table 20–2.

IV. PYROMETERS

The upper limit of a mercury-in-glass thermometer is 300°–400°C; beyond this point the mercury boils and the glass softens. An instrument called a pyrometer is used for measuring extremely high temperatures. There are many kinds of pyrometers, but here we shall concern ourselves only with the thermocouple.

Thermocouples. A thermocouple consists of two dissimilar wires welded together at one end. The welded end, called the "hot junction," is placed in the kiln, and the free ends are connected to an instrument from which the temperature can be determined. A thermocouple composed of two chromium alloys is shown in Fig. 20–2. These wires may be uncovered or may be enclosed in a stainless-steel tube, which has a use limit of 1250°C.

For extremely high temperatures, wires of platinum alloys inside a porcelain tube may be used (Fig. 20–3). These couples are more

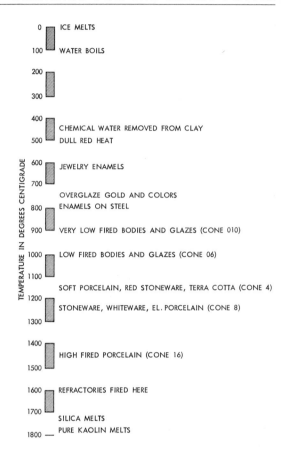

Fig. 20-1. The centigrade temperature scale, with points of interest in ceramics work.

expensive, and are unnecessary except for temperatures beyond 1250°C.

When the hot junction of the thermocouple is heated, it acts as a battery, and produces a small voltage which increases with the temperature. Each kind of thermocouple has its own particular temperature-voltage characteristics. These are listed in Tables A15 through A20 in the author's *Elements of Ceramics.*

Measuring instruments. The usual measurement indicator for thermocouples is a delicate instrument called a millivoltmeter (Fig. 20–4). Instead of a millivolt scale (1 millivolt = 1/1000 volt), this instrument

may be equipped with a scale that is calibrated directly in degrees of temperature. Many kinds of millivoltmeters are available; a relatively inexpensive one is sufficient for the potter.

It is also possible to obtain instruments that will record the temperature on a chart, but these cost several hundreds of dollars and are necessary only for large-scale production.

How to use a pyrometer. The best instruments in the world will not give satisfactory results unless they are properly used, and it is important to use your pyrometer correctly.

The hot junction of the pyrometer should be extended into the kiln far enough so that it will not be cooled by conduction of heat out through the wires and the protecting tube. For the average thermocouple, the junction should be 6 to 8 inches inside the

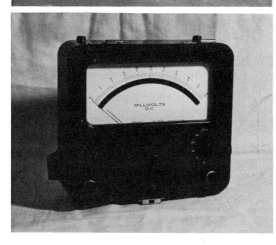

Fig. 20-2. A base-metal thermocouple removed from its casing.

Fig. 20-3. A platinum thermocouple with a porcelain protection tube; its cold junction is in a thermos bottle of ice.

Fig. 20-4. A precise millivoltmeter for temperature measurement.

kiln wall. A thermocouple measures the temperature *difference* between the hot junction and the connection to the leads of the measuring instrument (called the cold junction), and therefore a high room temperature will make the kiln seem cooler than it actually is. For precise work, the cold junction is kept in a thermos flask of ice and water. (Some pyrometers compensate automatically for room temperature.)

V. PYROMETRIC CONES

The simplest and least expensive method of determining firing temperatures is by the use of pyrometric cones. These are small pyramids of ceramic material made in a graded series, so that at certain temperatures and times they soften and bend. It should be emphasized that these cones do not measure *temperature* as such, but rather measure temperature and time combined, which, after all, is what the potter needs to know.

These cones are obtainable commercially in various series, each suited to a particular firing condition (Table 20–3). The temperatures listed in the table correspond to a temperature rise of 20C° per hour.

TABLE 20–3
TEMPERATURE EQUIVALENTS OF CONES[1]

Cone No.	°C	°F	Cone No.	°C	°F
022	585	1085	1	1125	2057
021	595	1103	2	1135	2075
020	625	1157	3	1145	2093
019	630	1166	4	1165	2129
018	670	1238	5	1180	2129
017	720	1328	6	1190	2174
016	735	1355	7	1210	2210
015	770	1418	8	1225	2237
014	795	1463	9	1250	2282
013	825	1517	10	1260	2300
012	840	1544	11	1285	2345
011	875	1607	12	1310	2390
010	890	1634	13	1350	2462
09	930	1706	14	1390	2534
08	945	1733	15	1410	2570
07	975	1787	16	1450	2642
06	1005	1841	17	1465	2669
05	1030	1886	18	1485	2705
04	1050	1922	19	1515	2759
03	1080	1976	20	1520	2768
02	1095	2003	23	1580	2876
01	1110	2030	26	1595	2903

[1]Orton cones heated at rate of 20°C per hour. A recent check by the Bureau of Standards shows some slight deviation from these values.

How to use the cones. Figure 20–5 shows how the cones should be set at an angle into the plaque furnished by the manufacturer (the lower portion of the figure). The cone that is to act as the "control" for the particular piece to be fired is placed in the third socket, two lower cones are placed to the left of the control cone, and one higher cone is placed to its right. For example, Cone 7 is the control for parian ware; therefore Cone 7 is placed in the third position, Cones 5 and 6 are placed to its left, and Cone 8 is placed to its right. As the lower cones bend, they give warning that the peak of the firing is being approached; the higher cone serves as a check against overfiring. The upper part of Fig. 20–5 shows a plaque properly fired to Cone 7; the tip of Cone 7 has bent so that it just touches the plaque.

Advantages and limitations of cones. Pyrometric cones have the advantage of being relatively foolproof, and they enable the potter to repeat a successful firing again and again. They are also inexpensive and easy to read.

Cones are unsatisfactory for special firing schedules, such as those required for crystalline glazes, and they are not reliable indicators in a strongly reducing atmosphere. Pyrometers are required in these instances.

VI. DRAW TRIALS

Method. In Europe particularly, draw trials are used as a gauge of firing temperature. A number of small pieces of ware, identical both as to body and glaze with the pieces to be fired, are placed among the pieces in the kiln in line with a sight hole. These small pieces have holes in them, so that they can be withdrawn from the oven with an iron hook. When it is estimated that

Fig. 20-5. A set of cones after and before firing. Cones 5, 6, 7, and 8 have been used, and Cone 7 is just down.

the kiln is approaching the correct heat, a trial is drawn and examined. This is repeated until the piece drawn is of the proper maturity, when the kiln can be shut off with the assurance that the ware is correctly fired. Specimens like those in Fig. 20–6 are quite useful for this purpose.

Advantages of draw trials. Draw trials tell the potter the exact condition of the ware in the kiln at any time and, of course, the method is inexpensive and simple. This process is especially useful when the exact firing range is unknown, and it would seem that artist potters should make more use of it than they now do.

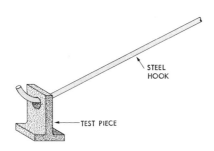

STEEL HOOK

TEST PIECE

Fig. 20-6. Specimen for draw trial.

VII. TEMPERATURE CONTROLS

When a great deal of firing is to be done, it is good economy to equip the kiln with a device that not only indicates the temperature, but controls it. We are all familiar with the devices on electric ranges that do just that. Some bring the temperature to the desired point and keep the oven at that temperature; others bring the oven to the correct heat, hold it at that temperature for a specified period of time, and then automatically shut off.

Some of these controls are expensive, and are used for the most part only in large potteries. However, a simple cut-off switch that is set like a mousetrap and uses a pyrometric cone as bait is inexpensive and well worth while.

VIII. KILN ATMOSPHERE

In an electric kiln, the atmosphere is close to normal, that is, 23.2% oxygen and 76.8% nitrogen by weight. A gas-fired or oil-fired kiln may have an atmosphere containing 88% nitrogen, 6% carbon dioxide, and 6% oxygen by weight. Both of these conditions are known as "oxidizing fires."

It is sometimes desirable to maintain a "reducing" atmosphere in the kiln (for example, when hard porcelains or copper red glazes are being fired). This atmosphere is deficient in oxygen, and the atmosphere contains something like 88% nitrogen, 10% carbon dioxide, and 2% carbon monoxide. This condition is attained in combustion kilns by reducing the air supply, which gives a smoky flame. In electric kilns a reducing atmosphere may be obtained by introducing a small amount of gas, coke, or naphthalene into the interior of the firing chamber.

Instruments which give an exact analysis of the gases in a kiln are obtainable, but these are expensive and require considerable experience to use. It is easy to learn to judge the conditions in other than electric kilns by the kind of flame coming from the stack. A pale yellow flame indicates oxidizing conditions; a white, blue, or smoky flame indicates reducing conditions. Old-timers often hold a splinter of dry wood in the kiln exhaust, and if it burns (inside the flue), it is an indication that there is free oxygen present. If it just chars, the atmosphere is reducing.

IX. REFERENCES

1. FAIRCHILD, C. O., AND M. F. PETERS, Characteristics of Pyrometric Cones, *J. Am. Ceram. Soc.* **9**, 701 (1926).

2. FOOTE, P. D., C. O. FAIRCHILD, AND T. R. HARRISON, Pyrometric Practice. *Nat. Bur. of Standards, Tech. Paper No.* 170, 1921.

3. WOOD, W. P., AND J. M. CORK, *Pyrometry,* 2nd ed., University of Michigan Press, Ann Arbor, 1941.

CHAPTER 21

Ceramic Sculpture

I. INTRODUCTION

Because the author has been asked innumerable questions by sculptors who wish to use ceramic media, and because many ceramic sculptors would like to be informed about the availability of adequate tools, we shall devote this entire chapter to the subject of ceramic sculpture.

As a medium, clay has much to recommend it to the sculptor, and it is only lack of knowledge that has handicapped its use. One outstanding advantage of sculpturing in clay is that the finished piece may be of the same material as the model. To model in clay and then reproduce in bronze or marble is inherently unsound: either the form of the model must be incompatible with the plastic clay to achieve the desired result in the final medium (e.g., slender parts in bronze), or the final result will give the impression of a soft and pliable material transformed into something quite different and frozen into shape.

Ceramic materials allow a very wide range of surface textures and colors and, perhaps just as important, they permit a translucency approaching that of marble and human flesh.

In this country, the professional sculptor has been confronted with a handicap in using ceramic materials, for it is difficult to find a source for the molding and firing. Some of the companies specializing in terra cotta have done excellent work with large pieces, but there is no equivalent place to which the sculptor may turn for his small pieces. We hope that this chapter will encourage the sculptor to learn how to carry out the ceramic processes himself.

It is easy and natural for children to form small figures and animals from clay. (See the tiger in Fig. 21-1, modeled by a five-year-old.) Adults, too, often have the urge to model, and even without formal training they sometimes make interesting pieces. However, if a potter is to seriously consider sculpturing, he must subject himself to the rigid discipline of learning to draw. Ceramic shows are filled with piddling sculpture submitted by "sculptors" who thought it unnecessary to learn the fundamentals of the art.

It would be unprofitable to the reader to attempt to set down here the principles and techniques of producing fine sculpture; again, there is no substitute for working with a good teacher. One thing, however, should be borne in mind: the composition should be compact. Rodin once remarked that good sculpture can be rolled down hill without breaking off external parts. Remember, too, that sculpture should have tranquillity and dignity; it is not a medium for caricature.

II. DIRECT MODELING

The simplest way to make a piece of ceramic sculpture is by modeling directly in the plastic body, drying, and firing. However, reproduction is difficult, and no molds are

Fig. 21-1. A tiger directly modeled by a five-year-old girl.

available to remake a piece if something happens in the firing. On the other hand, this is an ideal way of preserving the freedom and spontaneity of a sketch.

Tools. Modeling tools are commercially available, but many sculptors prefer to make their own. A hard, close-grained wood like sugar maple, boxwood, or holly is best for this purpose. Of the many kinds of modeling tools, the selection shown in Fig. 21-2 is enough for a beginner.

Calipers and dividers are very necessary, and except in the very small sizes, should be made of wood (for lightness). Proportional dividers are extremely helpful for enlarging a piece or for reducing its dimensions, but they must be precision made. Some of these tools are shown in Fig. 21-3.

Modeling small, solid objects. These are modeled directly in the clay, with perhaps a little hollowing out at the base. Grog bodies may be fashioned 2 or 3 inches thick, but fine-grained bodies should be limited to 1-inch thickness.

Hollow pieces. Pieces such as full-sized heads may be directly modeled on a simple armature, and later hollowed out. Figure 21-4 shows how a head has been cut with a wire, and then (Fig. 21-5) carefully hollowed out, leaving a wall thickness of about ¾ inch. At the same time the armature is withdrawn. The two sections are then painted with slip and rejoined; the joint can be made practically invisible. It is important, of course, that the two sections be equally dry when they are joined, so that unequal shrinkage will not

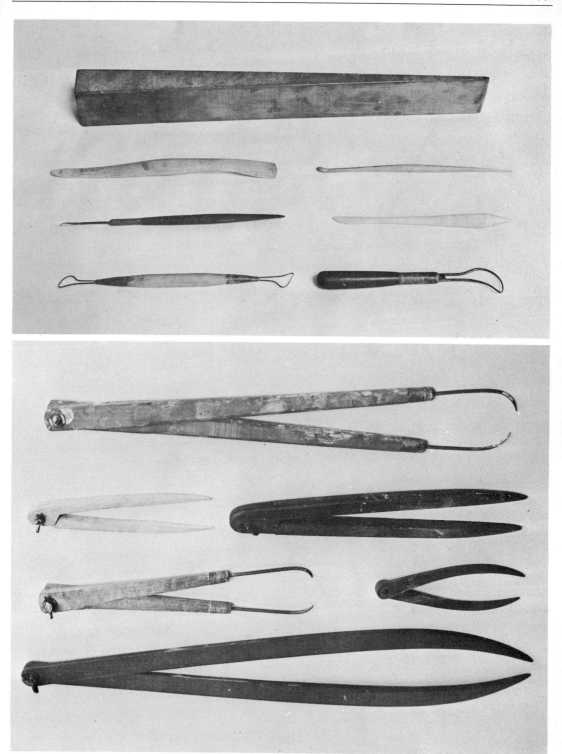

Fig. 21-2. Modeling tools.

Fig. 21-3. Calipers and dividers.

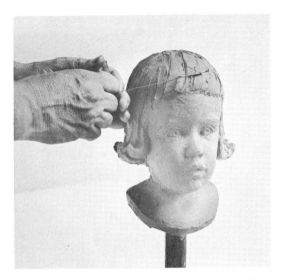

Fig. 21-4. Using a wire to cut a cap off the top of a head.

Fig. 21-5. Hollowing out the head.

later cause cracks. (To avoid distortion of large heads, it is advisable to pour a plaster cap over the crown before cutting.)

The process of solid modeling and later hollowing gives good results, but it is time-consuming. Also, because the piece will shrink when it is fired and dried, it is necessary to make the original model oversize if a life-sized piece is desired. Failure to take shrinkage into account is responsible for the unpleasing "monkey-sized" heads that we so often see in ceramic pieces.

Pointing from a model. The process of making the final piece of sculpture from the dimensions of the model by direct measurement is called *pointing*. Many kinds of pointing machines are commercially available, but the simple machine shown in Fig. 21–6 can be made from parts to be found in any studio. The process of pointing is as follows:

Starting at the base of the piece, a hollow shell is made with coils or by pinching the clay. The outer surface is controlled by the pointing and the inner surface is formed a

uniform distance inside it. For small pieces, a wall ¼ inch thick is satisfactory; the wall must be correspondingly heavy for large pieces. The whole piece cannot be pointed up at one time; the base must be allowed to dry somewhat before the height is built up, to avoid slumping.

Fig. 21-6. A simple pointing machine.

Pointing has much to recommend it. Pieces of any size or complexity can be quickly and precisely made, and the finish modeling can be carried out while the clay is still plastic. By proper setting, the pointing machine also permits enlargement of the piece to compensate for drying and firing shrinkage, and this is a real advantage.

Modeling over a temporary core. A core for this kind of modeling can be made in many ways. A simple core can be made from damp crumpled paper, tied with string into the desired shape. When the piece is finished, this kind of core can be removed by pulling it out piece or by piece, or it can be burned out. A rubber balloon filled with dry sand and evacuated with a sink aspirator makes a satisfactory core. It can be squeezed into any shape, and after the model is finished the sand is allowed to run out the neck of the balloon (Fig. 21–7).

It takes considerable experience to make a core large enough to give a reasonably thin wall of clay and yet not have it show at the surface at some stage of the modeling. The core also makes any major change in pose or arrangement impossible.

It would be helpful if wire armatures could be left in the arms and legs of a model. Wires

Fig. 21-8. Pâte-sur-pâte relief decoration.

made of aluminum are easily removed during firing because they melt, but the difficulty there is that they prevent normal drying shrinkage. Coiled wire would solve the shrinkage problem, but would not give sufficient support.

Pâte sur pâte. Literally translated, this means "paste on paste," and this method is so called because it consists of building up a series of layers of white slip to form a low relief. It is used particularly for making porcelain reliefs, and the layers are formed on a flat, colored background of freshly cast body. A skilled artist is able to produce very beautiful pieces by this method, because the translucency of the white layers permits the background to show through in varying degrees, dependent upon the thickness of the layers. Not many artists are successful with this work, primarily because it is time-consuming and requires much patience. The cross section of Fig. 21–8 illustrates the procedure.

III. CASTING

The casting process has been described in Chapter 4; it is particularly adapted to sculptured pieces.

Reliefs. A relief is the simplest kind of cast piece, but even here care is required to give good results. For example, casting in an open mold is seldom successful, because the relatively thin piece is apt to warp as it dries (the reasons are given in Chapter 22). Casting into a double-surfaced mold, as shown in Fig. 21–9, avoids this difficulty.

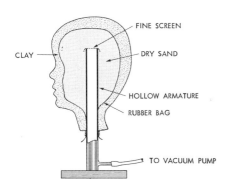

Fig. 21-7. A sand-filled rubber balloon as a core for modeling a head.

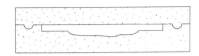

Fig. 21-9. Cross section of a two-surfaced mold for casting a relief.

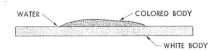

Fig. 21-10. Wedgwood method of making colored reliefs.

Reliefs of the cameo type, with white modeling against a colored background or vice versa, can be made in several ways.

(1) The most common method is that used by Wedgwood, where the modeled piece is formed separately by casting or pressing, and is then attached to a smooth, colored background while still damp (Fig. 21–10). Water is used to attach the pieces to the background, and this is sufficient if the pieces are gently pressed together (slip cannot be used because it would smear the background colors). Great skill is required to make such delicate pieces as those shown in Figs. 29–6 and 29–7.

(2) A method used by the early potters of Bennington, Vermont, consists in painting white slip into the modeled portions of the plaster mold and then casting a colored slip over it. Variations in the thickness of the white slip permit the background color to show through in different degrees after translucency has been developed in the firing. The effect is the same as that obtained by the pâte-sur-pâte method. The steps of this process are shown in Figs. 21–11 through 21–13, and Fig. 21–14 is a photograph of a finished piece.

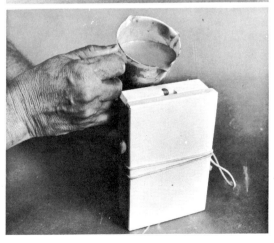

Casting a relief plaque:
Fig. 21-11. Mold with tree-frog design.
Fig. 21-12. Painting the plaster mold surface with green slip.
Fig. 21-13. Pouring white slip into the mold.

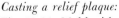

Fig. 21-14. The finished tree-frog tile, green on white.

job easier. An overhead north light is best for this work, with provisions for side lighting when it is needed, as shown in Fig. 21–15. The source of light should be high enough so that substantially the same light falls on the model and on the work. A good modeling stand is of tremendous help. The one pictured in Fig. 21–16 was developed by the author, and has proved to be more satisfactory than anything commercially available. The hydraulic automobile jack raises and lowers the heaviest piece smoothly and with little effort. The large, rubber-tired casters permit moving the stand easily and quickly to obtain varied lighting effects. Most useful of all is the tilting head, which makes it easy to look down on the work without climbing a ladder (Fig. 21–17). (This feature is also useful for making reliefs.)

Heads in the round. *The model.* The model for a head to be cast is usually made of plasticine. Again we must remember that if a slip with high shrinkage is to be used the head must be larger than life size to start with, to avoid the "monkey-size" result we have previously mentioned.

We cannot pretend here to teach the art of sculpturing, but we shall mention some of the physical requirements that will make the

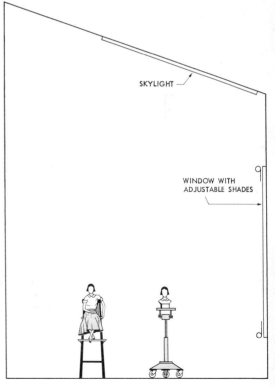

SKYLIGHT

WINDOW WITH ADJUSTABLE SHADES

Fig. 21-15. Well-lit sculpture studio.

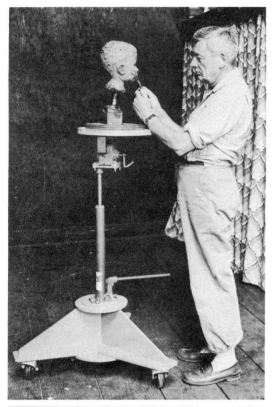

Fig. 21-16. The author modeling a head on a modeling stand with a hydraulic jack for raising and lowering, large casters, and a tilting head.

Fig. 21-17. The tilting head of the modeling stand in Fig. 21-16.

Fig. 21-18. An armature for heads. Note the ball-and-socket joint and the attachments for a centering caliper.

Fig. 21-19. The same armature with a balsa skull slipped in place, ready for the addition of clay.

The improved type of armature shown in Figs. 21–18 and 21–19 is of sturdy construction, with a vertical pipe corresponding to the backbone. The ball-and-socket joint at the top of the pipe permits tilting of the head, and it is arranged so that the center of motion is at a point corresponding to the base of the skull, where the human head naturally turns. This important feature assures that any position of the head will be a natural one.

Casting the head. The first step is to make a piece mold, as described in Chapter 19. For the casting itself, it is best to use the underflow technique discussed in Chapter 4. Knowing how long to let the cast pieces dry before removing the molds is largely a matter of experience. If they dry too long, cracking will result, and if they are not sufficiently dry, the piece will slump out of shape. As we mentioned earlier, the first few casts in a new mold are apt to pick up some plaster, and it is well to discard these.

After the cast piece has stood for a few hours in an enclosed space, the parting lines may be removed from it by scraping, and additional modeling may be done. However, parts of the surface that have been reworked will have a texture different from the rest of the piece after firing; therefore the entire surface should be brushed with a wet sponge at this stage, or should be treated with fine sandpaper after it is dry.

Although there is some interest in polychrome sculpture, little has been done in this field in modern times. There seems to be no doubt that early sculptors used some color even in their classic marble pieces— primarily for the eyes, lips, hair, and eyebrows. Ceramics offers an excellent opportunity for the sculptor to develop polychrome methods, for colored slips are easily painted on the cast surface. Care must be taken to

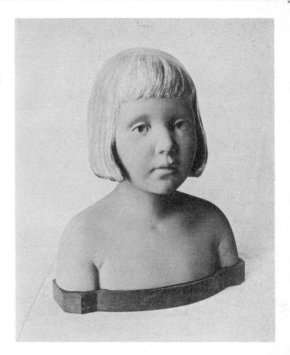

Fig. 21-20. Portrait head cast in a soft red body. The hair is waxed.

avoid too great a contrast in shading, or the modeling will be repressed.

After the cast head is dried in the usual way, it is set on an unfired plate to permit even shrinkage. If the body is soft, the fired piece may be molded in much the same way as marble. The small head in Fig. 21–20 shows the excellent surface that can be obtained in this way, and it is interesting to note the contrast given to the hair by the use of beeswax applied to the finished piece by brushing on a solution in benzol.

Soft bodies offer the advantage of good workability, and they are also low in shrinkage. However, they tend to chip easily and they readily collect dust that is almost impossible to remove. A glaze will solve the cleaning problem, but it must be applied carefully if the delicate modeling is to remain undamaged. A wax coating on the biscuit works well, but the color is apt to change.

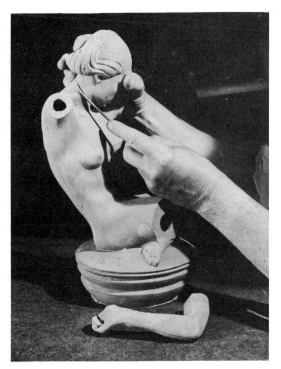

Fig. 21-21. Assembling a figurine from separately cast parts. The head is being attached to the torso with slip; the arms and legs will be attached in the same way.

Figurines. Figurines are usually cast in a porcelain body. Quite complicated pieces can be modeled to be made in a two-piece mold, but it is better to use as many pieces as required than to arbitrarily limit the number to two. It is desirable to dissect the model into as many parts as are required, make a piece mold of each part, and then assemble the cast parts into a whole. Remember that for successful joining, the moisture content of the various parts must be the same; it is advisable to store all the parts together in a damp box for several days before they are joined. The surfaces to be joined are scored with a fine-toothed tool, painted with slip, and immediately pressed together (see Fig. 21–21). The finished figurine is shown in Fig. 21–22.

It is difficult to remove the seams in a cast porcelain body. Because of the orientation of the particles of the clay, the seams reappear after firing, no matter how carefully they have been smoothed out beforehand. There are several ways of solving this problem: (1) the clay can be cut from the surface in a narrow groove along the seam, immediately after joining, and plastic clay can be forced into the groove (Fig. 21–23); (2) the body can be lightly hammered around the joint to break up the orientation of the clay particles, and then the joint can be smoothed out; (3) the piece can be fired just below the maturing temperature, removed from the kiln for grinding the surface smooth, and then refired.

When figurines are set, all of the extended parts must be carefully supported, as explained in Chapter 10. Skill in setting is gained with experience.

Figures 21–24 and 21–25 are photographs of excellent porcelain sculptures.

IV. PRESSING

This process, briefly described in Chapter 2, is used for making both the fine biscuit porcelain figurines of Sèvres and full-sized terra-cotta figures. Coarse grog bodies are particularly suited for this method.

The surface texture of modeled surfaces varies greatly with the technique employed, especially when grogged bodies are used. A slicking action of the tool forces the grog below the surface and gives a smooth finish. Scraping or brushing brings up the grog to give a rough texture. Whatever surface is used must be deliberate; indecision results in an unpleasing spotty texture.

V. SUMMARY

There are many processes and materials that are suited to ceramic sculpture, and

Fig. 21-22. The porcelain figurine of Fig. 21-21
(modeled by George Demetrius) after assembly and
firing.

selection of the best one for a particular
purpose requires considerable experience.
All of the requirements must be kept in mind
when selection is made: the body, the glaze,
and the desired color—and then it is wise to
make a test tile before combining the ingredients for the final work.

(a)　　　　　(b)　　　　　(c)　　　　　(d)

Fig. 21-23. Elimination of the parting line in a joint,
step by step.

Fig. 21-24. Beautifully modeled porcelain eagle, poised as though ready to spring into the air. Piece designed by Dahl-Jensen, made by Bing and Gröndahl of Copenhagen. (Courtesy of The Metropolitan Museum of Art, New York.)

VI. REFERENCES

1. ANON., Relief Modeling, *Ceram. Age* **52**, No. 3, 151 (1948).

2. BOGATAY, P., Ceramic Sculpture, *Bull. Am. Ceram. Soc.* **22**, 66 (1943).

3. ECKHARDT, E., A Way with Animals, *Ceramic Monthly* **2**, No. 6, 10 (1954).

4. GREGORY, W., Ceramic Sculpture, *Design* **43**, No. 4, 12 (1941).

5. KENNY, J. B., *Ceramic Sculpture*, Greenberg: Publisher, Inc., New York, 1953.

6. HUGHES, G. B., English Statuary Parian Ware, *Country Life* **108**, 1986 (1950).

7. MARTZ, K., Decorate Clay with Clay, *Ceramic Monthly* **1**, 9, 17 (1953); **1**, 10, 11 (1953); **1**, 12, 14 (1953).

8. RANDALL, RUTH, *Ceramic Sculpture*, Watson-Guptill Pub., New York, 1948.

9. RICKERT, A., *Das Bilden in Ton*, R. Maier, Rowensburg, 1952.

10. RUSCOE, W., Ceramic Sculpture, *Pottery Gaz.* **67**, 702 (1942).

11. SLOBODKIN, L., *Sculpture*, World Publishing Company, Cleveland, 1949.

12. TOFT, A., *Modeling and Sculpture*, Seeley, Service and Company, Ltd., London, 1921.

13. WINTER, T. F., The Art of Ceramic Sculpture, *Ceramic Age* **63**, No. 1, 42 (1954).

Fig. 21-25. Modern Percheron stallion by Edward Marshall Boehm. (Courtesy of The Metropolitan Museum of Art, New York.)

CHAPTER 22

Control of Shrinkage, Warpage, and Cracking

I. INTRODUCTION

The reduction in size which invariably accompanies the drying and firing of a piece of pottery introduces problems which are often most bothersome to the potter. In this chapter we shall discuss the reasons for this shrinkage, as well as means for its control.

From the standpoint of the finished size of the piece, high shrinkage is a serious problem for the industrial potter and for the sculptor, who must produce finished pieces to a predetermined size. The artist potter is seldom concerned with this particular result of shrinkage, but shrinkage introduces other problems that must be dealt with.

For example, warping is a serious problem, particularly in thin-walled pieces, and this is true even in commercial pottery making. Recently the manager of a large commercial pottery reported that an epidemic of warping in the manufacture of cups was causing rejection of forty out of every one hundred pieces.

Cracking due to shrinkage is a more serious problem for the beginner than for the experienced potter, for it is comparatively easy to control this failure when the causes are known.

II. NATURE OF PLASTIC MASSES

Why a clay-water mixture is plastic. A plastic lump of moist clay has the unique property that it may be deformed under moderate pressure to take on a new shape without cracking, and the new shape will remain after the pressure is removed. The reasons for this plasticity were unknown for a long time, but modern research has given us a partial answer.

Let us refer back to Figs. 15–1 and 15–2, where the highly magnified photographs show that clay is composed of small, thin plates, with two flat surfaces. If the magnification could be made as great as a million to one, each plate would closely resemble the bread board that used to be in every kitchen. When water is added to the clay, it wets the surfaces of these plates and forms thin films between them. These water films serve two purposes: (1) they lubricate the surfaces so that the plates can readily slide over each other when the clay is deformed, and (2) they hold the particles together.

If greatly enlarged, two plates of plastic clay would look something like the illustration of Fig. 22–1. The plates are aligned with thin water films between them, and there is also a water film on the surface that acts very much like a thin, stretched rubber membrane holding the plates firmly together. When light forces are applied no change results, because this surface film is quite rigid, but appreciable force will cause the plates to slide over one another to form a new shape. If a great deal of force is applied, deformation will cause the outer film to rupture, and the plates will be moved out of contact with each other.

Plastic properties vary greatly with different clays. Fine-grained clays, with many particles and consequently many water films, are more plastic than coarser-grained clays. One may well ask, "Why are not finely ground flint and feldspar plastic?" The answer is clear if Fig. 22–2 is studied. This greatly magnified cross section of two very fine quartz particles coated with a film of water shows that because the surfaces are not flat, the particles cannot glide over each other, and because the film is not continuous, they are not tightly bound together.

Effects of addition of nonplastics to clay.

Very few clays are pure in the first place, and nonplastics like flint and feldspar are sometimes purposely added to them. Because these nonplastics are not as fine-grained as clay and do not have flat surfaces, they reduce the plasticity of the mixture, and for this reason they are usually limited to 50% of the body. However, these nonplastics offer definite advantages, among them a decrease in shrinkage.

Influence of particle alignment.

When clay is formed, by no matter what process, the motion inside the mass rotates the tiny plates of the clay, and also the plates of the

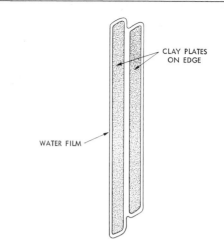

Fig. 22-1. Two clay plates separated by a water film.

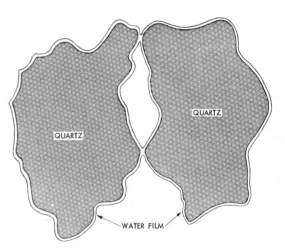

Fig. 22-2. Two fine quartz particles with their water films.

nonplastic bodies that are present, so that they more or less line up in one direction, very much like the stems of grass in a bale of hay. We shall discuss later the profound effect that this alignment has on the drying and firing properties of the body.

III. WHAT HAPPENS WHEN CLAY DRIES

Pottery must be dried *slowly* to prevent warping and cracking, and *thoroughly* to prevent explosions in the biscuit fire. The potter needs to understand the mechanism of drying, and the causes of warping and shrinking. These are discussed in this section.

Removal of water. Because drying starts at the surface of the ware, it is obvious that the water in the interior must flow to the surface to be evaporated. The force that causes this flow is the moisture gradient, or the difference in the water content inside the clay and on the surface. In rapid drying, the water is removed from the surface quickly, the moisture gradient is large, and consequently the water on the inside tends to move rapidly toward the surface. Figure 22–3 shows the difference in slabs of clay that have been dried quickly in one case and slowly in the other.

The first water removed in drying is that between the clay plates that originally looked like those shown in Fig. 22–4 (a). As the drying proceeds the plates draw closer together, and the whole mass shrinks until all of the films have disappeared, the plates touch each other, and little further shrinkage can take place. The clay is now in the "leather-hard" condition. Nevertheless, about half of the original amount of water still remains in the clay in the irregular spaces between the angles of the grains, as shown in part (b) of the figure. This water (often called pore water) now proceeds to disappear, but the drying is slowed considerably because the capillary channels are interrupted and it is more difficult for the water to reach the surface. The final stages of drying are internal, rather than from the surface, and eventually all of the water is gone, as shown in part (d) of the figure.

The rate at which drying takes place during the first, or shrinkage, period depends on three factors: (1) the temperature of the surrounding air, (2) the moisture content of the

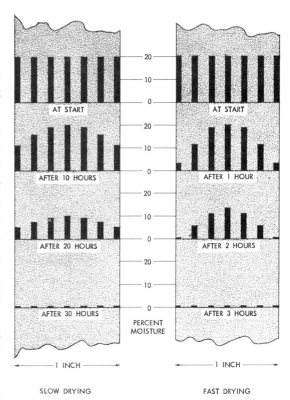

Fig. 22-3. Comparison of moisture distributions throughout a one-inch slab of clay: left, dried slowly; right, dried rapidly.

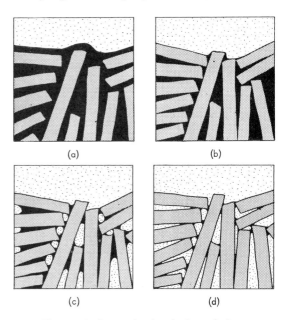

Fig. 22-4. Stages in the drying of clay.

air, (3) the velocity of the air. For fast drying, the air should be hot, dry, and moving rapidly, and conversely for slow drying.

During the first period, the drying rate at the surface is exactly the same as for a free body of water, as is evident from Fig. 22-4, where it can be seen that the clay plates are covered with a continuous film of water. This rapid drying continues until the leather-hard stage is reached, when it slows progressively until the piece is completely dry (Fig. 22-5).

Drying shrinkage. Shrinkage during drying is due to the gradual loss of the water films between the plates, as shown in Fig. 22-4. The finer the clay, the more films there will be, and the higher the shrinkage. Coarse-grained, nonplastic materials like quartz and feldspar, therefore, will obviously tend to reduce shrinkage (Fig. 22-6).

Practically all of the shrinkage occurs in the first portion of the drying cycle (Fig. 22-7). After the leather-hard stage is reached there will be little change in size, because the particles are then touching and can get no closer together. Table 22-1 lists the linear drying shrinkage values for some clays and bodies.

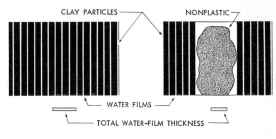

Fig. 22-6. How nonplastic reduces drying shrinkage.

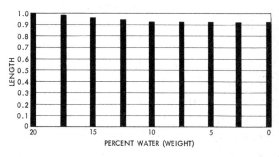

Fig. 22-7. Change in length with drying.

TABLE 22-1
DRYING SHRINKAGE VALUES

Clay or body	Linear drying shrinkage[1]
Residual kaolin (washed)	2-5
Sedimentary kaolin	5-7
Plastic kaolin (washed)	6-8
Fine-grained ball clay	8-11
Coarse-grained ball clay	6-8
Stoneware clay	5-6
Glacial brick clay	3-7
White earthenware body	3-5
High-fired porcelain body	3-5
Terra-cotta body	1-3

[1] With plastic length as base.

Dry strength. We have no satisfactory explanation of the high strength of most clays when they are thoroughly dry. It is believed that when the surfaces of clay plates come together they are held by a bond of some kind, and this, of course, accounts for the fact that fine-grained clays, with many surfaces, are stronger than coarse-grained clays.

Warping and cracking during drying. There are three principal reasons for warping during the drying process:

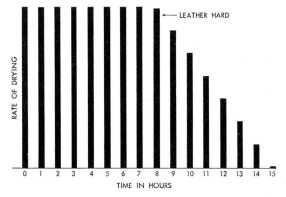

Fig. 22-5. How the drying rate of moist clay changes with time.

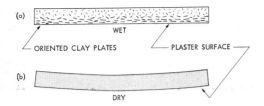

Fig. 22-8. Warping of a tile cast on a plaster slab.

(1) Nonuniformity of the structure; that is, one portion of the body consists of well-aligned particles, while the particles in other parts of the body are arranged in a helter-skelter fashion. For example, a tile cast in a one-surface plaster mold (Fig. 22–8) will invariably curl on drying [part (b) of the figure]. The reason becomes clear when we realize that the clay particles at the surface are laid down parallel to the mold surface, very much like shingles on a roof, while farther inside they are randomly placed. It is clear that shrinkage along the mold surface will be small, since there are few water films along this direction. On the other hand, the shrinkage of the rest of the clay will be normal, and therefore the tile curls toward the low-shrinkage (the mold) side.

This uneven alignment of particles may also cause warping in thrown and pressed ware. The author once saw a fluted candlestick being made in the Wedgewood factory by throwing and turning, and asked the reason for the flutes being applied at a slight angle. It was explained that the candlestick would twist sufficiently in drying and firing to make the flutes straight.

(2) A second cause of warping is the strains set up in handling the plastic or nearly dry piece. These strains may not be great enough to be immediately visible, but they may be the cause of serious warping at a later stage. At one factory, the cause of warped plates was found to be the fact that workmen were picking up the plates with one hand in such

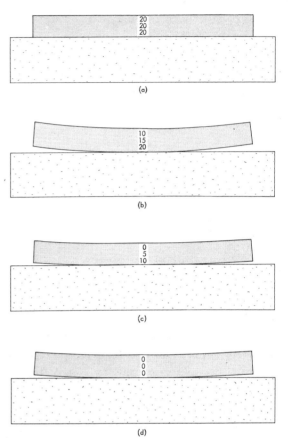

Fig. 22-9. Why unevenly dried tiles warp.

a way as to strain them; when the plates were lifted carefully with both hands the trouble vanished.

(3) A third cause of warping is uneven drying. This is one of the most common and most annoying faults in making flat pieces. For example, if a molded tile is allowed to dry fairly rapidly on a plaster bat, the results will be something like those shown in Fig. 22–9. At (a) the tile has just been formed and the moisture is uniform, let us say, at 20%. Part (b) shows the conditions that will obtain when the upper face has a moisture content of 10% and the lower face remains at the original 20%. This causes the upper face to shrink in relation to the lower face and causes the tile to curl up at the ends, a con-

dition with which every potter is familiar. Further drying produces the condition at (c), with all of the water removed from the upper surface. In part (d) the tile is completely dry, and it is set in the warped position because the upper surface is by now too rigid to be pulled back by the shrinkage of the lower surface.

We are all familiar with the tendency for the sides of a box made by the slab method to bow in. The inside of the box holds moisture, much like the plaster bat, while the outside dries much more quickly. If the outside of the box is covered to slow up the drying there, this warpage is eliminated (Fig. 2–40).

Cracking occurs when the drying strains are greater than the clay can support. The stronger the clay, the less its drying shrinkage, and the less apt it is to crack. Ordinary pottery has little tendency to crack if it is dried slowly enough. Remember that it doesn't pay to try to hurry the process of pottery making!

IV. THE FIRING PROCESS

It is important for the potter to thoroughly understand the firing process, so that costly spoilage can be avoided. A brief description of this process is given here.

Completion of drying by firing. Even when a piece is well dried before firing, some moisture remains to be driven off in the kiln. Many potters have experienced the great disappointment of having pieces of ware blow up in the kiln, and this is directly due to too high a temperature before the moisture has evaporated. If the initial temperature is too high, the water in the interior of the piece turns to steam too quickly for it to be able to escape through the fine pores of the clay, and the steam builds up inside the piece until the

pressure becomes so great that the piece explodes. If there is only biscuit ware in the kiln, only the piece that explodes is lost, but any glost ware in the kiln is very likely to be spoiled by the specks of body from the explosion that will adhere to its glaze. (This is one very good reason for never setting biscuit and glost ware together.)

Removal of chemical water. In addition to free water, chemically combined water is present in the clay, usually in an amount ranging from 5 to 15% of the total weight. This water can be driven off only at temperatures between 500°C and 700°C (red heat), and the clay or body is left quite weak. Here again, the rate of temperature increase must not be too rapid, or cracking will result, not only because of the building up of steam from the moisture, but because there is shrinkage at this stage. The chemically combined water in talc bodies requires even higher temperatures for expulsion.

Decomposition of carbonates and sulfates. Many clays contain calcium, magnesium, and iron in the form of carbonates (such as $CaCO_3$). These carbonates are rather unstable and decompose into the oxides, giving off carbon dioxide, at temperatures of from 600°C to 1000°C. Sulfates are broken up at roughly the same temperatures, giving off sulfur dioxide. However, the quantities of these minerals found in clays are usually so small that these reactions cause no trouble.

Oxidation of organic matter. Many clays (especially ball clays) contain organic matter, which first blackens and then burns off at about red heat. If thick ware is fired too rapidly, oxidation is not complete and a black core remains.

Recrystallization. When clay minerals are broken down by loss of their chemically combined water, there is little change in their form. However, when temperatures of from 950°C to 1000°C are reached, the minerals recrystallize into fine needlelike particles called mullite ($3 Al_2O_3 \cdot 2SiO_2$), embedded in a glass. At extremely high temperatures or in the presence of fluxes, these needlelike crystals do much to add strength to the body. In a similar manner, talc also recrystallizes to more stable minerals which add strength to the body.

The formation of glass. Above red heat the fluxes in a clay or body start to soften and a glass is formed which acts like cement, to make a strong body. The translucency in porcelain bodies is attributable to this same glass, which fills all the pores.

Feldspar is the most commonly used flux. It starts to soften at temperatures of from 900°C to 1100°C in its pure form, and at lower temperatures when iron minerals are present. Nepheline-syenite is a more active flux than feldspar and softens at lower temperatures, while very low-temperature vitreous bodies contain powdered glass or frit which melts at very low temperatures.

Figure 22–10 shows schematically the microscopic changes that occur in a pure kaolin and a porcelain body upon firing. Figure 22–11 shows the amounts of minerals formed when the temperature is increased. A careful study of these two figures will be helpful in gaining insight into what happens in the kiln.

Firing shrinkage. Firing shrinkage varies considerably among the different kinds of clay; in some it is sufficient to cause cracking, and in others shrinkage is almost negligible. In this section we shall discuss the causes and control of firing shrinkage.

When the clay body is dry, it consists of many small particles clustered together with small openings (pores) between them. One cubic centimeter of clay contains only about

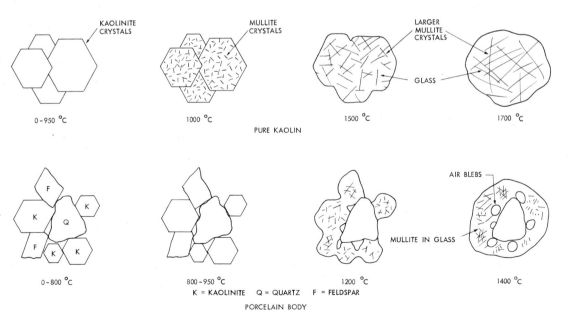

Fig. 22-10. Microscopic changes which occur during firing.

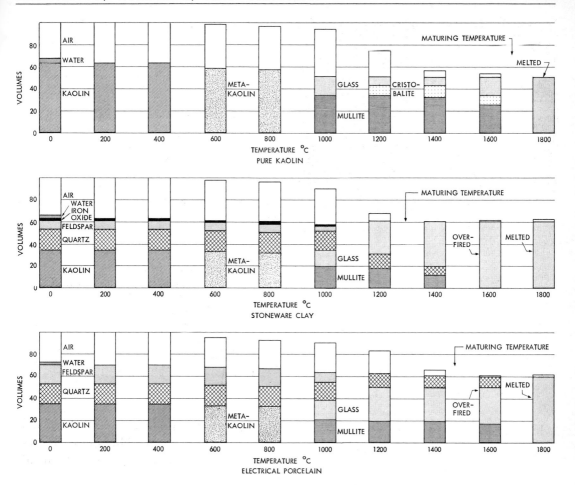

Fig. 22-11. Quantities of minerals formed in firing.

0.6 cc of the clay itself, and 0.4 cc of air in the pores. When this cubic centimeter of clay is fired to a temperature which will leave it with zero porosity, the final volume will be only 0.6 cc, and the percent volume shrinkage will be

$$100 \times \frac{1.0 - 0.6}{1.0} = 100 \times \frac{0.4}{10} = 40\%.$$

Translated to linear shrinkage, this value is 15.7, as indicated by Table 22–2.

The chief causes of firing shrinkage are: (1) a decrease in volume due to the expulsion of water, carbon dioxide, or sulfur dioxide, and (2) the drawing together of the

TABLE 22-2
SHRINKAGE CONVERSION [1]

Volume shrinkage	Linear shrinkage	Volume shrinkage	Linear shrinkage
1	0.33	26	9.55
2	0.67	27	9.96
3	1.01	28	10.37
4	1.35	29	10.79
5	1.69	30	11.21
6	2.04	31	11.63
7	2.39	32	12.06
8	2.74	33	12.50
9	3.09	34	12.93
10	3.45	35	13.38
11	3.81	36	13.82
12	4.17	37	14.27
13	4.54	38	14.73
14	4.50	39	15.19
15	5.27	40	15.66
16	5.65	41	16.13
17	6.02	42	16.90
18	6.40	43	17.09
19	6.78	44	17.57
20	7.17	45	18.07
21	7.56	46	18.57
22	7.95	47	19.07
23	8.34	48	19.59
24	8.74	49	20.10
25	9.14	50	20.63

[1] Based on initial volume and initial length.

Fig. 22-12. High translucency of a frit porcelain plate (Lenox Inc.).

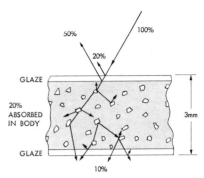

Fig. 22-13. Passage of light through a translucent body.

TABLE 22-3
FIRED PROPERTIES OF BODIES

Type of body	Maturing temp., °C	Lin. shrinkage based on dry size	Absorption, in percent
Red earthenware	1000	6	9
Parian	1150	10	0
Red stoneware	1150	9	6
Gray stoneware	1250	8	5
Semi-vit. earthenware	1250	9	4
Porcelain, elect.	1250	11	0
Porcelain, high fired	1450	11	0
Terra cotta	1150	4	11
Sculpture body	1015	1.5	20

crystals by the capillary forces of the glass and the consequent expulsion of air from the pores.

Ceramic bodies shrink in much the same way as clay, but since they contain larger particles of stable quartz to act as a skeleton, the shrinkage is not as great. It is desirable to keep the firing shrinkage of any body as low as possible, but it is unavoidable that it should be high for vitreous bodies—in the neighborhood of 10% to 14% on a linear basis. Table 22-3 gives the firing shrinkage values for a few typical bodies fired to maturity. The shrinkage may be greatly reduced by adding grog to the body, as is done with terra cotta. Special bodies are sometimes fired at very low temperatures and with a small clay content to reduce the firing shrinkage; sculptured bodies are in this category.

Translucency. As we have mentioned earlier, the degree of translucency is due to the amount of glass in the fired body. Light passes through glass, while it is scattered by the crystals of quartz and mullite. Obviously, the more glass, the greater the percentage of transmitted light and the greater the translucency. This effect is pictured in Fig. 22-12, where the hand can be clearly seen through the frit porcelain plate when it is held against the light. The simple optical diagram of Fig. 22-13 further explains this phenomenon.

The absorption of fired bodies. Absorption is a measure of the amount of water taken up in the pores of the body when a piece is immersed in boiling water for 1 hour and allowed to stand for 24 hours. For example, if a fired piece weighs 103.5 grams when dry, and 109.2 grams when saturated (with the surface water wiped off), its absorption is

$$\frac{109.2 - 103.5}{109.2} \times 100 = \frac{5.7}{109.2} \times 100 = 5.2\%$$

Because the water will enter only the open pores (and not those completely enclosed by particles), there may be a small amount of porosity not indicated by the absorption test.

The absorption value of a fired body is very useful, because it tells us how well the body has been fired, whether it is a vitreous or earthenware body, and something about its strength and watertightness.

As the firing temperature increases, absorption decreases. Absorption is in the range of 4 to 10% for earthenware, 1 to 6% for stoneware, and 0 to 3% for porcelain. Figure 22–11 shows how absorption values decrease during the firing cycle for stoneware (as indicated by the decreasing volume of air). When firing temperatures are too high, the absorption for stoneware becomes too low, and the body is said to be overfired. The absorption of porcelain should fall to zero at the correct firing temperature; when this body is overfired, absorption usually increases again, because bubbles form in the glassy stage of firing. Table 22–3 lists the absorption values of some properly fired ceramic bodies.

V. CONTROL OF SHRINKAGE AND WARPAGE IN DRYING

Influence of composition. We discussed earlier the reasons why coarse-grained clays shrink less than fine-grained clays, and how the addition of flint, feldspar, and coarse grog reduce the total shrinkage of the body. Remember, however, that low shrinkage is obtained only with the sacrifice of plasticity and green strength.

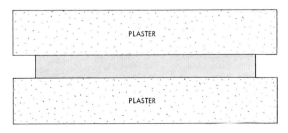

Fig. 22-14. Drying a tile between plaster bats.

Influence of forming methods. The experienced potter knows that a body cast from a slip shrinks less in drying than the same body molded in the plastic state, since in a cast the clay plates along the surface of the mold are aligned parallel to it and thus shrink very little.

Influence of drying methods. If a pressed tile is dried between two plaster slabs, so that both sides dry at the same rate, no warping will result (Fig. 22–14). Drying the tile on a screen will give similar results (Fig. 6–6). It is sometimes advisable to assure even drying by placing the piece inside a damp plaster box and allowing it to dry very slowly.

Warping of hollow ware with very thin walls may be prevented by use of a plaster ring, with a 45° level, placed in the mouth of the piece, as was shown in Fig. 6–7. As the drying progresses, the ring slips upward but maintains a constant force on the clay.

VI. CONTROL OF SHRINKAGE AND WARPAGE IN FIRING

Influence of composition. Low firing shrinkage is achieved in the same way as low drying sh.inkage—by the addition of grog and other nonplastics to the body. If 50% grog and 50% clay are combined, the firing shrinkage will be only about one-half that for the clay alone.

Influence of forming methods. Because the plastic body becomes more dense when pressure is used in forming it, and because the denser the body the less the shrinkage, forming methods do have some effect on firing shrinkage. This is much more of a problem for the commercial potter than for the artist potter, because the high pressures used in industry are usually not available to the artist. It is possible, however, that variations in the pressure used on different parts of a piece may account for some of the warpage encountered on firing.

Influence of firing methods. Evenness of temperature throughout the kiln is extremely important. If one part is hotter than another, the shrinkage will vary and cause warping.

Influence of setting methods. When a special body is used that becomes so soft on firing that it sags down onto a preformed setter, warping is no problem. However, plates, bowls, and other thin pieces must be carefully handled in the setting to avoid uneven strains that will warp the piece.

Warping can often be avoided by use of the proper setting method. We have discussed setting procedures in Chapters 7 and 10, but a review of some of the cardinal rules will be useful here:

(1) Delicate pieces should be set on an un- fired bat of the same body, so that all will shrink together.

(2) Thin hollow ware should be mounted on conical setters of unfired body, to maintain its roundness.

(3) Highly translucent flat ware should have a smooth, level bed to rest on when it sags in firing. This bed may be an alumina-washed fire-clay setter or a formed bed of flint.

(4) Delicate sculptured ware must be supported by props of unfired body.

VII. SUMMARY
All of the above boils down to just this: the potter must learn to know the character, the idiosyncrasies, and the mood of the clay with which he is working; he must know just how much he can hurry the various stages of production; he must live with his media until they seem like old friends.

VIII. REFERENCES
1. ANDREWS, A. I., *Ceramic Tests and Calculations,* John Wiley & Sons, Inc., New York, 1928 (Chaps. II and III).
2. NORTON, F. H., *Elements of Ceramics,* Addison-Wesley Publishing Company, Inc., Cambridge, Mass., 1952 (Chap. 12).

Elements of Glazing

I. INTRODUCTION

The author can still remember his acute disappointment when, as a small boy, a batch of cupcakes which had made the kitchen fragrant finally came to the table without frosting. The glaze on a piece of pottery is much like frosting—it is the finishing touch that makes the perfect piece.

Glazing presents no particular problems for the beginner. It is easy to master the technique of applying a thin layer of the glaze suspension, just like paint, onto the surface of a body, and firing to the proper temperature. Glazes are commercially available in a great variety of colors and textures, and these can be used with very good results. More advanced potters may wish to make their own glazes, following the well-tried formulas to be found in the literature. Serious students will prefer to experiment in making their own glazes, and consequently will need to know something about the nature of different glazes and about methods of calculation. It is for this third group that this chapter is written.

Purpose of glazes. A glazed surface on a fired body serves several useful purposes: (1) it adds a smooth, nonabsorbent surface that is easily cleaned; (2) it permits the production of a variety of colors and textures not possible on the body itself; (3) it serves as a protective coating for underglaze decorations.

From the decorative point of view, glazes enhance the appearance of a piece, for example in the encaustic process and for transparent relief-modeled surfaces in color.

Glaze formation. Glaze is a thin layer of glass, or glass and crystals, that adheres to the surface of the body. It is made by mixing the finely ground glass with water to make a suspension, and it is applied to the surface of the piece in a thin coat with a brush, by dipping, or by spraying. When the piece is fired, the glaze particles fuse into a continuous glossy layer.

How glass is formed. It is interesting to know of what glass is composed and how it is formed, so that we will know why we use glass-forming compounds for glazes.

Glass is really a liquid, but it is so viscous at ordinary temperatures that it acts like a solid. Because it is actually a liquid, however, it easily forms a thin film when it is heated. The glass used for glaze must have such special properties as stability against atmospheric conditions, resistance to soaps, and extreme hardness so that it will not be easily scratched. It must also contract on cooling at about the same rate as the body to which it has been applied, to avoid crazing (cracking) of the glaze.

Glasses are composed of various oxides, combined in proportions that will yield the desired properties. The acid oxides, silica (SiO_2) and boric oxide (B_2O_3), are the glass formers, but by themselves would not give a satisfactory result for glazing. Basic oxides, such as sodium oxide (Na_2O), potassium oxide (K_2O), calcium oxide (CaO), and lead oxide (PbO), and the neutral oxide, aluminum oxide (Al_2O_3), are combined with the acid oxides to form the compound best suited for the particular glaze desired. By suitable selection of the oxides it is possible to make glazes that may be fired at a wide range of temperatures. For example, glazes that are high in silica content must be fired at high temperatures, while the addition of lead, boric, or sodium oxide lowers the firing range. In general, the high-firing glazes are more stable and harder than those that will fire in the low-temperature range.

Because an oxide like calcium oxide is unstable, and boric oxide, for example, is soluble in water, these cannot be added directly to the glaze mixture. In these cases, a compound such as a carbonate which breaks down to the desired oxide when heated is substituted. This will be further discussed in the next section.

II. CALCULATION OF GLAZE FORMULAS

The serious worker in ceramics will often find it necessary to convert the equivalent formula of a glaze to the batch formula, or vice versa. This requires only simple arithmetic calculations; no knowledge of chemistry is required. It is the purpose of this section to explain such calculations.

Equivalent formula. Seger, the father of scientific ceramics, was the first to propose that the components of glazes should be expressed in terms of oxide equivalents. Although it is quite true that we seldom find oxides in the finished glaze, because they have combined to form a glass, it is most helpful to think of the glaze compound in terms of oxides rather than in weights of raw materials. To work intelligently, we need to become familiar with the symbols for the various elements used in the ceramic process, and this requires some knowledge of the structure of matter and of atomic weights. The average person can easily grasp enough of this knowledge for our purposes. Don't let the words "atom" and "atomic" frighten you!

Atomic weight. All matter is composed of atoms, as we discussed in Chapter 15. A piece of copper is entirely composed of copper atoms, while a piece of burnt limestone is one-half calcium atoms and one-half oxygen atoms. There are about one hundred different kinds of atoms that make up all matter as we know it. Some, like oxygen and silicon, are very common and compose more than half of the earth's crust; others, like gold and cobalt, are quite rare.

These various atoms all have different weights, and when properly listed they form a uniform series, progressing from the lightest to the heaviest atoms. These weights, known as *atomic weights,* are listed in Table 15–2. Because the weight of a single atom is extremely small, the figures given are only relative values, with hydrogen, the lightest atom, taken as unity (one unit). Note that each kind of atom is expressed by a symbol, which simplifies the writing of formulas (for example, Ca for calcium). We need to become familiar with the symbols for those elements used in ceramics.

Formula weight. The chemical compounds we shall deal with are a combination of one or more metallic-type atoms with unit numbers of nonmetallic atoms. For example, in lime (CaO), one atom of calcium combines with one of oxygen. A molecule of alumina (Al_2O_3) consists of two atoms of aluminum and three atoms of oxygen. All the ratios are small integers, like 1, 2, 3, and 4.

It is convenient to express the atomic weights of the elements in grams, because then the expression for the weight of any element, called the *gram-atomic weight,* in every instance contains the same number of atoms as that for every other element. For example, 40 (the atomic weight) grams of calcium (Ca) contains the same number of atoms as 16 (the atomic weight) grams of oxygen (O), and the two would combine to form 56 (the formula weight) grams of calcium oxide (CaO) with nothing left over. The sum of the atomic weights of all the components of a compound is known as the *formula weight* (listed in Table 15–3 for some of the common ceramic materials). This system applies even to such complex materials as potash feldspar ($K_2O \cdot Al_2O_3 \cdot 6SiO_2$), whose formula weight is 557 grams, just the sum of the atomic weights of the several constituents. Formula weights are used in many calculations, as we shall show.

Equivalent weight. The formula weight is often used directly in calculations, but more often it must be multiplied or divided by a small integer to take into account those portions of a compound in which we have no interest for our purpose. For example, the formula weight of white lead, written $2PbCO_3 \cdot Pb(OH)_2$, is 776 grams. If we rewrite the formula on the basis of the oxides (which are what we are interested in), we have $3PbO \cdot 2CO_2 \cdot H_2O$. (Note that to arrive at this formula we may think of the $Pb(OH)_2$ as giving up a molecule of water to leave one molecule of PbO, and of the $2PbCO_3$ as expelling two molecules of CO_2 to leave two more mole-

cules of PbO. This gives a total of 3PbO, $2CO_2$, and $1H_2O$, which is just what our new formula states.) Therefore one formula weight of white lead will yield three formula weights of lead oxide (PbO) for introduction into the glaze. Thus the formula weight of 776 is divided by 3 to give the *equivalent weight* of 259.

As another example, suppose that a glaze formula calls for ferrous oxide (FeO), but only ferric oxide (Fe_2O_3) is available. The formula weight of ferric oxide is 160, but we get two weights of FeO for each one of ferric oxide, and therefore the 160 is divided by 2 to get the equivalent weight, 80. In other words, 80 grams of ferric oxide added to a glaze will give the same results as 72 grams of ferrous oxide.

Similarly, sodium nitrate ($NaNO_3$), with a formula weight of 85, yields only ½ a formula weight of Na_2O, which is what we require. Therefore the equivalent weight of sodium nitrate is 170.

As a general rule, the equivalent weight is obtained from the formula weight by dividing or multiplying by the number of times the oxide of interest occurs. Compounds may have different equivalent weights with respect to different components. For example, potash feldspar ($K_2O \cdot Al_2O_3 \cdot 6SiO_2$), with a formula weight of 557, has an equivalent weight of 557 on the basis of potassium oxide and aluminum oxide, but the equivalent weight is only 93 on the basis of silica, because the formula weight of this oxide is only ⅙ that of potash feldspar.

Some equivalent weights are listed in Table 15–3.

Seger formula for glazes. In formulating his expression for glazes, Seger divided the oxides into three groups: the basic oxides, the neutral oxides, and the acidic oxides. He also found it convenient to keep the sum of the equivalents of the basic oxides equal to unity (one) and to calculate the others in terms of this. This system permitted classification of the oxides commonly used in glazes in the manner shown in Table 23–1. Let us use this information to calculate the formula for a good raw-lead glaze to be fired at 900°C (Cone 010).

For firing at temperatures from 750° to 800°C (Cones 016 to 014), a very simple glaze is expressed by the formula

$$1.0 \text{ PbO} \qquad 1.0 \text{SiO}_2$$

However, this glaze is hard to use, because it is very fluid and too soft. It can be improved by the addition of alumina and an increase in the silica content:

$$1.0 \text{ PbO} \quad 0.15 \text{ Al}_2\text{O}_3 \quad 1.45 \text{ SiO}_2$$

But this glaze has a slight yellow tinge, and a still better composition will result if we replace some of the lead with other basic oxides:

$$0.65 \text{ PbO}$$
$$0.25 \text{ CaO} \quad 0.15 \text{ Al}_2\text{O}_3 \quad 1.45 \text{ SiO}_2$$
$$0.10 \text{ Na}_2\text{O}$$

Now we have the formula we require.

It will be seen from the above example that there is considerable advantage in comparing one glaze with another by the use of equivalents because systematic alterations are easily made. With experience, it is easy to tell just by examining its formula what kind of glaze will result from a particular compound.

Converting formulas to batch weights. *Raw glazes.* The formulas above tell us how much of a particular *oxide* we need to mix the glaze we want, but they fail to tell us

TABLE 23–1
OXIDES COMMONLY USED IN GLAZES

Basic oxides	Neutral oxides	Acid oxides
Sodium oxide (Na_2O) Potassium oxide (K_2O) Calcium oxide (CaO) Magnesium oxide (MgO) Zinc oxide (ZnO) Barium oxide (BaO) Lead oxide (PbO)	Alumina (Al_2O_3)	Silica (SiO_2) Boric oxide (B_2O_3) Tin oxide (SnO_2)

just what *ceramic material* to use in our batch to assure the presence of the oxides we want. In other words, we must convert the equivalent weights to batch weights, in terms of actual amounts of materials to be mixed together. This is a simple process when it is accomplished in logical steps. Let us again take the simple formula we used above as a starting point:

$$1.0 \text{ PbO} \qquad 1.0 \text{ SiO}_2$$

The lead can be supplied by using either red lead (Pb_3O_4) or white lead ($3PbO \cdot 2CO_2 \cdot H_2O$), and the silica can be obtained from potter's flint (SiO_2). The equivalent weights are: red lead, 229; white lead, 259; flint, 60 (from Table 15–3). Therefore the glaze should consist of

$$1.0 \times 229 = 229 \text{ grams of red lead}$$
$$1.0 \times 60 = \underline{60} \text{ grams of flint}$$
$$289 \text{ grams total}$$

or

$$1.0 \times 259 = 259 \text{ grams of white lead}$$
$$1.0 \times 60 = \underline{60} \text{ grams of flint}$$
$$319 \text{ grams total}$$

To find the weight percent of each ingredient, we divide by the total weight, which gives

> 79% red lead
> 21% flint

and

> 81% white lead
> 19% flint

The alert student will perhaps wonder why it requires 259 grams of white lead to do the same work as 229 grams of red lead. To find the answer, let's look at the formulas for these two compounds:

White lead $= PbO \cdot \frac{2}{3}CO_2 \cdot \frac{1}{3}H_2O$
Red lead $\quad = PbO \cdot \frac{1}{3}O$

Because everything but the PbO is volatilized in firing, white lead loses 35 grams of equivalent weight in the firing, while the loss for red lead is only 5 grams. The difference between the equivalent weights of white lead and red lead is just this 30 grams.

Let us cite another example. Again we take a formula that we used above:

1.0 PbO   0.15 Al_2O_3 1.45 SiO_2

For our batch formula, we will again use 259 grams of white lead. However, if 0.15 equivalent of clay (39 grams) is added to give the alumina, 0.30 equivalent of silica must be added with it. Therefore only 1.15 $\times$ 60 or 69 grams of potter's flint are needed. The batch formula will then be

259 grams of white lead
39 grams of clay
69 grams of flint
367 grams total

or, in percents:

71% white lead
10% clay
19% flint

Our next formula is more difficult to convert, so we will resort to a tabular form of calculation that can be used for the calculation of all future batches.

0.65 PbO
0.25 CaO   0.15 Al_2O_3 1.45 SiO_2
0.10 K_2O

The following rules are to be followed systematically in making the conversion:

(1) Set up a table with the equivalents of each oxide in the Seger formula listed as a column head.

(2) Now add a column at the left of the table, and in it list first the raw material and the number of equivalents required to form the first oxide listed at the top of the table.

(3) Now subtract all of the oxides introduced by this material from the whole glaze listed at the heads of the columns, which eliminates at least one oxide.

(4) Write in a second raw material in the left-hand column in the amount required to supply the correct weight of the second oxide listed at the top of the table.

(5) Subtract as before, and repeat the operation until all of the oxides listed at the tops of the columns have been accounted for. Usually flint (SiO_2) is the last material eliminated.

(6) Now multiply the number of equivalents associated with each raw material by its corresponding equivalent weight to give the batch weight in grams.

The application of these rules is made clear in Table 23–2. This form should always be used in calculating batch weights.

Figure 23–1 graphically illustrates the same procedure. In the upper chart, the original glaze expressed in equivalents is laid out horizontally on the top line—the sum of the

TABLE 23-2

GLAZE CALCULATION

Raw materials added, in equiv.	Equivalents of oxides in glaze				
	0.65 PbO	0.25 CaO	0.10 K$_2$O	0.15 Al$_2$O$_3$	1.45 SiO$_2$
0.65 White lead	0.65 PbO				
Difference	0	0.25 CaO	0.10 K$_2$O	0.15 Al$_2$O$_3$	1.45 SiO$_2$
0.25 Whiting		0.25 CaO			
Difference		0	0.10 K$_2$O	0.15 Al$_2$O$_3$	1.45 SiO$_2$
0.10 Feldspar			0.10 K$_2$O	0.10 Al$_2$O$_3$	0.60 SiO$_2$
Difference			0	0.05 Al$_2$O$_3$	0.85 SiO$_2$
0.05 Kaolin				0.05 Al$_2$O$_3$	0.10 SiO$_2$
Difference				0	0.75 SiO$_2$
0.75 Flint					0.75 SiO$_2$
Difference					0

Raw material	Equivalent added	Equivalent weight	Relative wt. in grams[1]	Percent weight[2]
White lead	0.65	259	169	55
Whiting	0.25	100	25	8
Feldspar	0.10	557	56	18
Kaolin	0.05	258	13	4
Flint	0.75	60	45	15
Total			308	100

[1] From product of figures in 2nd and 3rd columns.

[2] From figures in 4th column divided by 2.95.

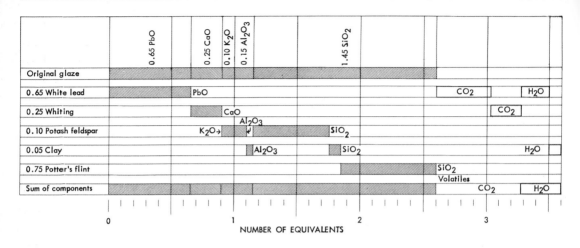

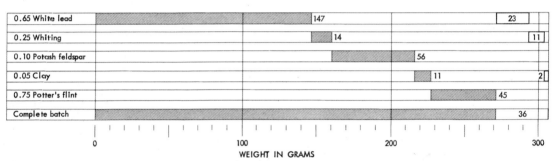

Fig. 23-1. Calculation of a raw glaze.

basic oxides, of course, being equal to unity. The lead oxide (PbO) resulting from 0.65 equivalent of white lead ($3PbO \cdot 2CO_2 \cdot H_2O$) appears on the next line, and on the same line, to the right, is shown the carbon dioxide (CO_2) and the water (H_2O) lost from 0.65 equivalent of white lead. On the third line we list the calcium oxide ($CaCO_3$), and the CO_2 that is lost. This procedure is followed for all of the remaining ingredients, and then the totals are given in the lower line. Note that this last line corresponds to the formula for the original glaze except for the volatile materials which are lost in firing.

The lower chart follows a similar scheme, except that the weights of the materials are used as a base. The total raw material is 295 grams, but 36 grams are lost in the firing.

Fritted glazes. It is often desirable to use water-soluble compounds in a batch of glaze. Because soluble salts may be drawn into the body or may form a scum on the surface, they cannot be added directly to the suspension. Instead such salts are melted in a crucible with all or some of the other ingredients to form a glass, or frit, which is then ground and suspended in water as before. Fritting also improves the working properties of the glaze suspension, allows better dispersion of color, and minimizes poison hazards. Frits may be readily made in the studio, but many kinds are commercially available (Table 23-3).

Let's start with the following formula and make up a batch of fritted glaze:

TABLE 23-3

STANDARD COMMERCIAL GLAZE FRITS

Group	Frit no.	CaF_2	K_2O	Na_2O	CaO	MgO	BaO	SrO	ZnO	PbO	Al_2O_3	B_2O_3	SiO_2	ZrO_2	Formula weight	Coef. of exp.
PEMCO FRITS	P-54			0.32	0.68							0.64	1.47		191	8.9
	P-67		0.12	0.19	0.69						0.37	1.16	2.17		311	7.0
	P-311		0.02	0.29	0.69						0.27	0.57	2.49		311	6.7
	P-786		0.09	0.09	0.58			0.24			0.19	0.36	2.80		284	7.2
	P-926		0.01	0.31	0.68						0.11	0.61	1.90		225	8.4
	Pb-63			0.21	0.29					0.50	0.12	0.66	2.60	0.07	379	6.1
	Pb-83			0.28						0.72		0.56	0.90		271	8.2
	Pb-197		0.07	0.18	0.29				0.32	0.14	0.20	0.26	2.43		276	6.7
	Pb-316									1.00	0.25		1.92		364	5.9
	Pb-349		0.09	0.09	0.58					0.24	0.19	0.36	2.80		313	6.4
	Pb-545									1.00	0.11		2.16		364	6.4
	Pb-723			0.07						0.93	0.07		1.21		291	8.9
	Pb-742			0.21	0.29					0.50	0.12	0.66	2.60	0.03	363	6.1
FERRO FRITS	3124		0.02	0.28	0.70						0.27	0.55	2.56		279	
	3134			0.32	0.68							0.63	1.47		210	
	3169		0.06	0.39	0.55						0.15	0.53	2.13		243	
	3185			1.00								4.43	7.27		808	
	3191			0.50	0.50							1.00	2.00		249	
	3193		0.06	0.42	0.52						0.30	0.62	2.46		283	
	3211				1.00							1.11			133	
	3223			1.00								2.00	5.00		502	
	3230		0.25	0.64			0.03		0.08				2.27		213	
	3256			0.07	0.45	0.12	0.11	0.06	0.19		0.08	0.41	1.82		219	
	3257				0.43	0.04	0.53				0.16	0.19	2.09	0.06	267	
	3417		0.07	0.10	0.31					0.53	0.12	0.69	2.72	0.75	464	
	3419			0.28						0.72		0.57	0.89		276	
	3300		0.06	0.03	0.27	0.08	0.08		0.27	0.21	0.19		1.34		207	
	3304			0.07						0.93	0.15		2.61		384	
	3386		0.02	0.08						0.90	0.13	1.77	4.42		499	
	3396			0.50						0.50		1.00	2.00		332	
	3403		0.04	0.02						0.94	0.07		1.45		309	
	3435		0.04	0.22	0.39					0.35	0.07	0.71	2.14		295	
	3457			0.23	0.35						0.62	0.53	1.74		337	
O. HOMMEL FRITS	291		0.26	0.32	0.60					0.05	0.05	0.31	1.98		213	
	244			0.62	0.31					0.08		0.78	2.34		268	
	288			0.83	0.77						0.15	0.16	0.79	4.48		429	
	126		0.17	0.20	0.38					0.40	0.27	0.37	2.15		308	
	22			0.47						0.53		0.98	2.88		385	
	235			0.84	0.30					0.52	0.13	0.68	2.72	0.07	197	
	245			0.84	0.21				0.26	0.44	0.14	0.29	1.40		251	
	240			0.28						0.72		0.56	0.90		271	
	13				0.30					0.70		0.39	0.41		227	
	243		0.34	0.03						0.94	0.07		1.23		295	
	242			0.33	0.67							0.65	1.48		192	
	69	0.10	0.14	0.15	0.22		0.11		0.41		0.02	0.29	1.36	0.17	205	
	285		0.11	0.90							0.21	0.94	2.72		315	
	90		0.02	0.29	0.69						0.28	0.56	2.60		284	
	40		0.25	0.75							0.42	1.26	2.67		351	
	253		0.29	0.30			0.41				0.31	0.69	1.99		310	
	267		0.13	0.31	0.56						0.29	1.24	2.05		301	
	266			0.33	0.68						0.32	1.10	1.31		245	
	249			0.05	0.35		0.40		0.20		0.02	0.48	1.55		228	
	313			0.20	0.61						0.20	0.86	1.54		262	

0.5 PbO

0.2 CaO   0.15 Al$_2$O$_3$ 2.2 SiO$_2$

0.3 Na$_2$O

It will be noted at once that if enough soda feldspar (Na$_2$O·Al$_2$O$_3$·6SiO$_2$) is used to give 0.3 sodium oxide (soda), too much alumina will be added. Therefore part of the soda must be added as frit. Such a frit can be an ordinary bottle glass with the composition

0.5 CaO
                  3.0 SiO$_2$
0.5 Na$_2$O

which can be rewritten as

CaO·Na$_2$O·6SiO$_2$

This can be treated just like other glaze materials, for it has a formula weight of 478, and the same equivalent weight on the basis of Na$_2$O. When we make up our table (Table 23–4), we see that the frit is taken care of nicely.

If we wish to make up the frit by melting the raw materials, the calculations are made just as for raw glaze. Of the required amount of raw material, 88 grams of volatile material are lost, making the formula weight of the finished frit 478 grams. The calculation is shown in Table 23–5.

Now we shall take a more complicated example. Let's make a batch formula of Cone 6

TABLE 23–4

CALCULATION OF A FRITTED GLAZE

Equiv. of raw materials added	Equivalents of oxides in glaze				
	0.5 PbO	0.2 CaO	0.3 Na$_2$O	0.15 Al$_2$O$_3$	2.2 SiO$_2$
0.5 White lead	0.5 PbO				
Difference	0	0.2 CaO	0.3 Na$_2$O	0.15 Al$_2$O$_3$	2.2 SiO$_2$
0.2 Frit		0.2 CaO	0.2 Na$_2$O		1.2 SiO$_2$
Difference		0	0.1 Na$_2$O	0.15 Al$_2$O$_3$	1.0 SiO$_2$
0.1 Soda feldspar			0.1 Na$_2$O	0.10 Al$_2$O$_3$	0.6 SiO$_2$
Difference			0	0.05 Al$_2$O$_3$	0.4 SiO$_2$
0.05 Kaolin				0.05 Al$_2$O$_3$	0.1 SiO$_2$
Difference				0	0.3 SiO$_2$
0.3 Flint					0.3 SiO$_2$
Difference					0

Raw material	Equivalents added	Equivalent weight	Relative wt. in grams	Percent weight
White lead	0.5	259	149	45
Frit	0.2	478	95	29
Soda feldspar	0.1	525	53	16
Kaolin	0.05	258	13	4
Flint	0.3	60	18	6
Total			328	100

TABLE 23–5

CALCULATION OF A FRIT

Equiv. of raw materials added	Equivalents of oxides in glaze		
	1.0 CaO	1.0 Na$_2$O	6.0 SiO$_2$
1.0 Whiting	1.0 CaO		
1.0 Sodium carb.		1.0 Na$_2$O	
6.0 Flint			6.0 SiO$_2$
Difference	0	0	0

Raw material	Equivalents added	Equivalent weight	Relative wt. in grams
Whiting	1.0	100	100
Sodium carb.	1.0	106	106
Flint	6.0	60	360
Total			566

whiteware glaze, with the following composition:

0.43 CaO

0.26 PbO
            0.27 Al$_2$O$_3$ 2.60 SiO$_2$
0.18 Na$_2$O   0.31 B$_2$O$_3$

0.13 ZnO

Since the glaze contains soluble boric oxide (B$_2$O$_3$), a frit must be used. One of the standard frits listed in Table 23–3 will be most economical, and taking P-54 as a possible choice, we can make up Table 23–6. Part of the alumina is added as calcined clay, for it is usually undesirable to use more than 0.10 equivalent of raw clay (too much drying shrinkage results). The batch weights are given in Table 23–6. These results are shown graphically in Fig. 23–2.

The preceding glaze can be made with two frits, one containing the lead and the other the borax. This is often done in making commercial glazes, because working properties are improved. Table 23–7 shows this calculation.

Correction for impurities in glaze materials.

Most of the raw materials used in glazes are so nearly pure that for practical purposes they can be assumed to be entirely so. A few minerals, however, contain sufficient impurities so that a correction must be made. In the average glaze calculation, feldspar is usually the only material for which a correction needs to be made. The chemical

TABLE 23-6

CALCULATION OF A FRITTED GLAZE

Equivalents of raw materials added	Equivalents of oxides in the glaze						
	$0.43\ CaO$	$0.26\ PbO$	$0.18\ Na_2O$	$0.13\ ZnO$	$0.27\ Al_2O_3$	$0.31\ B_2O_3$	$2.60\ SiO_2$
0.49 P-54 Frit	$0.33\ CaO$	-----	$0.16\ Na_2O$			$0.31\ B_2O_3$	$0.72\ SiO_2$
Difference	$0.10\ CaO$	$0.26\ PbO$	$0.02\ Na_2O$	$0.13\ ZnO$	$0.27\ Al_2O_3$	0	$1.88\ SiO_2$
0.26 White lead	-----	$0.26\ PbO$					
Difference	$0.10\ CaO$	0	$0.02\ Na_2O$	$0.13\ ZnO$	$0.27\ Al_2O_3$	-----	$1.88\ SiO_2$
0.13 Zinc oxide				$0.13\ ZnO$			
Difference	$0.10\ CaO$	-----	$0.02\ Na_2O$	0	$0.27\ Al_2O_3$	-----	$1.88\ SiO_2$
0.02 Soda feldspar			$0.02\ Na_2O$		$0.02\ Al_2O_3$		$0.12\ SiO_2$
Difference	$0.10\ CaO$	-----	0	-----	$0.25\ Al_2O_3$	-----	$1.76\ SiO_2$
0.10 Whiting	$0.10\ CaO$						
Difference	0	-----	-----	-----	$0.25\ Al_2O_3$	-----	$1.76\ SiO_2$
0.10 Kaolin					$0.10\ Al_2O_3$	-----	$0.20\ SiO_2$
Difference	-----				$0.15\ Al_2O_3$	-----	$1.56\ SiO_2$
0.15 Calcined kaolin					$0.15\ Al_2O_3$	-----	$0.30\ SiO_2$
Difference					0	-----	$1.26\ SiO_2$
1.26 Flint						-----	$1.26\ SiO_2$
Difference						-----	0

Raw materials	Equiv. added	Equiv. weight	Batch, grams
P-54 Frit	0.49	191	94
White lead	0.26	259	66
Zinc oxide	0.13	81	11
Soda feldspar	0.02	525	10
Whiting	0.10	100	10
Kaolin	0.10	258	26
Calcined kaolin	0.15	222	33
Flint	1.26	60	76
Total			326

TABLE 23-7

CALCULATION OF A FRITTED GLAZE

Equivalents of raw materials added	Equivalents of oxides in the glaze						
	$0.43\ CaO$	$0.26\ PbO$	$0.18\ Na_2O$	$0.13\ ZnO$	$0.27\ Al_2O_3$	$0.31\ B_2O_3$	$2.60\ SiO_2$
0.49 P-54 Frit	$0.33\ CaO$	-----	$0.16\ Na_2O$			$0.31\ B_2O_3$	$0.72\ SiO_2$
Difference	$0.10\ CaO$	$0.26\ PbO$	$0.02\ Na_2O$	$0.13\ ZnO$	$0.27\ Al_2O_3$	0	$1.88\ SiO_2$
0.26 Pb-545 Frit	-----	$0.26\ PbO$			$0.03\ Al_2O_3$		$0.56\ SiO_2$
Difference	$0.10\ CaO$	0	$0.02\ Na_2O$	$0.13\ ZnO$	$0.24\ Al_2O_3$	-----	$1.32\ SiO_2$
0.13 ZnO				$0.13\ ZnO$			
Difference	$0.10\ CaO$	-----	$0.02\ Na_2O$	0	$0.24\ Al_2O_3$	-----	$1.32\ SiO_2$
0.01 Soda feldspar			$0.02\ Na_2O$		$0.02\ Al_2O_3$		$0.12\ SiO_2$
Difference	$0.10\ CaO$	-----	0	-----	$0.22\ Al_2O_3$	-----	$1.20\ SiO_2$
0.10 Whiting	$0.10\ CaO$						
Difference	0						
0.10 Kaolin	-----				$0.10\ Al_2O_3$	-----	$0.20\ SiO_2$
Difference	-----				$0.12\ Al_2O_3$	-----	$1.00\ SiO_2$
0.12 Calcined kaolin	-----				$0.12\ Al_2O_3$	-----	$0.24\ SiO_2$
Difference					0	-----	$0.76\ SiO_2$
0.76 Flint						-----	$0.76\ SiO_2$
Difference						-----	0

Raw materials	Equiv. added	Equiv. weight	Batch, grams
P-54 Frit	0.49	191	94
Pb-545 Frit	0.26	364	95
Zinc oxide	0.13	81	11
Soda feldspar	0.02	525	10
Whiting	0.10	100	10
Kaolin	0.10	258	26
Calcined kaolin	0.12	222	27
Flint	0.76	60	46
Total			319

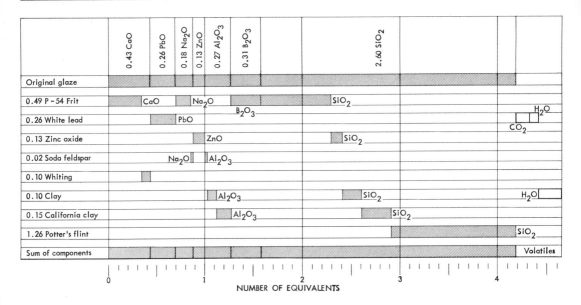

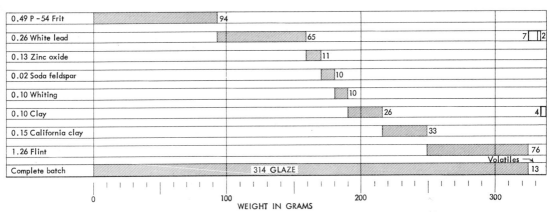

Fig. 23-2. Calculation of a fritted glaze.

formula for a particular feldspar should be obtained from the supplier, and an equivalent formula must be calculated from this. As an example, let us consider a Maine feldspar with the analysis

SiO_2	67.9%
Al_2O_3	18.4
Fe_2O_3	0.1
CaO	0.3
K_2O	10.0
Na_2O	3.0
Loss	0.3
	100.0%

The iron oxide is so small that it may be in-

cluded with the alumina. Then each percentage is divided by the formula weight:

$$\frac{67.9}{60} = 1.13\ SiO_2$$

$$\frac{19.5}{102} = 0.18\ Al_2O_3$$

$$\frac{0.3}{56} = 0.01\ CaO$$

$$\frac{10.0}{94} = 0.11\ K_2O$$

$$\frac{3.0}{62} = 0.05\ Na_2O$$

$$\frac{0.3}{44} = 0.01\ CO_2$$

which gives

$$0.11 \text{ K}_2\text{O}$$
$$0.05 \text{ Na}_2\text{O} \quad 0.18 \text{ Al}_2\text{O}_3 \quad \begin{array}{l} 1.13 \text{ SiO}_1 \\ 0.01 \text{ CO}_2 \end{array}$$
$$0.01 \text{ CaO}$$

The formula should now be multiplied by 5.9 to make the sum of the basic oxides unity. This gives

$$0.65 \text{ K}_2\text{O}$$
$$0.29 \text{ Na}_2\text{O} \quad 1.07 \text{ Al}_2\text{O}_3 \quad \begin{array}{l} 6.67 \text{ SiO}_2 \\ 0.06 \text{ CO}_2 \end{array}$$
$$0.06 \text{ CaO}$$

The above expression would then be used in place of the theoretical composition:

$$\text{K}_2\text{O} \cdot \text{Al}_2\text{O}_3 \cdot 6 \text{ SiO}_2$$

If only a small amount of feldspar is used, the more exact expression is not worth while, but in porcelain glazes where large amounts are needed, it is necessary to use the actual composition.

Converting batch weights to equivalent formulas. This conversion is relatively simple. The steps are as follows:

(1) Divide the weight of each material by its equivalent weight in terms of each component oxide in turn.

(2) Add similar oxides together and set up a Seger formula.

(3) Divide each of the sums obtained in step (2) by the sum of the basic oxides.

As an example of the above procedure, consider the following Cone 13 porcelain glaze:

Potash feldspar	25%
Whiting	11%
Clay	19%
Flint	45%

$$\text{Potash feldspar } \frac{25}{557} = 0.045 \text{ K}_2\text{O}$$

$$\text{Potash feldspar } \frac{25}{557} = 0.045 \text{ Al}_2\text{O}_3$$

$$\text{Potash feldspar } \frac{25}{93} = 0.270 \text{ SiO}_2$$

$$\text{Whiting } \frac{11}{100} = 0.110 \text{ CaO}$$

$$\text{Clay } \frac{19}{258} = 0.074 \text{ Al}_2\text{O}_3$$

$$\text{Clay } \frac{19}{129} = 0.148 \text{ SiO}_2$$

$$\text{Flint } \frac{45}{60} = 0.750 \text{ SiO}_2$$

Rearranging gives:

$$\begin{array}{l} 0.045 \text{ K}_2\text{O} \\ 0.110 \text{ CaO} \end{array} \quad 0.119 \text{ Al}_2\text{O}_3 \quad 1.17 \text{ SiO}_2$$

Dividing by 0.155 to make the basic oxides unity gives the final formula:

$$\begin{array}{l} 0.29 \text{ K}_2\text{O} \\ 0.71 \text{ CaO} \end{array} \quad 0.77 \text{ Al}_2\text{O}_3 \quad 7.5 \text{ SiO}_2$$

III. CLASSIFICATION OF GLAZES

There are many kinds of glazes, and the potter should be familiar with most of them. Here we shall give brief descriptions of the commonly used glazes.

Classification by transparency. Many glazes are as transparent as a piece of window glass and show decorations on the body clearly. In fact, these glazes actually add to the brilliance of the decorations, in much the same way that a pebble freshly picked from the bed of a brook is more brilliant in coloring seen through the water film than after it has dried. An excellent example is the way old New England redware, made of a dull orange-red body, is brought up to a brilliant orange by application of a clear lead glaze.

When it is desired to conceal the body, a white material like tin oxide (SnO_2) is added to the clear glaze to make it milky white. Delft ware is an excellent example; a tin-enamel glaze is used here to cover the buff body (in imitation of Chinese porcelain).

Plumbing fixtures and similar products are covered with an opaque glaze, to give a very white surface. These majolica or tin-enamel glazes were first developed in the Near East, and they were used by the Moors in Spain and on Italian and French Faience, as well as on Dutch and English Delft ware. The della Robbia sculptures made in Italy during the Renaissance are excellent examples.

Beautiful and varied results are obtained by the use of crystalline glazes. In *aventurine* glazes small crystals are formed below the surface, and when hematite (Fe_2O_3), for example, is added to the glaze, the appearance is that of colorful red spangles. Much larger crystals, up to 3 inches in diameter, can be produced also.

Classification by surface. One of the great charms of ceramic glazes is the variety of surfaces that can be produced. Utilitarian glazes have glossy surfaces, and are known as *bright* glazes. When the surface is dulled down to give a sort of eggshell finish by the growth of fine crystals on the glaze, the finish is known as *matte* glaze. This is the finish that is used a great deal on artware.

Other special surfaces are the crinkled surface known as vellum, and the bubbly surface produced by a substance such as manganese dioxide (MnO_2) which gives off gas during firing. These surfaces can be very effective in appearance, but they are dust collectors and are difficult to clean. A *crackle* effect is obtained by deliberate cracking of the glaze into a network of fine lines (crazing).

Classification by color. It is possible to produce nearly any color of nature in glazes, and the names applied to these colors— peachblow, sage green, etc.—attest this sim-

ilarity. Glaze colors are, to all intents and purposes, extremely stable over long periods of time; few other colors have this property.

Classification by composition. Glazes are rather arbitrarily classified as raw and fritted glazes, and each of these groups is further subdivided according to composition. Although it is evident that one type may grade into another, it is helpful to think of sets of glazes, as shown in Table 23–8. Besides those listed, there is a completely different kind of glaze that is applied when the piece is heated in the kiln and exposed to vapors in the combustion gases. Salt glaze is an example.

Some bodies are self-glazing; that is, sufficient glass comes to the surface from the body itself to form a thin surface film. Parian porcelain and Egyptian turquoise ware, the latter containing a soluble copper salt, are examples.

IV. REFERENCES

1. ANDREWS, A. I., *Ceramic Tests and Calculations,* John Wiley & Sons, Inc., New York, 1928.

2. BINNS, C. F., *The Potter's Craft,* 3rd ed., D. Van Nostrand Company, Inc., New York, 1948 (Chap. XV).

3. DEBEVOISE, N. C., The History of Glaze, *Bull. Am. Ceram. Soc.* **13**, 293 (1934).

4. DOAT, T., *Grande Feu Céramics,* Keramic Studio Publishing Company, Syracuse, N. Y., 1905 (Chap. IV).

5. Heatherington, A. L., *Chinese Ceramic Glazes,* Cambridge University Press, 1937.

6. KOENIG, J. H., AND W. H. EARHART, *Literature Abstracts of Ceramic Glazes,* College Offset Press, Philadelphia, 1951.

7. LEACH, B., *A Potter's Book,* Faber & Faber, Ltd., London, 1940.

TABLE 23-8

CLASSIFICATION OF GLAZES

Class	Type	Name	Typical formula			Maturing temp.
Raw	Lead-oxide containing	Raw lead	0.65 PbO 0.25 CaO 0.10 K_2O	0.15 Al_2O_3	1.45 SiO_2	900°C Cone 010
Raw	Zinc-oxide containing	Bristol	0.36 K_2O 0.24 ZnO 0.40 CaO	0.50 Al_2O_3	3.16 SiO_2	1170°C Cone 5
Raw	Lead- and zinc-free	Porcelain	0.30 K_2O 0.70 CaO	0.58 Al_2O_3	0.75 SiO_2	1250°C Cone 9
Fritted	Lead- and borax-free	Alkaline	0.50 K_2O 0.40 CaO 0.10 MgO	0.30 Al_2O_3	1.50 SiO_2	1200°C Cone 6
Fritted	Boric oxide, lead-free	Leadless fritted	0.60 K_2O 0.40 CaO	0.10 Al_2O_3	2.70 SiO_2 0.50 B_2O_3	930°C Cone 09
Fritted	Lead oxide, no borax	Fritted lead	0.40 K_2O 0.25 Na_2O 0.35 PbO	0.15 Al_2O_3	2.30 SiO_2	930°C Cone 09
Fritted	Both lead and boric oxide	Fritted whiteware	0.43 CaO 0.26 PbO 0.18 Na_2O 0.13 ZnO	0.27 Al_2O_3	2.60 SiO_2 0.31 B_2O_3	1200°C Cone 06

CHAPTER 24

Compounding Glazes

I. INTRODUCTION

The preparation of a glaze from the various materials specified in the batch formula is a very simple operation, and should hold no more fear for the beginner than the making of a pie or cake. The simplest of arithmetic suffices, and no background of chemistry is required.

II. MIXING AND WEIGHING

Weighing the ingredients. It makes no difference what unit of weight is used for the ingredients of a glaze batch—pounds, ounces, or grams—provided that the *same* unit is used throughout. As with any recipe, all the quantities for a batch formula may be multiplied or divided by the same number to make larger or smaller batches. For example, the batches of glaze in Table 24–1, each different in total volume, will be identical in their properties.

There is less chance of error if all weighings are in grams rather than in pounds or ounces, and the calculations are simpler. Recall that there are approximately 30 grams in one ounce, and 454 grams in one pound. The metric unit of volume is one cubic centimeter (cc), and it is convenient that 1 cc of water weighs exactly 1 gram.

For weighing ingredients for glazes, the platform balance shown in Fig. 24–1, with sliding weights on the beam up to 10 grams and with a minimum reading of 1/10 gram, will be found most convenient. For large batches, separate weights up to 1000 grams can be used. The balance should be checked before each weighing by setting all of the beam weights to zero and then noting whether the pointer comes to rest at zero or swings to equal angles on each side of the zero point (which is the same thing). If the balance is off, it should be adjusted until the proper balance is reached.

It is obvious that loose materials like powders should never be weighed directly on the platforms of the balance. A piece of paper of typewriter size, folded exactly across the center and torn on the fold will serve very well; one half of the paper is placed on each side of the balance, to assure accuracy. Now the required weight is moved into position on the beam, and the material to be weighed is placed on the paper to the left of the balance until equilibrium is reached. After the proper amount of material has been weighed out, *always* check the weight on the beams to be sure that no error has been made. Even a small mistake may ruin the entire batch of glaze. Learn to weigh accurately and to verify each step as you go along.

If the batch being mixed is so large that the required amount of an ingredient exceeds the capacity of the balance, the quantity may be weighed in several small lots which total the correct amount.

Mixing the ingredients. The most efficient way of mixing the ingredients for a glaze

TABLE 24–1
GLAZE BATCHES

Raw materials	Grams	Grams × 12	Grams × 1/4
White lead	50	600	12.5
Whiting	10	120	2.5
Soda feldspar	18	216	4.5
Kaolin	7	84	1.8
Potter's flint	15	180	3.7
Total	100	1200	25

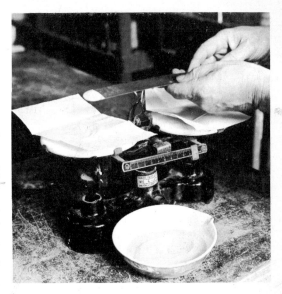

Fig. 24-1. Weighing a batch of glaze on a light balance.

is by milling them in a small ball mill (see Fig. 18–21). You will recall that this consists of a cylindrical porcelain jar containing porcelain balls or flint pebbles. When the jar is rotated about its axis, the load is tumbled about with the pebbles and thoroughly mixed. The grinding action that accompanies the mixing reduces the particle size of the brittle materials like feldspar and flint. There are many ways of rotating the jar, some of which are described in Chapter 30.

Remember the instructions given earlier: the jar should be only half-filled with pebbles and the load with the water should just fill the voids between the pebbles. In other words, the pebbles, dry ingredients, and water combined should occupy no more than half the volume of the jar. Remember, too, that a check should be made after the mill has been running for a few minutes, to be certain that the cover on the jar is tight—there must be no leakage.

Ball mill jars are available in many sizes; the pint, quart, and gallon sizes will be most useful to the potter. The smaller the mill, the faster it must turn to grind efficiently. Recommended speeds and charges are listed in Table 24–2. Maturing temperatures are directly influenced by the milling time, and

this factor must be carefully controlled. It will be found that one hour in a quart mill will grind the load finer than the same length of time in a pint mill. Therefore, grinding times must be varied with mill size.

The consistency of the glaze slip is a factor in the grinding time required: thick slips grind more slowly than thin ones. It will also be found that thin slips thicken after several hours of grinding; a good rule of thumb is that 100 grams of water are needed for each 100 grams of dry glaze in the mill.

All of the above factors must be considered when the grinding time for a particular glaze mixture is to be determined, and it is important to end the grinding just at the appointed time. An automatic shutoff switch is inexpensive and will prove invaluable.

Many of the materials used in glazes are expensive, and it is important to lose as little of the mixture as possible in removing it from the mill. The contents of the jar, including the pebbles, should be poured through a coarse (¼-inch mesh) screen into

TABLE 24–2
CHARACTERISTICS OF BALL MILLS

Outside diameter of jar	Total capacity of jar, in quarts	Weight of charge, in grams[1]	Volume of charge, in quarts	Diameter of pebbles, in inches	Best speed, in rpm
3 in.	0.25	90	0.08	3/8	150
5 in.	1.00	360	0.25	1/2	100
6 in.	2.00	680	0.50	3/4	90
9 in.	6.00	2300	1.50	1	60
13 in.	12.00	4500	3.00	1	40

[1] Dry sand.

Fig. 24-2. Emptying a ball mill properly.

Glaze slips. The experienced potter can quite easily judge the consistency of glaze slip by stirring it, but the beginner should check the specific gravity of the batch to be certain it is of the correct thickness. This is easily done by placing a 100-cc graduate on the scales and balancing it exactly, pouring the well-stirred slip slowly into the graduate up to the 100-cc mark and balancing again (Fig. 24-3). The difference between the two weights, divided by 100, gives the specific gravity. For example:

Wt. of graduate and 100 cc of slip	256.8 grams
Wt. of graduate alone	115.4 grams
Difference	141.4 grams

$$\text{Specific gravity} = \frac{141.4 \text{ grams}}{100 \text{ cc}} = 1.41$$

Glaze slips for dipping should have a specific gravity between 1.4 and 1.5. For spraying they may be slightly thinner.

a bowl, as shown in Fig. 24-2. Next, rinse the jar with a small amount of water and pour this over the pebbles to wash them off. This process can be repeated. The extra water may thin the glaze more than is desirable, but this is easily remedied by allowing it to settle in the bowl over night and then decanting off the clear water.

Some potters pass their glaze slips through a 100-mesh screen to remove any oversized pieces. This is usually not necessary for raw glazes, but it is desirable for a fritted glaze, because an occasional frit particle may have remained unground.

The pebbles and the mill must be thoroughly washed before they are put away. Cleanliness is extremely important in every step of the ceramic process, because the slightest contamination is likely to show up as streaks or specks in the finished piece. If the pebbles or the jar become stained beyond the point where they can be properly cleaned by rinsing or by the use of a brush, a charge of potter's flint and water should be ground in the mill overnight. This treatment is sure to remove all of the stains.

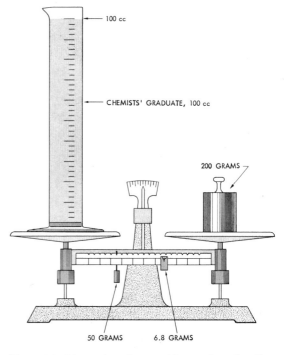

Fig. 24-3. Measuring the specific gravity of a slip.

Remember to always use nonrusting containers, such as glass jars, stoneware crocks, or wooden tubs, for slips.

The use of gums in glazes. Commercial potteries seldom use gums in their glazes, but the artist potter often finds them desirable because they improve the working properties. This is especially true for glazes with a high frit content and for glazes that are to be brushed on. Gum arabic or gum tragacanth may be used.

The gum solution is made up by soaking 10 grams of dry gum in 250 cc of cold water overnight, bringing the mixture to a boil, stirring thoroughly with an eggbeater, and passing it through a 35-mesh screen. This solution will sour within a few days in warm weather, and if it is to be kept for any length of time, 1 cc of formaldehyde should be added as a preservative.

This gum solution is added to the slip in quantities of 5 to 10 cc for each 500 cc of slip. The gum serves to slow up the absorption of water in porous bodies, keeps the glaze in suspension longer, and gives a tougher glaze layer on drying.

Fig. 24-5. Melting the frit in a gas-fired pot furnace.

Making glaze frits. In view of the excellent frits that are commercially available, there are few occasions when it will pay the potter to make his own. However, some glazes, such as turquoise or crystalline, require special frits.

The frit batch is thoroughly mixed in the dry state, preferably by passing it through a 20-mesh screen two or three times. The dry frit is then placed in a fire-clay crucible (Fig. 24-4), and is heated in a pot furnace (Fig. 24-5). The crucible should be no more than two-thirds full.

After the charge has melted down, more batch is added and the melting process is repeated. This procedure is followed until the crucible is about three-quarters full of melted frit. Now the temperature is slowly raised until the melt is free of bubbles, as determined by a fiber drawn from the melt on the tip of an iron rod. The temperature must be increased sufficiently to produce good fluidity of the mixture.

Fig. 24-4. Filling a fireclay crucible with a frit batch.

When the melt appears to be ready, the furnace is shut off, the crucible is removed, and the contents are poured rapidly into a pan of cold water. The stream should be moved about during the pouring, so that not all of the frit falls in the same place. The sudden cooling will shatter the frit so that it will grind easily. Any frit that adheres to the sides of the crucible may be removed by returning it to the furnace until it is melted sufficiently to pour. A crucible may be used a number of times for the same kind of frit, but a new crucible should be used for a frit of different composition (crucibles are inexpensive).

The cooled frit is now broken up in a porcelain mortar and is passed through a 20-mesh screen. It is then ball milled with water for about 12 hours, passed through a 100-mesh screen, and dried. Other materials, such as clay, are usually added to form the glaze, and these should be milled with the frit for a short time to assure thorough mixing.

III. SYSTEMATIC BLENDING OF GLAZES

Varying one component. When a glaze is to be developed for a particular purpose, it is usually necessary to make a number of trials. If this is done systematically, the process is speeded up. For example, suppose that a raw-lead glaze maturing at Cone 06 (1000°C) is to be prepared for a certain body. The basic formula is

0.6 PbO
0.3 CaO   0.2 Al_2O_3 1.6 SiO_2
0.1 Na_2O

It will be found that the amount of silica (SiO_2) must be adjusted to give the proper contraction with the body to be glazed. It would be possible, of course, to make up a whole series of glazes with different values of SiO_2, but it is certainly simpler to make only two glazes—one with a very high concentra-

TABLE 24-3
BLENDING GLAZES, ONE VARIABLE

Volume of glaze A	Volume of glaze B	Equivalents, SiO_2
100 cc	0 cc	1.40
87	13	1.45
75	25	1.50
62	38	1.55
50	50	1.60
38	62	1.65
25	75	1.70
13	87	1.75
0	100	1.80
Glaze A	0.6 PbO 0.3 CaO 0.1 Na_2O 0.2 Al_2O_3 1.4 SiO_2	
Glaze B	0.6 PbO 0.3 CaO 0.1 Na_2O 0.2 Al_2O_3 1.8 SiO_2	

tion of SiO_2 and another with a low concentration. These two mixtures are then adjusted to the same specific gravity and are blended by volume, as shown in Table 24-3, to give a total of 9 different glazes with uniform variations in SiO_2 content. Each glaze is now applied to a tile and the whole lot fired at one time. The results might be something like those shown in Fig. 24-6. It is then evident that for use on this particular body, 1.65 equivalents of silica is the correct value.

Varying two components. The procedure above may also be followed to determine the effect of varying two components of the glaze. For example, let us develop a porcelain glaze for Cone 14 (1390°C) by varying both the silica and alumina content. Four glazes will be needed here, one each for high silica, low silica, high alumina, and low alumina content. The following formulas will serve:

(a)   0.3 K_2O
      0.7 CaO   0.5 Al_2O_3 4.0 SiO_2

(b)   0.3 K_2O
      0.7 CaO   0.5 Al_2O_3 12.0 SiO_2

(c)   0.3 K_2O
      0.7 CaO   2.5 Al_2O_3 4.0 SiO_2

(d)   0.3 K_2O
      0.7 CaO   2.5 Al_2O_3 12.0 SiO_2

Fig. 24-6. The effect of silica content on crazing.

TABLE 24-5

APPEARANCE OF A CONE 14 PORCELAIN GLAZE

Equiv. silica	Equivalents of alumina				
	0.5	1.0	1.5	2.0	2.5
4	C	S.M.	S.M.	S.M.	S.M.
6	C	B	S.M.	S.M.	S.M.
8	C	B	B	S.M.	S.M.
10	C	B	B	S.M.	M.
12	C	C	S.M.	M.	M.

C = Crazed, B = Bright, S.M. = Semi-matte, S = Matte

TABLE 24-4

BLENDING GLAZES, TWO VARIABLES

Volumes of glaze, in cc				Equivalent of SiO$_2$	Equivalent of Al$_2$O$_3$
A	B	C	D		
100	0	0	0	4	0.5
75	0	25	0	4	1.0
50	0	50	0	4	1.5
25	0	75	0	4	2.0
0	0	100	0	4	2.5
75	25	0	0	6	0.5
56	19	19	6	6	1.0
38	12	38	12	6	1.5
19	6	56	19	6	2.0
0	0	75	25	6	2.5
50	50	0	0	8	0.5
38	38	12	12	8	1.0
25	25	25	25	8	1.5
12	12	38	38	8	2.0
0	0	50	50	8	2.5
25	75	0	0	10	0.5
19	56	6	19	10	1.0
12	38	12	38	10	1.5
6	19	19	56	10	2.0
0	0	25	75	10	2.5
0	100	0	0	12	0.5
0	75	0	25	12	1.0
0	50	0	50	12	1.5
0	25	0	75	12	2.0
0	0	0	100	12	2.5

Again, these glaze slips must be adjusted to the same specific gravity and blended by volume (Fig. 24–7 and Table 24–4).

When this series of porcelain glazes is fired on test tiles, a tabulation will give the values listed in Table 24–5, from which it can be seen that a good bright glaze will be

$$0.3 \text{ K}_2\text{O} \quad 1.0 \text{ Al}_2\text{O}_3 \quad 8 \text{ SiO}_2$$
$$0.7 \text{ CaO}$$

and a good matte glaze will be

$$0.3 \text{ K}_2\text{O} \quad 2.5 \text{ Al}_2\text{O}_3 \quad 12 \text{ SiO}_2$$
$$0.7 \text{ CaO}$$

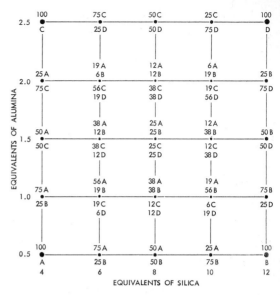

Fig. 24-7. Diagram of porcelain glazes.

Varying three components. Occasionally it may be necessary to vary three constituents independently. As an example, consider the following base glaze:

$$0.3 \text{ K}_2\text{O} \quad 0.6 \text{ Al}_2\text{O}_3 \quad 3.8 \text{ SiO}_2$$
$$0.7 \text{ CaO}$$

This is a bright porcelain glaze firing at Cone 9 (1250°C). If part of the lime (CaO) is replaced by other alkaline earth oxides such as barium oxide (BaO) and magnesium oxide (MgO), a higher gloss will result. To find just the right composition, we shall make three glazes, as follows:

(a) $0.3 \text{ K}_2\text{O}$
0.7 CaO $0.6 \text{ Al}_2\text{O}_3$ 3.8 SiO_2

(b) $0.3 \text{ K}_2\text{O}$
0.4 CaO $0.6 \text{ Al}_2\text{O}_3$ 3.8 SiO_2
0.3 BaO

(c) $0.3 \text{ K}_2\text{O}$
0.4 CaO $0.6 \text{ Al}_2\text{O}_3$ 3.8 SiO_2
0.3 MgO

Once more, these glazes are brought to the same specific gravity and are then blended volumetrically to give a uniform series. For

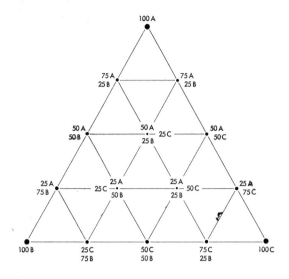

Fig. 24-8. Three-component diagram.

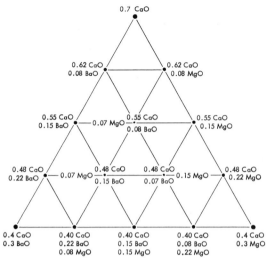

Fig. 24-9. Triangular plot of porcelain glazes.

those unfamiliar with the means of expressing three variables, a diagram is given in Fig. 24–8. Each point in the equilateral triangle represents the sum of the three compositions at the corners.

Now we shall draw a similar triangle (Fig. 24–9) with the glazes at the corners, but the composition will be abbreviated to represent only the alkaline earth. In this way, 12 mixtures are made from the three end members. Of course, it is possible to make many more compositions inside the triangle, if necessary.

Storing glazes. Glaze slips are best stored in tight bottles or jars for indefinite periods;

large quantities are stored in stoneware crocks with covers. Even if the glaze should dry out completely, it can be made usable by mixing with water, but care must be taken to exclude dust and dirt, which cannot be removed and may cause specking. Again let us emphasize that only rustproof containers should be used for glaze.

IV. REFERENCES

1. BINNS, C. F., *The Potter's Craft,* 3rd ed., D. Van Nostrand Company, Inc., New York, 1947 (Chap. XV).

2. PARMELEE, C. W., *Ceramic Glazes.* Industrial Publications, Inc., Chicago, 1948.

CHAPTER 25

Maturing and Fitting Glazes

I. INTRODUCTION

The processes involved in the proper maturing of a glaze seem quite complicated at first glance, but if the problem is approached logically it is quite simple to master the technique. The factors that must be taken into account to assure proper fitting of the glaze to the body are extremely important also, and a serious potter should thoroughly understand them.

II. THE LIFE HISTORY OF GLAZES

Every potter should understand the changes that take place in glazes during firing. Essentially, the granular layer of applied glaze, as if touched by a magic wand, is changed by the heat of the kiln to a thin, continuous layer of glass. The following sections describe in detail what actually happens in the firing process.

Fritted glazes. As a first simple case, let us consider a glaze composed entirely of frit. Frit, it will be remembered, is a finely powdered glass. The life history of such a glaze is diagramed in Fig. 25–1.

When the glaze is heated slowly, no change occurs until the particles start to soften (at about 600°C), when the angular particles become rounded by surface tension forces and are welded together at the points of contact. At temperatures of 800°C or higher, the particles have completely lost their identity and are drawing together into a continuous layer, with bubbles forming in the spaces between the particles. At about 900°C, when the frit has become comparatively fluid, the bubbles coalesce and many of them rise to the surface, where they burst and form pits which soon smooth out. When the glaze is completely matured, we will have a smooth, solid layer of glaze, such as that shown at 1050°C in Fig. 25–1.

Some glazes act on the body in much the same way as water dissolves sugar, leaving tiny crystals at the interface of glaze and body when the body is cooled, which act as anchors to hold the glaze in place.

It is interesting to actually see the changes as they take place in the kiln, and this can be done by glazing a tile and setting it flat in a small kiln where it can be seen through a peephole at a slight angle, as shown in Fig. 25–2. As the temperature increases, the dull glaze becomes more and more glossy. At a certain stage, the bubbles may be seen breaking on the surface like twinkling stars. At maturing temperature, the bubbles have all escaped, and the surface settles down to mirrorlike smoothness.

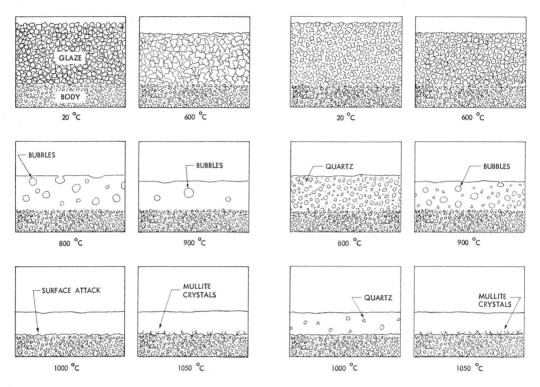

Fig. 25-1. Life history of the firing of a fritted glaze.

Fig. 25-3. Life history of the firing of a raw glaze.

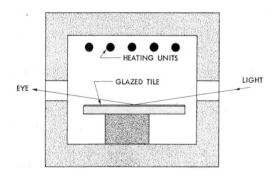

Fig. 25-2. Observing the maturing of a glaze in the kiln.

Raw glazes. The maturing of raw glazes is somewhat different from that for frit glazes because these contain no premelted glass; instead, the raw materials must react with each other to form the glass. In the first stages of firing, raw glaze simply shrinks together, as shown in Fig. 25–3. At about 600°C the amount of glass has increased because of dis-

solution of the raw materials, and at the same time bubbles appear in the glass. As the temperature continues to increase, the bubbles gradually rise to the surface and disappear, and this continues until all of the raw material except some of the potter's flint has dissolved. At maturity the glaze is completely free of solid particles and bubbles, as shown at 1050°C in Fig. 25–3.

III. FITTING OF GLAZES

In this section we shall explain the proper fitting of the glaze to the body being fired. A most annoying defect of glazing is crazing, which produces a network of cracks in the finished glaze. This defect is directly due to the improper fitting of the glaze to the body, and to avoid it we need to know how a glaze can be properly made for the body it is to cover.

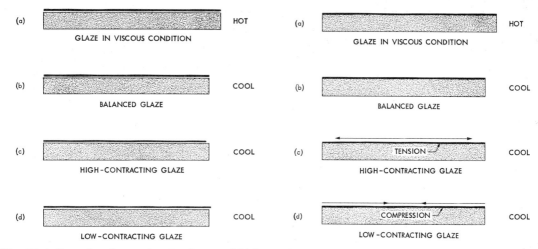

Fig. 25-4. Free glaze layer, showing low- and high-contracting compositions.

Fig. 25-5. The same glazes as in Fig. 25-4, but bonded to the body, showing the stresses that arise on firing.

Cause of crazing. At the glost firing temperature, the glaze is of about the consistency of thick maple syrup, and it flows in an even layer. As it starts to cool, it becomes more and more viscous, until it reaches a temperature where it is completely rigid. From this point down to room temperature, if the glaze and the body contract at the same rate, there will be no strains in the finished glaze; a difference in contraction is what causes crazing.

Figure 25–4 shows the edge of a small tile which has been glazed on one face. For purposes of demonstration only, the face of the tile was coated with fine quartz to prevent the glaze from adhering to the surface of the tile (this would never actually be done, of course). In part (a) of the figure, the tile is shown in the cooling kiln just as the glaze becomes firm enough to have a little strength, and it will be seen that the length of the glaze layer is the same as that of the tile. In (b) the tile has cooled to room temperature, and we note that the glaze has contracted exactly as much as the tile, and is still the same length as the tile. In (c), however, a different glaze, with a high coefficient of expansion, has been

used, and it has contracted more than the tile. The opposite situation is shown in (d); a glaze was used that contracted less than the body used for the tile, and consequently at room temperature the glaze is longer than the tile.

Now we shall repeat this experiment with a normally glazed tile, where the glaze layer adheres strongly to the body, as it should. This condition is shown schematically in Fig. 25–5. In parts (a) and (b) of this figure, the glaze of Fig. 25–4(c) has been cooled and shows no resulting stress. In (c) the glaze of Fig. 25–4(c) has been cooled, but here the glaze is in tension, for it must now be stretched from its normally short length to the size of the tile. In part (d) of Fig. 25–5 the normally longer glaze must be squeezed down to the size of the tile and is thus in compression.

Because glaze is very strong under compression, the glaze in Fig. 25–5(d) might not be harmed, but because glaze is very weak under tension, the glaze in Fig. 25–5(c) would almost certainly crack or, as a potter would say, "It crazes."

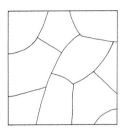 

Fig. 25-6. Tiles with crazed glazes.

Samples of crazed tiles are shown in Fig. 25-6. The larger "mesh" of the cracks is due to low-tension stresses, while the fine mesh of cracks is due to high stresses. Sometimes this crazing is deliberately produced to make what is known as "crackle" ware.

When a glaze fails by cracking under very high compression, it is called "shivering." Figure 25-7 shows a cross section of a glaze that has shivered, to illustrate the difference between this condition and crazing.

Delayed crazing. Experienced potters know that although some glazes are quite acceptable when taken from the kiln, they develop crazing after a period of time (this may be from several days to as long as a month). This imperfection may result for two reasons: (1) there may be a delayed contraction of the glaze, because it takes some time for a glaze to reach equilibrium at room temperature; (2) the body, if it is porous, may have expanded slightly because of the moisture in the air. To be reasonably well assured that such delayed crazing will be avoided, the glaze should be in some compression when it is removed from the kiln. It must be remembered, however, that a state of high

Fig. 25-7. Cross sections of a glaze, enlarged to show crazing and shivering.

compression will cause the glaze to fail at corners and edges.

We can test a piece to see if it will craze with time by heating the piece in steam immediately after it has been removed from the kiln. This is done in an autoclave, which is simply a more powerful version of an ordinary pressure cooker. If crazing does not appear after one hour at 150 pounds pressure, it is safe to assume that the piece will not craze if it is to be used indoors.

Prevention of crazing. If the reasoning in the previous section has been closely followed, it is obvious that there are two ways of preventing crazing: (1) the body can be corrected to contract *more,* or (2) the glaze can be corrected to contract *less.*

If the first method is to be used, then the ingredient having the greatest tendency to contract should be increased, which would automatically increase the contraction of the entire body. Experiments have shown that potter's flint (quartz) has high contraction; therefore it is logical to increase the amount of this material used in the mixture for the body.

When the body composition cannot be changed, we change the glaze composition. The contraction potential of the glaze is decreased by increasing the amounts of minerals that contribute to low contraction. Silica (potter's flint) is one of these, and increasing the boric oxide while at the same time decreasing the amounts of the alkalies (soda and potash) will lessen the contraction of the glaze. (Increasing the amount of silica to lessen contraction of the glaze may seem like a contradiction, since we recommended the same procedure for *increasing* contraction in the body. However, in a body the silica is in a crystal form which *encourages* contraction, while in a glaze it is in a glassy form which *discourages* contraction.)

As outlined above, the solution to the problem of crazing seems simple, but, as we have learned, when one ingredient of a mixture is changed it is necessary to alter others if we are to avoid equally bad faults. For example, in our attempts to avoid crazing by increasing or decreasing the amount of a single material, we may seriously alter the temperature range required for maturing, or some other equally important factor.

The beginner is well advised to use tested glazes and bodies at first, so that a fit will be assured. There are many suitable commercial frits available, and by proper selection a glaze suited to any body can be purchased.

Bodies high in talc contract less on cooling than normal bodies, and the glazes for these should have a particularly low coefficient of expansion. Matte glazes have less tendency to craze than bright glazes, for the crystals act as reinforcement and consequently permit some tensile stress without failure.

Systematic fitting of glazes. While glazes may be properly fitted by the trial-and-error method if sufficient time is allowed, it is much better to follow a logical plan. As an example, let us consider the following standard porcelain glaze:

$$\begin{matrix} 0.30 \text{ K}_2\text{O} \\ 0.70 \text{ CaO} \end{matrix} \quad n\,\text{Al}_2\text{O}_3 \quad m\,\text{SiO}_2$$

and systematically vary the amounts of alumina and silica. The results are shown in Table 25–1, and it is evident that the crazing region is easily avoided.

IV. GLAZE DEFECTS

It is not possible to discuss here all of the glaze defects that constantly annoy the potter, but we shall talk about the more important ones, with emphasis on their causes and prevention. Crazing has been discussed above, and we shall briefly describe other defects.

Crawling. This common defect was mentioned in Chapter 9. It is caused by cracks set up in drying, either because the glaze film shrank too much, or because the film was too weak. Unfortunately, if the shrinkage is reduced by using less raw clay and less grinding, the weakness is increased, as pointed out by Danielson (2). However, a compromise can usually be made; for example, the use of organic materials such as gums toughen the film. Glazes high in frit seldom give crawling trouble.

Fine bubbles. Bubbles in the glaze are apt to give trouble, particularly when a clear glaze is used over a dark body or a dark underglaze decoration. Although the bubbles are below the surface, they are often so numerous that they give a milky appearance to the finished piece. These bubbles are to be found where the glaze deposit is heavy, and in commercial ware they usually appear, for example, around the foot of a plate. A thinner glaze layer and longer firing at higher temperatures are the remedies for this defect, because these are bubbles that did not escape when the glaze was fused to the body.

TABLE 25-1

APPEARANCE OF CONE 10 PORCELAIN GLAZE

Equiv. silica (m)	Equivalents of alumina (n)							
	0.3	0.4	0.5	0.6	0.7	0.8	0.9	1.0
4	C	C	B	B	S.M.	S.M.	S.M.	M
5	C	C	B	S.M.	S.M.	S.M.	M	M
6	C	C	C	S.M.	S.M.	S.M.	M	M
7	C	C	C	S.M.	S.M.	M	M	M
8	C	C	C	C	M	M	M	M
9		C	C	C	C	M	M	I
10		C	C	C	C	C	I	I
11			C	C	C	C	C	C
12			C	C	C	C	C	C

$$\begin{matrix} 0.30 \text{ K}_2\text{O} \\ 0.70 \text{ CaO} \end{matrix} \quad n\,\text{Al}_2\text{O}_3 \quad m\,\text{SiO}_2$$

C = Crazed, B = Bright, S.M. = Semi-matte, M = Matte, I = Immature

Blisters and pinholes. One cause of these defects is the air that is trapped in pockets in the body and which forces its way out through the glaze. A well-prepared body minimizes their occurrence. Blisters are sometimes caused in raw glazes by the gases given off by some of the ingredients. Finer grinding will help.

Dirt. This is a very common defect that is primarily due to refractory particles that settle in the glaze before or during firing. Sometimes the dirt comes from the kiln or the kiln furniture. Before setting a glost kiln, the dust should be blown out and the shelves brushed off. A wash on the kiln furniture will help.

Specks. These colored spots are sometimes green and sometimes brown. The former are due to copper particles that enter the glaze from a screen or some other copper article. The latter come from iron. Cleanliness, care, and the avoidance wherever possible of copper and iron utensils will prevent these.

Wavy surface. A wavy surface is an indication that the firing temperature was too low to allow the glaze to become fluid enough to smooth out.

Pebbly surface. This usually occurs when the glaze has been sprayed on, and is an indication that the coat was not evenly applied.

Scum. This is caused by the use of soluble material in the glaze (perhaps a partially soluble frit).

Attack on underglaze colors. Zinc-containing glazes tend to react with many of the colors used for underglazes, and glazes that are high in lead tend to dissolve some of them.

Uneven color. When the glaze color appears in specks and spots, it is an indication of insufficient grinding of the slip. To get an even color, add the stain to the frit, rather than to the finished glaze batch.

Run-off. This fault is due to excessive fluidity of the glaze. Either the firing temperature should be lowered, or the viscosity of the glaze should be increased by the addition of alumina or silica.

V. REFERENCES

1. BLAKELY, JR., A. M., The Life History of a Glaze, II. Measurement of Stresses in a Cooling Glaze, *J. Am. Ceram. Soc.* **21**, 243 (1938).

2. DANIELSON, R. R., Crawling of Glazes, *Bull. Am. Ceram. Soc.* **33**, 73 (1954).

3. Harmon, C. G., Suggestions for Solution of Difficult Glaze-Fit Problems, *J. Am. Ceram. Soc.* **27**, 231 (1944).

4. JOHNSON, A. L., Stresses in Porcelain Glazes, *J. Am. Ceram. Soc.* **22**, 363 (1939).

5. MATTYASOVSZKY-ZSOLNAY, L., Investigations on Crazing, I-III, *J. Am. Ceram. Soc.* **29**, 200 (1946).

6. SCHURECHT, H. G., AND G. R. POLE, Method of Measuring Strains between Glazes and Ceramic Bodies, *J. Am. Ceram. Soc.* **13**, 369 (1930).

7. SCHURECHT, H. G., Fitting Glazes to Ceramic Bodies, *J. Am. Ceram. Soc.* **26**, 93 (1943).

CHAPTER 26

Practical Glazes

I. INTRODUCTION

In this chapter, we shall give some specific glaze formulas that are representative of the standard types, as well as a few special ones. These formulas have all been adjusted to one of four temperature levels and in most cases are planned to fit specific bodies. We have tried to make the directions for compounding and applying these glazes sufficiently complete so that the most inexperienced potter can successfully follow them. Additional information about practical glazes can be found in the extensive list of references at the end of the chapter.

II. STANDARD GLAZES

Raw lead glazes. The following simple glazes are easy to apply because they flow out smoothly on firing. They are brilliant, but easily scratched.

A bright glaze firing at Cone 08–04 (950°–1050°C):

$$0.6 \, PbO$$
$$0.3 \, CaO \qquad 0.2 \, Al_2O_3 \qquad 1.6 \, SiO_2 \quad (1)$$
$$0.1 \, Na_2O$$

A similar opaque glaze maturing at the same temperatures:

$$0.72 \, PbO \qquad\qquad 1.93 \, SiO_2$$
$$0.17 \, CaO \quad 0.17 \, Al_2O_3 \qquad\qquad (2)$$
$$0.11 \, ZnO \qquad\qquad 0.33 \, SnO_2$$

An opaque matte glaze with the same maturing range:

$$0.50 \, PbO$$
$$0.35 \, CaO \quad 0.35 \, Al_2O_3 \quad 1.55 \, SiO_2 \quad (3)$$
$$0.15 \, Na_2O$$

The batch formulas for these three glazes are given in Table 26–1.

These glazes can be readily colored by adding oxides or stains and grinding with the batch. Table 26–2 lists the colors formed in the bright glaze; the colors in the other glazes will be similar in hue but not so brilliant. Addition of color to the batch will cause specking unless the grinding time is long, but since long grinding may spoil the working properties of the glaze, it is better

TABLE 26–1
RAW LEAD GLAZES[1]

Raw materials	Bright (1)	Opaque (2)	Matte (3)
White lead	49 grams	48 grams	52 grams
Whiting	10	7	9
Soda feldspar	18		28
Edgar plastic kaolin	5	5	5
Calcined kaolin	3	6	4
Potter's flint	15	20	2
Tin oxide	– – – –	12	
Zinc oxide	– – – –	2	
Water	150 cc	125 cc	125 cc
Grind in qt mill	15 min	15 min	15 min
Specific gravity of slip	1.4	1.5	1.5
Application, cc/sq cm	0.1	0.2	0.2
For use on body No.	1,2,6	1,2,3,6,7,12	1,2,3,6,7,12

[1] Fire at Cone 08–04 (950 - 1050°C)

TABLE 26–2
COLORS PRODUCED IN RAW LEAD GLAZE NO. 1

Oxide added	Amount added	Color	Munsel specifications
Chromic oxide	0.05% 0.01	Deep yellow Bright yellow	2.5 Y 8/12 7.5 Y 6/10
Cupric oxide	6 2	Grass green Light green	2.5 G 6/6 2.5 G 8/4
Manganese oxide	0.7 0.1	Lilac Pale lilac	RPR 5/2 RPR 8/2
Ferric oxide	7 2	Orange[1] Buff[1]	YR 5/10 YRY 7/6
Nickel oxide	16 1	Olive green[1] Cream	5 GY 6/4 2.5 Y 8/6
Cobalt oxide	0.3 0.1	Medium blue Pale blue	5 PB 4/4 5 PB 6/4

[1] Contains crystals.

to grind the coloring oxide with only about one-third of the flint or feldspar for 2 hours, and then add the remainder of the batch and grind for the required 15 minutes.

Fritted glazes. These glazes are readily made from standard frits, usually have good working properties, and are less poisonous than the raw-lead glazes. They are recommended for the beginner.

A few glazes recommended by Pemco are listed in Table 26–3. Laboratory tests show that they are simple to use and give good results. Numbers 4 and 5 are low-temperature glazes, while 6 and 7 are for Cone 3 and Cone 4 firing. Number 8 is a low-expansion glaze for talc bodies, while 9 is a higher-temperature opaque glaze.

Porcelain glazes. These glazes are simple to mix, hard, durable, and nonpoisonous. We are all familiar with the very fine ware that is made from porcelain, and the chief reason for its limited use by the artist potter is that he lacks equipment for producing the very high firing temperatures required for porcelain.

TABLE 26–4
PORCELAIN GLAZES

Raw materials	For Cone 8–9 (1225–1250°C)		For Cone 16 (1450°C)	
	Bright (10)	Matte (11)	Bright (12)	Matte (13)
Whiting	18 grams	23 grams	17 grams	6 grams
Potash feldspar	43	55	17	14
Edgar plastic kaolin	8	9	11	4
Calcined kaolin	9	7	9	–
Potter's flint	22	–	49	50
Aluminum hydrate	–	6	7	26
Water	125 cc	125 cc	125 cc	125 cc
Grind in quart mill for	1 hr	1 hr	1 hr	1 hr
Specific gravity of slip	1.5	1.5	1.5	1.5
Application, cc/sq cm	0.1	0.2	0.1	0.2
For use on body No.	7, 13	7, 13	14	14

The four glazes described below and in Table 26–4 are more or less standard. They are particularly suited for application to low-fired biscuit.

Bright, Cone 8–9 (1225°–1250°C):

$$\begin{matrix} 0.30 \ K_2O \\ 0.70 \ CaO \end{matrix} \quad 0.50 \ Al_2O_3 \quad 4 \ SiO_2 \qquad (10)$$

Matte, Cone 8–9 (1225°–1250°C):

$$\begin{matrix} 0.30 \ K_2O \\ 0.70 \ CaO \end{matrix} \quad 1.00 \ Al_2O_3 \quad 8 \ SiO_2 \qquad (11)$$

Bright, Cone 16 (1450°C):

$$\begin{matrix} 0.30 \ K_2O \\ 0.70 \ CaO \end{matrix} \quad 1.10 \ Al_2O_3 \quad 10 \ SiO_2 \qquad (12)$$

Matte, Cone 16 (1450°C):

$$\begin{matrix} 0.30 \ K_2O \\ 0.70 \ CaO \end{matrix} \quad 2.50 \ Al_2O_3 \quad 11 \ SiO_2 \qquad (13)$$

TABLE 26–3
FRITTED GLAZES[1]

Materials	Bright (4)	Bright (5)	Bright (6)	Bright (7)	Bright (8)	Opaque (9)
Pemco Pb–63 Frit	92	46				
Pemco Pb–349 Frit	– – – –	46				
Pemco P–311 Frit	– – – –	– – – –	51.5			
Pemco Pb–316 Frit	– – – –	– – – –	25.1			
Pemco Pb–197 Frit	– – – –	– – – –		46.1		
Pemco Pb–545 Frit	– – – –	– – – –		8.7		
Pemco P–806 Frit	– – – –	– – – –		13.1		
Pemco Pb–629 Frit	– – – –	– – – –		– – – –	66.6	
Pemco P–675 Frit						54.0
Kaolin	8	8	4.7	9.2	6.8	6.8
Whiting	– – – –	– – – –	4.0	– – – –	4.1	
Potter's flint	– – – –	– – – –	14.7	5.2	9.3	16.8
Soda feldspar	– – – –	– – – –		13.2	13.2	19.5
Zinc oxide				4.5		
Tin oxide	– – – –	– – – –			– – – –	2.9
Water	100 grams	100 grams	100 grams	100 grams	100 grams	100 grams
Grind in qt mill	15 min	15 min	15 min	15 min	15 min	15 min
Sp. gravity of slip	1.5	1.5	1.5	1.5	1.5	1.4
App., cc/sq cm	0.1	0.1				0.3
Maturing condition	Cone 08–04 950–1050°C	Cone 08–04 950–1050°C	Cone 3–4 1145–1165°C	Cone 3–4 1145–1165°C	Cone 3–4 1145–1165°C	Cone 8–9 1225–1250°C
Use on body No.	1,6,12	1,6,12	6,7,12	6,12	12	3

[1] Formulas suggested by Pemco.

TABLE 26-5

COLORS PRODUCED IN PORCELAIN GLAZE, NO. 10

Oxide added	Amount added	Color	Munsel specifications
Cobalt oxide	4.0%	Deep purple	7.5 PB 3/8
	1.5	Purple-blue	7.5 PB 4/8
	0.2	Pale blue	7.5 PB 7/8
Chromic oxide	5.0	Deep green	5 G 5/4
	1.5	Green	2.5 G 6/4
	0.2	Pale green	7.5 GY 8/2
Nickel oxide	4.0	Olive brown	5 Y 6/4
Ferric oxide	4.0	Coral red	RYR 3/8

These glazes can be colored by the addition of oxides or stains, as indicated in Table 26-5.

Bristol glazes. These raw glazes contain considerable amounts of zinc oxide. They are suitable for terra cotta and other heavy clay bodies, but because of the limited range of colors, they are seldom used for artware.

A typical bright glaze maturing at Cone 3–4 (1145°–1165°C):

$$0.36 \text{ K}_2\text{O} \atop 0.24 \text{ ZnO} \quad 0.50 \text{ Al}_2\text{O}_3 \quad 3.16 \text{ SiO}_2 \quad (14) \atop 0.40 \text{ CaO}$$

An opaque matte glaze for the same temperature:

$$0.24 \text{ K}_2\text{O} \atop 0.27 \text{ ZnO} \quad 0.39 \text{ Al}_2\text{O}_3 \quad 2.00 \text{ SiO}_2 \quad (15) \atop 0.49 \text{ CaO}$$

The batch mixes for these glazes are given in Table 26-6.

TABLE 26-6

BRISTOL GLAZES[1]

Raw materials	Bright (14)	Opaque (15)
Potash feldspar	60 grams	51 grams
Zinc oxide	6	9
Calcium carbonate	12	19
Kaolin	9	15
Potter's flint	13	6
Water	125	125
Grind qt mill for	15 min	15 min
Sp. gravity of slip	1.4	1.4
Thickness of app.	0.1 cc/sq cm	0.2 cc/sq cm
For use on body No.	6	2,6,7

[1] Mature at Cone 3–4 (1145–1165°C)

III. SPECIAL GLAZES

Crystalline glazes. Many kinds of crystalline glaze are described in the literature, but those that produce zinc silicate crystals are the most satisfactory. The co[l]... quired for firing crystalline glaze[s] ... exact, and successive satisfactory firings are obtained only with the use of an accurate pyrometer.

The following glaze produces crystals as large as 3 inches in diameter, and it permits a wide range of color variations.

$$0.235 \text{ K}_2\text{O} \atop 0.087 \text{ CaO} \atop 0.052 \text{ Na}_2\text{O} \quad 0.162 \text{ Al}_2\text{O}_3 \quad {1.700 \text{ SiO}_2 \atop 0.202 \text{ TiO}_2} \quad (16) \atop 0.051 \text{ BaO} \atop 0.575 \text{ ZnO}$$

The batch formula for the above glaze is given in Table 26–7.

Because of the low clay content, this glaze is difficult to apply, but it can be sprayed on the body if the slip is kept agitated. This kind of glaze runs down vertical surfaces quite freely, and therefore stilts must be placed under the pieces when they are fired. The firing schedule is as follows:

Fig. 26-1. Large crystals grown in a glaze by controlled firing.

TABLE 26-7

SPECIAL GLAZES

Raw materials	16 Crystalline	17 Aventurine	18 Opalescent	19 Copper red[1]	20 Copper red[1]	21 Copper red[1]	22 Copper red[1]	23 Turquoise
FRIT BATCH								
Potassium carbonate	40.0		3.7					
Sodium carbonate	6.7			4.9	6.8			8.0
Barium carbonate	12.4		4.0					
Calcium carbonate			1.1	8.3	5.9			
Sodium nitrate				11.9				
White lead								
Ferro frit #3304		79						
Zinc oxide	57.5		19.4					
Ferric oxide								
Tin oxide				1.0	2.6			
Potash feldspar			9.6	16.9				
Borax			27.4	32.0				
Boric oxide					14.5			
Titanium dioxide	19.7							
Kaolin								11.2
Potter's flint	89.5		35.2	13.8	17.8			36.7
Cupric oxide				1.2	5.9			2.4
Ferro frit No. 3191						13.0	4.0	
Ferro frit No. 3396							16.0	
Pemco frit No. P-283							16.0	
Soda feldspar					46.7			24.4
Potassium nitrate								17.3
Red lead								
GLAZE BATCH								
Calcium carbonate	3.9				5.0	14.0	2.0	
White lead				8.30			22.0	
Soda feldspar						44.0		
Zinc oxide							3.0	
Tin oxide						1.0	1.0	
Cupric oxide						0.2		
Copper carbonate							0.2	
Ferric oxide		16						
Silicon carbide						0.2	0.3	
English china clay				12.5	12.1	3.0	10.0	
Edgar plastic kaolin	18.2	5						
Potter's flint	4.5			2.9	8.5	25.0	27.0	
Glaze No. 1			39.8					
Frit from table above	73.4	79	60.2	76.3	74.4	13.0	36.0	All
Water	100	120	125	125	125	125	125	100
Grind in quart mill	2 hr	1.5 hr	1 hr	1 hr	1 hr	2 hr	2 hr	2 hr
Specific gravity of slip	1.4	1.5	1.5	1.4	1.4	1.5	1.5	1.6
Thickness of app.	0.3 cc/sq cm	0.2 cc/sq cm	0.2 cc/sq cm	0.1 cc/sq cm	0.1 cc/sq cm	0.2 cc/sq cm	0.2 cc/sq cm	0.3 cc/sq cm
Maturing conditions	Special firing[1]	Cone 3-4 1145-1165°C	Cone 04 1050°C	Cone 08-04[2] 945-1050°C	Cone 8[2] 1225°C	Cone 9-10 1250-1260°C	Cone 04-03 1050-1080°C	Cone 09 930°C
For use on body No.	13	6,7	3	3,7,12	3	3,7	7	3,13

[1] Requires a special firing with controlled cooling. [2] Requires alternate oxidation and reduction.

Heat to 1275°C in 1 hour.
Hold at 1275°C for ½ hour.
Cool suddenly to 1100°C.
Hold at 1100°C for 1 to 4 hours.
Cool to room temperature.

Large, circular crystals should be produced with this formula, as shown in Fig. 26-1. The colors listed in Table 26-8 are formed by the addition of coloring oxides to the batch.

Aventurine glazes. These glazes are made by supersaturating the batch with iron oxide, which, on cooling, crystallizes out in the form of small, glistening crystals of hematite (Fe_2O_3). It is important to know exactly how much iron to use, because too much will cause surface crystallization. Of the many formulas for this type of glaze, No. 17, listed in Table 26-7, has been found by Schurecht (6) to be most satisfactory. This glaze is fired to Cone 3-4 (1145°-1165°C) and cooled slowly.

TABLE 26-8

COLORS IN CRYSTALLINE GLAZES

Oxide added	Background color	Crystal color
0.50% CaO	Pink	Light green
0.25% CoO	Tan	Brilliant blue
0.50% Fe_2O_3	Slate blue	Gray
0.50% MnO_2	Yellow	Gray
0.50% Cr_2O_3	Olive green	Green and blue

Flow glazes. These beautiful glazes reached their highest development in France. We know little about their specific composition, but they certainly contain such crystallizing elements as titania. They are applied thickly and with mixed colors, so that on firing they flow down the vertical surfaces of the piece and intermingle to give a varied pattern. Here again the pieces must be set on high stilts to allow room for some of the glaze to drip off.

The Rockingham ware made in England is typical of this kind of glaze. The Rockingham effect is obtained by dipping a cream-colored glaze on the body and immediately spattering a brown glaze on top of it with a stiff brush. The two colors blend together when the piece is fired, to give the familiar mottled appearance.

Fenton's flint enamel glaze, made in Bennington, Vermont, about the middle of the 19th century, is one of the few glazes that has been patented. This was similar to the Rockingham glaze, but with the addition of flecks of green and blue coloring. Marked pieces of this ware are collectors' items.

Opalescent glazes. These glazes must be very thick, and must have very fine crystals suspended in them. However, the crystals must not be so numerous that they completely prevent transparency. Like a natural opal, this finish should show a slight cloudiness. Many kinds of crystals will give opalescence, but usually these glazes are made crystalline by the use of boric oxide and silica. It is believed that very fine crystals of silica are formed when the glaze is cooled after firing. Of course, color is usually added to this glaze. Glaze No. 18 in Table 26–7 gives a good opalescent effect.

Reduction glazes. Some of the most beautiful glazes are in this group, but the exacting firing requirements discourage the beginner from attempting their use. However, the results are well worth the difficulties involved. These glazes reached their highest state of perfection in China, during the Sung and Ming dynasties. The reds (oxblood, peachblow, etc.) were made with a copper-containing glaze, while the gray-green celadons were made with a glaze containing ferrous iron.

The copper reds have been discussed in the literature at great length, but we are still not sure what produces this color. A paper by Mellor (96a) probably gives the best summary of the facts. This author is of the opinion that the red is due to a metallic copper colloid stabilized with tin oxide (SnO_2). However, there is some evidence that red copper oxide (Cu_2O) is the cause. Good reds are obtainable with a wide variety of glaze compositions, but the atmosphere in firing must be carefully controlled, usually with alternating periods of reduction and oxidation.

Depending on the atmosphere of the kiln, black, green, colorless, and various shades of red glaze can be obtained from the same glaze mixture. Baggs has shown that the reduction needed to produce good reds can also be attained by adding a reducing agent such as silicon carbide (SiC) to a slip under the glaze and then firing under conditions of oxidation. The author has often noticed that when copper-containing frits are melted under oxidizing conditions and are poured from a fire-clay crucible, they leave a residue with an excellent red color. It is believed that the ferrous oxide in the fire clay acts as a reducing agent, although this has yet to be proved.

Chinese celadon glazes are pale green, very thick, and more or less opaque. The opacity is due to the myriad bubbles in the glaze; under a microscope they look like a mass of frog's eggs. The fractured edge of a celadon cup often will show a glaze thickness that is greater than that of the body itself. In other words, it is essentially a thin layer of porcelain sandwiched between two thick layers of glaze. These glazes contain dissolved iron in the ferrous state and must be fired in a reducing atmosphere. All of these glazes show some crazing. Celadon glazes are produced by adding 1 to 3% ferrous oxide to a porcelain glaze and firing in a reducing atmosphere.

The Cone 08–04 (950°–1050°C) copper-red glaze (Harder), which follows, gives good reds if properly fired. The batch formula is given in Table 26–7.

$$
\begin{array}{lll}
0.10\ K_2O & & \\
0.33\ Na_2O & & 2.05\ SiO_2 \\
0.27\ CaO & 0.38\ Al_2O_3 & 0.54\ B_2O_3 \quad (19) \\
0.25\ PbO & & 0.02\ SnO_2 \\
0.05\ CuO & &
\end{array}
$$

The firing schedule for this glaze is:
Oxidation to 600°C.
Reduction from 600° to 860°C.
Oxidation from 860° to 960°C.
Reduction from 960° to 1000°C.
Slow cooling in air.

The alternate firing schedule below gives good results:
Oxidation in 2 hr to 825°C.
Reduction from 825° to 875°C.
Oxidation from 875° to 925°C.
Reduction from 925° to 950°C.
Oxidation from 950° to 975°C.
Reduction from 975° to 1000°C.
Oxidation from 1000° to 1025°C.
Reduction from 1025° to 1050°C.
Oxidation for 10 min at 1050°C.
Reduction for 10 min at 1050°C.
Oxidation for 10 min at 1050°C.
Cooling in air.

The following glaze for Cone 8 (1225°C), also taken from Harder, gives good reds. The batch formula is given in Table 26–7.

$$
\begin{array}{lll}
0.08\ K_2O & & 3.75\ SiO_2 \\
0.52\ Na_2O & 0.49\ Al_2O_3 & 0.06\ SnO_2 \quad (20) \\
0.40\ CaO & & 0.70\ B_2O_3 \\
& +\ 0.05\%\ CuO &
\end{array}
$$

Glaze No. 22 in Table 26–7 works well at Cone 04–08 (950°–1050°C) on bodies 6 and 7, and No. 21 is a similar glaze for use at Cone 8–9 (1225°–1250°C).

Theoretically, it should be possible to produce a good copper red by placing a piece coated with clear glaze into a tight sagger with a volatile copper compound, so that the transfer can occur in the vapor phase. Reducing conditions would have to be maintained in this case, also.

A few potteries, like Doulton's in England and Gladding McBean in California, have been able to produce good copper reds commercially. The artist potter, however, must be prepared for many disappointments before a good red can be consistently produced.

Turquoise glazes. A pure blue copper glaze can be obtained only within a narrow range of composition, outside of which a greenish tint creeps in. The author has found glaze No. 23 in Table 26–7 most successful, although it is difficult to apply because it is all frit (no clay may be used). However, it can be sprayed on the piece if great care is taken. The equivalent formula is

$$
\begin{array}{lll}
0.40\ K_2O & & \\
0.25\ Na_2O & 0.15\ Al_2O_3 & 2.3\ SiO_2 \quad (23) \\
0.25\ PbO & & \\
0.10\ CuO & &
\end{array}
$$

Natural glazes. For many years, red-burning clays have been used for stoneware and electrical porcelain. These clays can be used as they come from the ground, or they can be made into a slip that will pass through a 100-mesh screen. The composition is sometimes altered by the addition of small amounts of flux and by ball milling. Many clays are suitable for this purpose, but the best known are the slip clays from Albany, New York, of the following approximate composition:

$$0.20\ K_2O$$
$$0.45\ CaO \qquad 0.61\ Al_2O_3$$
$$0.35\ MgO \qquad 0.08\ Fe_2O_3 \qquad 3.97\ SiO_2$$

This glaze has a wide firing range ($1200°$–$1300°C$, Cone 6–12) and gives a reddish-brown color. There seems to be little tendency for it to craze, whether used for one-fire or two-fire work.

The above slip clay can be made somewhat more workable by the addition of other materials, like those listed for the insulator glaze, No. 24 in Table 26–9, maturing at Cone 8–9 ($1225°$–$1250°C$).

Glazes can also be made from natural rock mixtures. Glaze No. 25 in Table 26–9 is an example. This glaze fires at Cone 8–9 ($1225°$–$1250°C$) to give a golden brown matte.

Many of the early Chinese and Japanese stoneware glazes were made from wood ashes and a natural flux, and very interesting effects are obtained with such glazes. Leach discusses these in his book and gives a number of formulas. Because the ash from different woods varies a good deal in composition, the source of the ash must be carefully controlled. Formula No. 26 in Table 26–9 is an example of this kind of glaze.

Blister glazes. Glazes that froth up in firing to leave a rough surface of broken blisters are sometimes used by studio potters. This kind of finish can be used quite effectively on heavy pieces, although it is difficult to wash. The effect is secured by adding to the glaze a small amount of granular material that decomposes at the temperature of glaze fluidity. The material used depends on the maturing temperature of the glaze, but it is often a carbonate or manganese dioxide. The following is a list of decomposition temperatures of several suitable ingredients.

TABLE 26-9

SPECIAL GLAZES

Raw materials	Slip glaze (24)	Granite glaze matte (25)	Ash glaze (26)	Crackle matte (27)	Crackle matte (28)	Crackle bright (29)	Crackle bright (30)	Self glaze (31)
Borax	2							
Whiting				9.0	19.8	12.8	8.2	
Aluminum hydrate					2.3	3.7	6.4	
Sodium carbonate								10.6
Red lead				32.0				
Albany slip clay	47							
Ball clay	9	5	20					
Edgar plastic kaolin				12.0	3.7	3.3	1.5	10.5
Calcined kaolin				12.0				
Potash feldspar	37		40	20.0	47.1	30.4	19.6	34.2
Potter's flint				10.0	27.1	41.8	64.3	34.2
Granite (Cape Ann)		50						
Marble (Vermont)		45						
Ferric oxide	5							
Zinc oxide				5.0				
Copper carbonate								2.6
Dextrine			40[1]					7.9
Water	100	100	100	120	100	100	100	150
Grind in qt mill	15 min	1 hr		15 min	15 min	15 min		
Sp. gravity of slip	1.35	1.5		1.4	1.4	1.4		
Thickness of app.	0.2 cc/sq cm	0.2 cc/sq cm	0.2 cc/sq cm	0.2 cc/sq cm	0.1 cc/sq cm	0.2 cc/sq cm	0.1 cc/sq cm	
Maturing conditions	Cone 8-9 1225-1250°C	Cone 8-9 1225-1250°C	Cone 3-4 1145-1165°C	Cone 08-04 950-1050°C	Cone 8-9 1225-1250°C	Cone 8-9 1225-1250°C	Cone 16 1450°C	Cone 08 945°C
For use on body No.	3,5,13	3,7	6,7	3,7,12	13	13	14	Special

[1] Ashes from beech wood, washed.

Material	Decomposition temperature
Calcium carbonate ($CaCO_3$)	600°–1050°C
Magnesium carbonate ($MgCO_3$)	400°– 900°C
Calcium sulfate ($CaSO_4$)	1250°–1300°C
Manganese dioxide (MnO_2)	1100°–1300°C

Crackle glazes. These glazes give the interesting crackle effect simply because they have higher coefficients of expansion than the bodies to which they are applied, and so craze on cooling. Low stresses produce coarse networks of cracks, and high stresses give fine ones. The crackle effect is emphasized by boiling the piece in strong tea or by rubbing it with cobalt oxide. It is said that the Chinese were able to produce crackle in definite patterns, such as a spider web, and although the author has never seen such pieces, it seems as though it might be possible to accomplish this by making fine, sharp ridges on the body to concentrate the stress at these lines. The batch formulas for the following crackle glazes are given in Table 26–9.

A good opaque crackle glaze, Cone 08–04 (950°–1050°C), for body No. 7 or 12:

$$\begin{matrix} 0.42 \text{ PbO} \\ 0.28 \text{ CaO} \\ 0.19 \text{ ZnO} \\ 0.11 \text{ K}_2\text{O} \end{matrix} \quad 0.41 \text{ Al}_2\text{O}_3 \quad 2.23 \text{ SiO}_2 \quad (27)$$

A matte crackle for porcelain body No. 13 at Cone 8–9 (1225°–1250°C):

$$\begin{matrix} 0.30 \text{ K}_2\text{O} \\ 0.70 \text{ CaO} \end{matrix} \quad 0.4 \text{ Al}_2\text{O}_3 \quad 3.5 \text{ SiO}_2 \quad (28)$$

A bright crackle for the same body and temperature:

$$\begin{matrix} 0.30 \text{ K}_2\text{O} \\ 0.70 \text{ CaO} \end{matrix} \quad 0.5 \text{ Al}_2\text{O}_3 \quad 6.5 \text{ SiO}_2 \quad (29)$$

A bright crackle for body No. 9 at Cone 16:

$$\begin{matrix} 0.30 \text{ K}_2\text{O} \\ 0.70 \text{ CaO} \end{matrix} \quad 0.7 \text{ Al}_2\text{O}_3 \quad 11 \text{ SiO}_2 \quad (30)$$

Self-glaze. Porcelains that are high in feldspar, such as parians, fire with a high gloss that is very much like a glaze. This is an advantage for sculptured pieces, for there is then no thick glaze to obscure the fine modeling.

Blue Egyptian ware, which is self-glazing, is made by adding to the body a soluble copper salt which comes to the surface as scum and, on firing, produces a sort of blistery glaze of intense blue. Formula No. 31 in Table 26–9 is a composition by Binns that gives this effect.

Vapor glazes. The best-known glaze of this kind is salt glaze, which was used on stoneware in Germany and in the Low Countries as early as the 12th century and which was introduced into England about 1720. This ware, which is much in demand by collectors, was often decorated by modeling or by the use of colored enamels. Because of the orange-peel texture of the surface, however, it was hard to wash, and consequently it was soon displaced by the well-glazed earthenware known as Queen's ware. Much of the early stoneware in the United States was salt-glazed, often over cobalt-blue decorations. Some of the jars and jugs are masterpieces of design, and the modern potter would do well to study them. Ware of this type that was made in Bennington, Vermont, is part of most collections of antiques, but the process is seldom used now.

Salt glaze is made by adding common salt (NaCl), usually moistened with water, to the coal fires of a special kiln. The vapor that results passes through the kiln and combines with the surface of the biscuit to form a sodium-aluminum silicate. The glaze layer is thin, has a typical "orange-peel" surface, and is almost always finely crazed. To take a good salt glaze, the alumina in the clay body must be between 0.24 and 0.40 of the silica and the iron oxide should be not more than 6% of the total body.

The glaze itself is rather pebbly, and it has particular aesthetic appeal when it is used over bold underglaze decorations. A separate kiln is needed for this kind of glaze, because the vapors permeate the oven to an extent that makes it unsuitable for other firing. Salt-glazing can be done only on bodies that mature at fairly high temperatures; Cone 8 (1225°) is an average temperature.

The vapor glaze known as "smear" glaze is used quite generally for small sculptures. The biscuit piece is placed in a tight sagger which is coated on the inside with a volatile glaze, usually containing lead oxide or borax. The vapor formed in the sagger on firing combines with the surface of the piece and produces a very thin glaze which does not obscure the modeling.

IV. REFERENCES

Aventurine Glazes

1. BERDEL, E., Iron Oxide as a Coloring Agent in Bodies and Glazes, *Keram. Rund.* **39**, 403, 423 (1931).

2. HALDEMAN, V. K., Aventurine Glazes, *J. Am. Ceram. Soc.* **7**, 824 (1924).

3. KONDO, S., Aventurine Glaze, *Tokio Tech. School Bull.* **3**, No. 1, 13, 23 (1925).

4. PARMELEE, C. W., AND J. S. LOTHRUP, Aventurine Glazes, *J. Am. Ceram. Soc.* **7**, 567 (1924).

5. SANDERS, H. H., Aventurine Glazes, *Ceramic Age* **63**, No. 6, 48 (1954).

6. SCHURECHT, H. G., Experiments in Aventurine Glazes, *J. Am. Ceram. Soc.* **3**, 971 (1920).

Bristol Glazes

7. PURDY, R. C., Further Studies on White Bristol Glazes, *Trans. Am. Ceram. Soc.* **5**, 136 (1903).

8. WATTS, A. S., The Practical Application of Bristol Glaze Compounded on the Eutectic Basis, *Trans. Am. Ceram. Soc.* **XIX**, 301 (1917).

Crackle Glazes

9. ANON., Leadless Craquelle in Glazes, *Ceram. Ind.* **52**, 131 (April, 1949).

10. SANDERS, H. H., Crackle Glazes, *Ceramic Age* **63**, No. 3, 53 (1950).

Crystalline Glazes

11. BRASS, A., The Growth of Crystals in Glazes, *Sprechsaal* **58**, 591 (1925).

12. KRANER, H. M., Colors in a Zinc Silicate Glaze, *J. Am. Ceram. Soc.* **7**, 868 (1924).

13. KONDO, S., Crystal Glazes, *J. Jas. Ceram. Ass.* **33**, 165, 182, 188, 387, 399 (1925).

14. MELLOR, J. W., Crystallization in Pottery, *Trans. Eng. Ceram. Soc.* **4**, 49 (1904–05).

15. MINTON, L. H., Discussion of the So-called Zinc Crystals, *Trans. Am. Ceram. Soc.* **IX**, 782 (1907).

16. NORTON, F. H., Control of Crystalline Glazes, *J. Am. Ceram. Soc.* **20**, 217 (1937).

17. PUKALL, W., My Experience with Crystal Glazes, *Trans. Am. Ceram. Soc.* **X**, 183 (1908).

18. PURDY, R. C., AND J. F. KREHBIEL, Crystalline Glazes, *Trans. Am. Ceram. Soc.* **IX**, 319 (1907).

19. RAND, C. C., AND H. G. SCHURECHT, A Type of Crystalline Glaze at Cone 3, *Trans. Am. Ceram. Soc.* **XVI**, 342 (1914).

20. RIDDLE, F. H., A Few Facts Concerning the So-called Zinc Silicate Crystals, *Trans. Am. Ceram. Soc.* **VIII**, 336 (1906).

21. STULL, R. T., Notes on the Production of Crystalline Glazes, *Trans. Am. Ceram. Soc.* **VI**, 186 (1904).

22. WOLF, J., Crystal Glazes, *Sprechsaal* **64**, No. 20, 371 (1931); **64**, No. 21, 391 (1931).

23. WORCESTER, W. G., The Function of Alumina in a Crystalline Glaze, *Trans. Am. Ceram. Soc.* **X**, 450 (1908).

24. ZIMMER, W. H., Crystallized Glazes, *Trans. Am. Ceram. Soc.* **IV**, 38 (1902).

Defects in Glazes

25. ANON., Defects in Glazed Ware, *Ceram. Ind.* **44**, 82 (June, 1945).

26. ANON., Common Defects in Pottery Bodies and Glazes, *Ceram. Ind.* **18**, 242 (1932).

27. MELLOR, J. W., Crazing and Peeling of Glazes, *Trans. Eng. Ceram. Soc.* **34**, 1 (1935).

28. MELLOR, J. W., Spitting of Glazes in the Enamel Kiln, *Trans. Eng. Ceram. Soc.* **35**, No. 1, 355 (1935–36).

29. MOORE, B., AND J. W. MELLER, The Adsorption and Dissolution of Gases by Silicates—"Spit Out," *Trans. Eng. Ceram. Soc.* **21**, 289 (1921).

30. PLANT, H. C., Pinholes and Some Other Things, *Trans. Eng. Ceram. Soc.* **24**, 302 (1924–25).

31. SCHURECHT, H. G., Methods of Overcoming Crazing on Glazed Ceramic Products, *Ceram. Ind.* **37**, No. 2, 44 (1941).

Encaustic Glazing

32. RHEAD, F. H., Types of Glazes Suitable for Decorative Inlay Processes, *J. Am. Ceram. Soc.* **5**, 259 (1922).

Engobes and Slip Coatings

33. AMBERG, C. R., Terra Sigillata, Forgotten Finish, *Ceram. Ind.* **51**, 77 (December, 1948).

34. ANON., Use of Engobes, *Ceram. Ind.* **45**, 82 (August, 1945).

35. JENKINS, R. H., Engobing, *Ceramic Age* **53**, 373 (June, 1949).

36. LINDENER, F., Manufacture of Terra Sigillata, *Keram. Rund.* **44**, 151 (1936).

37. McDOWELL, S. J., Terra Cotta Slip Coatings, *J. Am. Ceram. Soc.* **16**, 134 (1933).

38. MONTGOMERY, E. T., AND C. F. TEFFT, Roofing Tile Slips and Glazes, *Trans. Am. Ceram. Soc.* **XVI**, 144 (1914).

39. MOSER, A., Terra Sigillata, *Tonind. Zeit.* **62**, 21 (1938).

40. PARMELEE, C. W., Engobes, Slips and Underslips, *Ceram. Ind.* **47**, No. 2, 74 (1946); **47**, No. 3, 98 (1946); **47**, No. 4, 82, 105 (1946); **47**, No. 5, 98 (1946); **47**, No. 6, 94 (1946).

Fluoride Glazes

41. ALZNER, F., AND E. HINRICKS, Practical Experience with Glazes Free from Lead and Boron, *Ber. Deut. Keram. Ges.* **22**, 150 (1941).

42. CORBETT, P. M., AND N. J. KREIDL, Development of Leadless Glazes Containing Fluorides, *Ceram. Ind.* **39**, 46 (February, 1942); **39**, 64 (March, 1942).

43. STEGER, W., Fluorine in Whiteware Glazes Free of Lead and Boron, *Ber. Deut. Keram. Ges.* **22**, 73 (1941).

44. THURMER, A., The Use of Alkali Fluorides in Transparent Glasses, *Ceram. Ind.* **28**, 162 (February, 1937).

Fritted Glazes

45. BERDEL, E., Azurite Glasses and Glazes, *Keramos.* **10**, 385 (1931).

46. DANIELSON, R. R., Low-lead, Bright Opaque Glazes at Cones 08–06, *J. Am. Ceram. Soc.* **30**, 245 (1947).

47. DANIELSON, R. R., AND D. V. VAN GORDON, Leadless Opaque Glazes at Cone 04, *J. Am. Ceram. Soc.* **33**, 323 (1950).

48. GELLER, R. F., E. N. BUNTING, AND A. S. CREAMER, Some Soft Glazes of Low Thermal Expansion, *Nat. Bur. of Standards, J. of Res.* **20**, 57 (1938).

49. KOENIG, J. H., Lead Frits and Fritted Glazes, *Ceram. Ind.* **26**, 134 (February, 1936); **27**, 108 (1936).

50. MARQUIS, J., Cone 01 Glazes for Low Temperature Vitreous Ware, *J. Am. Ceram. Soc.* **27**, 358 (1944).

51. MARQUIS, J., Ceramic Leadless Glazes for Dinnerware, *Ceramic Age* **45**, 192 (1945).

52. PARMELEE, C. W., AND K. C. LYON, A Study of Some Frit Compositions, *J. Am. Ceram. Soc.* **17**, 60 (1934).

53. PARMELEE, C. W., Leadless and Colored Fritted Glazes, *Ceram. Ind.* **45**, No. 5, 84 (1945).

54. PURDY, R. C., AND H. B. FOX, Fritted Glazes, *Trans. Am. Ceram. Soc.* **IX**, 95 (1907).

55. STALEY, H. F., The Compounding of Frits, *Trans. Am. Ceram. Soc.* **X**, 113 (1908).

General

56. ANON., Pottery Glazes, *Ceram. Ind.* **54**, No. 1, 148, 157 (1950).

57. COX, P. E., The Use of Iowa Clays in Small Scale Production of Ceramic Art, *Iowa Eng. Exp. Stat. Bull.* 133 (1937).

58. HENZE, W., Glazing Practice of An Art Pottery, *Keram. Rund.* **39**, 17 (1931).

59. HOLSCHER, H. H., AND A. S. WATTS, A Graphical Representation of the Molecular Formulas of Ceramic Glazes, *J. Am. Ceram. Soc.* **14**, 583 (1931).

60. KOENIG, C. J., Nepheline Syenite in Low-Temperature Vitreous Wares, *Ohio State Univ. Eng. Exp. Stat. Bull.* 112 (1942).

61. PEARSON, B. M., Ceramic Glazes and Enamels, *Ceramic Age* **I**, 54, 257 (1949); **II**, 54, 325 (1949); **III**, 55, 45 (1950).

Matte Glazes

62. ANON., Mat and Crystalline Glazes for Fireplace Tile, *Keram. Rund.* **45**, No. 16, 175 (1937).

63. BINNS, C. F., Matte Glazes at High Temperatures, *Trans. Am. Ceram. Soc.* **VII**, Part 1, 115 (1905).

64. BINNS, C. F., The Development of the Matte Glaze, *Trans. Am. Ceram. Soc.* **V**, 50 (1903).

65. BLUMENTHAL, G., Producing a Chrome-Tin Matte Glaze, *Ceram. Ind.* **20**, 222 (May, 1933).

66. ORTON, E., JR., A Study of a Type of Matte Glaze Maturing at Cone 2–4, *Trans. Am. Ceram. Soc.* **X**, 547 (1908).

67. PARMELEE, C. W., AND W. HORAK, The Microstructure of Some Raw Lead Mat Glazes, *J. Am. Ceram. Soc.* **17**, 67 (1934).

68. RHEAD, F. H., Matte Glazes, *Trans. Am. Ceram. Soc.* **XI**, 157 (1909).

69. WILSON, H., Mat Glazes and the Lime-Alumina-Silica System, *Bull Am. Ceram. Soc.* **18**, 447 (1939).

Natural Glazes

70. COX, P. E., Silts and Slip Clays as Ingredients in Art Pottery Glazes, *Ceramic Age* **47**, 206 (1946).

71. LING, M. C., Chinese Ash Glaze, *Bull. Am. Ceram. Soc.* **26**, 7 (1947).

72. THURN, H. L., Use of Wood Ash in a Low Fire Mat Glaze, *J. Am. Ceram. Soc.* **28**, 261 (1945).

Opacifiers

73. SINGER, F., *Ceramic Glazes*, Borax Consolidated Ltd., London, 1940.

74. STUCKERT, L., Tin Oxide in Ceramic Glazes, *Sprechsaal* **73**, No. 2, 13 (1940); No. 3, 21 (1940); No. 4, 29 (1940); No. 5, 37 (1940); No. 6, 43 (1940).

Opalescent Glazes

75. ANON., Opalescent Effects in Colored Glazes, *Ceram. Ind.* **53**, 118 (October, 1949).

76. MELLOR, J. W., Retrospection, Chinese Red Glazes and Other Things, *Trans. Eng. Ceram. Soc.* **36**, 44 (1937).

Porcelain Glazes

77. BERDEL, E., AND G. DANNHEIM, Alkalie-Free Lead Glazes, *Ber. Deut. Keram. Ges.* **13**, 20 (1932).

78. PARMELEE, C. W., Porcelain Glazes, *Ceram. Ind.* **47**, 76 (July, 1946); **46**, 20 (April, 1946); **46**, 76 (June, 1946).

79. SORTWELL, H. H., High Fire Porcelain Glazes, *J. Am. Ceram. Soc.* **4**, 718 (1921).

80. TWELLS, R., The Field of Porcelain Glazes Maturing Between Cones 17 and 20, *J. Am. Ceram. Soc.* **5**, 430 (1922).

81. TWELLS, R., Further Studies of Porcelain Glazes Maturing at High Temperatures, *J. Am. Ceram. Soc.* **6**, 1113 (1923).

82. BERDEL, E., Turquoise Glazes, *Ceram. Ind.* **17**, 195 (1931).

83. FRENCH, M. M., Further Experiments in the Problem of the Turquoise Alkaline Glaze, *J. Am. Ceram. Soc.* **8**, 143 (1925).

84. LITTLEFIELD, E., A Copper Blue at Cone 9, *J. Am. Ceram. Soc.* **15**, 269 (1932).

85. MERRIT, C. W., Raw Leadless Glazes for Pottery and Tile at Cone 2, *J. Am. Ceram. Soc.* **19**, 23 (1936).

86. RICHARDSON, F. W., Use of Lithium Carbonate in Raw Alkaline Glazes, *J. Am. Ceram. Soc.* **22**, 50 (1939).

Raw Lead Glazes

87. FRENCH, M. M., AND C. M. HARDER, Low Fire Glazes Using Rutile, *J. Am. Ceram. Soc.* **10**, 268 (1927).

88. PARMELEE, C. W., Raw Lead Glazes, *Ceram. Ind.* **46**, 78 (February, 1946); **46**, 76, 96 (March, 1946).

Reduction Glazes

89. BAGGS, A. E., AND E. LITTLEFIELD, The Production and Control of Copper-Reds in an Oxidizing Kiln Atmosphere, *J. Am. Ceram. Soc.* **15**, 265 (1932).

90. BLOTTEFIERE, DE R., Flambé Glazes, *Rev. Mat. Constr. Trav. Pub.*, No. 318, 33 (1936); No. 319, 51 (1936).

91. BREITENFELDT, E., Experiments on Copper-Red Glazes, *Keram. Rund.* **37**, 393 (1929).

92. COX, P. E., Low Temperature Copper Reds, *Ceramic Age* **48**, 22 (July, 1946).

93. COX, P. E., Copper Red for the Amateur, *J. Am. Ceram. Soc.* **6**, 685 (1923).

94. HARDER, C. M., Red Glazes and Underglaze Red by Reduction, *J. Am. Ceram. Soc.* **19**, 26 (1936).

95. ISHII, K., Experiments on the Tenriuji-Celadon Glaze, *Rept. Pottery Lab. (Kioto)* **2**, 55 (1923).

96. KLITZKE, G., Researches on Chinese-Red Glazes, *Keramos.* **5**, 133 (1926).

96a. MELLOR, J. W., The Chemistry of Chinese Copper-red Glazes. *Trans. Ceram. Soc.* **35**, 364 (1936); **35**, 487 (1936).

Self-glazes

97. BINNS, C. F., M. KLEM, AND H. MOTT, An Experiment in Egyptian Blue Glaze, *J. Am. Ceram. Soc.* **15**, 271 (1932).

98. EVERHART, J. O., Production of a Salt Glaze by the Application of a Slip to the Ware, *J. Am. Ceram. Soc.* **13**, 399 (1930).

99. FOSDICK, M. L., Salt Glazing at Cone 02 by Slip Application, *J. Am. Ceram. Soc.* **17**, 219 (1934).

Slip Properties of Glazes

100. BOWMAN, J. R., Studies of the Changes in Viscosity of Clay Slips and Glaze Suspensions on Aging and by Treatment with Electrolytes, *J. Am. Ceram. Soc.* **10**, 508 (1927).

101. BROWN, L. H., Preparing of Slips and Glazes for Best Results, *Ceram. Ind.* **22**, 376 (1934).

102. FOSTER, E. S., Organic Agents as Aids to Adhesion and Suspension of Glazes, *J. Am. Ceram. Soc.* **12**, 264 (1929).

103. HARMON, C. G., C. F. SHAEFER, *et al.*, Study of Factors Involved in Glaze Slip Control, *J. Am. Ceram. Soc.* **27**, 202 (1944).

104. KOENIG, J. H., AND F. C. HENDERSON, Particle Size Distribution of Glazes, *J. Am. Ceram. Soc.* **24**, 286 (1941).

105. PARMELEE, C. W., Recent Advances in Grinding, Control of Particle Size in Glaze Slips, *Ceram. Ind.* **35**, 48, 46 (January, 1940).

106. SCHRAMM, E., AND R. F. SHERWOOD, Some Properties of Glaze Slips, *J. Am. Ceram. Soc.* **12**, 270 (1929).

Vapor Glazes

107. ANON., Fuming Colors, *Ceram. Ind.* **50**, 115 (March, 1948).

108. BARRINGER, L. E., The Relation Between the Constitution of a Clay and its Ability

to Take a Good Salt Glaze, *Trans. Am. Ceram. Soc.* **IV**, 211 (1902).

109. DINGLEDINE, H. F., Salt Glazing a Clay of Low Vitrifying Temperature, *J. Am. Ceram. Soc.* **15**, 82 (1932).

110. DRISCOLL, H., Stoneware Pottery, *Ceramic Age* **53**, 148, 248 (1949); Studio Stoneware Glazes, *ibid.* **54**, 118, 174, 248, 318 (1949); Studio Stoneware Decoration, *ibid.* **55**, 181 (1950); Studio Stoneware Firing, *ibid.* **55**, 267, 344; Salt Glaze Firing, *ibid.* **56**, No. 4, 66 (1950).

111. FOSTER, H. D., Résumé of Technical Studies of Salt Glazing, *Bull. Am. Ceram. Soc.* **20**, 239 (1941).

112. FOSTER, H. D., Salt Glazes for Structural Building Units, *J. Am. Ceram. Soc.* **26**, 60 (1943).

113. HURSH, R. K., AND E. C. CLEMENS, Effect of Body Composition and Firing Treatments on Salt Glazes, *J. Am. Ceram. Soc.* **14**, 482 (1931).

114. LAMPMAN, C. M. AND H. G. SCHURECHT, Zinc-Vapor Glazing of Clays, I and II, *J. Am. Ceram. Soc.* **22**, 91 (1939); **23**, 167 (1940).

115. LONGENECKER, H. L., Vapor Glazing and Color Flashing of Pre-Cambrian Shales, *J. Am. Ceram. Soc.* **13**, 794 (1930).

116. SCHURECHT, H. G., Salt Glazing of Ceramic Ware, *Bull. Am. Ceram. Soc.* **22**, 45 (1943).

CHAPTER 27

Color
and Its Measurement

I. INTRODUCTION

One of the great charms of ceramic pieces is the wide range of possible colors, and it is interesting to know that these colors, as compared with paints or inks, are permanent. Every serious student of pottery making should have some understanding of color, and it is the purpose of this chapter to give a nontechnical description of color and its measurement.

II. THE HUMAN EYE

Nowhere in all nature will one find a more remarkable organ than the human eye. Originally a mere pit in the skin of some prehistoric amphibian for the purpose of collecting the heat of the sun, it has gradually evolved, through millions of years, to its present form.

The structure of the eye. Figure 27–1 is a simplified cross section of the human eye. It is very much like a tiny camera, with a lens that focuses an image on the retina, which rests at the back of the eyeball. The retina is a very fine grid of special cells, each one attached to a fiber in the optic nerve. There are approximately one million such cells and corresponding nerve fibers transmitting impulses to the brain. Not only does the eye resolve fine details, but it will operate efficiently over an amazing range of light intensity; for example, the ratio of the intensity of light on a sunlit desert to that prevailing on a starlit night is about a million to one. This adaptation is accomplished by dilation and contraction of the pupil of the eye, which regulates the amount of light that enters the eye itself; the retina, too, has a wide range of adaptation.

The mechanism of color vision. So far as we know, only man, the primate apes, birds, lizards, turtles, and fish have the ability to distinguish colors. To the cat and dog, for example, everything looks gray. The mechanism by which we are able to distinguish colors is not completely understood, but it is believed that some of the cone-shaped cells in the retina respond to red, others to yellow-green, still others to blue. If one or more sets of these color-responsive receptors is absent, partial or complete color blindness results. The eye is not equally sensitive to all colors, however. As Table 27–1 indicates, yellow-green appears most brilliant to the normal eye.

We also know that we need considerable light if the eye is to properly respond to different colors. For example, on a moonlit night all but the strongest colors in a flower garden look gray.

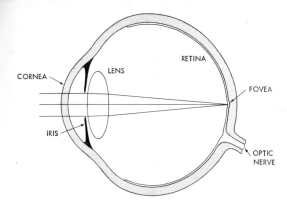

Fig. 27-1. Cross section of the human eye (somewhat enlarged).

TABLE 27-1

COLOR SENSITIVITY OF THE NORMAL EYE

Color	Percent response for normal eye
Red	20
Orange	50
Yellow	80
Yellow-green	100
Green	70
Blue	15
Violet	5

III. WHAT COLOR IS

Selective absorption. Light is actually a wave motion, much like radio waves. Daylight consists of a wide range of wavelengths which, when separated by a prism, show the spectrum colors of the rainbow. The long waves give the sensation of red, and the short waves give the sensation of violet. When all of the waves are mixed together, we have "white" light.

Various transparent materials, called filters, are capable of stopping certain of these wavelengths and allowing others to pass through. For example, if we observe a white cloud through a piece of red glass it looks red, because the orange, yellow, green, blue, and violet colors have been absorbed, or stopped (Fig. 27-2). In other words, the color of an object depends on the selective absorption of some of the wavelengths from white light.

Reflection. A transparent red glaze looks red because light passes into the glaze layer and is then reflected back to the eye, as shown in Fig. 27-3. In other words, the layer of glaze acts as a filter that absorbs all but the red wavelengths. The transparent fibers in a piece of colored paper or cloth similarly act as filters which cut out certain wavelengths.

Lusters. Lusters are the only exception to the general rule that glaze colors are produced by absorption of all other light. Here the light is uniquely reflected from metallic films.

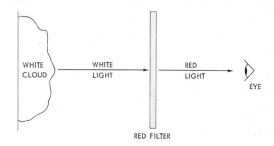

Fig. 27-2. Action of a light filter.

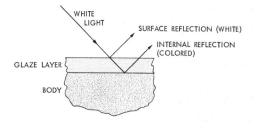

Fig. 27-3. How a colored glaze acts as a filter.

IV. DEFINITION OF COLOR

Now that we have tried to give a simple explanation of *why* we see color, let's try to define it from several different points of view. To the ceramist, color is a stain; to the physiologist, color is a retinal stimulus; to the physicist, color is a certain wavelength of vibration; to the artist, color is a sensation based on experience. The artist and the ceramist often define a particular color by comparing it with some natural object: peach, lilac, turquoise, etc.

V. MEASUREMENT OF COLOR

Photometric methods. Color can be measured with scientific precision by means of an instrument called a spectrophotometer, which compares the transmittance or reflectance of a sample with a standard. From this measurement the exact specifications for a particular color are known. Such equipment is costly and not really necessary for the ceramist.

Measurement of color by comparison. Another way to measure color is by comparison with a series of standard samples. Either of two standard color series, the Munsell system and the Ostwald system, is satisfactory for the ceramist. We shall not describe these in detail here; full information is given in the references at the end of this chapter.

Bear in mind that colors vary in appearance when exposed to different sources of light. Colors that seem to match in daylight may be completely dissimilar under artificial illumination.

VI. THE SENSATION OF COLOR

The apparent color of a ceramic glaze is influenced materially by several factors not easy to define or to measure. It is these factors that lend variety and charm to a glaze as compared, for example, with painted surfaces.

Surface texture. Figure 27–3 illustrates how the color in a glaze is caused by absorption and reflection of light through the layer of glaze itself. However, some of the

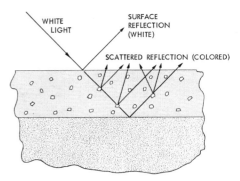

Fig. 27-4. How an opaque glaze shows color.

entering light is not absorbed at all and is reflected back as white light, which mixes with and dilutes the apparent color. Surface reflection is governed by the character of the glaze; a matte glaze, for example, will not look as brilliant as a clear glaze with the same amount of stain.

Translucency. Figure 27–3 shows how light penetrates through the glaze to the body surface and is then reflected back to the source. When the glaze contains fine suspended particles that make it more or less opaque, some of the entering light is reflected by these particles, as shown in Fig. 27–4, and consequently the color sensation will to some extent depend upon the thickness of the glaze layer and the number and size of the particles. The charm of many glazes is due to this internal reflection, which adds depth and quality.

Adjacent colors. The apparent color of a particular area, as every artist knows, is influenced by the color of adjacent areas, and this factor must be taken into account in ceramics as well as in painting.

VII. COLOR FORMATION IN GLAZES

To work intelligently toward desired colors, the ceramist must have some insight into the mechanism of color formation in glazes. A simple discussion, adequate for this purpose, is given in this section.

Solution colors. Most of the colors used for glazes are what are known as "solution" colors, that is, they are substances like ferric oxide (Fe_2O_3), which completely dissolve in the clear glaze. Only a few natural elements will produce colors when used in this way; therefore the ceramist is limited to these so-called "transition" elements. However, the color produced by one particular element can be varied somewhat by alteration of the mixture to which it is added. For example, copper produces a brilliant green when added to a glaze that is high in lead, but an intense blue in an alkaline glaze. Table 27–2 lists the different colors produced by transition elements in solution in two dissimilar batches of glaze.

It should be borne in mind that a transition element will produce the same solution color in a particular glaze, no matter in what form the element is added. For example, the same blue will be produced whether the additive is 0.1 equivalent of cobalt oxide or 0.1 equivalent of cobalt carbonate.

A given glaze is capable of dissolving only a certain amount of coloring element; if more than this is added crystals will be formed when the piece is cooled, and the glaze will not be clear. This is sometimes deliberately done to obtain a special effect.

TABLE 27-2

SOLUTION COLORS

Element	In raw lead glaze	In porcelain glaze
Cobalt	Blue–purple	Blue–purple
Chromium	Deep yellow	Green
Iron	Tan	Coral red
Nickel	Pale yellow–green	Olive brown
Manganese	Lilac	–
Copper	Grass green	–
Uranium	Brilliant orange	Black

Crystal colors. The crystal effect mentioned immediately above is one way of coloring by the use of crystals. Another method is to add to the glaze batch stable crystals of color that remain intact on firing. The use of such crystals sometimes permits a greater range of effects than the solution colors.

Colloid colors. Some colors, particularly the gold-reds, are believed to be due to the very fine suspension of metal particles that produce a color in much the same way that the water droplets in clouds produce the colors of the sunset. These colloidal colors are difficult to control, and we need to know much more about them than we do now.

VIII. COLOR FORMATION IN BODIES

Many clays are naturally colored, and this is usually due to the particles of iron oxide that are present. Whiteware bodies are colored by adding oxides or stains in finely divided particle form. These particles partially dissolve in the glassy phase of firing, forming tiny colored spheres which lend color to even the most opaque body.

IX. REFERENCES

1. Anon., *Munsell Book of Color*, Munsell Color Company, Inc., Baltimore, 1929.

2. Anon., *Color Harmony Index and Manual* (Ostwald System), Container Corporation of America, Chicago.

3. Birren, F., Application of the Ostwald Color System to the Design of Consumer Goods, *J. Optical Soc. of Am.* **34**, 396 (1944).

4. Hardy, A. C., *Handbook of Colorimetry*, Technology Press, Cambridge, Mass., 1936.

5. Judd, D. B., and K. L. Kelley, Method of Designating Color, *J. Res. Nat. Bur. of Standards* **23**, 355 (1939).

6. MOON, P., AND D. E. SPENCER, Geometric Formulation of Classical Color Harmony, *J. Optical Soc. of Am.* **34**, 46 (1944).

7. MOON, P., AND D. E. SPENCER, Area in Color Harmony, *J. Optical Soc. of Am.* **34**, 93 (1944).

8. MOON, P., AND D. E. SPENCER, Aesthetic Measure Applied to Color Harmony, *J. Optical Soc. of Am.* **34**, 234 (1944).

9. NICKERSON, D., AND S. M. HEWHALL, Central Notations for OSCC-NBS Color Names, *J. Optical Soc. of Am.* **31**, 587 (1941).

10. Optical Soc. of Am. Colorimetry Comm., *On The Science of Color*, Thomas Y. Crowell Company, New York, 1953.

11. WEYL, W. A., *Coloured Glasses*, Soc. of Glass Tech., Sheffield, 1951.

CHAPTER 28

Ceramic Stains

I. INTRODUCTION

Ceramic stains are compounds of coloring elements mixed with other ingredients, fired to a high temperature, finely ground, and then washed free of soluble salts. Their purpose is to impart color to the body, to the glaze, under the glaze, or over the glaze.

Even the large potteries no longer make their own stains, because excellent uniform stains are commercially available at reasonable cost. The making of good stains is exacting work, and it is recommended that the beginner use commercial products. If the potter wishes to experiment with producing his own colors, the necessary information is given in this chapter.

II. COMPOSITION OF STAINS

Coloring elements. Ceramic stains must be made from colored crystals of high chemical stability if they are to resist the attack of the molten glaze or flux. The simplest stain is a single oxide; for example, Fe_2O_3. Other compounds, however, have greater stability, and "spinels," which are a combination of two oxides, are extremely stable. Table 28–1 lists some of the common coloring elements.

Modifiers. The color produced by the use of a single coloring element can be modified by using another element with it. For example, chromic oxide produces green, but the shade of green can be varied by also adding lead oxide, which by itself is white.

Fluxes. When the ingredients of a stain are highly refractory, so that extremely high temperatures would be required to cause them to react, a flux is added as a sort of catalyst to bring the reaction temperature within reach of the potter's kiln. Sodium chloride, borax, and the phosphates can be used for this purpose. When the stain is heated, some of the flux vaporizes out and the rest forms water-soluble compounds that are washed out at a later stage. (This kind of flux is not to be confused with that added to the stain to form an overglaze color.)

Diluents. A diluent is an insoluble, neutral substance whose sole purpose is to dilute the color to make it lighter in hue. Ground whiteware body, flint, or alumina can be used as diluents.

III. PREPARATION OF STAINS

Mixing the stain. As we mentioned above, the preparation of stains is an exacting process which requires great care. The finely ground raw materials are weighed out and are thoroughly mixed by passing through a 65-mesh screen several times. Usually the soluble materials are made up as a concentrated solution which is then mixed with the dry powder to form a paste, which is then dried, broken up, and thoroughly mixed.

TABLE 28-1

CHIEF ELEMENTS THAT PRODUCE CERAMIC COLORS

Element	Color
Antimony	Yellows
Chromium	Greens and reds
Cobalt	Blue, purple, pink
Copper	Green (red when reduced)
Gold	Stable red and pinks
Iron	Yellow, brown, red
Manganese	Browns, purple
Nickel	Greens
Platinum	Fine blacks and grays
Uranium	Reds and orange, blacks
Vanadium	Yellows and greens

Calcining the stain. The next step is to pack the mixture into a fire-clay crucible and heat to the required temperature. Some stains must be fired at very high temperatures to complete the reaction, while others will decompose if the temperature is raised beyond a certain point. The directions for the particular stain should be carefully followed in every instance. Even when the crucible containing the stain is covered, it is inadvisable to place it too near whiteware in the kiln during this process, because it is possible for color to be transferred in the vapor state to neighboring pieces.

In this stage of the process, control of the atmosphere in the kiln is sometimes very important. For example, a slightly reducing atmosphere produces more brilliance in calcium-chromate greens, while oxidation is necessary for green stains containing copper.

Grinding. After calcining, the mass is broken free from the crucible, care being taken not to get any pieces of the container in the mix. Some compounds melt completely and form a solid crystalline mass, while only fritting takes place in other compounds, and the mass is friable.

This mass must now be broken up sufficiently to pass through a 20-mesh screen. This is usually done with a large iron mortar, and it is a slow job. Now the material is wet ball milled with flint pebbles (usually in a quart jar) until the largest particle is less than

10 microns in size. This often requires *several hundred hours,* and because particle size is extremely important, the directions should be followed carefully.

Washing. This step is one of the most important. All of the soluble salts must be carefully removed. This is done by stirring the slip from the ball mill into a large volume of hot water, allowing the mixture to settle, and then pouring off the clear water. This process must be repeated five or six times. If the stain is too fine to settle out in a reasonable length of time, the suspension may be filtered onto a vacuum filter and washed with hot water there.

Additives. If it is necessary to add clay or other materials to the colored stain, the mixing should be done by grinding for a short period in the ball mill. No additions are generally necessary for a body stain or a glaze stain, but the working properties of underglaze colors are often enhanced by the addition of 5% clay and 5% glaze. Considerable amounts of low-fusing frit are often added to overglaze colors.

IV. USE OF STAINS

In bodies. Colored bodies are used for such diverse purposes as floor tiles (unglazed); tableware, where a uniform color such as ivory is desired; and artware, for cameos. The intensity of color can be varied, of course, by varying the amount of stain used; 1% is an average amount of stain, although amounts may vary from 0.1% to 20%.

To obtain uniform color, the stain must be thoroughly mixed with the body. Vitreous bodies are colored by wet ball milling the batch after the stain has been added to the raw materials; for earthenware the stain is added in the blunger.

Table 28–2 shows how to blend a parian body to obtain a good flesh tone. Note that only three slips are prepared, rather than many small batches. After the slips have been milled for 15 hours in a one-gallon jar, they are blended by volume to give a systematic series. It is better to make this series by successively doubling or tripling one component than by adding a constant amount. Several mixture series are given in Table 28–3; Table 28–4 shows the blends and Table 28–5 lists

the resulting amount of stain in each blend. Note that the amount of stain in any row is just one-half that in the row above. The compositions marked off with heavy lines give good flesh tones.

Color often varies with the composition of the body, and it is therefore necessary to test the stain in the particular body to be used. Color also varies with firing temperature and degree of vitrification. Table 28–6 lists some common body stains and their firing conditions.

TABLE 28–2

COLORED BODIES

Raw materials	White body	Pink body	Yellow body
Feldspar	600	600	600
Plastic kaolin	150	150	150
N. C. kaolin	150	150	150
Ky. Old Mine #4 B.C.	100	100	100
Yellow stain	–	–	50
Pink stain	–	200	–
Water	1500	1800	1575

TABLE 28–5

RESULTANT AMOUNT OF STAIN IN PERCENT

5 Y	3.75 Y + 5 P	2.5 Y + 10 P	1.25 Y + 15 P	20 Y
2.5 Y	1.88 Y + 2.5 P	1.25 Y + 5 P	0.62 Y + 7.5 P	10 Y
1.25 Y	0.94 Y + 1.25 P	0.62 Y + 2.5 P	0.31 Y + 3.75 P	5 Y
0.62 Y	0.47 Y + 0.62 P	0.31 Y + 1.25 P	0.16 Y + 1.88 P	2.5 Y
0.31 Y	0.24 Y + 0.31 P	0.16 Y + 0.62 P	0.08 Y + 0.94 P	1.25 Y
0.16 Y	0.12 Y + 0.15 P	0.08 Y + 0.31 P	0.04 Y + 0.47 P	0.62 Y
0 Y	0 Y + 0 P	0 Y + 0 P	0 Y + 0 P	0 Y

TABLE 28–3

GEOMETRIC SERIES OF MIXTURES

Number of mixtures							
3		5		9		19	
% A	% B	% A	% B	% A	% B	% A	% B
0	100	0	100	0	100	0	100
6	94	3	97	3	97	2	98
50	50	13	87	6	93	3	97
94	6	50	50	13	87	4	96
100	0	87	13	25	75	6	94
		97	3	50	50	9	91
		0	0	75	25	13	87
				87	13	18	82
				94	6	25	75
				97	3	36	64
				100	0	50	50
						64	36
						75	25
						82	18
						87	13
						91	9
						94	6
						96	4
						97	3
						98	2
						100	0

TABLE 28–6

COMMERCIAL BODY STAINS

Color	Type of stain	Stability limit, °C	Comments
Red	Iron	1050	Bleached by lime
Pink	Manganese aluminate	1400	
Pink	Gold	1500	Colloidal color
Orange	Antimony – titanium – chromium	1300	
Brown	Iron – chromium – zinc	1300	
Brown	Iron	1100	
Tan	Titanium – chromium	1300	
Tan	Iron – chromium – zinc	1300	
Tan	Iron – antimony	1300	
Yellow	Antimony – titanium – chromium	1300	Varies with vit.
Yellow	Tin – vanadium	1300	
Yellow	Zirconium – vanadium	1300	
Green	Chromium	1500	
Green	Vanadium – chromium	1300	
Blue	Cobalt	1500	
Blue	Cobalt – aluminate	1500	
Blue	Vanadium – zirconium	1300	
Black	Cobalt – chromium – iron	1500	

TABLE 28–4

VOLUMES OF SLIPS BLENDED

1 Y	$\frac{3}{4}$ Y + $\frac{1}{4}$ P	$\frac{1}{2}$ Y + $\frac{1}{2}$ P	$\frac{1}{4}$ Y + $\frac{3}{4}$ P	1 P
1 Y + 1 W	$\frac{3}{4}$ Y + $\frac{1}{4}$ P + 1 W	$\frac{1}{2}$ Y + $\frac{1}{2}$ P + 1 W	$\frac{1}{4}$ Y + $\frac{3}{4}$ P + 1 W	1 P + 1 W
1 Y + 3 W	$\frac{3}{4}$ Y + $\frac{1}{4}$ P + 3 W	$\frac{1}{2}$ Y + $\frac{1}{2}$ P + 3 W	$\frac{1}{4}$ Y + $\frac{3}{4}$ P + 3 W	1 P + 3 W
1 Y + 7 W	$\frac{3}{4}$ Y + $\frac{1}{4}$ P + 7 W	$\frac{1}{2}$ Y + $\frac{1}{2}$ P + 7 W	$\frac{1}{4}$ Y + $\frac{3}{4}$ P + 7 W	1 P + 7 W
1 Y + 15 W	$\frac{3}{4}$ Y + $\frac{1}{4}$ P + 15 W	$\frac{1}{2}$ Y + $\frac{1}{2}$ P + 15 W	$\frac{1}{4}$ Y + $\frac{3}{4}$ P + 15 W	1 P + 15 W
1 Y + 31 W	$\frac{3}{4}$ Y + $\frac{1}{4}$ P + 31 W	$\frac{1}{2}$ Y + $\frac{1}{2}$ P + 31 W	$\frac{1}{4}$ Y + $\frac{3}{4}$ P + 31 W	1 P + 31 W
1 W	1 W	1 W	1 W	1 W

In glazes. When the glaze stain is dissolved in the glaze, the solution color produced by the transition element results. Stain composition has no effect on the hue. For example, a lead glaze will be grass green in color when copper is added in any one of the following forms:

1.0% of CuO
12.4% of $CuO \cdot 4B_2O_3 \cdot 3PbO$ (frit)
1.4% of $CuCO_2$

On the other hand, if the stain is relatively insoluble, its characteristic color will persist in the glaze. It is difficult to obtain insoluble stains for the highly fluid lead glazes, but the less active porcelain glazes are readily colored. Remember, too, that a completely transparent glaze can be produced only with solution colors, which considerably limits the choice of color.

Certain glaze stains, like cobalt blues or gold reds, are stable to very high temperatures, while such stains as antimony yellow can be used only at comparatively low temperatures. The composition of the glaze influences the color; for example, chrome-tin pinks can be used only with zincless glazes, and chrome greens must be used with glazes free from tin oxide. On the other hand, some of the copper turquoise colors are more brilliant in zinc-containing glazes.

The recommendations of the manufacturer should be closely followed for all stains (Table 28–7).

In underglazes. Stains used under glazes must be resistant to the attack of the glaze during firing, and they must have high stability. Underglaze colors are discussed more thoroughly in Chapter 29 but, in general, the specifications listed in Table 28–7 should be followed.

In overglazes. Because these colors are ordinarily a mixture of stain and flux that is

TABLE 28 –7
COMMERCIAL GLAZE STAINS

Color	Type of stain	Stability limit, °C	Type of glaze recommended
Pink	Chromium – tin	1300	Zinc-free
Maroon	Chromium – tin	1300	Zinc-free
Brown	Iron – chromium – zinc	1300	Best in zinc
Tan	Antimony – chromium – titanium	1050	High-lead
Ivory	Iron – antimony	1050	High-lead
Buff	Chromium – titanium		Low-temperature
Yellow	Tin – vanadium	1300	Any
Yellow	Lead – antimony	1050	High-lead + zinc
Green	Calcium – chromium	1300	No tin or zinc
Green	Tin – vanadium – copper	1250	Zinc-containing
Green	Cobalt – chromium	1300	Zincless
Green	Chromium	1300	Zincless
Green	Copper	1050	High-lead
Blue	Cobalt – aluminum	1300	Any
Blue	Cobalt – zinc – tin	1300	Any
Blue	Cobalt – silica	1300	Any
Turquoise	Copper	1250	Alkaline
Turquoise	Vanadium – zirconium	1300	Any
Black	Cobalt – iron – manganese	1300	Any
Black	Cobalt – iron – chromium	1300	Any

fired on the glaze at relatively low temperatures for short periods of time, many colors can be used that are not sufficiently stable at higher temperatures. This subject is covered in detail in Chapter 29.

Commercial stains. The following advertisers are listed in the *Ceramics Data Book* as suppliers of stains.

Ceramic Color and Chemical Mfg. Co.
New Brighton, Pa.

Croxall Chemical & Supply Co.
East Liverpool, Ohio

B. F. Drakenfeld & Co., Inc.
45 Park Place
New York 7, N. Y.

Ferro Corp.
4150 E. 56th St.
Cleveland 5, Ohio

Harshaw Chemical Co.
1945 E. 97th St.
Cleveland 6, Ohio

The O. Hommel Company
Pittsburgh 30, Pa.

Vitro Manufacturing Company
60 Greenway Drive
Pittsburgh 4, Pa.

TABLE 28-8

RED, YELLOW, AND BROWN STAIN BATCHES

Raw materials	1 Rose pink	2 Crimson	3 High-t. pink	4 Iron red	5 Gold rose	6 Naples yellow[2]	7 Naples orange[2]	8 Rutile yellow	9 Rosen. yellow	10 Patent yellow[1]	11 Dark brown	12 Red brown	13 Vandyke brown	14 Faun	15 Gold brown
Tin oxide	73	47													
Whiting	15	17	1												
Lead chromate	2													12	
Porcelain body		9			84.3										
Calcium fluoride		4													
Potassium dichromate		2													
Borax			9	13											
Precip. alumina			81	0.05		5				18	12				
Manganous carbonate			9												
Lead oxide				50			40								
Sodium hydroxide					6.5										44.9
Ferric oxide				20			14			7	45	23	6	12	
Gold chloride					3.2										11.3
Potter's flint	10	21		17											
Chromic oxide										2	43	22			
Zinc oxide								17				55	24	15	
Potash alum								30					58		
Tin oxide								16						61	
Kaolin															26.2
Silver carbonate															1.6
Bismuth oxide															0.25
Potassium carbonate													12		
Antimony trioxide						15	26								
Potassium nitrate							20								
Lead nitrate						34									
Sodium chloride						46									
Rutile								37							
Uranium nitrate									17						
Zirconia									83						
Titania										73					
Glycerine					6.0										15.7
Calcining temp., °C	1200	1230	1230	850	1400	1160	1160	1160	1125	1300	1260	1260	1260	1260	1400
Grinding time, hr	100	150	200	150	250	100	100	200	180	150	150	150	150	150	250
Raw kaolin added, %[3]	5	5	5	5	5	6	5	5	6	5	6	5	5	5	12
Porc. glaze added, %[3]	5	5	5	5	20	4	5	5	6	4	6	5	5	5	

[1] U. S. Pat. No. 1945809 [2] Poisonous. [3] For use as an underglaze color.

TABLE 28-9

GREEN, BLUE, AND BLACK STAIN BATCHES

Raw materials	16 Victoria green	17 Sage green	18 Blue green	19 Ultramarine	20 Blue green	21 Turquoise	22 Copen. blue	23 Sèvres blue	24 Rosen. blue	25 Thenard blue	26 Black	27 Black	28 Ice gray	29 Mouse gray	30 Black
Potassium dichromate	35		20												
Calcium chloride	13														
Whiting	20														
Flint	20	66	32	12			11								
Chromic oxide		24		50	23										
Feldspar		10													
Cobaltous oxide			8	38			30	37							23
Zinc oxide			16												
Borax			24												
Fluorspar	20														
Cupric phosphate						56									3
Tin oxide						44					9				15
Zinc oxide							8								
Precipitated alumina								49	44						
Boric acid								14							
Cobaltous phosphate					16				26	80		11	18		
Zinc carbonate					25				30			25	35		
Aluminum hydrate					36										
Porcelain glaze							51								
Ferric chromate											52				32
Nickel oxide											9				
Cobaltous carbonate											21				
Manganese dioxide											9	16	31		25
Zinc carbonate												29	8.5		
Uranium oxide												19	7.5		
Porcelain body										20					
Zirconia														85	
Cobaltous chloride														15	
Calcining temp., °C	1160	1160	1160	1260	1400	1200	None	1160	1400	1200	1260	1400	1400	1125	1200
Grinding time, hr.	200	200	200	200	200	100	100	200	450	200	200	400	300	150	200
Raw kaolin added, %	5	5	5	5	10	6	5	5	5	5	5	10	10	5	5
Porc. glaze added, %[1]	5	5	5	5	6	6	5	5	5	5	5	-	-	5	5

[1] For use as an underglaze color.

V. STAIN COMPOSITIONS

We recommended earlier that the beginner should use commercial stains, but for the potter who wishes to experiment with his own colors, Tables 28–8 and 28–9 list a few typical compositions that give satisfactory results when carefully prepared.

VI. SUMMARY

We must again emphasize that the art of making stains is extremely exacting, and we are fortunate that such a variety of colors is available commercially at reasonable cost. Remember, however, to carefully follow the recommendations of the manufacturer.

VII. REFERENCES

Stains

1. ANON., Slants on Yellow Stains, *Ceram. Ind.* 53, 79 (August, 1949).

2. ANON., Using Victoria Greens in Glazes, *Ceram. Ind.* 51, 92 (September, 1948).

3. ANON., Ceramic Colors, *Ceram. Ind.* 35, 87 (October, 1940).

4. BOSE, H. N., Note on Chrome-Tin Pink Colors, *Ceramic Age* 53, 17, 29 (1948).

5. CHAMBERS, A., AND A. F. RIGG, Notes on Antimony Yellows, *Trans. Eng. Ceram. Soc.* 25, 101 (1925–26).

6. FUNK, W., High Fire Colors for Porcelain, *Ber. Deut. Keram. Ges.* 1, 24, (1920).

7. HEUBACH, A. R., Notes on the Production of Ceramic Red Colors, *Trans. Am. Ceram. Soc.* 11, 48 (1909).

8. HEUBACH, A. R., Light Green Chromium Stains, *Trans. Am. Ceram. Soc.* 14, 418 (1912).

9. HULL, W. A., Chrome-Tin Pink, A Further Discussion, *Trans. Am. Ceram. Soc.* 6, 148 (1904).

10. HULL, W. A., The Constitution of the Chromium-Tin Pink, *Trans. Am. Ceram. Soc.* 4, 230 (1902).

11. KOHL, H., Red and Yellow Colors in Ceramics: II. Yellow Colors, *Ber. Deut. Keram. Ges.* 17, 597 (1936).

12. KRUSE, O., AND W. THEIL, Spinel Coloring Materials, *Ber. Deut. Keram. Ges.* 15, 101 (1934); 15, 111 (1934); 15, 169 (1930).

13. MAYER, E. W. T., Study in Chrome-Tin Pink, *Trans. Eng. Ceram. Soc.* 17, 104 (1917–18).

14. MELLOR, J. W., Cobalt and Nickel Colors, *Trans. Eng. Ceram. Soc.* 36, 1 (1937).

15. MELLOR, J. W., Cobalt Blue Colors, *Trans. Eng. Ceram. Soc.* 6, 88 (1908).

16. PENCE, F. K., Colors Produced by Nickel Oxide in Ceramic Mixtures Containing Zinc, *Trans. Am. Ceram. Soc.* 14, 143 (1912).

17. PILLAI, D. S., The Effect of Zinc Oxide on the Coloring Properties of Chromium, Cobalt and Iron Oxides, *Trans. Eng. Ceram. Soc.* 25, 209 (1925–26).

18. PURDY, R. C., AND G. H. BROWN, A Study of Chromium-Tin Pinks, *Trans. Am. Ceram. Soc.* II, 228 (1909).

Color in Glazes

19. ANON., Chrome Red Crystal Glazes, *Ceram. Ind.* 52, 82 (1949).

20. ANON., How to Make Green, Blue-Green Glazes, *Ceram. Ind.* 51, 110 (November, 1948).

21. ANON., Selenium Red Glazes, *Ceram. Ind.* 15, 188 (1930).

22. BARRETT, W. E., Colored Glazes with Molybdenum Compounds, *Ceram. Ind.* 4, 211 (1925).

23. BARRETT, W. E., Glazes Colored by Molybdenum, *J. Am. Ceram. Soc.* 8, 306 (1925).

24. BINNS, C. F., AND E. CRAIG, A Chromium Red Glaze, *J. Am. Ceram. Soc.* 10, 73 (1927).

25. CARTER, O., Notes on the Constitution of Chrome-Tin Pink, *Trans. Am. Ceram. Soc.* 5, 242 (1903).

26. COLLIE, J. N., Notes on the "Sang de Boeuf" and the Copper-Red Chinese Glazes, *Trans. Eng. Ceram. Soc.* 17, 379 (1918).

27. CORDT, F. W., Suggestions for the Production of Red Glazes, *Ceram. Ind.* 21, 172 (1933).

28. CORDT, F. W., Rot als Glasur und Dekorationsfarbe, *Keram. Rund.* 41, 307 (1933); 41, 433 (1933).

29. DIETZEL, A., Beobachtungen an Chromroten Glasuren, *Ber. Deut. Keram. Ges.* 26, 12 (1949); 26, 15 (1949).

30. GEYSBEEK, S., Red Glazes at High Temperatures, *Trans. Am. Ceram. Soc.* 1, 62 (1899).

31. HEIDE, H., Die Ordnung der farbigen Glasuren in der Wandplatten und Kachelofen-Industrie, *Ber. Deut. Keram. Ges.* 26, 88 (1949).

32. HILL, E. C., Chromium Green Stains, *J. Am. Ceram. Soc.* 15, No. 7, 378 (1932).

33. McVAY, T. N., AND C. W. PARMELEE, Effect of Iron and Its Compounds on Color and Properties of Ceramic Engobes and Materials, *J. Am. Ceram. Soc.* 20, 336 (1937).

34. MELLOR, J. W., Chemistry of the Chrome-Tin Colors, *Trans. Ceram. Soc.* 36, 16 (1937).

35. MINTON, R. H., The Effect of Variation of RO Elements upon Chromium Oxide as a Coloring Agent in a Mat Glaze, *Trans. Am. Ceram. Soc.* 16, 248 (1914).

36. MINTON, R. H., Chrome-Tin Colors at Cone 9, *Trans. Am. Ceram. Soc.* XIX, 378 (1917).

37. MONTGOMERY, E. T., AND I. A. KRUZON, Colored Porcelain Glazes at Cone 10, *Trans. Am. Ceram. Soc.* 16, 347 (1914).

38. POLGREAN, J. H., "Selenium Red" as a Ceramic Color, *Trans. Ceram. Soc.* 28, 87 (1929).

39. RADCLIFFE, B. S., AND C. L. WALDUCK, Chrome-Tin Red Glazes Between Cones 2 and 8, *Trans. Am. Ceram. Soc.* 17, 278 (1915).

40. RAMSDEN, C. E., Notes on the Chromium Red Glaze, *Trans. Eng. Ceram. Soc.* 12, No. II, 239 (1914).

41. RODGERS, F. J., AND J. W. MELLOR, Notes on the Crimson-Chromium-Tin Glaze, *Trans. Eng. Ceram. Soc.* 4, 66 (1904–05).

42. WALKER, F. W., Notes on the Development of Greens from Cupric Oxide in Glazes, *Trans. Am. Ceram. Soc.* 4, 278 (1902).

43. WHITMER, J. D., Nickel Oxide in Glazes, *J. Am. Ceram. Soc.* 4, 357 (1921).

44. WHITMER, J. D., A Glaze Study Involving Some Interesting Colors Produced by Nickel Oxide, *J. Am. Ceram. Soc.* 3, 663 (1920).

CHAPTER 29

Special Methods of Decoration

I. INTRODUCTION

Some of the simpler methods of decorating pottery were described in Chapters 8 and 11. Here we shall elaborate on these and describe other techniques. Decorative methods have remained essentially unchanged since antiquity; most of these processes have been in use for many centuries.

II. SURFACE MODELING

Scratched outlines. This is the most primitive of all methods of decoration, for the only tool needed is a sharp-cornered stone. Nevertheless, this kind of modeling can be very effective and it permits many variations. For example, outlined areas may be filled with an earth color to give some contrast with the body color, or a glaze that pulls away from the scratches to leave a pattern may be used.

Sprig work. This ancient method consists of forming small decorative elements in molds, applying mold and all to the surface of a plastic piece, and then removing the mold. Early English potters used this method quite effectively, as illustrated in Fig. 29–1, and it would seem that it could be adapted to a modern approach quite easily.

Modeled surfaces. Surface modeling is very effective if the modeling is not too deep and if it conforms to the general shape of the piece. The Grueby Pottery used this method effectively during the early part of this century. The simple fluted jar shown in Fig. 29–2, made by William Shakespeare of Newton a few years ago, is a fine example of this kind of work. The modeling is done while the piece is in the plastic state, so that clay can be added without difficulty. After the modeling is completed, the piece is allowed to dry slowly and the surface is finished by scraping and sponging.

Pierced work. Whether it is eggshell porcelain of the Ming dynasty or the meticulous work of Mrs. Robineau, finely pierced ceramic work is intriguing. The method is quite simple.

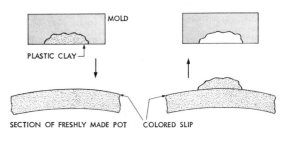

Fig. 29-1. Application of sprig decoration.

270

Fig. 29-2. Fluted jar made by William Shakespeare of Newton, Massachusetts.

Fig. 29-3. Drilling a leather-hard bowl, to start perforated decoration.
Fig. 29-4. Cutting out the drill hole with a thin-bladed knife.

A piece is thrown on the wheel, allowed to become leather hard, and then turned to give a thin, even wall thickness. The design is applied by marking through a piece of tracing paper. Then, using very little pressure, so as to avoid chipping, a hole is drilled through the wall with an ordinary twist drill held in a pin vise, as shown in Fig. 29–3. Now a very thin-bladed knife is used to pare the clay back to the outline, as shown in Fig. 29–4. This work requires a great deal of patience, for it must be done slowly and gently to avoid damage. The process is repeated for each cut-out area.

A much faster method of piercing is to use a hollow punch for cutting the openings, and to do the punching when the clay is quite soft. However, only a few sizes of openings can be made by this method, and it is used only in semi-production work.

Applied reliefs. Wedgwood cameo ware is the best known example of this kind of work. The reliefs are molded from a plastic body (usually white), in small, finely detailed molds. If only a few pressings are required, the molds may be made of hard plaster, but for production work the molds are made of fired biscuit, which stands up for many years.

When the mold has been filled, the excess body is scraped off and the surface is lightly rubbed with the back of a spoon to make the relief curl sufficiently to fall out. The relief is now placed on a damp plaster bat, as shown

Fig. 29-5. Making cameo ware in the Wedgwood Pottery. Note the small mold being filled and emptied onto a damp plaster bat.

Fig. 29-6. Cameo decoration being applied to the border of plates in the Wedgwood Pottery.

Fig. 29-7. A piece of Wedgwood jasper ware with applied decoration.

in Fig. 29–5 and 29–6 (this is a photograph taken in the Wedgwood factory by the author some years ago).

Now the different portions of relief are taken up with a spatula and applied to the leather-hard piece, the surface of which has been brushed with water. The relief is gently pressed onto the surface and, as the water dries, it is sucked firmly into place. Care must be taken not to deform the relief or to mark it with fingerprints and, of course, slip must not be used if background smear is to be avoided. This is a highly skilled art; it requires patience and a delicate hand. A finished piece is shown in Fig. 29–7.

Slip painting in the mold. You will recall that we talked about this process in Chapter 21. The procedure is quite simple. A clean mold is sponged to give it some moisture and is then painted with a colored casting slip in the desired areas. The mold is immediately assembled and white slip is cast over it in the usual manner. English potters and the potters of Bennington, Vermont, used this process extensively for making blue-and-white parian ware.

Inlay. This effective method of decoration was commonly used for the floor tiles in the old English cathedrals. It consists of cutting out areas of the tile surface and pressing in plastic clay of a different color. When the tile is scraped smooth, the design is clearly evident. (The finishing must be done by scraping, as a sponge will smear the edges of the design.) The steps in this process are shown in Fig. 29–8.

Pâte sur pâte. This difficult method of surface decoration, so effectively used by Solon at Minton's, was described in Chapter 21.

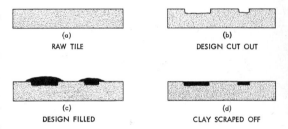

Fig. 29-8. Inlaying with colored clay, step by step.

III. UNDERGLAZE DECORATION

This kind of decoration was discussed briefly in Chapter 8; here we shall go into greater detail.

Underglaze colors. These are composed of a stain, a small amount (5%) of flux (such as a glaze), and perhaps 5% clay to keep the color in suspension. A great variety of colors can be obtained commercially, but it must be borne in mind that some colors cannot be used under certain glazes. For example, chrome greens cannot be used under glazes containing tin.

TABLE 29-1
COLORED SLIPS

Materials	Red	Brown	Blue	Green	Black	White
Body No. 11	92	90	98	95	89	100
Manganese dioxide		4			6	
Ferric oxide	8	6			4	
Cobalt oxide			2		1	
Chromic oxide				5		

Grind wet in qt. mill for 12 hrs. Use on green body No. 5.

Under slips. A solid colored piece can, of course, be made by using a colored body, but this requires a great deal of stain for coloring. The same effect is obtained by dipping a white piece into stain, or by spraying it. Wedgwood Jasperware was colored in this manner, and this method is quite commonly used for production work. By using templates or wax resists the color can be confined to specific areas.

Colored slips and bodies are made by adding a coloring oxide like chromic oxide (Cr_2O_3) or cobalt oxide (CoO) to a white body, or by using body stains, as explained in Chapter 28. The stains (limited to about 15%) must be milled with the slip to give an even color. The formulas for some colored slips are given in Table 29–1.

Slip trailing. This method is suitable for bold designs, and it was used extensively for Staffordshire earthenware, for stoneware, and for New England and Pennsylvania redware. Examples are shown in Figs. 29–9 and 29–10. The procedure is simple. A bulb with a quill (an atomizer bulb attached to an ink dropper is excellent) is used to apply the slip, as shown in Fig. 29–11. Although, with practice, the line widths can be varied considerably, the application must be boldly and quickly done or the effect is spoiled.

Fig. 29-9. Cobalt blue slip decoration on a stoneware jar.
Fig. 29-10. Slip-decorated plate made in Pennsylvania, early 19th century. (Courtesy of The Metropolitan Museum of Art, N. Y.)
Fig. 29-11. Slip-trailing on an unfired vase.

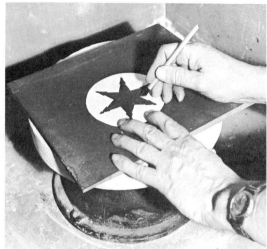

Fig. 29-12. Decorating a vase by the sgraffito method. Note the clean outline.

Sgraffito. This effective and simple method consists of applying colored slip to a leather-hard piece of a different color. When the slip is wholly or nearly dry, it is scraped away from portions of the piece to allow the body color to show. The procedure is shown in Fig. 29–12.

Frisket stenciling. This simple method was described in Chapter 8; it is an excellent technique for the beginner.

Stenciling. This process is more suited to production methods than for use by the artist potter. The method consists of holding a stencil against the biscuit surface (or a short distance from it) and spraying on the color. (Figures 29–13 through 29–15.)

Stenciling:
Fig. 29-13. Cutting a stencil.
Fig. 29-14. Spraying the plate with underglaze color, with the stencil in place. Note the weights holding the stencil down.
Fig. 29-15. Cleaning up the outline after the stencil has been removed.

Painting. This method was discussed in Chapter 8. The results depend on the skill of the artist; written instructions are of little help.

Underglaze crayoning. Commercial crayons are available in a wide range of colors for this kind of work. This is an excellent medium for the beginner, as explained in Chapter 8.

IV. DECORATION IN THE GLAZE

Designs that are painted in the glaze are seldom pleasing, because the outlines are indistinct. The following methods of decorating in the glaze are preferable.

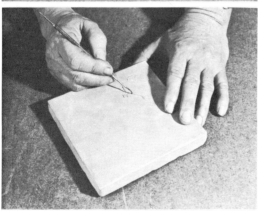

Encaustic glazing (inlay). For this kind of decorating, different areas of colored glaze are separated by (1) ridges on the body, (2) grooves in the body, or (3) underglaze black lines. Generally speaking, only flat, horizontal surfaces can be treated in this way.

The design is first transferred to the surface of a leather-hard piece, like the tile in Fig. 29–16; the impression of the pencil point through the tracing paper is easily seen in the clay. Now the design is outlined with narrow grooves cut into the clay surface, as in Fig. 29–17. These grooves should be uniform in width and have clean edges. The areas of the design are then covered with colored glaze, using a bulb, as shown in Fig. 29–18 (a separate bulb for each color). If glaze accidentally runs into the grooves, it must be scraped out when it is dry. It re-

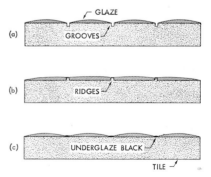

Encaustic decoration:
Fig. 29-16. Transferring a design to a raw tile.
Fig. 29-17. Scratching the design outline.

Fig. 29-18. Applying glaze to the biscuit tile.
Fig. 29-19(a). The three methods of separating areas for different colors.

Fig. 29-19(b). A fine example of encaustic decoration, made by the Grueby Pottery in Boston.

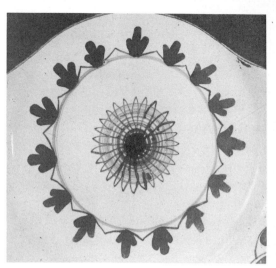

Fig. 29-20. A simple decoration in blue on a Delft plate.

quires practice to get the correct glaze thickness. Figure 29–19(a) shows a cross section such a tile to indicate the three methods, and Fig. 29–19(b) shows a fine example of encaustic decoration by the Grueby Pottery in Boston.

Delft decorations. This characteristic decoration is unique in that a stain (usually cobalt) is painted directly on the dry, unfired glaze surface. The glaze is a tin-enamel, to prevent the buff-colored body from showing through. The painting must be carried out rapidly with a full brush; there can be no hesitation and no correcting. For this reason, the method lends a freedom and boldness not found elsewhere. An example is shown in Fig. 29-20.

V. OVERGLAZE DECORATION

Because overglaze decorations are fired at relatively low temperatures, many of the more brilliant but less stable colors can be used. On the other hand, these decorations do not seem to be as well integrated with the piece as underglaze colors; they give the feeling of a surface treatment.

Production methods such as decals, copper-plate transfers, and photographic printing are used in many potteries, but since they are not adapted to the studio pottery, we shall not elaborate on them here. However, we shall discuss silk-screen printing.

Overglaze colors. Stains for overglaze decorations are much like those used for underglaze colors, except that the range of suitable colors is wider. These stains were described in Chapter 28. Because these colors mature at fairly low temperatures (about Cone 016, 750°C), a soft flux must be added to cause fusion with the glaze surface. Although many kinds of flux can be used, they generally are of the lead boro-silicate type (Table 29-2).

TABLE 29-2
OVERGLAZE FLUXES

Material	For blues	For purples	For gold cols.
Red lead	50-80	37	50
Potter's flint	50-20	15	25
Borax		48	
Melted borax			25

The flux is fused in a crucible, poured into water, ground, and washed. It is then ready to be added to the stain for further grinding. Commercial fluxes are quite satisfactory.

When an opaque overglaze color is required, an opacifying agent can be added to the frit batch or can be added in the mill at a later stage. The usual opacifying ingredients are tin oxide, zinc oxide, zirconia, and titania. (Remember that zinc and tin cannot be used with chromium greens.)

Overglaze colors are not so readily blended as oil paints. For example, iron-containing colors often change the hues of other colors mixed with them. Experience teaches how the colors can be effectively used.

For the convenience of the potter who would like to experiment with his own colors, we have listed in Table 29–2 the fluxes that can be used with the stains described in Chapter 28.

Application by brush. The application of these colors has been generally described in Chapter 8. The vehicle carrying the color is usually a fat or an essential oil which is sold commercially. The references at the end of this chapter will prove helpful in learning the techniques of painting designs over the glaze, but again we must urge that working under the tutelage of an expert can help immeasurably.

Figure 29–21 shows how overglaze decorations are applied by hand in a large pottery; Figure 29–22 shows an artist applying decoration to a vase at the Royal Danish Porcelain Works; and Figure 29–23 pictures a bowl with a simple black overglaze design that is very effective.

Fig. 29-21. Decorating ware in a large pottery (Wedgwood Pottery).

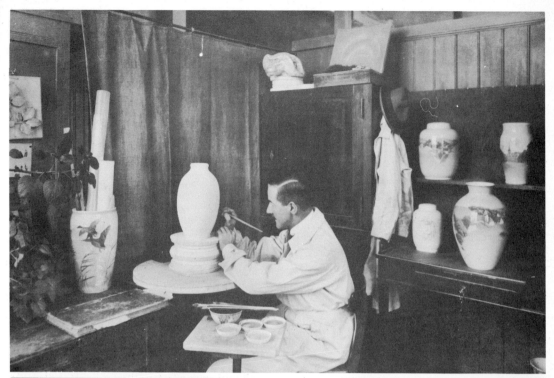

Fig. 29-22. Artist decorating a vase in his studio at the Royal Danish Porcelain Works.

Fig. 29-23. Simple overglaze decoration on a Worcester porcelain bowl.

Silk-screen printing. This process is well adapted to use by the studio potter, and we shall describe it in some detail. A stencil is formed on a tightly stretched silk cloth which holds it just above the ceramic surface, and the mixture of color and vehicle is forced through the meshes of the silk onto the surface of the ware. These steps are shown schematically in Fig. 29–24.

The silk screen for this process is specially woven from raw silk, and is usually 124 meshes per inch (#12) or 156 meshes per inch (#16). It is obtainable from artist supply houses.

The first step is to stretch the silk tightly on a wooden frame, which can be made or purchased. The stencil is cut from special duplex paper, and care must be taken to cut through the stencil, but not through the backing. The stencil, with the backing, is placed on the silk and is cemented down with a hot iron (the stencil paper has a layer of shellac very much like dry mounting tissue). The backing is then stripped off, leaving the stencil firmly fixed to the silk screen.

Now the screen is mounted about ⅛ inch above the ceramic surface (carefully registered into position), and the color, with its vehicle, is placed on one edge of the stencil and is dragged over the surface with a rubber squeegee. This dragging action presses the screen tightly against the ceramic surface and at the same time forces the color through the meshes of the screen. It is possible to produce many pieces in a short time by this method.

Gilding. This operation consists of depositing a thin layer of a noble metal on top of the glaze. Gold is most often used, but platinum and silver are not uncommon. Gilding mixtures can be purchased com-

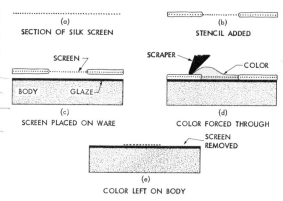

Fig. 29-24. Silk-screen printing, step by step.

mercially. The better (and more expensive) ones are made from powdered coin gold, a flux, and a vehicle. It is not recommended that the potter go through the exacting process of making his own solutions.

The gilding mixture is applied to the glaze surface, dried, and then fired at a low temperature (700°–800°C). When the metal is cooled, it looks brown, but burnishing transforms it to a gleaming surface. (A matte gold finish is obtained by burnishing with a pencil of spun glass.) Gold decorations are sometimes applied by painting a design on the glazed surface with a varnish and then dusting with powdered gold, which sticks to the varnished surface.

A less expensive gilding solution can be made from gold chloride, a flux, and a vehicle. Upon firing at about 700°C the gold chloride is reduced to the metal, which is deposited in a thin, bright layer on the glaze surface. This finish requires no burnishing, but it does not wear as well as the coin gold application.

Lusters. Lusters are very thin films of metal deposited on the glaze. They are commercially available in a variety of colors and are of three general types.

(1) A metal resinate, which usually contains compounds of gold, silver, or copper, with bismuth. The vehicle is an oil such as oil of lavender, and the mixture is applied to the glazed surface and fired at 600° to 900°C in a muffle. The carbon which is formed in this process reduces the resinates and deposits a thin metallic film on the glazed surface.

(2) Metal salts (including bismuth), which are mixed with a vehicle and applied to the glaze. The piece is then fired in a reducing atmosphere until a metal film is formed.

(3) An overglaze "reflect" made up of 1 part flint, 2 parts borax, and 15 parts red lead, fritted and used like a fritted glaze. After the piece has been fired under overglaze conditions, it is dipped for a few seconds into a 2% solution of acetic acid. It is important to watch closely, so that the piece is removed from the acid bath and quickly rinsed as soon as the proper colors have appeared. This type of luster is seldom used today.

Ground laying. This method of overglaze decoration produces an even-colored surface. The first step is to apply a resist consisting of a strong sugar solution colored with a dye to those parts of the surface which are to be free of color. Next the piece is painted with a drying oil (linseed oil and turpentine) and the surface is patted with a cotton pad to remove all brush marks. After the oil has

become tacky, the color is pounced on with a cheese-cloth bag, and the excess is shaken and blown off.

When the piece has dried for 24 hours, it is washed with warm water to remove the resist, and is fired at the usual overglaze temperature. For some colors, a second coat and a second firing are needed. The application of color by this process is shown in Fig. 29–25.

Encrustation. In this process, the areas to be left intact are coated with a film of wax. The piece is then immersed in dilute hydrofluoric acid until the glaze is etched down a few hundredths of an inch. (It is dangerous to inhale this acid. Good ventilation is essential.) This encrusted area is often gilded to bring out the relief. The steps of this process are shown in Fig. 29–26, and a finished piece is shown in Fig. 29–27.

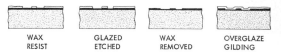

WAX RESIST   GLAZED ETCHED   WAX REMOVED   OVERGLAZE GILDING

Fig. 29-26. Resist-etching a glaze, step by step.

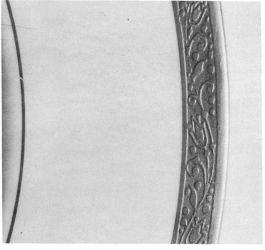

Fig. 29-27. Example of glaze etching (encrustation) on the edge of a plate.

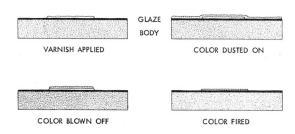

VARNISH APPLIED   GLAZE BODY   COLOR DUSTED ON

COLOR BLOWN OFF   COLOR FIRED

Fig. 29-25. Laying a ground, step by step.

Relief enamels. The enamels used for this purpose are lead disilicates with a few per cent of potash, lithia, alumina, and an opacifier such as zirconia. Voorhies (17) gives a number of satisfactory formulas. The relief pattern is built up on the glaze surface, and is sometimes gilded. A very fine example of this kind of work is shown in Fig. 29–28.

Fig. 29-28. Fine example of gilded relief enamel on a vase decorated by E. Lycett.

VI. REFERENCES

Silk-screen Printing

1. JURISCH, M., Practical Silk Screen Decorating for Ceramic Products, *Ceram. Ind.* **30**, 42 (April, 1938); **30**, 44 (May, 1938).

2. STAPLEFORD, G. H., Silk Screen Printing and its Application to the Dinnerware Industry, *Bull. Am. Ceram. Soc.* **20**, 188 (1937).

Overglaze Decoration

3. ANON., Applying Decals, *Ceram. Ind.* **55**, 83 (December, 1950).

4. ANON., Raised Paste Decorating, *Ceram. Ind.* **55**, 93 (November, 1950).

5. ANON., Acid Etching, *Ceram. Ind.* **55**, 111 (October, 1950).

6. ANON., Applying Lusters, *Ceram. Ind.* **55**, 85 (August, 1950); **55**, 93 (September, 1950).

7. ANON., Spraying Color and Stippling, *Ceram. Ind.* **55**, 99 (July, 1950).

8. ANON., Groundlaying, *Ceram. Ind.* **54**, 107 (June, 1950).

9. ANON., Hand Painting, *Ceram. Ind.* **54**, 97 (May, 1950).

10. ANON., Printing Gold, *Ceram. Ind.* **54**, 139 (April, 1950).

11. ANON., Lining Overglaze, *Ceram. Ind.* **53**, 83 (December, 1949).

12. ANON., Overglaze Decorating, *Ceram. Ind.* **45**, 92 (December, 1945).

13. ANON., How to Use Metallic Decoration, *Ceram. Ind.* **34**, 47 (June, 1940).

14. BURNHAM, F., AND C. M. HARDER, Practical Production of One-Fire Luster Glazed Pottery, *J. Am. Ceram. Soc.* **27**, 62 (1944).

15. JACKSON, C. E., Notes on Decorating Kilns and the Problems of Overglaze Decoration, *Trans. Am. Ceram. Soc.* **IX**, 408 (1907).

16. POLLOCK, L. A., Fundamentals of China Painting, *Ceramic Age* **55**, 178, 274, 350, 436 (1950); **56**, 48 (1950).

17. VOORHIES, J. H., Cone 015 Relief Enamels for Decorating Vitreous China, *J. Am. Ceram. Soc.* **28**, 170 (1945).

18. WILSON, H., Note on Overglaze Colors at Cone 6–7, *Trans. Am. Ceram. Soc.* **XIX**, 653 (1917).

General Decoration

19. ANON., Preparation of Gold Luster for Pottery, *Keram. Rund.* **47**, 26, 293 (1939).

20. ANON., Pottery Decorating, *Pottery Gazette* **75**, 209 (1950).

21. BREITENFELDT, E., Experiments with Luster Glazes, *Keram. Rund.* **37**, 329 (1929).

22. MEIR, G. E., AND J. W. MELLOR, The Ferric Oxide Colors, *Trans. Eng. Ceram. Soc.* **36**, 31 (1936).

23. PERKINS, D. W., Overglaze, *Ceramic Age* **51**, 215 (April, 1948).

24. BINNS, C. F., *The Potter's Craft*, D. Van Nostrand Company, Inc., New York, 1948.

25. PERKINS, D. W., Brief Survey of Ceramic Decorative Processes, *Ceramic Age* **48**, 23 (July, 1946); **48**, 83 (August, 1946).

CHAPTER 30

Pottery Equipment

I. INTRODUCTION

In this chapter we shall describe the equipment needed for setting up a small pottery. Names of suppliers are listed for those who wish to purchase equipment commercially, and instructions for constructing his own equipment are given for the potter who wishes to do so.

II. EQUIPMENT FOR BODIES AND SLIP

Scales. Scales are readily and economically purchased commercially. Chapter 18 describes the most satisfactory types.

Blungers. A blunger is a mixer for body or glaze slips. For small batches, an ordinary eggbeater is satisfactory; for larger amounts, an electrically driven kitchen mixer is quite suitable. For batches over 5 pounds, the portable mixer shown in Fig. 30–1 is recommended. It may be clamped to a bench for convenient use in a large crock or a galvanized iron pail.

Screens. Mechanical screens are hardly justified for the small pottery; fairly large batches of mix may be processed in the 16-inch wood-rimmed riddles shown in Fig. 18–5. Remember that screens (especially fine screens) must be carefully handled; they should be cleaned (always with a soft brush) and rinsed after each use.

The mesh of a screen is expressed in terms of the number of meshes per linear inch. For example, a 100-mesh screen has 100 openings to one inch (actually each opening is less than 1/100 inch, because the wires occupy some of the space). Screens are usually made of bronze wire, and the finer the mesh, the more expensive the screen. The artist potter will need screens of 10, 20, 65, 100, and perhaps 150 mesh.

Magnetic separators. It is not always necessary to run slip through a magnetic separator to remove iron specks, but it is certainly desirable to subject porcelain bodies to this treatment. The excellent small separators that are now available for this purpose require direct current.

Filters. Dewatering the slip is a troublesome process, but with suitable equipment the operation can be smoothly performed. Small batches can be filtered with a glass funnel and a flask, as described in Chapter

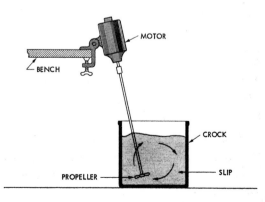

Fig. 30-1. High-speed blunger for mixing slip.

18. A metal filter operating on the same principle works quite well for somewhat larger batches, as shown in Fig. 30–2. (This is made from the cover of an ash barrel!)

The filter shown in Fig. 30–3, which was developed by William Shakespeare of Newton, Massachusetts, is a very fine piece of equipment for handling 60 pounds of body at a time. A welder can make the main body of the filter from half of an old tank, and the vacuum is produced by a simple aspirator pump in the sink. The chief advantages of this piece of equipment over the standard filter press are that the cleaning is simple, the filter cloths last indefinitely, there is no problem of blowouts or leaks, and no pumping is required.

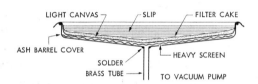

Fig. 30-2. Cross section of a vacuum filter for dewatering a few pounds of slip.

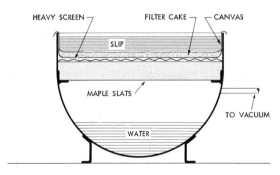

Fig. 30-3. Section of a large vacuum filter to handle 60 pounds of body.

Ball mills. The ball mill is one of the most useful pieces of equipment a potter can have. It not only grinds mixtures finely, but mixes them thoroughly. For glaze work, the usual porcelain jar mills with flint pebbles are

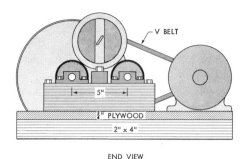

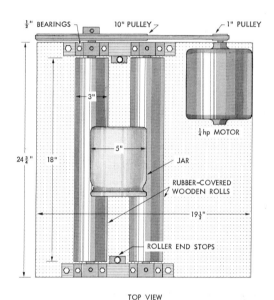

Fig. 30-4. A simple ball-mill drive.

most useful. Sizes and capacities are listed in Table 24–2. Frames for rotating the jars are commercially available, but the simple set of rolls shown in Fig. 30–4 is quite adequate because, no matter what the size of the jar, the rolls will turn the jar at the proper speed. These rolls can be purchased, or may be homemade.

A larger mill is needed for grinding bodies, and one-piece jars with a capacity of up to 60 pounds are obtainable. For larger batches, steel mills lined with porcelain blocks are required. The large mills are mounted on heavy bearings and need good-sized motors to drive them, as explained in Chapter 18.

Pug mills. Wedging a sizeable quantity of plastic body by hand is a time-consuming process, and there are many small pug mills, or pug mills with augers, on the market that are quite suitable for the small pottery. A vacuum attachment permits a better and faster job. These machines operate on the principle of a meat grinder, forcing the clay through a die by means of a screw. They are expensive, and are justified only if they are to be extensively used. Figure 18–20 shows one machine of this type.

Wet pans. Mixes containing grog (refractory or terra-cotta bodies, for instance) are difficult to handle in a small pug mill because the grog catches between the worm and the housing and causes excessive wear. Such mixes are best handled in a wet pan, like that shown in Fig. 18–26, but these are also fairly expensive.

Wedging table. A surface on which to wedge clay is a must in even the smallest pottery. Wedging may be done on a soapstone or marble slab resting on a stout table, or a heavy plaster slab can be used. The latter is cast in a wooden frame at least 2 feet square and 4 inches deep. It should be placed near the throwing wheel. It is convenient to stretch a piece of piano wire along one side, about 10 inches above the slab, for cutting the clay (a turnbuckle will keep it taut).

Storage facilities. Plastic bodies must be stored so that they lose no water, and where they are protected from dust and dirt. Large covered stoneware crocks are satisfactory for amounts up to 100 pounds, but for larger quantities wooden bins lined with zinc are desirable. Care must be taken to store the body away from iron utensils, to avoid rust stains.

III. EQUIPMENT FOR PLASTER WORK

Mixers. Small batches of plaster can be worked by hand or with a spoon, but better results are obtained by the simple mixer shown in Fig. 30–5. This mixer consists of a light electric drill with a shaft in its chuck, on the end of which is a rubber disk 2 to 4 inches in diameter. Rotating this disk in the plaster mixes it thoroughly, and if the disk should strike the mixing vessel, no harm is done. The drill should be connected to a ground to avoid shock.

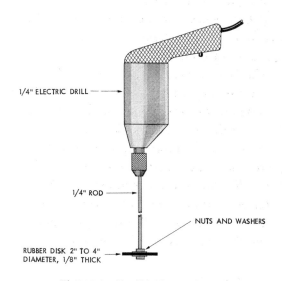

1/4" ELECTRIC DRILL

1/4" ROD

NUTS AND WASHERS

RUBBER DISK 2" TO 4" DIAMETER, 1/8" THICK

Fig. 30-5. Simple plaster mixer.

Bowls. Small batches of plaster can be mixed in rubber or plastic bowls (half of a rubber ball will do), which are easily cleaned by squeezing after the plaster has set. Large, self-cleaning bowls of thin brass are available for larger mixes. For production work, plaster is mixed in large tinned pitchers.

Bench. The plaster bench should be a solid table about 3 by 6 feet in size, with a flat, smooth top. A soapstone or marble slab is excellent. (Wood is unsatisfactory, because the wet plaster will cause it to warp.)

Tools. A set of marble or soapstone blocks is very convenient for setting up molds, and such tools as spoons, spatulas, brushes, and scrapers can be obtained from any pottery supply house.

IV. FORMING EQUIPMENT

The wheel. This is one of the most important pieces of equipment in the pottery, and a good one is worth what it will cost. Wheels are available commercially, or they are quite easily made.

Kick wheels are equipped with either a lower disk or a treadle, and it is purely a matter of preference which is used. Power wheels are strongly recommended, however, because they are more easily controlled, are certainly less tiring to use, and they actually cost little more than kick wheels to build. Figure 30–6 shows a power wheel made from standard parts; anyone can set this up in a few hours at no great expense. No matter what kind of wheel is used, it is essential that the speed control work smoothly and that the head be vibrationless.

The jigger. A jigger is required for the production of flat pieces such as plates. This may be an adjunct to the throwing wheel or may be a separate piece of equipment. Figure 30–7 shows a jigger attachment that can be easily made.

Storage closet. Even the smallest pottery needs a place to store partially finished pieces so that they will not dry out before they can be completed. Individual pieces can be placed under a metal or plastic cover for a day or two, but they cannot be kept moist for long periods in this way. Plastic display boxes make excellent storage containers, as they are both airtight and transparent. (These

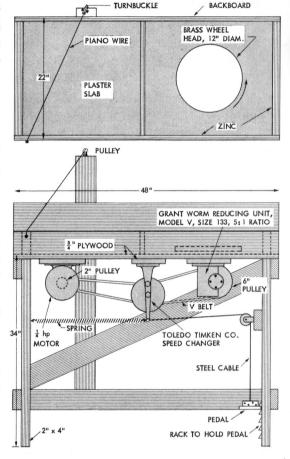

Fig. 30-6. Top and side views of a power-driven potter's wheel made from standard parts. (Scale 1/16″ = 1″.)

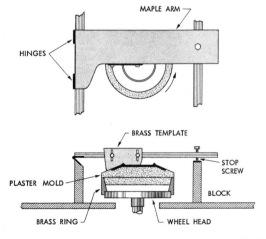

Fig. 30-7. A jigger attachment on a potter's wheel. (Scale 1/16″ = 1″.)

are particularly useful for schools; each pupil can have his own container at small expense.)

For large pieces of pottery a storage cabinet or closet is essential. An old ice box is often used, but any airtight box with a zinc or aluminum lining is satisfactory. The interior can be kept moist by placing a saturated plaster slab in the bottom. Large potteries and schools will find that a special damp room, lined with shelves and with water sprayers to maintain high humidity, is very useful.

Dryers. The artist potter has little use for dryers, for small pieces will dry quickly at room temperature, and large pieces should be dried slowly anyway. The gentle drying that is sometimes required just before firing can be done over a radiator or on top of the kiln. If a special dryer is needed, it can be made from a metal cabinet and a hot plate, or a small dryer can be purchased at reasonable cost.

V. GLAZING EQUIPMENT

We have already discussed scales and ball mills, and these are the same for both glaze and body work. Containers for storing glazes should be glass jars, stoneware crocks, or wooden tubs.

Spray gun. This is exactly the same as the guns used for spraying paint, and they are commercially available from any number of manufacturers. A good gun is worth the initial investment. It should be supplied by a compressor that has a capacity of at least 6 cubic feet per minute at 50 pounds pressure per square inch. The air line from the compressor should be equipped with a filter to remove oil. Recently developed spray guns

that are powered by self-contained blowers or CO_2 cartridges are suitable for pottery work and they eliminate the necessity for the rather costly compressor. Also, some vacuum cleaners have spray attachments that can be used for glazing.

An airbrush is needed for very fine underglaze spraying, and there are many excellent ones on the market.

Spray booth. Spraying should be done in a well-ventilated booth, so that the operator is completely protected from the mist, whether or not the medium is especially poisonous. It is easy to set up a hood like that in Fig. 30-8. The exhaust can extend into a vacant lot, or the fumes can be carried through a flue to the roof. Although the glaze passing through the exhaust fan is salvaged in commercial potteries, it is hardly worth while for the artist potter to attempt this. Excellent spray booths can be purchased ready-made.

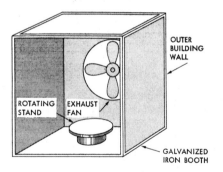

Fig. 30-8. Ventilated spray booth.

VI. KILNS

We talked about the many kinds of commercial kilns in Chapter 7, but if the potter wishes to build his own, the designs shown here will be helpful.

Gas-fired kiln. Figure 30-9 is a modified version of the muffle kiln shown in the au-

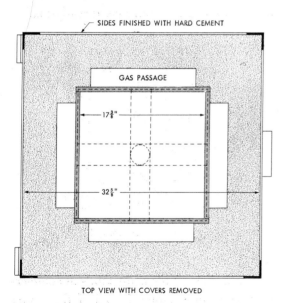

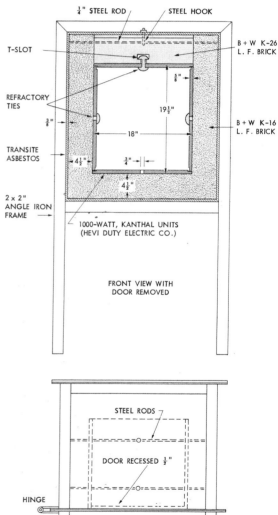

thor's *Elements of Ceramics*. Although the temperature is not as uniform as in the original model, it is easier to construct and is adequate for most purposes.

Electric wire-wound kiln. The large kiln shown in Fig. 30–10 is about the same size as that shown in *Elements of Ceramics* but is more rugged and far easier to construct. Eight commercial 1000-watt heating units

Fig. 30-9. Vertical section and top view of a muffle kiln for a small pottery.

Fig. 30-10. Front and top views of an electric kiln for firing to Cone 10.

wound with Kanthal wire are used; if a unit burns out, it is easily replaced in a few minutes. The elements are placed in parallel across a 220-volt line, and a 5-kva autotransformer acts as the control, although the temperature could be controlled by means of a separate switch on each element. This kiln will fire to Cone 10 (1260°C) and, taking everything into consideration, is the best all-around kiln that we know of for the serious potter. Figure 7–2 is a photograph of this kiln.

A similar kiln can be made up less expensively by using four 1000-watt elements on the sides only, and will fire up to Cone 01 (1100°C). Because there are no heating elements on the top, a simple suspended roof construction is possible.

Electric globar kilns. *Elements of Ceramics* contains an illustration of an excellent kiln for firing stoneware and porcelain at temperatures up to Cone 18 (1500°C). This kiln is easily constructed, but it requires an expensive transformer for satisfactory control. Globar kilns are recommended for schools and for large potteries.

Kiln furniture. It is important to have adequate furniture to set a kiln properly. In its simplest form, kiln furniture consists of plates separated by blocks or posts, as illustrated in Chapter 7. The refractory may be a fireclay-grog body, a high-alumina body, or silicon carbide bonded with clay. For low temperatures the fireclay is satisfactory, but for high fires the alumina or silicon carbide bodies are worth the extra cost. It is recommended that the potter purchase kiln furniture, although it is possible to make it.

Occasionally it is necessary to cut down a kiln plate to a smaller size, and this is quite easily done, even when they are of silicon carbide, if the following procedure is used. The cutting line is first marked on both sides of the plate, and a shallow groove is chipped along these lines with a cold chisel and a light hammer, working slowly to avoid cracking the plate. Now the plate is clamped on the bench with a piece of 2 x 4 exactly aligned with the groove, and the edge is broken off with a heavy pair of pliers or by tapping with a hammer.

Saggers are sometimes needed to support and protect the ware, especially in a wood-fired kiln. Here again it is better to purchase this equipment than to make it.

Insulating firebrick. Modern pottery kilns owe much of their efficiency to the insulating firebrick with which they are lined. Not only does this refractory cut down heat loss, but it permits fairly rapid heating and cooling. Insulating firebrick has the advantage, too, that it is easily cut and fitted. The bricks can be cut to size with an ordinary saw or a heavy hacksaw. The supplier will recommend the proper mortar for cementing the bricks, and this same mortar can be thinned and painted on the inside surface to keep down the dust (unless the coat is very thin, it will peel off and take some of the brick with it).

Firebrick comes in several grades, which are specified by the numbers 16, 20, 23, 26, 28, and 30. These numbers are an indication of the temperatures that the bricks will withstand; for example, #16 may be used to 1600°F (870°C), etc. The higher the number, the heavier and stronger the brick, and the higher the temperature at which it can be used. For small kilns, #26 or #28 bricks are best for lining, although a back-up layer of #16 can be used.

VII. SUPPLIERS OF CERAMIC EQUIPMENT

A few of the many suppliers of ceramic equipment are listed here. The basis for selection is the author's personal acquaintance with the products, but there are, of course, other manufacturers who make excellent equipment. The advertisements in ceramic magazines should be consulted for local suppliers.

Screens

The W. S. Tyler Company
3614 Superior Ave.
Cleveland 14, Ohio

American Art Clay Co.
Indianapolis 24, Ind.

The O. Hommel Company
Pittsburgh 30, Pa.

Abbé Engineering Co.
50 Church St.
New York 7, N. Y.

Magnetic Separators

S. G. Frantz Co., Inc.
Kline Ave.
Trenton 6, N. J.

Filter Presses

The Crossley Machine Company
301 Monmouth St.
Trenton 9, N. J.

Patterson Foundry and Machine Co.
Helene St.
East Liverpool, Ohio

International Engineering Inc.,
Dayton 1, Ohio

Ball Mills

Abbé Engineering Co.
52 Church St.
New York 7, N. Y.

The O. Hommel Company
Pittsburgh 30, Pa.

U. S. Stoneware Co.
Akron 9, Ohio

Pug Mills

International Engineering Inc.
Dayton 1, Ohio

The Crossley Machine Company
301 Monmouth St.
Trenton 9, N. J.

Wet Pans

National Engineering Co.
603 Machinery Hall Bld.
Chicago 6, Ill.

Lancaster Iron Works, Inc.
Lancaster, Pa.

Complete Slip House Equipment

The Crossley Machine Company
301 Monmouth St.
Trenton 9, N. J.

International Engineering Co.
Dayton, Ohio

Potter's Wheels

The O. Hommel Company
Pittsburgh 30, Pa.

American Art Clay Co.,
Indianapolis 24, Ind.

Ferro Corp.
214 Northfield Road
Bedford, Ohio

Craft Tools Inc.
401 Broadway
New York 13, N. Y.

Jiggers

The Crossley Machine Company
301 Monmouth St.
Trenton 9, N. J.

Scales

Central Scientific Co.
Cambridge, Mass.

Standard Scientific Supply Co.
34 West 4th Street
New York 12, N. Y.

Fairbanks Morse and Co.
178 Atlantic Avenue
Boston, Mass.

Glaze Spray Guns
Binks Manufacturing Co.
3114 Carroll Ave.
Chicago 12, Ill.

DeVilbiss Co.
300 Phillips St.
Toledo 1, Ohio

The O. Hommel Company
Pittsburgh 30, Pa.

Sullivan-Becker Co.
Kenosha, Wis.

Spray Booths
The O. Hommel Company
Pittsburgh 30, Pa.

General Pottery Supplies
Milligan Hardware & Supply Co.
115 E. 5th Street
East Liverpool, Ohio

Craftools Inc.
401 Broadway
New York 13, N. Y.

The O. Hommel Company
Pittsburgh 30, Pa.

Ferro Corp.
214 Northfield Road
Bedford, Ohio

American Art Clay Co.
Indianapolis 24, Ind.

B. F. Drakenfeld & Co., Inc.
45 Park Place
New York 7, N. Y.

Potters Supply Co.
East Liverpool, Ohio

Electric Kilns
Harrup Ceramic Service Co.
3470 E. 5th Ave.
Columbus, Ohio

Electric Kilns Manufacturing Co.
Chester 11, Pa.

B. F. Drakenfeld & Co., Inc.
45 Park Place
New York 7, N. Y.

Pereny Equipment Co.
893 Chambers Road
Columbus 12, Ohio

Harper Electric Furnace Corp.
39 River St.
Buffalo 2, N. Y.

Dickenson Pottery Equipment Co.
2424 Glover Place
Los Angeles 31, Calif.

Electric Hotpack Co., Inc.
5079 Cottan St.
Philadelphia 35, Pa.

Gas & Oil Kilns
Denver Fire Clay Co.
Denver, Col.

Richard C. Remmey Son Co.
Philadelphia 37, Pa.

Peterson Kiln Co.
11823 Sherman Way
North Hollywood, Calif.

Kiln Furniture
Norton Company
Worcester 6, Mass.

Electro-Refractories and Abrasives Corp.
344 Delaware Ave.
Buffalo 2, N. Y.

Carborundum Co.
Perth Amboy, N. Y.

Babcock & Wilcox Co.
Chrysler Bld. Annex
New York, N. Y.

Newcastle Refractories Co.
Newcastle, Pa.

Insulating Firebrick
Babcock & Wilcox Co.
Chrysler Bld. Annex
New York, N. Y.

VIII. REFERENCES

1. ALLEN, L. G., A Note on Kiln Construction, *Ceramic Age* **63**, No. 3, 50 (1954).

2. ANON., Cone 04 Electric Kiln, *Ceramic Age* **53**, No. 1, 39 (1949).

3. ANON., *Ceramic Data Book*, Ceramic Publishers, Inc., Chicago, 1954.

4. NORTON, F. H., AND V. J. DUPLIN, JR., A Muffle Kiln of High Efficiency, *J. Am. Ceram. Soc.* **16**, 152 (1933).

5. NORTON, F. H., *Elements of Ceramics*, Addison-Wesley Publishing Company, Inc. Cambridge, Mass., 1952 (Appendix).

6. WEBBER, I. E., AND D. S. EPPELSHEIMER, Making an Electric Kiln, *Univ. of N. H. Exp. Stat. Eng. Pub.* January, 1943.

CHAPTER 31

Laying Out the Pottery

I. INTRODUCTION

Because most studio potters start with very little equipment and expand their facilities only as they need to, the workshop, like Topsy, often "just grows," and eventually it is filled with a jumbled assortment of pieces. Even though all the equipment cannot be purchased or made at the start, it is much better to plan ahead for the most efficient use of available space, and this chapter is aimed in that direction.

II. THE ONE-MAN POTTERY

Space and services. It is surprising how little floor space is needed for any project if its use is well planned, as we can see from the tiny kitchens of dining cars that serve hundreds of people. The pottery is no exception.

Several important points must be taken into account when space for the pottery is considered. If a gas-fired kiln is to be used, there must be a flue connection for the waste gases; an electric kiln usually does not require a flue. There must be sufficient window area to adequately ventilate the room when the kiln is operating; in the summertime the heat would become unbearable without good ventilation.

It is essential that the local building inspector and your own insurance company be consulted. In some localities a kiln cannot be installed unless it has an underwriter's approval (the author knows of potters who purchased unapproved kilns and were not allowed to connect them!), and most cities and towns have zoning ordinances that impose restrictions which must be observed.

It is important to check the supply of gas and electricity to make sure that it is adequate for the intended kiln. The average lighting circuit can safely supply only about 1200 to 1500 watts (1.2 to 1.5 kva). A large electric kiln will need special wiring, like that for an electric stove. Your local gas and electric companies will gladly advise you on these points.

Although the author has seen small potteries that seem to get along very well without sinks with running water, they are certainly desirable and convenient.

Equipment. For the potter who plans to buy his body and glaze readymade, the following comprises all the essential equipment:

A well-lighted work bench
2 or 3 stools of good working height
Storage facilities for body (stoneware crocks)
A wedging table
A damp closet
Storage facilities for glaze (jars)
Storage facilities for drying ware
A kiln
Storage space for kiln furniture
Small tools (brushes, scrapers, sponges, etc.)
Bowls, pans, pitchers

Screens of various meshes
A sink with running water
A potter's wheel, if throwing is to be done

If the potter plans to make his own glaze and body, he will need the following additional equipment:

Storage space for raw materials
Scales, large and small
A mortar for grinding
A blunger (a kitchen mixer)
2 16″ screens, 65 mesh and 100 mesh
2 10″ screens, 4 mesh and 100 mesh
A filter and a sink aspirator
Ball-mill rolls
Gallon and quart jars for the mill
A large pan and smaller containers

The additional items required if the potter is to make his own body and glazes will cost several hundreds of dollars, and this expense must be balanced against the long-run anticipated savings. It is true, however, that many desirable bodies are not commercially available, and this may have some bearing on the decision.

If space and the pocketbook permit, the following additional equipment is desirable:

An air compressor and a spray gun
A ventilated spray booth
A plaster working table
A trial kiln
A desk
A drawing board

Placing the equipment. When the potter has decided what equipment he must have or wants to have, he should plan its placement for maximum efficiency. The easiest way is to make a scale drawing of the available space, with a scale of perhaps 1 inch for each foot. Similarly, a cutout is made for each piece of equipment, to the same scale. Now the cardboard equipment can be jockeyed about on the drawing of the space until the best arrangement is found. Figures 31–1 through 31–3 show possible arrangements for the small pottery.

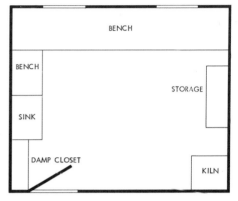

Fig. 31-1. Plan for a very small pottery. (Scale 3/16″ = 1′.)

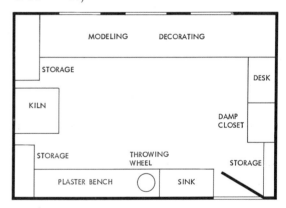

Fig. 31-2. Plan for a small pottery workshop. (Scale 3/16″ = 1′.)

III. THE SMALL PRODUCTION UNIT

Although it is not within the scope of this book to discuss production methods as such, a small art pottery sometimes produces in sufficient volume so that efficient repetitive procedures become necessary. In general, the equipment required is much the same as that listed above, but the capacity must be greater. If such operations as casting and jiggering are to be included, a small continuous kiln is desirable.

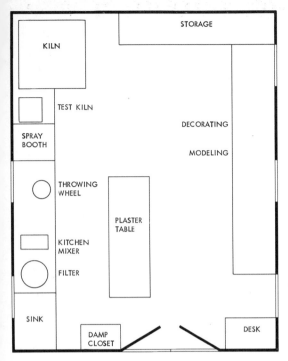

Figures 31–4 and 31–5 show suggested layouts for small production potteries; each potter should plan his own unit for maximum efficiency.

IV. POTTERY SCHOOLS

Obviously, a pottery school will need more table and seating space than the small pottery, and usually more kiln capacity will be required. Large damp rooms and storage shelves are needed to accommodate the many pieces that will be in process at one time. Figures 31–6 and 31–7 show suggested layouts.

Fig. 31-3. Plan for a well-equipped studio pottery. (Scale 3/16″ = 1′.)

Fig. 31-4. A small pottery for limited production. (Scale 3/16″ = 1′.)

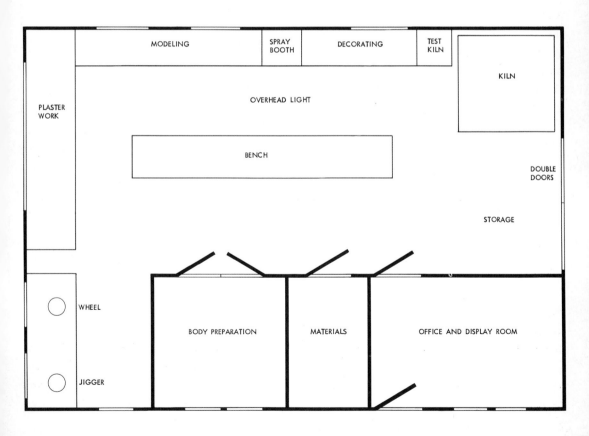

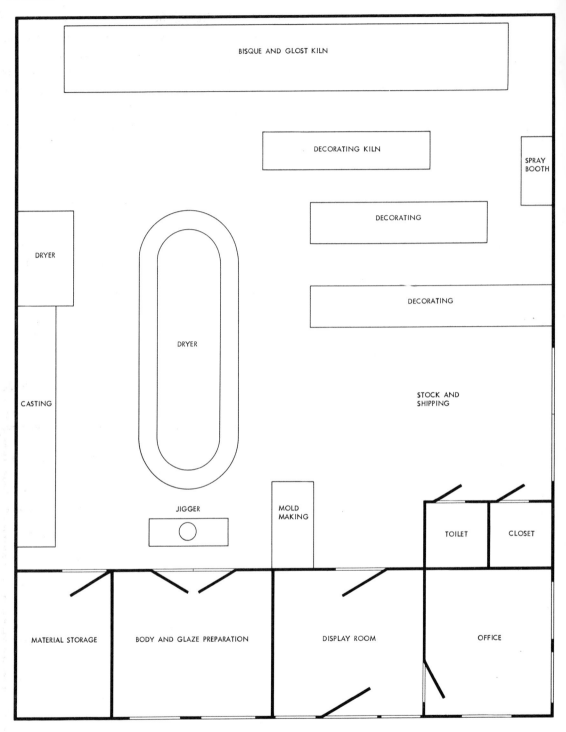

Fig. 31-5. A small production pottery. (Scale 3/16″ = 1′.)

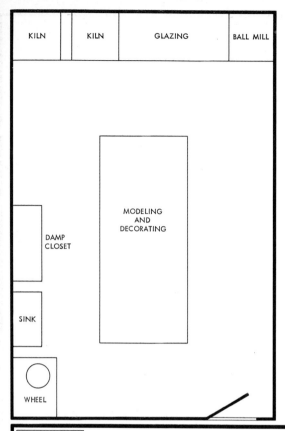

V. REFERENCES

1. ANON., Craft Potters of North Carolina, *Bull. Am. Ceram. Soc.* **21**, No. 6, 79 (1942).

2. BINNS, C. F., *The Potter's Craft*, D. Van Nostrand Company, Inc., New York, 1948 (Chap. X).

3. BORD, P., Charges for Custom Firing, *Ceramic Age* **53**, No. 2, 70 (1949).

4. COLE, R. D., AND P. B. STARR, *Making Pottery for Profit*, Sterling Publishing Co., New York, 1951.

5. ELSTERMAN, R. V., Starting a Small Pottery Business, *J. Can. Ceram. Soc.* **16**, 33 (1947).

6. JENKINS, R. H., *Practical Pottery*, The Bruce Publishing Co., Milwaukee and New York, 1941.

7. RANDALL, T. A., The Potter's Production Problems, *Ceramic Monthly* **1**, No. 3, 20 (1953).

Fig. 31-6. A small school pottery. (Scale 3/16″ = 1′.)

Fig. 31-7. A pottery laid out for class work. (Scale 3/16″ = 1′.)

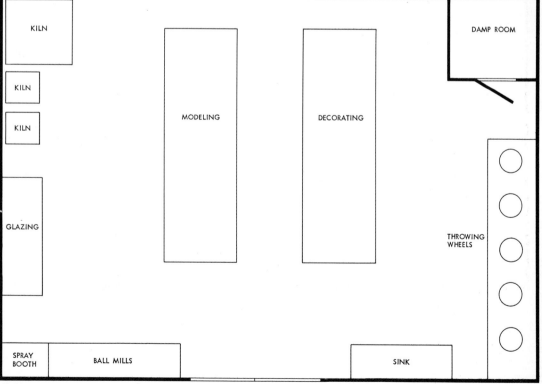

CHAPTER 32

Good Pottery: Past and Future

How can we tell good pottery from bad? What sort of standard can be set up that will enable us to judge pottery of the past and to produce good pottery in the future? These are most difficult questions to answer specifically, but we can give a general answer.

Much has been written on this subject and, as might be expected, each author has his own point of view. Perhaps the most satisfactory discussion is that given by Bernard Leach in the first chapter of *A Potter's Book*. Every potter should read this work.

I. THE CYCLIC DEVELOPMENT OF ARTS AND CRAFTS

The development of the arts and crafts in all the great civilizations have followed similar patterns:

(1) The first stage is the production of crude, simple articles purely utilitarian in nature. The struggle for bare existence left no time for elaboration.

(2) Repeated production of useful articles led to greater uniformity in this second stage, and some attempt was made to better adapt them for their purposes. Simple decorations were also occasionally used.

(3) In this third period of development, still greater refinement is evident, materials are more carefully chosen to fit their use, and although the pieces are still simple and strong, ornamentation is more common. By this time a tradition of style has developed, and proportions have become pleasing to the eye as well as utilitarian.

(4) Now the traditional style is well established, ornamentation is generous and varied, and technical advances have provided new materials and techniques. Many believe this to be the period of highest development.

(5) After the peak has been reached, the inevitable decline sets in. New materials and techniques continue to appear, and the decorations become more elaborate—there is a distinct departure from the simple, honest products of the previous periods.

(6) In this final stage, definite decadence appears. Relaxed moral principles are reflected in overdecoration and ostentation. This is the end of an era.

Sculpture in Ancient Greece. The rise and fall of the art of sculpture in Ancient Greece is an excellent example of the above cyclic process. In the archaic period, sculptured figures were simple and strong, but anatomically incorrect. By the 6th century B.C., the figures had been refined, with little loss of strength. In the 5th century B.C., this sculpture reached its zenith; these simple, beautifully proportioned heads and figures have never been equalled. In the 4th century B.C., it was fashionable to try for elaborate and tricky effects, and the decadence that rapidly set in paralleled the decline in the moral standards of the people.

Pottery making in China. Here, again, materials and techniques were at first crude, and refinement was a gradual process. The peak was reached in the Tang and Sung Dynasties, when the ware produced happily combined the honesty and simplicity of earlier times with improved methods and materials. Many students believe that this period produced the finest pottery ever known. New glazes and methods of decoration were developed in the later Ming Dynasty, but it is felt by some that the luxury of this period had a deleterious effect. In any event, this was the beginning of the decline, for definite decadence set in not long after.

Pottery making in the United States. Before the machine age, nearly every town in this country had its own pottery, where redware was made from local clays (much like the slipware of England). These pieces had an honest, down-to-earth quality, but because they lacked watertightness they were soon superseded by salt-glazed stoneware which was usually made in fairly large potteries from clay that often came from a considerable distance. Much of this ware was sound in design and construction, and well suited to its purpose. However, the making of folk pottery had pretty much died out by 1850, and most pieces were copies of fussy European ware with no real artistic merit.

Summary. The above examples make it clearly evident that as civilization advances and standards of living rise, the scope of art is broadened to include more than just the minimum required for usefulness, and that this inevitably leads to decadence. The historian Arnold Toynbee believes that people become strong only through adversity, and that when the struggle is over morals and art deteriorate. This seems to have been true in the art of pottery making.

II. THE ZENITH OF THE ART OF POTTERY MAKING

It will be instructive to examine the environments in which the world's finest pottery was produced.

In China. Let us first consider the period from the Tang Dynasty to the Sung Dynasty (618–1260 A.D.) in China.

A long, continuous tradition had been built up over the preceding millenium by the apprenticeship of young men to master potters, and pottery centers were well established. Fine pottery was so highly prized that the better potters were subsidized by the rulers, and it was unnecessary for them to be concerned with making a living. If the manufacture of a fine piece required half a lifetime, there was nothing to prevent the potter from spending that amount of time.

During this period, new materials were plentiful and technical developments had been making slow, steady progress. It was now possible to purify stoneware to produce white, translucent porcelain, and, more important, new methods of high-firing the ware made exciting new glazes possible.

Summary. The following important factors made the production of exquisite Chinese pottery possible in this period: the carrying on of a tradition from father to son, and from master potter to apprentice; gradual improvement of techniques and of materials; a public appreciation of fine pottery.

In England. Here the simple slipwares were made in a traditional fashion for many years, with little change, until stoneware was introduced from the Low Countries. At this point technical advance became rapid, and such bodies as Queen's ware, frit porcelain, bone china, parian, basalt, and jasper followed in close succession. Many new glazes, such as Rockingham glaze and matte glazes, were also developed.

During and following the Wedgwood period, little of the ware that was produced was soundly designed. It was common practice to copy classical pieces, even though these designs were not suited to the materials that were used. This unfortunate situation was directly attributable to the fact that technical advances were too rapid to allow the potter to keep pace. He wanted to use the new materials and techniques at once—and did—even though he had not yet learned how they could *best* be used.

In the Americas. In the United States, the situation was much the same as in England. Technical advances came along more rapidly than they could be properly assimilated, and the result was the fussy, overdecorated ware typical of the Empire Period. In Central and South America, on the other hand, technical advancement lagged, and it was possible for sound design to keep pace with what new materials and techniques became available.

Summary. To the summary of the factors that were important to the production of Chinese pottery at its peak of perfection, we can now add that technical advances must be gradual, if basically good design is to be maintained.

III. CAN GOOD POTTERY BE PRODUCED TODAY?

The answer, of course, is "yes," but a major reform is necessary before this can come about.

Much of the ware turned out by modern artist potters is judged excellent in both design and execution by other potters, but because all too often it is garish, overembellished, or trivial, it cannot be considered "good" by classical standards. A few years ago, Henry James said, "The great American disease is the appetite, morbid and monstrous, for color and form, for the picturesque and romantic at the same time." Perhaps this is because our potters have been trained in art schools rather than as apprentices to master potters, and consequently they lack the spirit of tradition. Most of them have only a superficial knowledge of pottery making and of the materials with which they work. Many have had no training at all.

Leach and others of our really good potters feel that we should revert to the use of local, unrefined clays for our pottery. Their premise is that a more honest, satisfying product results. I cannot altogether agree, for I believe that much greater variety and better control is possible with refined materials that have been properly blended. One of the chief troubles is that few modern potters have the skill to select from the thousands of possible combinations those that are best suited for the particular purpose both from the technical and the artistic viewpoints.

Too many modern potters strive to attract attention to their work by some tricky *tour de force*. Above all else, they want to be different, no matter how trivial or vulgar the result. The old system of apprenticeship to a master potter would check this trend. It has been remarked that good pots are made only when the potter himself throws them on the wheel, and it is true that these are the most satisfying pieces to the potter himself. Nevertheless, there is no reason why good pots cannot be made by a skilled artisan working under the direct supervision of the potter.

IV. WHAT IS THE STANDARD FOR JUDGING POTTERY?

Standards of any kind are difficult to set up, and in judging the excellence of any work of art, the personal opinion of the judges plays an important part. This is particularly true in the field of pottery: the verdict of a traditional potter, for example, would probably be quite different from that of an artist, and the general public would hold another opinion still. Traditional taste would veer toward a Tang stoneware bowl, or perhaps a modern piece by Leach or the Scheiers; a group of artists might favor pieces that break somewhat with tradition; the general public is quite apt to select gaudy, realistic, and perhaps inconsequential ware.

To the author it seems that pottery should be judged on the following points:

Is it fit for its purpose?
Is the material compatible with its use?
Does the piece exhibit good craftsmanship?
Does it have sensitivity and vitality?
And above all else,
Is it honest?

The reader has probably gathered from the above remarks that there is considerable disagreement among potters as to what constitutes fine pottery—and this is so. These differences of opinion in some cases approach the proportions of feuds in their intensity, but so long as they are *honest* differences, we shall have a healthy, vigorous atmosphere in which we can expect this ancient art to flourish anew.

Glossary of Ceramics Terms

Although the author makes no guarantee as to the completeness of this list, he has attempted to include here terms peculiar to ceramics that might be unfamiliar to the layman. Some of them the reader will have found and looked up while reading this book; others may be useful to him as he becomes more familiar with ceramics and reads other books and articles.

Absorption. Taking up of water in the pores of a body.

Accessory minerals. Nonclay minerals, such as mica, feldspar, and quartz, in a clay.

Agateware. Ware with irregular veins of color in the body.

Albite. Soda feldspar, $Na_2O \cdot Al_2O_3 \cdot 6SiO_2$.

Alkali. Strong base; mainly sodium and potassium hydroxide (NaOH, KOH). Alkalies combine with acidic substances (such as silica).

Alumina. Aluminum oxide, Al_2O_3.

American hotel china. A body, white or colored, moderately translucent, with less than 0.3% absorption, having great strength and covered with a moderately hard glaze.

American household china. A body similar to American hotel china but made in thinner sections and having greater translucency.

Anorthite. Lime feldspar, $CaO \cdot Al_2O_3 \cdot 2SiO_2$.

Arabesque. A florid type of decoration originated by Arabian artists.

Auger. A machine for extruding plastic clay through a die.

Autoclave. A vessel for developing steam pressures.

Aventurine glaze. A glaze with spangles, usually produced by hematite crystals, shimmering below the surface.

Ball clay. Highly plastic, fine-grained, sedimentary clay burning white or cream colored, often containing considerable organic matter.

Ball mill. A rotating jar containing pebbles and charge, used for mixing or fine grinding.

Bas-relief. Low modeling on a flat or curved surface.

Basalt ware. Fine, black, unglazed stoneware, first developed by Wedgwood.

Bat. A plaster slab or disk on which clay is worked, or on which objects are formed and dried. Sometimes, a fire-clay slab for setting in the kiln.

Batch. A mixture of weighed ingredients.

Belleek china. A thin, highly translucent, frit-containing body with no absorption, covered with a soft glaze. The name comes from Belleek in Ireland, the principal source.

Bentonite. Special clay used in small amounts to increase workability of bodies, or to suspend glazes.

Biscuit. Unglazed fired ware.

Bisque. *See* Biscuit.

Bitstone. Crushed silica used as a setting sand.

Blanc-de-chine. White, glazed, Chinese porcelains.

Blank. An undecorated piece.

Blunge. To mix thoroughly, as slip.

Blunger. A mixer with revolving paddles, used to form slip.

Boccaro ware. Red, unglazed stoneware with relief decorations. First made in China.

Body. A mixture of clays and nonplastics that is workable and has suitable firing properties.

Bone ash. Largely calcium phosphate. Used as an ingredient in bone china and as an opacifier for glazes.

Bone china. Soft porcelain of high translucency having 0.3 to 2% absorption, made with bone ash as a flux. Produced mainly in England.

Böttger ware. Dark red stoneware made at Dresden from 1709–1719 by Böttger to imitate boccaro ware.

Bristol glaze. Raw glaze containing zinc oxide, often used on terra cotta.

Bulk density. Over-all density, including pores.

Burning. Firing.

Burnishing. Polishing with a stone or steel tool, as on overglaze gold or leather-hard clay.

Calcine. To heat to a moderate degree to drive off chemical water or carbon dioxide.

Calipers. A tool for measuring diameter.

Cameo. A relief ornament in a color different from the background.

Casting. Process of forming objects in plaster molds from a slip.

Cauliflower ware. Cream-colored ware modeled and colored like a cauliflower. Made in England in the last of the 18th century.

Celadon glaze. Gray-green, semi-opaque glaze with reduced iron as the colorant.

Ceramics. Art and science of forming objects from earthy materials with the aid of heat.

Chuck. A form, mounted in a lathe, in which ware is set for turning.

Chum. A form, mounted in a lathe, on which hollow ware is set for turning.

China. Whiteware, vitreous and more or less translucent, biscuit-fired at a moderate temperature and glost-fired at a lower temperature. Its absorption is less than 2%.

China clay. Residual kaolin mined in southern England.

Clay. Fine-grained, earthy material containing a considerable amount of the mineral kaolinite. It is plastic when wet and strong when dry.

Coefficient of expansion. The rate of change of length with temperature.

Coiled ware. Ware made from clay coils.

Colloid. Any material in very finely divided form, with particles below one-half micron in diameter.

Combed ware. Ware with scroddled glaze made by combing several colored, wet glazes together.

Cornish stone. Rock containing largely feldspar and quartz, used as a whiteware flux in England.

Crackle finish. Intentional crazing of the glaze in a network to give a decorative effect. The cracks are often accentuated by staining.

Crawling (Eng.:parting). Drawing up of a glaze into drops, due to previous cracking in the dry state.

Crazing. Accidental, undesirable cracking of the glaze, due to tension in cooling or delayed expansion of the body.

Crank. A low sagger for holding one plate, used for hard porcelain.

Cream-colored ware. Fine earthenware first made by Astbury early in the 18th century in England. After 1765 it was called Queen's ware.

Cryolite. Sodium aluminum floride, Na_3AlF_6; used in glazes.

Crystal glazes. Glazes in which large crystals have grown during cooling.

De-airing (of clay). Process of removing air in plastic bodies by means of pugging in a vacuum.

Decalcomania (decal) A transfer pattern for decorating ware.

Deflocculant. A basic material, such as sodium carbonate or sodium silicate, used to deflocculate.

Deflocculate. To disperse a clay suspension so that it has little tendency to settle and has a low viscosity, together with a low water content.

Delft ware. A soft, buff-colored, majolica body covered with a white, tin-enamel glaze. Overglaze decorations are painted onto the unfired glaze, often using cobalt blue. First made in Holland and later in England.

Della Robbia ware. Richly modeled ware, especially tin-enamel reliefs, produced at Florence (15th century).

Density. Weight per unit volume, usually expressed in grams per cubic centimeter.

Dipping. Glazing by immersing the biscuit piece in a glaze slip.

Dolomite. Limestone containing magnesite.

Draw. To take ware from the kiln.

Dry. To remove free moisture (below 110°C).

Dry-foot. Ware with no glaze on the foot.

Dryer. A chamber with a heat supply for drying ware.

Dunting. Cracking of fired articles during the cooling period of the kiln (caused by too-rapid cooling).

Earthenware. Ware having no translucency and an absorption over 3%, covered with a soft or medium-hard glaze.

Eggshell porcelain. Very thin, translucent porcelain.

Elers ware. Fine red unglazed stoneware made first by Elers in Staffordshire about 1690.

Encaustic decoration. A kind of inlaid glaze. The glazes are placed in cells on a tile surface to prevent intermingling.

Engine-turned ware. Ware that is lined or fluted in a special lathe.

Engobe. White or colored slip applied to a fired or unfired body. It is more vitreous than the body, less so than the glaze. It may or may not be covered with a glaze.

Faience. Earthenware made in France, having a soft, porous body of light red or yellow color and generally covered with a thick, opaque, and usually white tin-enamel glaze. The name comes from the small Italian town of Faenza, a potting center.

Famille rose. A series of red colors obtained from gold (purple of Cassius). First used by the Chinese in the Ching Dynasty.

Fat oil. Thickened turpentine.

Feldspar. In ceramics, the potash-soda feldspars, which serve as an insoluble source of alkali for fluxing.

Fettle. To remove fins, mold marks, and rough edges from dry, or nearly dry, ware.

Filter press. A machine for removing some of the water from a slip to give a plastic material.

Fire. To heat in a kiln to the required temperature.

Fit. Adjustment of a glaze to a body.

Flambé glaze. Flow glaze with reduced copper, which gives variegated effects.

Flatware. Plates, saucers, platters, round and oval dishes, and trays.

Flint (potter's flint). In Europe, a crypto-crystalline variety of quartz ground from flint pebbles. In this country, finely ground quartz sand.

Flint-enameled ware. Rockingham-type pottery with a glaze flecked in yellow, brown, and blue. Patented at Bennington, Vt.

Flocculate. To thicken a clay suspension by the addition of an acid.

Flow glaze. Glaze with enough fluidity in the kiln to flow down the ware, usually having intermingling colors.

Flux. A body ingredient that softens or melts in firing to serve as a cement to bond the other materials together. Common fluxes are feldspar, bone ash, and frit.

Foot. Base of a piece of ware.

Frisket. A stencil, usually of paper, stuck to the ware to protect it from slip or glaze.

Frit. Special water-insoluble glass for use in a body or glaze.

Frit china. Belleek china.

Fritting. Melting ingredients into a glass, which can then be finely ground and suspended for use in bodies or glazes.

Gilding. Application of metals such as gold and platinum to the surface of a glaze.

Glaze. A thin layer of special glass used as a coating for biscuit. It may be clear, colored, or opaque, or contain crystals.

Glost firing. Firing of a glaze on a biscuit that has previously been fired to a higher temperature.

Granite ware. Earthenware with mottled glaze to imitate granite. First made by Wedgwood.

Grès. Stoneware.

Grog. Crushed hard-fired clay, used in terra-cotta and refractory bodies to reduce shrinkage.

Ground laying. Application of a uniform background color.

Gum arabic. Natural gum used in some glazes.

Gum tragacanth. Natural gum used in some glazes.

Gypsum plaster. Hydrated calcium sulfate, $CaSO_4 \cdot 2H_2O$, which sets after mixing with water to form a firm block. Used by the potter for molds.

Hardening on. Heating of underglaze-decorated ware at 600°C to burn off the organic matter in the colors.

Hard porcelain. True porcelain composed of china clay, feldspar, and flint, fired with the glaze at 1250°C or more.

Hollow ware. Cups, bowls, vases, pots, jars, vegetable dishes, soup tureens, etc.

Incised ware. Ware with surface carving.

Intaglio. Depressed surface decoration, the reverse of the usual relief.

Ironstone china. Strong earthenware, first made in England.

Jasper ware. Fine, unglazed stoneware, white or colored, containing a large proportion of barium, often with relief or cameo decoration. First made by Wedgwood.

Jigger. A machine like a potter's wheel with a profile template to form one surface of flatware.

Jolley. Like a jigger, but for use with hollow ware.

Kaolin. Pure, white clay, consisting largely of the mineral kaolinite. It may be either a residual or a sedimentary clay. China clay of England is a kaolin.

Kiln. A refractory-lined chamber, with means for heating it, in which ceramic ware is fired.

Kiln furniture. Refractory slabs, posts, and setters for supporting ware in the kiln.

Lawns. Screens.

Leather hard. Condition which a plastic clay or body reaches on drying, when the shrinkage has just ended and when the surface has not yet become light-colored.

Limestone. Calcium carbonate, $CaCO_3$.

Lining. Putting bands or lines on ware.

Luster. Surface iridescence caused by a very thin layer of metal on top of the glaze.

Magnesite. Magnesium carbonate, $MgCO_3$.

Magnetic separator. A machine for removing iron particles from slip.

Majolica glaze. Opaque glaze with a glossy surface. Tin oxide is often used to make it opaque.

Majolica ware. Earthenware with more than 15% absorption and relatively low mechanical strength. The name comes from the island of Majorca.

Marbled ware. Ware made from several colored bodies partially wedged together to give a veined effect like marble.

Matte glaze. Glaze with a dull or eggshell finish.

Maturing. Reaching the proper temperature to develop the desired properties.

Mazarine blue. Medium-dark cobalt blue.

Mica. A sheetlike mineral, often found in small flakes in many clays.

Microcline. Potash feldspar, $K_2O \cdot Al_2O_3 \cdot 6SiO_2$.

Micron. 1/1000 of a millimeter (equals 0.0000394 inch).

Model. Original form in clay, plasticine, or plaster.

Muffle. Inner chamber in a kiln to protect the ware from direct contact with the combustion gases.

Mullite. Needlelike crystals often found in fired bodies. It is an aluminum silicate ($3Al_2O_3 \cdot 2SiO_2$).

Naples yellow. Yellow stain, largely lead antimonate.

Natch. A key used to register two halves of a plaster mold. It may be of plaster or a brass insert (sometimes called joggle).

Nepheline-syenite. A rock like feldspar, but with more fluxing power. It contains the minerals albite and nephelite.

Nibber. The blade of a squeegee.

Nonplastic material. Material that shows no plasticity when mixed with water.

On-glaze. Overglaze (England).

Opalescent glaze. Glaze with a milky appearance.

Overglaze. Decoration put on over a glaze and fired on at a low heat.

Oxidizing condition. Excess of air in a kiln. The usual way of firing in the United States.

Palissy ware. Fine, French faience with tin-enamel glaze decorated in bright colors.

Parian ware. Porcelain high in feldspar, usually unglazed, resembling white marble from the island of Paros. First made in England about 1840.

Paste. Body of which porcelain is made.

Pâte dure. Hard porcelain (France).

Pâte sur pâte. Cameo-type decoration in which a relief is built up with successive layers of slip.

Peachbloom glaze. A copper-reduction glaze having the color of a ripe peach.

Pearl ash. Potassium carbonate, K_2CO_3.

Pebble mill. *See* Ball mill.

Peeling. Separation of glaze or engobe from the body.

Peephole. Small observation hole in the wall or door of a kiln.

Pin marks. Marks left by the pins on the underside of plate rims.

Pins. Triangular refractory rods on which glost flatware is set.

Pitcher. A fired pottery ground to a powder and used in bodies, glazes, and colors (a British term).

Plasticity. Property of yielding under pressure without cracking and then retaining the new shape after the pressure is released.

Plinth. The base of a figurine or vase.

Pointing. Point-by-point copying from a model, usually with a machine.

Porcelain (hard porcelain, European porcelain). Mechanically strong, highly translucent body with no absorption. The biscuit is low fired, but the glaze is fired to a very high temperature and is hard and resistant to abrasion.

Pottery. A loosely used term; often, pieces of the earthenware type, or a place where they are made.

Pressing. Forming plastic clay in a plaster mold by forcing it against the mold face.

Pug mill. A mill used to bring clay or bodies into the plastic state. It works very much like a meat grinder.

Pyrometer. Instrument for measuring high temperatures.

Pyrometric cones. A series of small pyramids of earthy materials, each of which softens with a specified heat treatment (combination of temperature and time). They are much used as indicators in firing.

Quartz. A common natural mineral that is the low-temperature, stable form of silica (SiO_2).

Queen's ware. *See* Cream-colored ware.

Raku. Very soft, porous earthenware with a lead borate glaze, made in Japan chiefly for the Tea Ceremony.

Raw glaze. Glaze containing no frit.

Red lead. Lead oxide, Pb_3O_4.

Reducing agent. Material in a body or glaze that gives off carbon monoxide on firing.

Reducing condition. Deficiency of air for combustion. European porcelain and reduction glazes are so fired.

Refractory. Material with a high fusion point for kilns and kiln furniture.

Resist. A thin layer of varnish covering portions of a glazed area to protect it from attack during decoration.

Rib. A tool used in throwing a pot.

Rockingham ware. Coarse earthenware of red or cream body covered with a mottled brown glaze, first made in Butler in England in 1757.

Rouge flambé (sang de boeuf). A reduced copper red glaze originating in China.

Rutile. A mineral, mainly titanium dioxide (TiO_2), often containing iron, used as a stain to give ivory and yellow.

Sagger. A refractory box in which ware is set for support and to protect it from the combustion gases.

Salt glaze. A vapor glaze formed by putting salt (NaCl) on the fires and letting the vapor combine with the surface of the ware. Used mainly on stoneware bodies.

Screen. A container having a bottom of woven bronze wires for sizing particles.

Secondary clays. Clays washed by nature from their source and settled in the quiet water of lakes and estuaries.

Semivitreous china. A white or ivory body with 4–10% absorption and fair strength, with a fairly hard glaze. The common tableware made in the United States.

Set. To place ware in a kiln; or to harden, as with gypsum plaster.

Sgraffito decoration. Decoration in which an engobe is incised to let the body color show through.

Shivering. Cracking of the glaze due to compression in cooling. Less common than crazing, but equally undesirable.

Short. Showing only slight plasticity, as a body or clay.

Shrinkage. Contraction of clays or bodies in drying or firing.

Silica. Oxide of silicon, SiO_2. Found abundantly in nature, as quartz.

Silicate of soda. A solution of sodium silicate, used as a deflocculant. The pottery industry uses "N" brand, with 36.7% solids, a ratio of soda to silica of 1 to 3.3, and a specific gravity of 1.395.

Sintering. Drawing together of the particles in a body or glaze to give a firm structure, but not going to the point of fusion.

Size. A soap coating, which prevents fresh plaster from sticking to old.

Slip. A suspension of ceramic materials in water, either bodies or glazes.

Smalt. Blue glass colored by cobalt.

Soda ash. Sodium carbonate, Na_2CO_3. Often used as a deflocculant.

Specific gravity. Density compared with that of water.

Spit-out. A defect of glazes caused by the breaking of blisters on the surface.

Sponging. Smoothing the surface of a leather-hard or dry piece with a damp sponge.

Sprigged ware. Ware, usually unglazed, with a relief decoration applied in the plastic state from a mold.

Spur. A pointed refractory setter for glost ware, usually in the form of a triangle.

Squeegee. A tool for rubbing color through a silk screen.

Stain. Ceramic color, usually one of the transition metals, in combination with other elements.

Steatite. A massive form of talc.

Stilt. A tripod-like setter for glost ware.

Stilt marks. Three marks left in the bottom of a glazed piece from the stilt.

Stone. See Cornish stone.

Stoneware. A body with 0 to 5% absorption but no translucency. The color is grey, red, or buff, and the piece may have a normal or a salt glaze.

Talc. Hydrated magnesium silicate, $3MgO \cdot 4SiO_2 \cdot H_2O$. Used in whiteware bodies.

Terra cotta. Unglazed body, generally of red color, used for sculpture, often containing grog.

Throwing. The operation of forming pieces on the potter's wheel from a plastic body.

Tin-enamel. An opaque glaze containing tin oxide.

Tortoise-shell ware. Cream ware with mottled brown and yellow mingled together to suggest a tortoise shell.

Trailing. A method of decorating with slip.

Transfer printing. Printing under or over the glaze decorations from an engraved plate by the intermediate step of a special transfer paper.

Translucency. Ability to transmit scattered light.

Transmutation glaze. See Flambé.

Tremolite. Talc mineral, $2CaO \cdot 5MgO \cdot 8SiO_2 \cdot H_2O$.

Turning. Trimming a piece in the leather-hard condition on a lathe or potter's wheel.

Underglaze. Decoration on the body, later covered with a transparent glaze.

Viscosity. Property of resisting flow; stickiness.

Vitreous. Glassy.

Volatilize. To change to the vapor form.

Wads. Rolls of plastic clay to seal a sagger to the one above.

Warping. Twisting out of shape in drying or firing.

Water glass. Thick solution of sodium silicate, often used as a deflocculant. *See* Silicate of soda.

Wedging. Working a plastic body to make it homogeneous and to eliminate the air.

Wet pan. A machine for working up a plastic body.

White lead. Basic carbonate of lead, $2PbCO_3 \cdot Pb(OH)_2$. Used in glazes.

Whiteware. Ware with a white- or ivory-burning body.

Whiting. Calcium carbonate, $CaCO_3$.

Appendix

The first three Appendix tables have appeared in various chapters in the book; the fourth is a temperature conversion table from *Refractories,* also by F. H. Norton, published by the McGraw-Hill Book Company, Inc. These tables have been enlarged and are repeated here for easy, and probably frequent, reference.

TABLE 15-2   ATOMIC WEIGHTS OF COMMON ELEMENTS

Element	Symbol	Atomic weight	Element	Symbol	Atomic weight
Aluminum	Al	26.97	Magnesium	Mg	24.32
Antimony	Sb	121.76	Manganese	Mn	54.93
Arsenic	As	79.91	Molybdenum	Mo	95.95
Barium	Ba	137.36	Nickel	Ni	58.69
Beryllium	Be	9.02	Nitrogen	N	14.01
Bismuth	Bi	209.00	Oxygen	O	16.00
Boron	B	10.82	Phosphorus	P	30.98
Cadmium	Cd	112.41	Platinum	Pt	195.23
Calcium	Ca	40.08	Potassium	K	39.10
Carbon	C	12.01	Silicon	Si	28.06
Chlorine	Cl	35.46	Silver	Ag	107.88
Chromium	Cr	52.01	Sodium	Na	23.00
Cobalt	Co	58.94	Strontium	Sr	87.63
Copper	Cu	63.57	Sulfur	S	32.06
Fluorine	F	19.00	Tin	Sn	118.70
Gold	Au	197.20	Titanium	Ti	47.90
Hydrogen	H	1.00	Tungsten	W	183.92
Iron	Fe	55.84	Uranium	U	238.07
Lead	Pb	207.21	Zinc	Zn	65.38
Lithium	Li	6.49	Zirconium	Zr	91.22

TABLE 15-3   FORMULA AND EQUIVALENT WEIGHTS OF CERAMIC MATERIALS

Material	Formula	Formula weight	Equivalent Weight		
			Basic oxides	Neutral oxides	Acic oxides
Alumina	Al_2O_3	101.9		101.9	
Aluminum hydrate	$Al_2O_3 \cdot 3H_2O$	155.9		155.9	
Ammonium carbonate	$(NH_4)_2CO_3 \cdot H_2O$	114.1	114.1		
Arsenious oxide	As_2O_3	197.8		197.8	
Barium carbonate	$BaCO_3$	197.4	197.4		
Boracic acid	$B_2O_3 \cdot 3H_2O$	123.7		123.7	
Boric oxide	B_2O_3	69.6		69.6	
Borax	$Na_2B_4O_7$	381.4	381.4	190.7	
Calcium carbonate[1]	$CaCO_3$	100.0	100.1		
Calcium oxide (lime)	CaO	56.1	56.1		
Calcium fluoride	CaF_2	78.1	78.1		
Chromic oxide	Cr_2O_3	152.0	76.0	152.0	
Clay (kaolinite)	$Al_2O_3 \cdot 2SiO_2 \cdot 2H_2O$	258.2		258.2	129.1
Clay (calcined)	$Al_2O_3 \cdot 2SiO_2$	222.2		222.2	111.1
Cobaltic oxide	Co_2O_3	165.9	83.0	165.9	
Cryolite	Na_3AlF_2	210.0	140.0	420.0	
Cupric oxide	CuO	79.6	79.6		
Feldspar (potash)	$K_2O \cdot Al_2O_3 \cdot 6SiO_2$	556.8	556.8	556.8	92.9
Feldspar (soda)	$Na_2O \cdot Al_2O_3 \cdot 6SiO_2$	524.5	524.5	524.5	87.6
Flint (quartz)	SiO_2	60.1			60.1
Ferrous oxide	FeO	71.8	71.8		
Ferric oxide	Fe_2O_3	159.7	79.8	159.7	
Lead carbonate[2]	$2PbCO_3 \cdot Pb(OH)_2$	775.6	258.5		
Lead oxide[3]	Pb_3O_4	685.6	228.5		
Lithium carbonate	Li_2CO_3	73.9	73.9		
Magnesium carbonate	$MgCO_3$	84.3	84.3		
Magnesium oxide	MgO	40.3	40.3		
Manganese dioxide	MnO_2	86.9	86.9		86.9
Nickel oxide	NiO	74.7	74.7		
Potassium carbonate	K_2CO_3	138.0	138.0		
Sodium carbonate	Na_2CO_3	106.0	106.0		
Sodium nitrate[4]	$NaNO_3$	85.0	170.0		
Strontium carbonate	$SrCO_3$	147.6	147.6		
Tin oxide	SnO	150.7			150.7
Titanium dioxide	TiO_2	80.1			80.1
Zinc carbonate	$ZnCO_2$	125.4	125.4		
Zinc oxide	ZnO	81.4	81.4		
Zirconium oxide	ZrO_2	123.0	123.0		

[1] Whiting   [2] White lead   [3] Red lead   [4] Niter

TABLE 20-3   TEMPERATURE EQUIVALENTS OF CONES[1]

Cone No.	°C	°F	Cone No.	°C	°F
022	585	1085	1	1125	2057
021	595	1103	2	1135	2075
020	625	1157	3	1145	2093
019	630	1166	4	1165	2129
018	670	1238	5	1180	2129
017	720	1328	6	1190	2174
016	735	1355	7	1210	2210
015	770	1418	8	1225	2237
014	795	1463	9	1250	2282
013	825	1517	10	1260	2300
012	840	1544	11	1285	2345
011	875	1607	12	1310	2390
010	890	1634	13	1350	2462
09	930	1706	14	1390	2534
08	945	1733	15	1410	2570
07	975	1787	16	1450	2642
06	1005	1841	17	1465	2669
05	1030	1886	18	1485	2705
04	1050	1922	19	1515	2759
03	1080	1976	20	1520	2768
02	1095	2003	23	1580	2876
01	1110	2030	26	1595	2903

[1]Orton cones heated at rate of 20°C per hour. A recent check by the Bureau of Standards shows some slight deviation from these values.

Temperature-Conversion Table

(Dr. L. Waldo, in *Metallurgical and Chemical Engineering*, March, 1910)

C	0	10	20	30	40	50	60	70	80	90
	F	F	F	F	F	F	F	F	F	F
−200	−328	−346	−364	−382	−400	−418	−436	−454	.....	.....
−100	−148	−166	−184	−202	−220	−238	−256	−274	−292	−310
− 0	+ 32	+ 14	− 4	− 22	− 40	− 58	− 76	− 94	−112	−130
0	32	50	68	86	104	122	140	158	176	194
100	212	230	248	266	284	302	320	338	356	374
200	392	410	428	446	464	482	500	518	536	554
300	572	590	608	626	644	662	680	698	716	734
400	752	770	788	806	824	842	860	878	896	914
500	932	950	968	986	1004	1022	1040	1058	1076	1094
600	1112	1130	1148	1166	1184	1202	1220	1238	1256	1274
700	1292	1310	1328	1346	1364	1382	1400	1418	1436	1454
800	1472	1490	1508	1526	1544	1562	1580	1598	1616	1634
900	1652	1670	1688	1706	1724	1742	1760	1778	1796	1814
1000	1832	1850	1868	1886	1904	1922	1940	1958	1976	1994
1100	2012	2030	2048	2066	2084	2102	2120	2138	2156	2174
1200	2192	2210	2228	2246	2264	2282	2300	2318	2336	2354
1300	2372	2390	2408	2426	2444	2462	2480	2498	2516	2534
1400	2552	2570	2588	2606	2624	2642	2660	2678	2696	2714
1500	2732	2750	2768	2786	2804	2822	2840	2858	2876	2894
1600	2912	2930	2948	2966	2984	3002	3020	3038	3056	3074
1700	3092	3110	3128	3146	3164	3182	3200	3218	3236	3254
1800	3272	3290	3308	3326	3344	3362	3380	3398	3416	3434
1900	3452	3470	3488	3506	3524	3542	3560	3578	3596	3614
2000	3632	3650	3668	3686	3704	3722	3740	3758	3776	3794
2100	3812	3830	3848	3866	3884	3902	3920	3938	3956	3974
2200	3992	4010	4028	4046	4064	4082	4100	4118	4136	4154
2300	4172	4190	4208	4226	4244	4262	4280	4298	4316	4334
2400	4352	4370	4388	4406	4424	4442	4460	4478	4496	4514
2500	4532	4550	4568	4586	4604	4622	4640	4658	4676	4694
2600	4712	4730	4748	4766	4784	4802	4820	4838	4856	4874
2700	4892	4910	4928	4946	4964	4982	5000	5018	5036	5054
2800	5072	5090	5108	5126	5144	5162	5180	5198	5216	5234
2900	5252	5270	5288	5306	5324	5342	5360	5378	5396	5414
3000	5432	5450	5468	5486	5504	5522	5540	5558	5576	5594
3100	5612	5630	5648	5666	5684	5702	5720	5738	5756	5774
3200	5792	5810	5828	5846	5864	5882	5900	5918	5936	5954
3300	5972	5990	6008	6026	6044	6062	6080	6098	6116	6134
3400	6152	6170	6188	6206	6224	6242	6260	6278	6296	6314
3500	6332	6350	6368	6386	6404	6422	6440	6458	6476	6494
3600	6512	6530	6548	6566	6584	6602	6620	6638	6656	6674
3700	6692	6710	6728	6646	6764	6782	6800	6818	6836	6854
3800	6872	6890	6908	6926	6944	6962	6980	6998	7016	7034
3900	7052	7070	7088	7106	7124	7142	7160	7178	7196	7214

°C.	°F.
1	1.8
2	3.6
3	5.4
4	7.2
5	9.0
6	10.8
7	12.6
8	14.4
9	16.2
10	18.0

°F.	°C.
1	0.56
2	1.11
3	1.67
4	2.22
5	2.78
6	3.33
7	3.89
8	4.44
9	5.00
10	5.56
11	6.11
12	6.67
13	7.22
14	7.78
15	8.33
16	8.89
17	9.44
18	10.00

Examples. 1347°C. = 2444°F. + 12.6°F. = 2456.6°F.; 3367°F. = 1850°C + 2.78°C = 1852.78°C.

Index